THE SCOTTISH INDEPENDENCE REFERENDUM

The Scottish Independence Referendum

Constitutional and Political Implications

Edited by

AILEEN McHARG

Professor of Public Law, University of Strathclyde

TOM MULLEN

Professor of Law, University of Glasgow

ALAN PAGE

Professor of Public Law, University of Dundee

NEIL WALKER

Regius Professor of Public Law and the Law of Nature and Nations, University of Edinburgh

OXFORD

UNIVERSITY PRESS

OXFORD
UNIVERSITY PRESS

Great Clarendon Street, Oxford, OX2 6DP,
United Kingdom

Oxford University Press is a department of the University of Oxford.
It furthers the University's objective of excellence in research, scholarship,
and education by publishing worldwide. Oxford is a registered trade mark of
Oxford University Press in the UK and in certain other countries

First Edition published in 2016

Published in the United States of America by Oxford University Press
198 Madison Avenue, New York, NY 10016, United States of America

British Library Cataloguing in Publication Data
Data available

Library of Congress Control Number: 2016934699

ISBN 978-0-19-875551-7

Preface

The Scottish independence referendum of 2014 marked a watershed in our legal, political, economic, and cultural history. For the first time since the 1707 Union the constitutional standing of Scotland was put seriously in question. Should Scotland remain part of the United Kingdom or should it pursue the course of autonomous sovereign statehood?

To understand how that question came to be asked with such urgency today and not before, why it was answered as it was (with a narrower than expected 'No'), why matters remain unsettled, and whether and how some final settlement might eventually emerge from the intense constitutional politics of the immediate post-referendum period, is a large and daunting task. It is a task that requires both a broad historical and comparative perspective and a detailed focus on the here and now. It demands that we examine the big picture, while remaining alert to the fact that it remains a fast-moving and incomplete picture.

It is, nevertheless, the task—or, rather, the multi-task—that we set ourselves in the present volume. As constitutional lawyers, the editors were naturally most concerned, and best equipped, to look at the referendum and its aftermath through a constitutional prism. However, we have tried to take as wide and generous view of constitutional matters as possible, and so have included contributions from historians, political scientists, and economists, from international and European lawyers, as well as from constitutional lawyers and theorists. All of our contributors are acknowledged experts in their field and all have contributed to the referendum debate in one way or another. The editors themselves, and some of the other contributors, are founder members of the Scottish Constitutional Futures Forum (SCFF) (<http://www.scottishconstitutionalfutures.org/>), which through its blog and busy schedule of public events was and remains closely involved in the constitutional debate.

We would like to thank our various academic homes, namely the Law Schools of Dundee, Edinburgh, Glasgow, and Strathclyde, for the support they have given to the SCFF, and also in the production of the present volume. We also owe a special debt of gratitude to our publishers, and in particular to our editor Elinor Shields, for recognizing that this was a volume which, such was its topicality, required to be produced promptly without compromising OUP's usual high standards.

In what follows, we do not pretend to pronounce the last or definitive word on the Scottish independence referendum. We do hope, however, to provide a cooler and more comprehensive view of a significant occurrence in the international calendar of constitutional events than has been available or possible until now, and to supply a resource that will prove helpful to those engaged in the continuing business of domestic constitutional reform.

The editors

December 2015

Table of Contents

PART IV. TERRITORIAL POLITICS AND THE UK CONSTITUTION AFTER THE REFERENDUM

List of Contributors

Nicholas Aroney is Professor of Constitutional Law and Fellow of Emmanuel College at the University of Queensland. He is a member of the governing council of the Australian Association of Constitutional Law and recently completed an Australian Research Council fellowship focussed on the study of comparative federalism.

Christine Bell is Professor of Constitutional Law and Assistant Principal (Global Justice) at the University of Edinburgh. She was a member of the Advocate General for Scotland's Legal Forum, the Scottish Constitutional Futures Forum, and *Lawyers for Yes*.

Sionaidh Douglas-Scott holds the Anniversary Chair in Law at Queen Mary Faculty of Law, University of London and is an Honorary Fellow of Lady Margaret Hall, Oxford. In 2015, she was special adviser to the Scottish Parliament's European and External Affairs Committee's inquiry into the implications of EU reform and the EU referendum for Scotland.

Jim Gallagher is a Member of Nuffield College, Oxford, and Visiting Professor in the School of Law at Glasgow University. As a civil servant he worked in government at both UK and Scottish levels. During the referendum he advised the Better Together Campaign.

Colin Kidd is Wardlaw Professor of Modern History at the University of St. Andrews and a Fellow of All Souls College, Oxford. Although not formally affiliated to any organization or party, he contributed articles to the press on the side of the No campaign, and collaborated with Labour politicians outside the fold of Better Together.

Nicola McEwen is Professor of Territorial Politics at the University of Edinburgh, and Associate Director of the Centre on Constitutional Change. She was a Senior Scotland Fellow under the ESRC *Future of the UK and Scotland* programme.

Aileen McHarg is Professor of Public Law at the University of Strathclyde. She is a founding member of the Scottish Constitutional Futures Forum, a member of the Law Society of Scotland's Constitutional Law sub-committee, and was a member of both *Academics for Yes* and *Lawyers for Yes*.

James Mitchell is Professor of Public Policy at the University of Edinburgh. He held an ESRC Senior Scotland Fellowship under the ESRC *Future of the UK and Scotland* programme.

Tom Mullen is Professor of Law at the University of Glasgow. He is a founding member of the Scottish Constitutional Futures Forum.

Alan Page is Professor of Public Law at the University of Dundee. He is a founding member of the Scottish Constitutional Futures Forum and was a member of the Advocate General for Scotland's Legal Forum.

Malcolm Petrie is Leverhulme Early Career Fellow in the School of History, Classics and Archaeology at the University of Edinburgh.

Andrew Scott is Professor of European Union Studies at the University of Edinburgh. Between 2012 and 2014, he was seconded as Adviser to the Scottish Government's European and External Relations Secretariat.

Andrew Tickell is Lecturer in Law and Risk at Glasgow Caledonian University. He was a member of a number of pro-independence campaign groups, including *Lawyers for Yes*, National Collective, and the Scottish National Party.

Stephen Tierney is Professor of Constitutional Theory at the University of Edinburgh, Director of the Edinburgh Centre for Constitutional Law, and a Senior Research Fellow under the ESRC *Future of the UK and Scotland* programme. He is a founding member of the Scottish Constitutional Futures Forum. He served as independent adviser to the Scottish Government on the technical aspects of the referendum in 2012, and as constitutional adviser to the Scottish Parliament's Referendum (Scotland) Bill Committee. He currently serves as Legal Adviser to the House of Lords Constitution Committee.

Neil Walker is Regius Professor of Public Law and the Law of Nature and Nations at the University of Edinburgh. He is a founding member of the Scottish Constitutional Futures Forum.

PART I

THE ROAD TO THE REFERENDUM

1

Introduction

Tom Mullen

The Scottish independence referendum on 18 September 2014 was a momentous political event. In one sense the outcome was clear; the people of Scotland voted by 55.3 per cent to 44.7 per cent to remain in the United Kingdom. However, it is already apparent that the referendum has not finally resolved the political questions relating to Scotland's future in the UK, far less removed the threat that the Union may be dissolved within the foreseeable future. This book aims to make sense of the referendum; to explain what happened and why; to consider its significance, including its likely effects on the future of Scotland and the United Kingdom, and generally to examine the issues raised by the referendum. It can only be a preliminary stocktaking as the full effects of the referendum may only unfold over a long time scale. A little over a year since the referendum is clearly too soon to attempt a definitive view, but there is merit in examining the referendum while it is reasonably fresh in our minds.

The book approaches the referendum from a variety of disciplinary perspectives: history, political science, law, and economics, and consists of fourteen essays divided into four parts: (i) the road to the referendum, (ii) the referendum process, (iii) the referendum debate, and (iv) territorial politics and the UK constitution after the referendum. Part I (the referendum process) consists of this introduction and a chapter setting the referendum in its historical and political context. Part II (the referendum process) consists of two chapters, one on the use of referendums in the UK constitution and another on the referendum campaign. The five chapters in Part III (the referendum debate) examine the key issues in the referendum debate covering the constitutional case for independence, the case for Scotland remaining in the Union, the specifically economic arguments for independence, the European Union dimension of the independence debate, and the general international law dimension. The five chapters in Part IV (territorial politics and the UK constitution after the referendum) cover the nature of the post-referendum proposals for constitutional reform and the power future Scottish Governments will have under them, the options for the future of the United Kingdom's territorial constitution, the present and future governance of Scotland, what can be learned from the constitutional experience of other countries whose systems are derived from the Westminster model, and finally prospects for a future referendum on independence.

The structure of this introduction is as follows: a brief narrative of events leading up to and shortly after the referendum, followed by analysis of the vote; some preliminary discussion of the referendum debate to set the scene for the chapters in Part III; a brief discussion of post-referendum constitutional issues to set the scene for the chapters in Part IV; and some concluding thoughts.

I. The road to the referendum and its aftermath: A brief narrative

A. The road to the referendum

Colin Kidd and Malcolm Petrie describe the historical background to the referendum in depth in Chapter 2 placing particular emphasis on the period since the mid-1950s and covering the growth of nationalism and electoral support for the Scottish National Party (SNP). As well as providing a narrative of events, they assess the political and economic forces influencing the rise of nationalism and the role played by each of the political parties (including those supporting the Union) in changing the character of Scottish politics. This section of the introduction merely seeks to provide a brief narrative of events leading up to the referendum and a summary of political and constitutional developments since the referendum.

At the elections for the Scottish Parliament in 2007, the SNP won 47 out of 129 seats making it the largest single party and allowing it to form a minority government. This was clearly a significant event. For the first time there was a party in government whose ultimate aim was for Scotland to become independent of the rest of the United Kingdom. The two previous elections in 1999 and 2003 had resulted in coalitions between the Labour and Liberal Democrat Parties. As a minority government the SNP was unable to legislate without the consent of the other parties, yet it lasted the full term and was able to demonstrate competence as a governing party on a day-to-day basis. Early in its term, in August 2007, the Scottish Government launched a *National Conversation* on Scotland's constitutional future.[1] That document set out possible options for Scotland's constitutional development including extending devolved powers and independence, the latter being the SNP's preferred option. The reaction of the pro-Union parties was to propose a review of the powers of the Scottish Parliament which led to the establishment by the Scottish Parliament and UK Government of a Commission on Scottish Devolution chaired by Sir Kenneth Calman. Its remit was to review the Scotland Act 1998 and to recommend changes to the existing constitutional arrangements that would enable the Scottish Parliament to serve

[1] The Scottish Government, *Choosing Scotland's Future: A National Conversation: Independence and Responsibility in the Modern World* (2007).

the people of Scotland better, improve its financial accountability, and secure the position of Scotland within the United Kingdom. The SNP did not participate in the deliberations of the Commission, although the Scottish Government did make submissions to it.

The Calman Commission published its first report in December 2008[2] and its final report in June 2009.[3] It recommended a modest extension of functional competence, including the regulation of airguns, power to determine the national road speed limit, and power to set blood alcohol limits for drink-driving. These recommendations were duly implemented by the Scotland Act 2012. The most substantial recommendations related to finance. Up to that point most of the funding of devolved government came from a block grant made by the UK Treasury with the remainder financed by local government taxes. The Scottish Parliament had power to vary the rate of income tax either up or down by three pence in the pound but had never used it.[4]

The Commission recommended devolution of four small taxes (Stamp Duty Land Tax, Aggregates Levy, Landfill Tax, and Air Passenger Transport duty) and giving the Scottish Parliament power to vary the rate of income tax by ten pence in the pound with a corresponding reduction in the block grant. A grant reduction on that scale would have forced a future Scottish Parliament to set a Scottish rate of income tax as otherwise drastic cuts in the Scottish Government's budget would have been required. The proposals to devolve stamp duty, land tax, and landfill tax were implemented in part by the Scotland Act 2012 and took effect from April 2015. The 2012 Act also enacted the enhanced income tax powers with the expectation that the new power to vary income tax would be operational from April 2016.

In November 2009, the Scottish Government published its White Paper: *Your Scotland, Your Voice: A National Conversation*, setting out four broad options for Scotland's future. These were (i) the status quo, (ii) implementing the recommendations of the Calman Commission, (iii) devolution of the maximum possible range of responsibilities to Scotland within the United Kingdom ('devolution max'), and (iv) independence. The White Paper stated that the Scottish Government favoured a referendum on independence and intended to bring forward a Referendum Bill early in 2010. In the event it did not do so, although it did publish a consultation on a referendum bill in February 2011.[5]

Therefore, there remained two competing versions of Scotland's constitutional future in play: one being the offer of a significant but arguably not major increase in devolved power and responsibility as set out in the report of the Calman Commission, and the other being the vision of an independent Scotland offered by the SNP. The Scottish Parliamentary elections of 2011 proved decisive

[2] *The Future of Scottish Devolution Within the Union: A First Report* (2008).
[3] *Serving Scotland Better: Scotland and the United Kingdom in the 21st Century* (2009).
[4] Scotland Act 1998, Part IV, ss 73–80.
[5] Scottish Government, *Scotland's Future: Draft Referendum (Scotland) Bill Consultation Paper* (2011).

in putting the option of independence before the voters. In May 2011, the SNP somewhat unexpectedly won a majority of seats in the Scottish Parliament elections (69 out of 129) and now formed a majority government. It had included in its election manifesto a pledge to hold a referendum. With a parliamentary majority it was able to deliver that pledge, but how this was to be achieved was disputed. The Scottish Government accepted that it would require legislation by the UK Parliament to make Scotland independent, but argued that the Scottish Parliament already had the power under the Scotland Act to hold a referendum to find out the wishes of the people.[6] The UK Government accepted (as UK Governments had for some years) the right of the Scottish people to determine their own future. However, it argued that the Scottish Parliament did not have the legal power to hold a referendum; only the UK Parliament had competence to legislate for a referendum.[7] What was at stake, apart from a concern for legality, was the right to control key aspects of the process including the framing of the questions, timing of the referendum, and voting age.

The arguments over competence were never tested in court. Both the question of competence and the other issues were resolved politically by the Edinburgh Agreement of 15 October 2012[8] which confirmed that there would be a referendum and set out the terms on which it would take place. These terms were given effect by an Order under section 30 of the Scotland Act 1998[9] which expressly stated that a referendum on the independence of Scotland would be within the powers of the Scottish Parliament provided that the referendum took place not later than 31 December 2014, that there would be only one ballot paper, and that ballot paper must give the voter a choice between only two responses.[10] The agreement also declared that the referendum should be conducted according to the principles underpinning the Political Parties, Elections and Referendums Act 2000 and that the franchise could be extended to 16- and 17-year olds if the Scottish Parliament chose to do so. Subject to those points the Scottish Parliament would decide how the referendum would be conducted.

The Edinburgh Agreement, therefore, gave some of what they wanted to both the Scottish Government and the UK Government. The UK Government got its wish that there should be a single question referendum with no third option of further devolution on the ballot paper. The Scottish Government got its wish for a lengthy referendum campaign and the extension of the franchise to 16- and 17-year olds. The details of the franchise were then set out in the Scottish Independence Referendum (Franchise) Act 2013. Apart from the enfranchisement of young people, the key decision taken was that the right to vote would be limited to European Union and Commonwealth citizens resident in Scotland.

[6] Scottish Government, *Your Scotland, Your Referendum* (January 2012).

[7] *Scotland's Constitutional Future: a consultation on facilitating a legal, fair and decisive referendum on whether Scotland should leave the United Kingdom*, Cm 8203 (January 2012).

[8] Agreement between the United Kingdom Government and the Scottish Government on a referendum on independence for Scotland.

[9] Section 30 permits the powers of the Parliament to be extended by delegated legislation.

[10] Scotland Act 1998 (Modification of Schedule 5) Order 2013, SI 2013/242.

Therefore, the right to vote was not limited to those of Scottish ancestry; conversely, those who were Scottish by birth but resident outside Scotland could not vote. The detailed framework for conducting the referendum was set out in the Scottish Independence Referendum Act 2013. The question eventually agreed was 'Do you agree that Scotland should be an independent country?' The referendum process is analysed by Stephen Tierney in Chapter 3. He explains how the referendum, which follows and reinforces a distinct recent pattern in the United Kingdom and elsewhere of submitting matters of major constitutional significant to plebiscite, was set up and regulated by legislation. This followed the principles of the existing UK model, the Political Parties, Elections and Referendums Act 2000, on matters such as the treatment of campaigning groups and campaign expenditure limits. Tierney considers how far the referendum legislation dealt with two of the standard criticisms of the use of referendums ('the elite control syndrome', and 'the deliberation deficit').[11]

The date chosen for the referendum was 18 September 2014. Arguably, the campaign really began with the Edinburgh Agreement and lasted nearly two years, although the regulated period, at sixteen weeks, was much shorter. The campaign intensified as polling day drew closer. James Mitchell gives a detailed analysis of the referendum campaign in Chapter 4, setting out the background and events leading up to the campaign and the way the referendum debate was structured. He also analyses the roles of political parties, umbrella groups, and the media in the campaign, the significance of public participation, and the impact of certain key events and issues and of the opinion polls. It is enough to note here that for much of the campaign, the 'No' side held a clear lead. That was in line with opinion surveys over a number of years, which had consistently shown support for independence well short of 40 per cent.[12] However, as the real poll approached, the gap narrowed and one survey published less than two weeks before the vote showed only a narrow majority for independence. This apparent narrowing of the gap suggested the result was genuinely in doubt and prompted the pro-Union parties to take swift action. On 8 September 2014, the former UK Prime Minister Gordon Brown, apparently with the approval of the UK Government, made a speech in Dundee in which he set out a timetable for rapid progress towards extensive further devolution, a 'modern form of Scottish home rule' if the Scottish people voted to remain in the United Kingdom. This was swiftly followed by the leaders of the Conservative, Labour, and Liberal Democrat Parties making a solemn 'vow'[13] which was published on the front page of the Daily Record on 15 September. It promised that 'extensive new powers' would be devolved to the

[11] The third being 'the majoritarian danger' which was less relevant to the Scottish independence referendum.

[12] See eg ScotCen Social Research (2014), *Has the Referendum Campaign Made a Difference?* <www.scotcen.org.uk/media/563071/ssa-2014-has-the-referendun-campaign-made-a-difference.pdf> accessed 30 November 2015.

[13] <www.dailyrecord.co.uk/news/politics/david-cameron-ed-miliband-nick-4265992> accessed 30 November 2015.

Scottish Parliament if Scotland voted to remain in the United Kingdom. In the event, the result was not as close as the late opinion poll had suggested.

B. After the referendum: Constitutional change and the 2015 UK general election

Three developments since the referendum are worth mentioning: the proposals for further devolution; the proposals to change the legislative process in the UK Parliament; and the 2015 UK general election.

1. Further devolution

The promise of further devolution having been made so clearly, it was necessary for the pro-Union parties to act on it. In the light of their vow the 'No' vote could not easily be interpreted as a vote for no change. However, the cooperative approach that had been evident in the promises of more devolution being made jointly by the three party leaders before the referendum disappeared overnight. The morning after the poll, the Prime Minister, apparently without consulting the other parties, announced UK Government plans for further devolution.[14] Lord Smith of Kelvin was to lead an all-party commission[15] that would present agreed proposals for further devolution of powers over tax, spending, and welfare. This was in line with what had been suggested before the referendum. More controversially, the Prime Minister appeared to link progress on devolution for Scotland with adjustment of the devolution settlements for the rest of the United Kingdom and reform of the UK Parliament stating that 'The question of English votes for English laws—the so-called West Lothian question—requires a decisive answer' and that 'all this must take place in tandem with, and at the same pace as, the settlement for Scotland.' This had certainly not been agreed by the parties before the referendum and the issue of English votes for English laws continues to divide the parties.

The timetable set for developing the proposals for further devolution was tight. The Smith Commission was obliged to report by the end of November and the Government had promised to produce draft legislative clauses by the end of January. The Smith Commission duly published its report, to which all the Scottish parties had agreed (with varying degrees of enthusiasm), on 27 November 2014.[16] Its recommendations were grouped under three 'pillars' relating to constitutional structure, additional functions, and financing devolved government. The most significant proposals were:

[14] <www.gov.uk/government/news/scottish-independence-referendum-statement-by-the-prime-minister> accessed 30 November 2015.

[15] ie the five parties represented in the Scottish Parliament (Conservative, Green, Labour, Liberal Democrat, and SNP).

[16] *Report of the Smith Commission for further devolution of powers to the Scottish Parliament* <www.smith-commission.scot/smith-commission-report/> accessed 30 November 2015.

a) Constitutional structure

- UK legislation should state that the Scottish Parliament and Scottish Government are permanent institutions;
- The Sewel Convention should be put on a statutory footing;
- The Scottish Parliament should have all powers in relation to elections to the Scottish Parliament, the electoral system, and the number of members of the Parliament; and
- The Scottish Parliament should have power to make decisions about all matters relating to the arrangements and operations of the Scottish Parliament and Scottish Government.

b) Additional functions

The Scottish Parliament should have devolved to it:

- Powers over certain existing social security benefits (including housing benefit,[17] and benefits for carers, disabled persons, and those who are ill);
- Power to create new social security benefits provided they are within devolved responsibility (eg new housing-related benefits);
- Power to top-up existing benefits which remain reserved to the UK Government (eg jobseekers allowance); and
- Regulation of abortion.

c) Financing devolved government

- Income tax should become a shared tax with the Scottish Parliament having power to set the rates of income tax and the thresholds at which these are paid by Scottish taxpayers (excluding income from savings and dividends). All other aspects of income tax, such as the tax-free personal allowance and tax reliefs would remain reserved to the UK Parliament;
- Both the tax on air passengers leaving Scottish airports and the tax on commercial exploitation of aggregate should be devolved;
- The receipts raised in Scotland by the first ten percentage points of the standard rate of value added tax (VAT) should be assigned to the Scottish Government's budget, but VAT itself should remain reserved;
- All other taxes would remain reserved including National Insurance, inheritance tax, capital gains tax, corporation tax, and taxation of oil and gas receipts; and

[17] This is a means-tested benefit which covers all or part of the rent in rented housing. The UK Government is implementing a reform which rolls all of the principal means-tested benefits into one new benefit, Universal Credit. Therefore, strictly speaking what will be devolved is the housing element of Universal Credit.

- The Barnett formula would continue to be used to calculate the amount of the annual block grant from the UK Treasury to support Scottish Public expenditure but its amount would be reduced to reflect the additional powers devolved over income tax.

The UK Government published a command paper which included draft bill clauses on 26 January 2015[18] and the Scotland Bill 2015–16 was given its first reading in the House of Commons on 28 May 2015. The Bill is broadly in line with the recommendations of the Smith Commission, with clauses corresponding to each of Smith's main proposals, although there has been considerable argument as to whether some of the Bill's provisions deliver exactly what the Smith Commission report had envisaged. At the time of writing, the Bill has completed all its stages in the House of Commons and is being considered by the House of Lords. It is intended that the Bill will have completed all its Parliamentary stages in both Houses and that the Scottish Parliament will have given its consent in the Spring of next year so that the Bill can receive Royal Assent before the next elections to the Scottish Parliament in May 2016. Whilst the Bill may be subject to amendment, the final version is not expected to differ greatly from the version available at the time of writing.

Even if one considers that the Bill does not fully implement the Smith Commission Report or other promises made before the referendum, it should be apparent that the package in the Bill represents a substantial increase in devolved power. Effective capacity to use those powers is, of course, a separate question. The most important new powers over substantive policy areas are those relating to social security, but the changes to taxation and public spending are arguably more significant. Until now, with only local government taxes devolved and the bulk of expenditure supported by the block grant from HM Treasury, the Scottish Government and Parliament have had full responsibility for expenditure on devolved public services and government functions, but very little responsibility for raising the taxation that finances that expenditure. Decisions have had to be taken about the levels of both council tax and non-domestic rates, both of which contribute to local government expenditure, but the council tax has been frozen for eight years and non-domestic rates are not paid by individuals. The (admittedly modest) power conferred in the original devolution framework to vary the rate of income tax by three pence in the pound has never been used. In effect, the Scottish Parliament has not yet had to make any difficult taxation decisions, that is, it has not felt the need substantially to raise taxes which are paid directly by individuals. The cut in the block grant that will accompany the extended powers of taxation will force the Scottish Parliament to set the level of income tax, which is the tax most visible to voters and, therefore, politically the most sensitive. Clearly, this will alter the dynamic of Scottish politics.

[18] *Scotland in the United Kingdom: An enduring settlement* (Cm 8990, 2015).

2. *The legislative process in the UK Parliament*

The UK Government has pressed on with its promise to change the legislative process in the UK Parliament ('English votes for English laws'),[19] although this is not being done on a cross-party basis. On 22 October 2015 the House of Commons voted by 312 votes to 270 to accept a Government proposal to introduce new standing orders for the House of Commons whereby only English MPs would decide whether to adopt legislation that was deemed to affect only England and not to affect other parts of the United Kingdom.[20] The Speaker of the House of Commons would certify whether a bill affected only England. The process for such a bill would include a stage at which only English MPs could vote. MPs from the rest of the United Kingdom would participate in all other stages of the Bill but crucially, English MPs would hold a veto over any bill affecting only England. The changes are opposed by the other main UK parties represented in the House of Commons (Labour and Liberal Democrat), by the SNP, and by Democratic Unionist party (representing Northern Ireland constituencies); so, in effect, the Government has used its majority in the House of Commons to force through a major constitutional change with potentially far-reaching consequences.

3. *The United Kingdom general election 2015*

Arguably, the most dramatic and most constitutionally significant political event since the referendum was the SNP's overwhelming success in the UK general election of 2015. Rather than suffering a post-referendum hangover, the SNP experienced a massive surge in party membership immediately after the referendum and the polls soon detected a marked shift in voting intentions for the 2015 general election. The SNP increased its share of the vote in the election on 7 May 2015 to 50 per cent of the vote. This, as a consequence of the first past the post system, was sufficient for it to claim fifty-six of the fifty-nine Scottish constituencies in the UK Parliament. Labour, the Liberal Democrats, and the Conservatives won only one seat each. Labour's share of the vote declined from 42 per cent at the 2010 election to 24.3 per cent and the Liberal Democrat's declined from 18.9 per cent at the 2010 election to 7.5 per cent.

Although the increase in the SNP's share of the vote to 50 per cent from 19.9 per cent at the 2010 election is particularly striking, it is also interesting to note how voting intentions seemed to have changed in quite a short time. Those polls which tracked voters' intentions for the 2015 election during the referendum campaign showed support of the SNP averaging 36 per cent during the first nine months of 2014 but there was then a substantial increase shortly after

[19] Cabinet Office, *English Votes for English Laws: An Explanatory Guide to Proposals* (2015) <www.gov.uk/government/uploads/system/uploads/attachment_data/file/441848/English_votes_for_English_laws_explanatory_guide.pdf> accessed 30 November 2015.

[20] H C Deb, Vol. 600, 22 October 2015, cols 1159–1239.

the referendum in those intending to support the SNP at the 2015 election.[21] It appeared that the fact of voting Yes at the referendum had encouraged many who had not previously supported the SNP to do so in the 2015 election. Clearly this altered the dynamics of both Scottish and UK politics. The parties that had supported the Union were left without a significant presence in the UK Parliament and Scottish representation in the Westminster Parliament now consists largely of MPs who wish to end the Union. The result also strengthens the position of the SNP within Scotland, and it appears on course to gain another overall majority at the 2016 elections for the Scottish Parliament.[22]

II. Explaining the outcome: Analysis of the vote

It is worth examining the vote in a little detail and considering why the Scottish people voted to remain in the UK rather than for independence, although this does not pretend to be a comprehensive analysis. The vote can be analysed in terms of a number of variables including the socio-economic status, gender, age, place of birth, and party affiliation of voters; and geography. Some analysis was published immediately after the referendum based on two polls of how people had voted conducted by YouGov[23] and by Lord Ashcroft.[24] However, the most comprehensive source of data on why people voted as they did is the Economic and Social Research Council Scottish Referendum study[25] from which preliminary results were released in March 2015. The data in this section draws on both these sources and on official returns which confirm the geographical distribution of votes.[26] This data can be set in the context of survey data over many years, particularly from the Scottish Social Attitudes Survey.

Taking Scotland as a whole, a higher proportion of men than women voted Yes (53.2 per cent to 43.4 per cent). Older people were also much more likely than younger people to vote No, with the 70 and over age group being least likely to vote Yes (34.3 per cent compared to 54 per cent for the 16–29 age group). These differences according to gender and age group were consistent with long-term trends evidenced by the Scottish Social Attitudes Survey.[27] Voters who had been born in Scotland were more likely to vote Yes (52.7 per cent) than those resident in Scotland but born elsewhere, with those born in the rest of the

[21] See J. Curtice, *Scotland 'One Year On': the Legacy of the Independence Referendum* (IPPI/David Hume Institute, 2015).

[22] Curtice, *Scotland 'One Year On'* (n. 21).

[23] <https://yougov.co.uk/publicopinion/archive/10934/> accessed 30 November 2015.

[24] <http://lordashcroftpolls.com/2014/09/scotland-voted/> accessed 30 November 2015. For analysis of these polls, see J. Curtice, *So Who Voted Yes and Who Voted No?* <http://blog.whatscotlandthinks.org/2014/09/voted-Yes-voted/>. See also *Scotland 'One Year On': the Legacy of the Independence Referendum* (IPPI/David Hume Institute, September 2015).

[25] ESRC Scottish Independence Referendum Study, ES/MOO3418/1.

[26] Data available at: <http://centreonconstitutionalchange.ac.uk/sites/default/files/Scottish%20Referendum%20Study%2027%20March%202015.pdf> accessed 30 November 2015.

[27] See *Has the Referendum Campaign Made a Difference?* (n. 12).

United Kingdom being least likely to vote Yes (27.9 per cent) and those born outside the United Kingdom rather more inclined to do so (42.9 per cent).[28] Differences in educational qualifications (eg degree/no degree) seem not to have been significant.

Party affiliation had a marked effect on voting with around 80 per cent of SNP voters voting Yes compared to only 43 per cent of Liberal Democrats, 31 per cent of Labour voters, and only 2 per cent of Conservative voters. Although there was, therefore, strong correlation between party affiliation and voting it is clear that there is also a substantial mismatch between support for the parties and support for independence, with a substantial minority of SNP voters voting against independence and even higher proportions of Liberal Democrats and Labour voters (both ostensibly pro-Union parties) voting for independence.

Socio-economic status appeared to correlate strongly with voting. In the Economic and Social Research Council (ESRC) survey, 41.7 per cent of middle-class respondents voted Yes compared to 53.6 per cent of working-class respondents. Housing tenure was also strongly correlated with voting, with 61.9 per cent of those who were tenants in the social-rented sector voting Yes compared to only 35.4 per cent of those who were owner-occupiers. There was a marked disparity in voting according to income with little difference between those in the upper three quartiles (ranging from 46.8 per cent to 42.4 per cent voting Yes) whereas fully 56.4 per cent of those in the lowest quartile voted Yes.

There were notable area patterns. In only four of the thirty-two local authority areas in Scotland was there a majority for independence although in a fifth there was a very even split with 49.9 per cent voting Yes. The highest majorities voting against independence were in those areas nearest to England and Wales (Scottish Borders, Dumfries, and Galloway) and furthest from the central belt of Scotland (Orkney and Shetland). To a large extent, the area patterns reflect the distribution of personal characteristics described above. Those areas with the highest proportion voting Yes were also the local areas with high levels of poverty and deprivation (eg Dundee, Glasgow, and North Lanarkshire). The effect is even more pronounced at a more local level. According to two polls conducted by Ipsos MORI before the vote, only 36 per cent of those living in the most affluent 20 per cent of areas in Scotland voted Yes, whereas fully 65 per cent of those living in the 20 per cent most deprived neighbourhoods voted Yes.[29] The areas noted above as least likely to vote Yes have relatively lower levels of unemployment and deprivation, and (except Shetland) relatively higher levels of older people. They also have higher proportions born in the rest of the United Kingdom and higher proportions identifying as British in opinion surveys.

The patterns of voting themselves do not tell us the substantive reasons why people voted as they did. Two possible reasons actively motivating voting behaviour

[28] All data in this paragraph drawn from the ESRC survey.
[29] Curtice, *So Who Voted Yes and Who Voted No* (n. 24).

that have been subject to opinion surveys are perceptions of national identity and perceptions of the economic consequences of independence. In general, opinion surveys have found a strong correlation between perceptions of national identity and expressed voting intentions, and the ESRC study was no exception with, for example, 86.6 per cent of those describing themselves as Scottish/not British voting Yes and 60.4 per cent of those describing themselves as more Scottish than British. Conversely, 90.0 per cent of those claiming to be British and not Scottish voted No and 87.6 per cent of those claiming to be more British than Scottish voted No. Of those who claimed to be equally British and Scottish 81.4 per cent voted No.

There is also evidence that voters were strongly influenced by their perceptions of the economic consequences of independence. In the ESRC study, those who thought cuts in public spending if Scotland remained part the United Kingdom after the referendum were 'very unlikely' were also very likely to vote No, whereas the great majority of those who thought spending cuts were 'very likely' voted Yes. Similarly, perceptions of whether the wealth gap between rich and poor would widen if Scotland remained part of the United Kingdom also correlated closely with voting, with most of those who thought a widening wealth gap was 'very likely' voting Yes. The 2014 Scottish Social Attitudes Survey (which was conducted between May and August 2014) found a very strong correlation between economic optimism and propensity to vote Yes,[30] as have other opinion surveys.[31]

The ESRC study also asked respondents to state the single most important reason for voting. Three reasons stood out for No voters: feeling British and believing in the Union (29.5 per cent), too many unanswered questions (27.8 per cent), and a sense that independence would have made Scotland worse off economically (26.3 per cent). Four reasons stood out for Yes voters: to ensure that Scotland always gets the government it votes for (24.8 per cent), the whole Westminster system is rotten (24.1 per cent), independence is the natural state of nations like Scotland (21.8 per cent), and Scotland would be better off economically (20.1 per cent).

We may reasonably infer from the data that voting decisions were strongly influenced by perceptions of national identity, perceptions of the economic consequences of independence, uncertainty about the consequences of independence, and dissatisfaction with Westminster government.

How far voters were influenced in their voting decisions by the arguments in the campaign is a separate question to which the answer cannot be conclusively determined. However, the ESRC study suggested that the importance of some issues changed over the last four weeks of the campaign with the issues of the degree of uncertainty about the consequences of independence, whether the

[30] See *Has the Referendum Campaign Made a Difference?* (n. 12).

[31] See J. Curtice, *How Scotland Voted: Economic Perceptions in the Scottish Independence Referendum* (International Public Policy Institute (IPPI), 2015) <https://pure.strath.ac.uk/portal/en/publications/how-scotland-voted(74320b62-3e51-4c2b-85bd-65e99b0ece2a)/export.html> accessed 30 November 2015 and *Has the Referendum Campaign Made a Difference?* (n. 12).

economy would get worse, whether Scotland would keep the pound, and whether Scotland would remain in the EU all becoming of less concern to voters by the fourth week.

Conversely, the question of more powers had become slightly more important as had concerns over whether the gap between rich and poor would narrow or widen. Whilst it is not possible to establish cause and effect from these correlations, the data does at least suggest that the campaign may have had an impact on preference formation.[32] A separate study based on analysis of successive Scottish Social Attitudes Surveys also suggested that campaigning had made a difference, and that voters were better informed towards the end of the campaign than at its beginning.[33] The next section considers the arguments that were put before the voters.

III. The referendum debate

The length of the referendum campaign meant that there was ample time for a wide range of issues to be raised and debated. During the long campaign both the Scottish and UK Governments published extensive commentary on the issues they thought should influence voters. The Scottish Government's vision for an independent Scotland—in effect their referendum manifesto was set out in a White Paper, *Scotland's Future* in November 2013.[34] It made the general case for independence in an opening chapter, followed by further chapters on finance and the economy, and the main areas of public policy, with a final chapter on the transition to independence, the adoption of a written constitution and governance issues. This manifesto specified the policies the SNP would pursue if elected as the first government of an independent Scotland. Other key documents included a series of reports by the Fiscal Commission Working Group such as its report on the macroeconomic framework, which included its analysis of currency options for an independent Scotland (which was to prove a highly contentious issue in the campaign).[35] For its part, the UK Government published a lengthy series of *Scotland Analysis* papers between February 2013 and June 2014, fourteen on specific topics and a fifteenth offering the conclusions of the analysis programme.[36]

In addition to these official documents there was extensive discussion of the issues in all the media and academic commentary, and a huge volume of discussion

[32] See Mitchell, Ch. 4 in this volume. [33] See Mitchell, Ch. 4 in this volume.

[34] Scottish Government, *Scotland's Future: Your Guide to an Independent Scotland* (November 2014) <www.gov.scot/resource/0043/00439021.pdf> accessed 30 November 2015.

[35] Scottish Government, *Fiscal Commission Working Group—First Report—Macroeconomic Framework* (2013); Fiscal Commission Working Group First Report—Annex, Assessment of key currency options (2013), both available at: <www.gov.scot/Publications/2013/02/3017/downloads> accessed 30 November 2015.

[36] All the papers are available at: <www.gov.uk/government/collections/scotland-analysis> accessed 30 November 2015. A conclusions paper was published in June 2015.

in cyberspace. There was, therefore, a huge range and quantity of information and comment potentially available to voters to assist them to make up their minds.

While James Mitchell provides an overview in Chapter 4 of some key issues in the referendum campaign, Part III of the book examines those issues in more detail and sets out the terms on which they were debated by the Yes and No sides during the campaign. In Chapter 5, Aileen McHarg explores the constitutional case for independence, considering four sets of arguments which provided a basis for it: those based on a democratic deficit; effective governance; the place of Scotland in the United Kingdom's territorial constitution; and the constitution of an independent Scotland. She evaluates the strength of these arguments in the light of the referendum and of subsequent events, arguing that a coherent constitutional case can be made for independence, although not necessarily a compelling one. In particular, she highlights the similarities in the constitutional case made for independence and those made previously for devolution, arguing therefore that devolution in its current form has not provided an adequate answer to the constitutional discontents identified by its proponents. In Chapter 6, Jim Gallagher makes the case for Scotland remaining in the Union, reviewing arguments made both by supporters of the Union and supporters of independence. He reviews the political and economic benefits of the Union and the link between political union and economic integration, stressing the benefits of access to UK markets, a stable currency, and sharing of economic risks, and argues that the primary purpose of fiscal sharing is to allow for social solidarity and common social citizenship. He concludes with an analysis of how further devolution of power might allow the Scottish political institutions greater freedom to reflect Scottish opinion without threatening the risk pooling that underpins the Union.

In Chapter 7, Andrew Scott examines the specifically economic arguments for independence, addressing from a contrasting view broadly in favour of Scottish independence many of the issues discussed by Gallagher in Chapter 6. Scott covers the issues that were particularly prominent in the debate including the domestic implications of the financial crisis, the currency controversy, and the state of Scotland's public finances, and also addresses some post-referendum questions such as the promise to devolve additional powers over finance.

In Chapter 8, Sionaidh Douglas-Scott discusses two aspects of the European Union dimension of the independence debate. First, she discusses whether and on what terms Scotland might remain in the EU on becoming independent (a hotly contested issue during the referendum), and what the route to EU membership for an independent Scotland would be in the light of the relevant EU law principles. Secondly, she considers the implications of a vote in favour of the United Kingdom leaving the EU in the referendum on membership that will be held on 23 June 2016. These implications include the possibility that a vote for leaving the EU might be argued to be a reason for holding a second Scottish independence referendum, and the effects on an existing devolution settlement that incorporates both EU law and the European Convention on Human Rights as limits on the competence of devolved institutions.

The external aspect of the debate was not confined to EU matters. In Chapter 9, Christine Bell considers the general international law dimension and discusses the way international law arguments were used by both sides during the campaign in strategically instrumental ways, to support their political claims as to the consequences of independence. The relevant international law issues included whether Scotland had a right to self-determination and issues of state succession to international rights and obligations, in particular whether after independence the rest of the United Kingdom would be treated as a 'continuing state', and Scotland a 'successor state'. Other issues included how break-up would affect both an independent Scotland and the remainder of the United Kingdom, including the division of UK assets and liabilities and the effects of independence on financial and military security.

The paragraphs above are enough to give an indication of the matters covered in these chapters, but to set them more fully in context, I will offer a few further comments about the way the debate was framed.

A. The choice on offer: Independence or more devolution

The basic referendum choice itself, and the ensuing political argument and public debate was originally framed by the Edinburgh Agreement as a binary choice between independence and remaining in the United Kingdom. Yet the intermediate option of further devolution within the United Kingdom, which opinion surveys had consistently shown in recent years to be the preferred option of most Scots, did not disappear from the agenda. During the campaign, both the Scottish Conservative and Labour Parties published reports of Commissions they had established to consider further devolution of powers to the Scottish Parliament, that is, measures beyond those proposed by the Calman Commission.[37] As a Commission appointed by the Scottish Liberal Democrats had reported in favour of a federal solution in 2012[38] and a second report followed in March 2014,[39] this meant that all three of the main UK parties had tabled proposals for giving greater powers to the Scottish Parliament shortly before or during the campaign. These proposals were followed up by joint statements by the three party leaders in both June and August 2014 promising that

[37] See Scottish Conservatives, *Commission on the Future Governance of Scotland* (2014) <www.scottishconservatives.com/wordpress/wp-content/uploads/2014/06/Strathclyde_Commission_14.pdf> accessed 30 November 2015; Scottish Labour (2014), *Powers for a purpose—Strengthening Accountability and Empowering People* <www.scottishlabour.org.uk/page//Scottish%20Labour%20Devolution%20Commission%20report.pdf> accessed 30 November 2015.

[38] Scottish Liberal Democrats, *Federalism: the best future for Scotland: The report of the Home Rule and Community Rule Commission of the Scottish Liberal Democrats* (2012) <www.smithcommission.scot/wp-content/uploads/2014/10/Scottish-Liberal-Democrats-Submission-1.pdf> accessed 30 November 2015.

[39] Scottish Liberal Democrats, CAMPBELL II: *The second report of the Home Rule and Community Rule Commission* (2014) <http://worldofstuart.excellentcontent.com/repository/CampbellIIreport.pdf> accessed 30 November 2015.

more powers would be devolved to the Scottish Parliament if there were a No vote in the referendum, and finally by the 'vow' made at the end of the campaign. These statements effectively put back on the ballot the very option—further devolution—that had been ruled out by the Edinburgh Agreement, and the vote became a choice between independence and further devolution and—unless voters disbelieved the promise of further devolution—the status quo was no longer an option. I return to the effects of the more powers pledge below when considering the post-referendum situation.

1. The choice on offer: The meaning of independence

Another important framing factor was the way in which the concept of independence was defined; what exactly did 'independence' mean? A few decades ago, the idea of independence carried little ambiguity. Independence equated to sovereignty. An independent nation state had complete or very substantial control over its own affairs. Its government decided all questions of domestic law and policy without outside interference and it carried on relations with other states as an independent entity. Independent states also had control over their populations and their borders, possessed their own armed forces, and had their own currency. Having membership of various international organizations did not substantially compromise the sovereignty of the nation state, and whilst in practice many states experienced severe political and economic constraints on their ability to act independently, the 'sovereigntist' view of independence was the ideal to which states and stateless nations aspired.

More recently, it has been increasingly recognized that in an increasingly interdependent world this level of autonomy may not be achievable or desirable for many states and that sovereignty can be shared and divided rather than having a single locus in the nation state. Independence has come to be seen more as a spectrum of possibilities for a nation than as a fixed indivisible package. This shift in understanding of independence is perfectly illustrated by the Scottish independence debate.[40]

The version of independence offered to the Scottish people by the SNP was very different to the traditional 'sovereigntist' version. The SNP had begun to move away from that position many years before the referendum campaign, and since they started the National Conversation had consistently argued that whilst much would change as a result of independence, much would also stay the same. It stated that the 'current parliamentary and political Union of Great Britain and Northern Ireland would become a monarchical and social Union—United Kingdoms rather than a United Kingdom ....'[41]

The precise package offered to the people of Scotland during the campaign included the following points:

[40] See, generally, M. Keating, *The Independence of Scotland—Self-government and the Shifting Politics of the Union* (Oxford University Press 2009) ch. 6.

[41] See *Choosing Scotland's Future*, para. 3.25.

- Scotland would be a separate state recognized as such by other states and a member of the United Nations;
- The Queen would remain as head of state;
- Scotland would be a member of the European Union and of the Council of Europe;
- Scotland would become a member of NATO and the OSCE;[42]
- all matters of domestic policy would be settled by the Scottish Parliament and Government; but
- Scotland's currency would continue to be the pound which would be shared with the rest of the United Kingdom.

As noted above, the SNPs approach was to emphasize continuity as well as change; much would stay the same after independence. It would not be a leap in the dark. This strategy was designed to allay the fear of the consequences of change that might put off voters not already converted to the independence cause. The possible downside of such a strategy is that it fails to satisfy voters already committed to independence who might see limitations on the autonomy of a future self-governing Scotland as an unwanted concession to 'independence-lite'. However, the SNP made the calculation that the benefits of allaying the fears of the undecided by stressing continuity outweighed any risk that a departure from the classical conception of independence would put off enthusiasts. Clearly, the commitment to the EU was incompatible with the traditional conception of independence because of the legal and de facto limits that membership places on a member state's autonomy of decision. The intention to join NATO was far less so since military alliances are a long-standing feature of international relations. However, it is unlikely that most Scottish voters would have seen anything odd in combining any of these commitments with an aspiration for independence, even those who were sceptical about the EU. Neither the continuation of the monarchy nor membership of the European Union would have seemed an unacceptable compromise.

The decision as to the currency of an independent Scotland—one of the key decisions that the SNP had to make—was more problematic. For some years, the SNP had been suggesting that an independent Scotland would use the euro as its currency. The financial crisis of 2007–8 and the subsequent troubles of the Eurozone prompted a rethink, and in the referendum campaign, the SNP adopted the position recommended by its Fiscal Commission that Scotland should enter a formal monetary union with the rest of the United Kingdom and continue to use the pound sterling with the agreement of the UK Government. In short, Scotland would have a currency union with the rest of the United Kingdom. This would leave important economic management powers with the UK Treasury and Bank of England. Even from within the perspective of independence as a spectrum

[42] Organization for Security and Cooperation in Europe.

of possibilities, this was an important concession. The currency was a genuine choice, as the euro, a distinctive Scottish currency, and the informal use of sterling were all viable options.

The obvious concern about the currency union proposal was that under it the Bank of England would make all necessary decisions regarding the currency, set interest rates, and act as lender of last resort. The feasibility and merits and demerits for both Scotland and the rest of the United Kingdom of a currency union were hotly contested in the campaign. Gallagher[43] and Scott[44] set out the arguments in this volume, reaching different conclusions. Whatever view one takes of the currency question, a currency union clearly results in a substantial loss of autonomy compared to the classical conception of independence. Monetary policy would be determined by the United Kingdom and the Scottish Government would in practice have to get the UK Government's agreement to its borrowing plans and the size of its permissible deficit. This might well limit the policies that an independent Scotland could pursue as most policies have significant expenditure implications. In particular, it might well limit the extent to which Scotland could make different policy choices from England when the ability to pursue different policies, including reversing or modifying policies pursued by the UK coalition government between 2010–15, had been one of the key arguments for independence.

The SNP's decision to propose a currency union indicates that, for it, independence did not necessarily mean maximum decision-making autonomy. It was prepared to sacrifice some of its potential autonomy in the service of other goals, for example, ensuring macroeconomic stability. This nuanced attitude to independence seemed to chime with voters' views. Although the prospects for the economy were clearly a key issue for voters, there was little evidence of potential supporters of independence being disillusioned by the limits on autonomy that a shared currency would impose.[45] Voters seemed to appreciate that independence is not a one-size-fits-all concept and that what it meant for Scotland could be varied by a pragmatic judgment of what was in Scotland's best interests. So, whilst the concept of independence was the key framing concept in the referendum campaign, it was a flexible rather than a rigid frame.

B. Practical politics and identity politics

One of the interesting features of both the official Yes and No campaigns was the extent to which they concentrated on the practical consequences of independence rather than identity politics. Perceptions of identity undoubtedly influenced voters' views on independence, but the campaign was not fought principally on that terrain. A campaign for independence based on identity might have been expected to invoke Scotland's history, particularly before the Union, as a source

[43] See Ch. 6. [44] See Ch. 7.

[45] Both Mitchell, Ch. 4 and Scott, Ch. 7 in this volume discuss the impact of the debate over the currency.

of national pride and assert that there was a distinct Scottish character which made Scots different from their neighbours in the rest of the United Kingdom. A campaign against independence based on identity might have been expected to stress post-Union history, similarity of national character, and common institutions such as the monarchy.

Neither of the official campaigns took that direction. According to the SNP's independence White Paper the central purpose of independence was 'to make life better for people living in Scotland' and there were three overriding reasons for Scotland to become independent: (i) to create a more democratic Scotland (in the sense that only the people of Scotland would choose their governors and that all important policy decisions would be made in Scotland), (ii) to create a more prosperous Scotland (ie economic growth would be higher), and (iii) to become a fairer society (ie there would be a reduction in inequality). Much of the White Paper was taken up with explanation of the policies that would be pursued across the full range of policy areas were the SNP to form a post-independence government, always emphasizing where the policies differed from those being pursued by the UK Government. Thus, in the field of social security benefits, a future SNP government would improve the state pension, abolish the bedroom tax, and halt the further rollout of Universal Credit and the Personal Independence Payment.[46] In the field of education, it would continue to provide higher education free of charge and in the field of defence Scotland would remain in NATO but would insist on withdrawal of nuclear weapons from Scotland. The official campaign did not seek to emphasize Scottish identity against any other kind of identity, for example, British or English; indeed the foreword stated that 'the social ties between Scotland and the rest of the UK will continue and thrive.' There was little by way of appeals to history or patriotic sentiment in the White Paper.

The No campaign paid even less attention to questions of identity. It did not seek to rely greatly on shared history or the flags and other symbols of 'banal nationalism',[47] emphasizing instead the negative consequences of independence (principally economic) and the obstacles which lay in the path of key SNP's proposals, for instance, the currency union and admission to membership of the EU.

These modes of campaigning were based on pragmatic calculations of what was the best approach to persuading the voters. The No campaign calculated that appeals to history and tradition would probably cut little ice with those who were not already committed to voting No. And a strong stress on British identity might not help it to persuade those who had a strong Scottish identity but were wary of the possible consequences of independence to vote No. The Yes side made a similar calculation; appeals to history and tradition might go down well with committed nationalists but might be off-putting for certain groups of waverers. For both

[46] This benefit replaced Disability Living Allowance, a benefit which met care and mobility needs, with effect (for new claims) from April 2013.

[47] M. Billig, *Banal Nationalism* (Sage 1995).

sides, it seemed that a strategy focusing on consequences would be more fruitful and public debate in the media focused largely on practical issues such as the prospects for the economy and the likely state of the Scottish public finances after independence, the feasibility and desirability of a currency union, social security policy, and the prospects of Scotland gaining entry to the EU.

That, of course, is to describe the official campaign. What happened at grass-roots level is harder to generalize about but here identity politics were clearly more prominent. In cyberspace in particular insults were traded, national epithets bandied about, and patriotism and loyalties questioned. In this respect the referendum campaign followed the temper of the times, online abuse having become a feature of public debate in recent years. This tendency to abuse political opponents led to accusations of intimidation from both sides in the referendum debate. However, unfortunate as these abusive interventions were, they were probably no more than was to be expected on such an important and potentially divisive issue. The campaign was on the whole conducted in a civilized manner, and it seems very unlikely that the bad behaviour of a minority of campaigners significantly affected the result.

IV. Beyond the referendum

The referendum has resulted in the rejection of one major constitutional change. At the same time it has been the catalyst for other substantial constitutional changes: further devolution and the introduction of 'English votes for English laws'. Part IV of this book therefore changes the focus from the independence question and the referendum debate to the territorial politics of the United Kingdom and its constitution after the referendum.

In Chapter 10, Nicola McEwen considers the particular path now being taken towards constitutional reform in the wake of the referendum by implementing the proposals of the Smith Commission. She examines the question whether we might be moving towards a federal United Kingdom. More generally, she assesses the extent and nature of the power future Scottish Governments will have under the Smith Commission proposals in a wider comparative perspective utilizing a multi-factorial test of decentralization.

In Chapter 11, Neil Walker examines the future of the United Kingdom's territorial constitution considering the different options for developing the territorial dimension of the UK constitution and Scotland's place within it. He addresses, amongst other things, the possible extent and intensity of Scottish self-government short of independence, the question of how far the governance arrangements of the constituent nations of the United Kingdom are or should be symmetrical, the forms of common governing institutions at the UK level that may be required to accommodate substate distinctiveness or to promote integration, and the question of the locus, terms, and feasibility of constitutional initiative in a context where the proper source(s) of constituent power is a matter of deep and continuing disputation.

In Chapter 12 Alan Page focuses on the present and future governance of Scotland in relation to both structures and accountability. He discusses the constitutional fundamentals of the devolution settlement in place before the referendum, the proposals set out in the referendum campaign by the SNP for the transition to independence (the interim constitutional platform) and the development of a permanent constitution of an independent Scotland. He also considers the Smith Commission proposals for further devolution as they relate to the constitutional structure and accountability of the Scottish Parliament and Government.

In Chapter 13, Nicholas Aroney considers what can be learned from the constitutional experience of Canada and Australia, these being countries whose systems of government are both constitutionally derived from Westminster and modelled with some modifications on the Westminster original. He considers whether these Westminster-centred examples of self-government can offer useful analogies for Scotland in terms of the process, shape, and long-term trajectory of constitutional reform.

The book closes with Chapter 14 by Andrew Tickell, entitled 'The Technical Jekyll and the Political Hyde: The Constitutional Law and Politics of Scotland's Independence "Neverendum"'. It examines the prospects for a future referendum, including the circumstances which might give rise to another referendum, the vexed and internationally resonant question of the legality of any such referendum, and how it would be constitutionally regulated.

V. Concluding thoughts

A. The referendum, democracy and public participation

Contrasting thoughts have been expressed on the significance for democratic politics of the referendum. The referendum process was certainly not politics as usual. There was much greater voter engagement than has been the case in recent election campaigns. This was apparent not just in the turnout which was, at 84.6 per cent, higher than at any UK general election, but also in the very high levels of voter engagement during the campaign. Both a high turnout and a high level of voter engagement were always likely given what was at stake. Nonetheless, in the light of the evident disillusionment with democratic politics felt by voters across the United Kingdom in recent years, many commentators were surprised by both trends. For them, the significance of the referendum lay not only in its result but also in the way voters experienced the process. It was proof that voters' disengagement from politics could be reversed. One well-known journalist described the referendum debate as 'a festival of democracy'.[48] Many similar comments could be cited and they are supported by evidence from the ESRC study in which

[48] I. Macwhirter, *Disunited Kingdom: How Westminster Won a Referendum but Lost Scotland* (Cargo Books 2014).

36.9 per cent said they had become a bit more or a lot more involved in politics than they normally would, and a further 50.6 per cent had noticed others becoming more involved even though it had made no difference to them. There was a marked difference between Yes and No voters with 50.4 per cent of Yes voters saying they had become a bit more or a lot more involved in politics than they normally would compared to only 24.7 per cent of No voters. So, the heightened engagement with politics that so evidently occurred during the referendum seems to have been far more on the side of Yes voters than no voters.

There is also evidence that Yes and No voters experienced the referendum differently in other ways, the former having a very positive view and thinking that it brought the country together and the latter thinking it divisive. In one survey carried out by YouGov towards the end of the campaign,[49] 46 per cent of No voters said that they had felt personally threatened by the Yes campaign at some point. By contrast, 24 per cent of Yes voters said that they had felt personally threatened by the No campaign. Similarly, about half of No voters felt that they had not always felt able to speak freely about their views during the campaign compared to a fifth of Yes voters. Moreover, 85 per cent of No voters said they felt Scottish society had become more divided as a result of the referendum campaign, whereas nearly 40 per cent of Yes voters felt it had become more united and a quarter felt that the campaign had made no difference.[50]

Interpreting these findings is not straightforward, particularly the high proportion referring to feeling 'threatened'. Respondents may, for example, have answered yes to this question merely because independence would affect them personally in ways they did not like. We would want to know more about what lies behind these responses before drawing firm conclusions from such surveys about any negative effects of the campaign, but they do suggest caution about seeing the undoubted increase in public engagement that occurred as an unqualified good.

Post-referendum developments also suggest there may be a difference between Yes and No voters in continued engagement with politics. In the ESRC study, Yes voters were far more likely than No voters to say both that they and the Scottish public generally would stay more involved in politics after the referendum as opposed to things going back to normal. This is supported by what has happened to political party membership. The SNP certainly experienced a great increase in membership. It had around 25,000 members before the referendum but this increased to 70,000 within a few weeks and had increased to around 112,000 one year later.[51] The Greens have also seen growth in membership increasing from

[49] Buzzfeed News, 'Scotland's No Voters Feel Threatened, Afraid To Speak Out, And Think Their Country Is More Divided' <www.buzzfeed.com/jimwaterson/scotlands-no-voters-feel-threatened-afraid-to-speak-out-and#.isVadNEXR> accessed 30 November 2015.

[50] A similar finding was made in a poll published by the Daily Telegraph. See Opinium/Daily Telegraph: <http://ourinsight.opinium.co.uk/survey-results/opiniumtelegraph-scottish-referendum-poll> accessed 30 November 2015.

[51] 'Independence referendum one year on: The Winners and Losers', available at: <http://beta.scotsman.com/news/independence-referendum-one-year-on-the-winners-and-losers-1-3891329> accessed 30 November 2015.

around 1,700 registered members to 9,000 members a year later.[52] The Labour Party appeared to suffer a decline in membership after the referendum. Numbers were boosted by the 2015 leadership election in Scotland although they remain low by historic standards.[53] So, it does appear as if many Yes voters have been inspired to get more involved in politics since the referendum, but this seems much less true of No voters.

So, despite the positive experiences many people had of the referendum campaign and the mainly positive commentary since, we must be open to the possibility that voters' experiences during the campaign may have been very different, and their propensity to maintain the stronger engagement with politics that was evident also different. We must also attend to the possibility that Scotland remains seriously divided and that it may be difficult to bridge that divide. The independence question has become the central question of Scottish politics and the people's views on it seem to have hardened during and since the referendum campaign.

B. An uncertain future

It has become almost a cliché to say that the referendum has not finally resolved the question of Scotland's future, or indeed that of the United Kingdom. On more than one occasion before the referendum, Alex Salmond, then leader of the SNP and First Minister, described the referendum as 'a once in a generation opportunity', implying that in the event of a No vote, another referendum on independence could not be called for many years. Similarly, the UK Government hoped that the referendum would be decisive and that the issue of independence would cease to be the central question of Scottish politics. However, the No vote has not turned out to be a decisive rejection of independence. At 45 per cent in favour of Yes, the result was close enough to give encouragement to supporters of independence and represented a significant increase compared to the early stages of the campaign. Since the referendum it has been the SNP that has strengthened its position while the parties supporting the Union have become weaker, and many individual supporters of the Union seem more pessimistic about its long-term prospects since the referendum than before it. In an Ipsos MORI survey carried out for STV, 54 per cent of respondents thought it likely that independence would happen by 2025, compared to 44 per cent who thought it was unlikely and two per cent who were unsure.[54]

So can the Union survive in the long-term? That is a large issue which cannot be answered in this introduction, but here are a few points. Two of the key determinants of how people voted appear to have been perceptions of identity and perceptions of the economic consequences of independence. The question of identity

52 'Independence referendum one year on' (n. 51).

53 <www.scotsman.com/news/politics/interview-kezia-dugdale-on-reform-of-scots-labour-1-3899416#axzz3pmSpXCVP> accessed 30 November 2015.

54 <https://www.ipsos-mori.com/researchpublications/researcharchive/3662/Scots-believe-independence-is-likely-to-happen-in-the-next-ten-years.aspx> accessed 30 November 2015.

has figured prominently in accounts suggesting that the United Kingdom cannot survive. The argument is that the factors which once held the United Kingdom together by creating a common sense of national identity no longer apply. Religion is no longer a unifying factor if it ever was. Neither is the British Empire which has largely gone, nor the existence of an external threat, the last major war having ended seventy years ago.[55] Evidence to support this thesis can be found in the changes that have taken place over time in perceptions of national identity. The Linz-Moreno question has been asked for many years and had shown a long-term increase in the proportion identifying themselves as 'Scottish and not British' or 'more Scottish than British' and a long-term decrease in the proportion identifying themselves as 'equally British and Scottish'. The weakness in this argument is that new reasons for perceiving a common identity can replace old ones. It has been argued, for example, that the welfare state created in the twentieth century funded by UK taxation and under which all enjoy common social rights helped to create a sense of common citizenship. It is also worth noting that since 2011 there has been a marked increase in the proportion of the population identifying themselves as 'equally British and Scottish' and a corresponding reduction in those identifying as 'Scottish and not British' or 'more Scottish than British'.[56] So perceptions of identity appear to be fluid to some extent and to change in response to changing circumstances. It would be wrong, therefore, to conclude that there will inevitably be further decline in 'Britishness' and a corresponding weakening of support for the Union.

In any event, the opinion survey data suggest that identity is not the only issue for Scottish voters in deciding on their governing arrangements. The likely economic consequences appeared to be a major issue and, as noted above, those who thought the economy would get worse under independence were very unlikely to vote Yes. How voters' perceptions of the economy will change in future can only be guessed at, but these perceptions are likely to be shaped to a considerable extent by government policy. Decisions on economic policies and their consequences both by UK and Scottish Governments may have important effects on the level of support for the Union.

More generally, the policies, decisions, and actions of political parties and their leaders and the image they present will have an important impact on voters' views of the Union. Keating commented in 2009, with respect to the apparent decline of the Union, that mainstream elites had lost the constitutional plot and neither Conservative nor Labour parties had found a new form of territorial accommodation to suit modern conditions.[57] This comment remains apposite. The Labour party currently lacks credibility in Scotland and, having lost most of its MPs from the UK Parliament, it is not in strong position to make the case for Union. The Conservative party seems to have a limited understanding of the possible consequences of its actions for the Union. The partisan approach being taken to the

[55] See eg L. Colley, *Britons: Forging the Nation 1707–1837* (Yale University Press 1992).
[56] See *Has the Referendum Campaign Made a Difference?* (n. 12).
[57] Keating, *The Independence of Scotland* (n. 40) at 77.

introduction of English votes for English laws risks alienating Scots by adding to their dissatisfaction with Westminster politics and there is the possibility that—as during the Thatcher years—unpopular Conservative economic policies may be seen as a Westminster imposition on Scotland. The SNP has never had a stronger grip on Scottish politics and can be expected to continue to make a persuasive case for independence.

That does not mean it will call for another referendum soon. The SNP's new leader, Nicola Sturgeon, will not necessarily feel herself to be bound by Salmond's 'once in a generation' but at the party's 2015 annual conference, she dampened speculation, saying there would be no call for another referendum until 'strong and consistent evidence' emerged of a change in public opinion. Subsequent briefing by senior party figures suggested this meant the opinion polls showing 60 per cent of voters in favour of independence for over a year. On the one hand, this cautious approach seemed to postpone the possibility of a second referendum into the distant future; on the other, no guarantee was given that a minimum time must elapse before a further referendum took place. The First Minister has also said that a second referendum would be justified if the UK electorate as a whole were to vote to leave the EU, but the majority of Scots chose to remain. As the EU referendum will take place on 23 June 2016, this brings the possibility of an independence referendum into the near future.

How important the further devolution proposed by the Smith Commission will be to the future of the Union is also unclear. Currently, it shows little sign of stabilizing the situation as polling evidence suggests that voters are distrustful of the ability of the pro-Union parties to deliver the promise of further devolution; further, while many have little grasp of the detail of proposals, they also think they do not go far enough. In a nutshell, as yet the process of devolving further powers does not seem to be leading to increased voter satisfaction with the Union. In light of this, one academic has recommended that a referendum be held to endorse the further devolution envisaged by the Scotland Bill and that it would be in the interests of the pro-Union parties to support this.[58]

In short, the current situation is one of uncertainty. The Union has been preserved for the time being but its long-term prospects remain in doubt. Yet, there is nothing inevitable about eventual dissolution of the Union. Short-term prospects are also unclear especially given the contrast between the relatively congenial political and economic circumstances in which devolution was first introduced and the far more challenging circumstances in which the enhanced devolution envisaged by the Scotland Bill will operate.

[58] House of Lords Select Committee on the Constitution, *Inquiry on The Union and Devolution*, evidence of Professor John Curtice, 4 November 2015 <http://data.parliament.uk/writtenevidence/committeeevidence.svc/evidencedocument/constitution-committee/the-union-and-devolution/oral/24237.html> accessed 30 November 2015.

2

The Independence Referendum in Historical and Political Context

Colin Kidd and Malcolm Petrie

I. Introduction

Proximity to events makes contemporary history a risky undertaking. The Scottish independence referendum of 2014 is a case in point. While the historian may curb his or her own political bias, and try to empathize with both sides,[1] it remains difficult to discern the deeper significance of the referendum, its antecedents, and outcome. Bias, it transpires, is less of a disadvantage than the fact that in matters of contemporary history one's vantage point keeps shifting. Until the Scottish National Party (SNP)'s surprise victory in the Scottish Parliamentary election in 2011 a referendum on independence was a remote hypothetical. After all, the SNP had won only six of Scotland's fifty-nine seats in the 2010 UK general election. Besides, the devolved settlement had inbuilt shock absorbers; the Additional Member voting system used in elections to the Scottish Parliament had been devised with the explicit intent of precluding single-party government. The SNP—whose ultimate goal was Scottish independence—was to be confined by electoral arrangements which should, in the last resort, compel cooperation with one or more of the 'Unionist' parties. Moreover, constitutional change did not belong within the remit of Holyrood, but was reserved to Westminster. When, in January 2012, the Prime Minister David Cameron indicated his willingness to endorse the legitimacy of a referendum on Scottish independence, opinion polls still predicted a resounding No vote, an outcome still seemingly likely when the Edinburgh Agreement—a concordat between the Scottish and UK Governments on the timing and character of the referendum—was concluded in October 2012. Only in the final weeks before the September 2014 referendum did it become obvious that support for the Union—and its central Scottish pillar, the Labour Party—was crumbling. Nevertheless, the outcome of the referendum remained a clear, if far from decisive, victory for supporters of the Union, by 55 per cent to

[1] It is perhaps worth noting that the two authors of this essay hold differing views on Scottish politics.

45 per cent. A further twist followed. Notwithstanding the electorate's rejection of the SNP's purported *raison d'être*, by early 2015, the SNP threatened a near clean sweep of Scottish seats in the UK general election, and in the end took fifty-six out of fifty-nine constituencies. Assessing the meaning of these bewildering events depended less on one's partisan preferences than on whether one observed the drama from the vantage point of 2011–12 or 2014–15.

Obviously, a quicksilver electorate provides a vital ingredient in the analysis. Since the first elections to the devolved Scottish Parliament in 1999, Scottish voters had—until 2015—been more willing to vote for the SNP in Scottish than in UK elections. However, in addition to these curious divergences in voting patterns, there were other wrinkles. In the independence referendum of 2014 twenty-eight of thirty-two districts, including areas with SNP representation at Westminster and Holyrood, voted No. Yet less than a year later much of Scotland had transferred its allegiance to the SNP. This leaves open the issue of whether voters were happy enough to support the SNP, but reluctant to endorse its flagship policy; or were acting tactically to secure further devolution; or had genuinely changed their minds about independence. The contemporary historian has no means of distinguishing deep and enduring changes from temporary swings of electoral mood. Did the low rumbles which preceded the referendum—such as the SNP's emergence as the largest party at Holyrood in the Scottish election of 2007—indicate an inexorable shifting of tectonic plates? Or were such events merely an index of growing electoral volatility?

Another area of perplexity is the problematic nature of Scottish constitutional vocabulary, especially the terms 'Unionism' and 'nationalism', which had pejorative overtones, strangely enough, for their *own* supporters. In the aftermath of the referendum, the Labour Party in Scotland acquired a new leader, Jim Murphy, who became the de facto leader of the forces of Unionism, yet promptly announced that, being from Irish Catholic stock, he had never been, and was not, a 'Unionist'.[2] Why was Unionism so toxic? For a start, between 1912 and 1965 the Scottish Conservatives had been known as the Unionists,[3] a legacy of their merger with the Liberal Unionists, who had split from the Liberals in opposition to the Gladstonian policy of Irish Home Rule. There are several matters to note here. Until at least the 1970s, the Anglo-Scottish Union was so uncontentious that it was rarely in need of defence, or indeed articulation. Thus Unionism, even in Scotland, meant a defence of the British-Irish Union;[4] and as late as the 1970s and 1980s Unionism was associated almost exclusively with a 'primordial' Ulster Unionism repellent to mainstream political opinion.[5] Unionism was, then, the

[2] M. Gardham, 'I Have Never Been a Unionist: Murphy' *Herald* (Glasgow, 14 January 2015) <www.heraldscotland.com/politics/scottish-politics/i-have-never-been-a-unionist-murphy.116094238> accessed 21 May 2015.

[3] D. Seawright, 'The Scottish Unionist Party: What's in a Name?' (1996) 14 *Scottish Affairs* 90.

[4] C. Macdonald (ed.), *Unionist Scotland 1800–1997* (John Donald 1998).

[5] I. McLean and A. McMillan, *State of the Union: Unionism and the Alternatives in the United Kingdom since 1707* (Oxford University Press 2005); A. Jackson, *The Two Unions: Ireland, Scotland, and the Survival of the United Kingdom, 1707–2007* (Oxford University Press 2011). Cf. G. Walker, *Intimate Strangers: Political and Cultural Interactions between Scotland and Ulster* (John Donald 1995).

ideology which dared not speak its name, even after the referendum campaign. 'Nationalism' was not constrained by the same taboo, yet there remained a discomfort in some quarters about the term. The novelist James Robertson declared that he did 'not subscribe to nationalism as an ideology', but did 'believe in the right of peoples and nations, if that is how they perceive themselves, to determine their own political futures.'[6]

There are further ambiguities. The SNP contains gradualists as well as fundamentalists; and for the former—arguably including Alex Salmond and Nicola Sturgeon—social justice matters as much as complete disengagement from the British state. Indeed, historians now recognize that Scottish political culture from the mid-nineteenth century has functioned largely in the middling range of a unionist-nationalist continuum, with politicians generally appealing to *both* Scottish and British values.[7] Despite the seemingly unbridgeable gulf between nationalism and Unionism, Salmond himself appropriated the term 'social union' to describe his vision of a post-independence Scotland's shared currency, shared monarchy, and, suggestively, common standards of welfare with the former United Kingdom. The SNP's promotion of a 'social union' further inhibited the clear articulation of a Unionist case for the British state, while Unionist politicians happily deployed the quasi-nationalist rhetoric of 'devo-max'. Furthermore, Labour, Liberal Democrats, and the SNP all used the rhetoric of 'home rule'—a vague synonym for devolution, which did not preclude other more daring possibilities, as in Salmond's invocation of Scotland's 'home rule journey'[8]—and all subscribed to the notion of Scottish popular sovereignty. During the 1970s, indeed, the intense competiveness between Labour and the SNP had not precluded a measure of flirtation, most notably in Gordon Brown's celebrated *Red Paper*.[9] The starkness of the Yes-No choice facing Scots in 2014 and the exclusion of a third way, the devo-max option, from the ballot paper tended to obscure such commonalities. In the circumstances, it was the SNP who proved most adept at triangulation. During the referendum campaign and its aftermath, the SNP made great efforts to woo Labour voters, despite denouncing the leaders of the Labour Party as 'Red Tories' for allying with the Conservatives under the umbrella of Better Together, the cross-party No campaign.

The historian is also faced with one of the biggest problems which confounded the No campaign: how to disentangle disappointment with the sitting

[6] Quoted in: D. Torrance, *The Battle for Britain: Scotland and the Independence Referendum* (Biteback Publishing 2013) 198.

[7] G. Morton, *Unionist-Nationalism: Governing Urban Scotland, 1830–1860* (Tuckwell Press 1999); C. Kidd, *Union and Unionisms: Political Thought in Scotland, 1500–2000* (Cambridge University Press 2008).

[8] S. Carrell and N. Watt, 'Alex Salmond hails historic day for Scotland after referendum deal' *Guardian* (London, 15 October 2012). <www.theguardian.com/politics/2012/oct/15/alex-salmond-scotland-referendum-deal> accessed 21 May 2015.

[9] G. Brown (ed.), *The Red Paper on Scotland* (Edinburgh University Student Publications 1975).

government of the United Kingdom from Scottish attitudes towards the British state in the abstract. The Yes campaign focused as much attention on remedying current policy affronts as on deeper structural flaws in the Anglo-Scottish constitutional relationship. Indeed, the referendum injected a demotic element into the constitutional question. In the final days of the campaign, it seemed as if the division was stark: a cleavage between Left and Right within Scottish society, between a downtrodden working class willing to risk independence and a comfortably complacent bourgeoisie. That was, of course, an oversimplification, yet poignant. Over the past forty years, as we shall see, identity politics has dominated Scottish debate. Nevertheless the Scottish Question has not been exclusively a matter of nationhood; it is also about class, and the self-identification of Scotland—even at the heart of the middle class—as a working-class nation.

II. Electing the Union

The Union of 1707 created a hybrid polity, a mixed-unitary state, which exhibited both pluralism and centralization. While Scotland retained its own legal system and established Church, there was, in the sovereign Westminster Parliament, a common focal point for British politics. Of the component parts of the United Kingdom, only Northern Ireland, with its own devolved assembly at Stormont and regional parties, has stood apart from the norms of mainstream British politics. Despite the presence on the fringes of Scottish politics from the inter-war period of, first, the National Party of Scotland (founded in 1928), and then, from 1934, the SNP—a fusion of the NPS with the right-of-centre Scottish Party[10]—several decades would pass before the nationalists made any impact on politics. Anglo-Scottish political convergence continued apace after 1945. The two-party dominance of Labour and the Conservatives in England and Wales was replicated in Scotland, with the two parties routinely sharing over 85 per cent of the vote both north and south of the border in the early 1950s. Scottish Unionists had traditionally opposed Home Rule; in 1958, Labour officially repudiated its commitment to establish a Scottish Parliament, which had been largely theoretical since the 1930s in any case. Mid-century Scottish politics outwardly assumed a largely British, and Unionist, hue.[11]

Just two decades later, however, this cross-border equipoise had vanished, and politics in Scotland had been transformed into a more fluid, and volatile, four-cornered contest. As John Mackintosh, Labour MP for East Lothian and a Professor in Politics at the University of Edinburgh, reflected in 1976, 'for the

[10] R. Finlay, *Independent and Free: Scottish Politics and the Origins of the SNP 1918–1945* (John Donald 1994).

[11] M. Keating, 'The Labour Party in Scotland, 1951–1964' in I. Donnachie and others (eds), *Forward! Labour Politics in Scotland, 1888–1988* (Polygon 1989); E. A. Cameron, *Impaled upon a Thistle: Scotland since 1880* (Edinburgh University Press 2010) 263–88.

first time in modern history there is ... something called Scottish politics, which has a life of its own'.[12] Commentators began to speak of the looming 'break-up' of Britain, or, less portentously, of the 'end of British politics'.[13] This was, in part, exaggeration: Scottish politics continued to be shaped by events at Westminster. Nonetheless, such perceptions mattered. By the end of the 1970s Scottish politics felt increasingly distinctive, and, more importantly, produced different outcomes from the rest of Britain.

It was the advent of a politically credible Scottish nationalism, coupled with the inability of Scottish Conservatives to equal the performance of their counterparts in England that fostered a specifically Scottish politics.[14] Conservative fortunes in Scotland waned steadily after the highpoint of Unionism in 1955, when the Party achieved an outright majority of both votes and parliamentary seats. In 1964 the Unionists polled just over 40 per cent; by October 1974 the Party—since 1965 known as the Scottish Conservative and Unionists—could claim the loyalties of less than one in four Scots, in contrast to almost four in ten across the United Kingdom as a whole. This decline was paralleled by the emergence of the SNP as a plausible political force. After decades of electoral irrelevance, the SNP recorded a remarkable victory at the Hamilton by-election of November 1967, when Winnie Ewing secured 46 per cent of the vote in the safest Labour seat in Scotland. The following year the Party topped the poll at the local authority elections. In the short term, the SNP failed to capitalize on these advances. At the 1970 general election Hamilton was reclaimed by Labour, with only the Western Isles returning a SNP Member. Nevertheless, in attaining 11 per cent of the vote, a platform had been laid, and, after further by-election success at Glasgow Govan in 1973, the SNP polled first 22 and then over 30 per cent of the vote at the two general elections of 1974. In February 1974 they returned seven MPs to Westminster, and eleven in the October election later that year. This represented astonishing progress for a party, which, barring Dr Robert McIntyre's six-week sojourn in the peculiar circumstances of spring 1945, lacked even a single Member of Parliament before 1967.

The speed with which the national question garnered prominence in British politics appeared startling.[15] Yet notwithstanding the electoral marginality of the SNP, national identity was far from irrelevant to Scottish political debate. The Scottish Covenant, a mass petition expressing a vague commitment to Home Rule, was inaugurated in 1949, and had reportedly acquired 1.7 million signatures by the following year. It relied, however, on moral suasion, and, lacking parliamentary support, was easily dismissed by the Labour government. A frustrated Scottish sentiment was similarly glimpsed in the reception afforded to the

[12] J. P. Mackintosh, 'Labour and Scotland' *New Statesman* (London, 16 January 1976) 55–6.

[13] T. Nairn, *The Break-up of Britain: Crisis and Neo-Nationalism* (New Left Books 1977); W. L. Miller, *The End of British Politics? Scots and English Political Behaviour in the 1970s* (Clarendon Press 1981).

[14] D. Torrance (ed.), *Whatever happened to Tory Scotland?* (Edinburgh University Press 2012).

[15] In Wales, Gwynfor Evans, the first Plaid Cymru MP, was returned at the July 1966 Carmarthen by-election.

temporary 'liberation' of the Stone of Destiny by some enterprising students in 1950, and the affront caused when the new Queen adopted the title Elizabeth II, when her namesake had, of course, been Queen only of England.[16] Of greater significance was the unease occasioned by Labour's post-war programme of nationalization, which aroused fears that such measures would lead to the erosion of a distinctive Scottish identity. During their time in opposition the Conservatives had taken care to indulge such sentiments. In May 1949 Winston Churchill addressed a Unionist rally in Glasgow, declaring that 'no sharper challenge could be given to Scottish national sentiment than [that] launched by the Socialism of Whitehall'.[17] The rhetorical vilification of 'Whitehall' centralization was enshrined in a pamphlet, *Scottish Control of Scottish Affairs*, which criticized the growing authority of central government as a 'new despotism', which emanated from a political philosophy that 'denies individuality either in men or in nations'.[18]

This has been viewed in retrospect as a cynical, if not unsuccessful, attempt by the Unionists to 'play the Scottish card' in order to undermine support for the Labour Party.[19] Whatever the sincerity of these flourishes, they certainly allowed the Unionists to pose as the defenders of Scotland. Although not in favour of a devolved parliament, the Conservatives, once returned to office in 1951, did bolster the remit and personnel of the Scottish Office. Beneath the ostensible 'Britishness' of Scottish politics in the 1950s, there remained certain Scottish facets; the achievement of Unionism was to accommodate a distinctive, yet still varied, 'Scottishness' within a larger British framework. If in West Central Scotland the Party embodied a popular Protestantism and imperialism, in the rural peripheries it was heir to a deeply entrenched provincial Liberalism, something reflected in the continued relevance of the National Liberal label, a relic of the 1930s, within post-war Unionism.[20] Thus Unionism was never merely synonymous with Conservatism, but was instead closer to a broad coalition of those non-Labour forces that were always a narrow majority within Scotland. By the 1960s, however, this coalition was fragmenting as the threat of socialism receded and, at a British level, politics began to centre upon questions of economic modernization. With the abandonment of the Unionist brand in 1965, the two-party model of Scottish politics vanished.

Under the direction of Jimmy Halliday (leader, 1956–60) and Arthur Donaldson (leader, 1960–9), the SNP improved its organization and electoral machinery, which

[16] J. Mitchell, *Strategies for Self-Government: The Campaigns for a Scottish Parliament* (Edinburgh University Press 1996) 144–8 and 259–69.

[17] 'Mr Churchill in Glasgow' *Scotsman* (Edinburgh, 21 May 1949) 7.

[18] *Scottish Control of Scottish Affairs* (Scottish Unionist Association 1949) 1–2.

[19] J. Mitchell, *Conservatives and the Union: A Study of Conservative Party attitudes to Scotland* (Edinburgh University Press 1990); for a more sympathetic treatment see M. Cragoe, '"We like local patriotism": the Conservative Party and the discourse of decentralisation, 1947–51' (2007) 122 *English Historical Review* 965.

[20] M. Dyer, 'The evolution of the Centre-Right and the state of Scottish Conservatism' (2001) 49 *Political Studies* 30. On the National Liberals, see: D. Dutton, *Liberals in Schism: A History of the National Liberal Party* (I. B. Tauris 2008).

in turn encouraged a steady rise in party membership. The first indications that this would produce political rewards came at the Glasgow Bridgeton by-election of November 1961, when the SNP candidate captured almost one-fifth of the vote. This trend was visible once more at the West Lothian by-election in June 1962, when William Wolfe claimed second place for the SNP, and subjected both the Unionists and the Liberals to the ignominy of forfeited deposits.[21] The SNP grew rapidly in the following years, party membership increasing from 2,000 to 100,000 between 1962 and 1968.[22] Organizational advances and a growing membership gave the SNP a stronger financial basis, enabling more seats to be contested and the profile of nationalist politics to be raised. Less clear, however, is why the national question began to assume a greater prominence in the 1960s. At a general level, the success of the SNP was but one aspect of a wider disenchantment with Labour and the Conservatives, and, indeed, with the British state. Anti-nuclear anxieties reinforced concerns about the British state apparatus and what it symbolized, and would find a home in the Campaign for Nuclear Disarmament (CND). During the 1960s, the Liberals, committed to devolution and representing a more modest estrangement from the establishment, enjoyed a revival, claiming three Highland seats in 1964; this was followed by David Steel's famous victory at the 1965 Roxburgh, Selkirk, and Peeblesshire by-election. Additionally, the emergence of the SNP was perhaps evidence of a loss of faith in British institutions and identity, stemming from imperial retreat and the failure of successive Conservative and Labour administrations to provide a solution to Scotland's entrenched economic problems.[23] As government agencies sought to respond to this discontent through the extension of regional economic policy and enhanced public expenditure, particularly during the 1960s, Scotland, it has been suggested, came to represent a discrete economic and administrative unit; yet by a further irony this in turn served inadvertently to fuel nationalism.[24]

The discovery of North Sea Oil brought into focus the Scottish dimension of Britain's lacklustre economic performance: the SNP posed the choice: Rich Scots, or Poor Britons?[25] However, the SNP also voiced a vigorous suspicion of the centralized state. As the Unionists sought to counteract their relatively poor performance at the polls in 1959, they too embraced regional planning. At the 1964 general election the Unionist message to the Scottish electorate eulogized economic 'progress', 'modernization', and 'improvement'.[26] Intriguingly, the SNP continued to promote that deeply individualist vision of politics, opposed to state interference, which had been typical, ironically, both of the SNP and the Unionists since the 1940s.[27] A 1964 pamphlet declared that the SNP stood for the

[21] W. Wolfe, *Scotland Lives* (Reprographia 1973) 10–25.

[22] H. J. Hanham, *Scottish Nationalism* (Faber and Faber 1969) 204.

[23] T. M. Devine, 'The Challenge of Nationalism' in Devine (ed.), *Scotland and the Union, 1707–2007* (Edinburgh University Press 2008).

[24] An argument advanced in: J. Brand, *The National Movement in Scotland* (Routledge and Kegan Paul 1978).

[25] P. Lynch, *SNP: The History of the Scottish National Party* (Welsh Academic Press 2013) 134.

[26] *Scotland with the Unionists* (Scottish Unionist Association 1964).

[27] Hanham (n. 22) 163–80.

'reversal of the policy of bureaucratic centralization, and over interference by government officials in private lives'.[28] Four years later, Arthur Donaldson addressed a rally gathered to commemorate the anniversary of Bannockburn, declaring that they stood 'united in the defence of democracy and the significance of the common man ... and of the individual and national rights and liberties from which he cannot safely be separated'.[29] Similar attitudes informed the SNP's opposition to membership of the European Community.

It was difficult for those opposed to Scottish independence to distinguish between economic and political motivations when calculating how to respond to the SNP: was this simply a protest vote, a reaction to the seemingly interminable crises that had come to characterize the British economy, and which had wrecked the ambitious plans of the Labour government of Harold Wilson? Or was it something deeper, a more essential rejection of the British political settlement, which would require substantial constitutional reform? The Conservatives moved first, with Edward Heath, from the comfort of opposition, abandoning his party's traditional opposition to Home Rule and pledging his support for a devolved Scottish Assembly at the 1968 Scottish Conservative Conference. Devolution presented a greater intellectual hurdle for Labour, which, in its commitment to the welfare state, redistributive regional policy, and national economic planning, had adopted an inflexible Unionism, predicated upon the belief that only central government could ensure economic growth and equality in social provision. Labour thus categorized nationalism as a barometer of *economic* discontent. The curt dismissal of the nationalists as 'Tartan Tories' by Willie Ross, Labour Secretary of State for Scotland between 1964 and 1970, and again from 1974 to 1976, and a vehement opponent of devolution, exposed a wealth of assumptions about the scope and meaning of politics.[30] As Donald Dewar argued when a young Labour MP for Aberdeen South, disillusionment with Westminster emanated 'from continuing economic crises and the failure of the parties to satisfy the expectations they themselves have done so much to raise'.[31] The belief that political discontent had economic roots led to a reticence to undertake constitutional reform; the response of the Labour government was rather to delay, and indeed to institute a Royal Commission on the Constitution in 1969.[32]

The failure of a SNP breakthrough to materialize at the 1970 general election allowed the Conservatives to disregard their earlier commitment to devolution once back in power. Although in late 1973 Labour's Royal Commission produced a majority report in favour of devolution, interest had dissipated, as

[28] *The Scottish National Party Stands For* (SNP 1964).

[29] A. Donaldson, SNP Speeches (1968), National Library of Scotland Acc. 10090/17.

[30] For a discussion of this particular epithet, see G. Hassan, 'The Auld Enemies: Scottish Nationalism and Labour' in Hassan (ed.), *The Modern SNP: From Protest to Power* (Edinburgh University Press 2009) 148–50.

[31] D. Dewar, 'Devolution and Local Government Reform' in N. MacCormick (ed.), *The Scottish Debate* (Oxford University Press 1970).

[32] D. Tanner, 'Richard Crossman, Harold Wilson and devolution, 1966–70: the making of government policy' (2006) 17 *Twentieth Century British History* 545.

industrial relations dominated politics.[33] Only the resurgence of nationalist support at the two elections of 1974 returned the constitution to the political agenda. The minority Labour administration which took office in February expressed support for devolution, yet this fresh enthusiasm was not reflected in Scotland, and in June 1974 the Party's Scottish Executive reiterated its longstanding opposition to devolution by a margin of one vote. Although this decision was overturned two months later at the behest of the national leadership, there remained an ultimately irresolvable conflict within Labour politics in the 1970s between those who supported devolution as a short-term tactic, and those who opposed what they saw as capitulation to narrow nationalism. Although some within Scottish Labour's ranks became committed advocates of devolution, most notably Jim Sillars, for most devolution was a political expedient pushed by the Cabinet, not an article of faith. In their scepticism they were supported by Labour MPs from Northern England, who feared that devolution would penalize their constituents, and by the parliamentary Left, who disapproved of nationalism on moral and theoretical grounds.[34]

This division became palpable when the UK Government attempted to pilot a bill establishing devolved Scottish and Welsh assemblies through the Commons. The proposals, which not only preserved the Secretary of State for Scotland and Scottish representation in the Commons, but granted the former considerable powers of veto over the work of the Assembly, fell well short of what the pro-devolutionists had expected. Sillars promptly left and formed a breakaway Scottish Labour Party in January 1976.[35] Conversely, it was too much for those opposed to devolution, and the bill collapsed in early 1977, but not before the principle of a referendum on a Scottish Assembly had been conceded. A Scotland Bill surfaced in late 1977, and was finally passed in February 1978. The Act provided for a Scottish Assembly with a set of enumerated powers. In the course of the bill's passage the anti-devolutionist Labour MP Tam Dalyell formulated what came to be known—after his constituency—as the West Lothian Question: why, under devolution, would a Scottish MP be able to vote at Westminster on matters of health and education in England, while health and education in his own constituency would be the preserve of the new Scottish Assembly, yet an English MP conversely had no say on health and education in Scotland?[36] However, a controversial provision within the Scotland Act 1978 constituted a significant obstacle in the way of devolution. George Cunningham, a Scot who sat as a London Labour MP, successfully secured an amendment requiring the Scotland Act to be placed before Parliament for repeal if the total number of 'yes' votes in the referendum was less than 40 per cent of the electorate. It proved an insurmountable barrier: the Yes campaign

[33] *Royal Commission on the Constitution* (Cmnd. 5460, 1973).

[34] M. Keating and D. Bleiman, *Labour and Scottish Nationalism* (Macmillan 1979) 164–75.

[35] H. Drucker, *Breakaway: The Scottish Labour Party* (Edinburgh University Student Publications 1978).

[36] V. Bogdanor, 'The West Lothian Question' (2010) 63 *Parliamentary Affairs* 156.

could only secure 51.6 per cent in the referendum, held on 1 March 1979, which was below the required level since turnout stood at 63 per cent (itself another indicator of an ambivalent public mood). The result was followed by the defeat of the Labour government on a motion of no confidence, by one vote, with SNP MPs voting alongside the Conservatives. In the ensuing election the SNP lost nine of its eleven MPs, and saw its share of the vote almost halved.

The failure of devolution in the 1970s has its curious aspects. There had long been considerable popular support for a Scottish Parliament, at least in opinion polls, and, whatever the splits within the Commons, the proposals had government backing. The fractured nature of the referendum campaign undoubtedly played a part. Labour, the dominant force in Scottish politics, offered the public campaigns both in favour and against devolution, and refused to work with the SNP in the cross-party 'Yes for Scotland' alliance. Under the leadership of Margaret Thatcher, who replaced Ted Heath in 1975, the Conservatives distanced themselves from previous commitments to devolution. While some prominent Scottish Conservatives such as Alick Buchanan-Smith and Malcolm Rifkind remained convinced proponents of devolution, and Alec Douglas-Home notoriously promised Scots that if they voted no a future Conservative government would deliver something better, the appointment of Teddy Taylor as Shadow Scottish Secretary denoted a significant change in the tenor of Toryism, and the adoption of a less pluralist style of Unionism.

More fundamentally, however, nobody could agree what devolution was intended to achieve: was it, as both the SNP and opponents of devolution such as Tam Dalyell claimed, a springboard to independence?[37] Or was it, as the Labour government hoped, a measure that would stymie the advance of nationalism by institutionalizing Scottish distinctiveness within the Union? If much nationalist rhetoric focused upon the evils of excessive centralization and government interference, was another layer of bureaucracy really the solution, especially given the two-tier structure of local government introduced in 1975? It would take the unwelcome policies pursued by the Conservative government during the 1980s to persuade a more decisive majority of Scots, and their politicians, of the necessity of devolution. Moreover, Conservative provocations in the 1980s also brought into focus a more compelling rationale for a Scottish Parliament—namely, the protection of Scots from the excesses of a government that lacked popular support north of the border.

III. Imagining difference

Traditionally, Scottish Unionism had been flexible, pragmatic, and sensitive to the distinctive identity of the Scottish nation within the Union. Conservatives, being temperamentally disinclined to accept the rigidly geometric rationality of socialist

[37] T. Dalyell, *Devolution: the End of Britain?* (Jonathan Cape 1977).

planning, took a certain delight in the lopsided irregularities of British constitutional arrangements. The Union, it was recognized, was a partnership of notional equals, notwithstanding the obvious disparities in scale between England and Scotland, and elementary politeness—as well as political reality—demanded an unfussy but scrupulous attention to Scottish susceptibilities. However, the advent of Thatcherism in 1979 changed all that.

Thatcher was, ironically, a committed, but clumsy, Unionist. She misunderstood the way the Union worked, and arguably did more than anyone else to undermine the British state. Thatcher's conception of the Union was hyper-unionist, verging on unitarist. While she subscribed to the ideal of individual freedom, she had little truck with regional policy, the autonomy of local government, or particularist exceptions to the will of Downing Street. There was no room in Thatcher's Unionism for the historic asymmetries of the Anglo-Scottish union-state. The defeat of socialism, as she saw it, required the untrammelled operation of the market. From her perspective, this was to lay out a level playing field; but from a Scottish perspective it seemed like the exportation of the values of the City and south-east of England to less prosperous parts of the Union, and most especially to one of its constituent nations, which had decisively rejected the Conservative Party at the ballot box. In the 1979 election the Conservatives took only twenty-two out of seventy-one Scottish seats.

It was not only Thatcher's policies and her obvious insensitivity to Scottish concerns which alienated Scots; so too did her stridency and her acutely strained version of received pronunciation, which jarred on Scottish ears. The whole package—personality as well as policy, and *that voice*—provoked a visceral reaction. During the 1980s disaffection from Thatcher and Thatcherism was to be found across almost the whole spread of the Scottish political spectrum, from socialists and nationalists to former Conservative voters and leading members of the Tory Party in Scotland, who found themselves out of favour or disenchanted or both. For, as Thatcherism established itself as the dominant strain within the Conservative Party,[38] other kinds of Conservatism, once respectable and honoured doctrines within the Party's broad church, took on an aura of heresy.[39] Pro-devolutionist sentiment was frowned on. So too was a distinctively Scottish form of corporatism, indebted to the 'godly commonwealth' ethos of the established Presbyterian Church of Scotland. If the Kirk in some respects resembled the Scottish Conservatives at prayer, then to insensitive Thatcherites the social gospel of traditional Scottish corporatism resembled a kind of Christian Socialism, or at best 'Wetness'; for 'Wet', during the 1980s, was the preferred Thatcherite term of abuse for mawkish paternalist Toryism.[40] The possibility of a right-wing populism in Scotland which spoke directly to the people—bypassing the comfortable

[38] D. Torrance, *We in Scotland: Thatcherism in a Cold Climate* (Birlinn 2009); D. Stewart, *The Path to Devolution and Change: A Political History of Scotland under Margaret Thatcher* (I.B. Tauris 2009).

[39] A. Kemp, *The Hollow Drum* (Mainstream 1993) 199–208.

[40] Cf. H. Young, *One of Us* (Pan Macmillan 1989).

middle classes, many of them in the pews of the Kirk—was never a serious one, perhaps; but the chance was lost with the defeat of Teddy Taylor, who would have been Thatcher's choice as Secretary of State for Scotland, at the 1979 general election. Until then Taylor had held the predominantly working-class seat of Glasgow Cathcart against the odds.[41] Taylor's replacement, George Younger, MP for Ayr, was thoroughly paternalist, but, as a product of Winchester and Oxford, he lacked the common touch necessary to woo the wider electorate; although moderate and politely diffident, Younger still seemed semi-foreign. Moreover, his commitment to consensus politics was too unobtrusive to counter the wider effect on the electorate of the brasher Thatcherite message. The Liberals, the Social Democrats, and the SNP all benefited from the alienation of dissident old-time Conservatives.

The prime beneficiary, of course, was the Labour Party in Scotland. Although Scotland was not immune to the jingoistic appeal of the 'Falklands Factor' in the general election of 1983, all this achieved was to staunch the haemorrhage of support from the Tories to the other parties in Scotland. By the 1987 general election, the Scottish Conservatives—despite their massive victory at the UK level—were reduced to a mere ten seats out of seventy-two. Labour had run away with the election in Scotland, taking fifty seats, but were helpless to protect their constituents from the insensitive application of Thatcherite policy to Scotland. The SNP—faring reasonably well by their standards in the 1980s, having obtained only two seats at the elections of 1979 and 1983—had won three seats in 1987; but they exploited Labour's constitutional predicament, denouncing Scotland's Labour phalanx at Westminster as the 'feeble fifty'. Indeed, it was in this period that the seeds of Labour's subsequent problems in Scotland were sown. Scottish Labour Action, a left-wing grouping with nationalist leanings, was formed in 1988, followed in 1992 by Scotland United, which included prominent Labour MPs such as George Galloway and John McAllion.[42] 1987 was a crucial turning point in Scottish politics. It placed firmly on the political agenda the question of Scotland's 'democratic deficit': did Thatcher's government possess a mandate to govern Scotland?

Such was the self-belief of leading Thatcherites after a third successive election victory that the solution to the Scottish problem seemed obvious: upping the dosage. Whereas Younger had served as a buffer between Downing Street and Scotland, Thatcher's Chancellor of the Exchequer, Nigel Lawson, a committed free marketeer, complained in a speech to businessmen in Glasgow in November 1987 that 'large areas of Scottish life' were 'sheltered from market forces'.[43] On the other hand, some intelligent Conservatives saw the need to reconfigure Thatcherite unitarism into something more versatile and receptive to Scottish opinion. Most prominent among these was the Secretary of State for Scotland, Malcolm Rifkind—a former devolutionist who paid some lip service to

[41] I. G. C. Hutchison, *Scottish Politics in the Twentieth Century* (Palgrave 2001) 112–13.
[42] G. Hassan and E. Shaw, *The Strange Death of Labour Scotland* (Edinburgh University Press 2012) 49 and 63.
[43] Mitchell (n. 19) 113.

Thatcherite orthodoxies for the sake of his career, but was never quite accepted as a true believer. In an April 1988 speech to the Aberdeen Chamber of Commerce Rifkind advanced a very different picture of the union-state. Union was not only about shared values and interests, Rifkind insisted, it was also about the enjoyment of a healthy pluralism under the security of a common umbrella. Rifkind recognized that the United Kingdom was a multinational state, which required neither 'uniformity' nor 'the Anglicisation of Scotland'; rather 'the unity of the kingdom [was] strengthened by diversity'.[44]

Rifkind's generous vision came too late, and its message was quickly blotted out; for already—against the advice of the far-from-fainthearted Lawson—the policy juggernaut of the poll tax was rolling. Not that the poll tax, or community charge, was, strictly speaking, an English imposition on Scotland. It had originated north of the border where Scottish Tories feared the effect of a rates revaluation on the strained loyalties of their own middle-class supporters. Indeed, the tax's provenance was distinctly 'Wet'.[45] Nevertheless, such niceties were lost on the Scottish electorate. The imposition of the tax on Scotland a year before its implementation in England looked vengeful at worst, at best a quasi-colonial treatment of Scotland as a laboratory for radical experiments in fiscal policy. Although Thatcher's stubborn refusal to abandon the poll tax after the calamitous extension of the measure to England led her own party to get rid of her in a dramatic coup d'état in the autumn of 1990, in Scotland the Conservatives were never forgiven.

There were other significant changes in the political landscape. Although the SNP had been an anti-Common Market party in the 1960s and 1970s, the arrival of Jim Sillars in the 1980s, after the implosion of his short-lived Scottish Labour Party, led to a dramatic reframing of SNP policy. The Scottish electorate did not like the idea of separatism; the notion that a small, historically poor country might go it alone. Sillars's policy prescription of 'independence in Europe'—formally adopted in 1988—changed perceptions of the Party's ambitions.[46] Henceforth, the SNP was to be the most enthusiastically Europhile of British political parties. Salmond, Sillars's *then*-friend and ally, became the leader of the SNP in 1990. Both Sillars and Salmond believed that the Scottish electorate was unlikely to sleepwalk to independence in a romantic reverie. Progressive social democracy—at the very least, if not full-blown socialism—was a necessary accompaniment. The new model SNP was, however, much less certain about Scottish devolution.

The campaign for devolution had continued on the fringes of Scottish politics in the aftermath of the disappointing referendum result in 1979 and Thatcher's abandonment of Tory devolutionism. A new pressure group, the Campaign for

[44] P. Hetherington, 'Rifkind tries to rally Scots Tories' *Guardian* (London, 16 April 1988) 24; C. Kidd, 'The Defence of the Union: Ironies and Ambiguities' in G. Hassan and J. Mitchell (eds), *After Independence: The State of the Scottish Nation Debate* (Luath 2013) 43–4.

[45] W. Waldegrave, *A Different Kind of Weather* (Constable 2015) 218–28.

[46] J. Sillars, 'Independence in Europe' in L. Paterson (ed.), *A Diverse Assembly: the Debate on a Scottish Parliament* (Edinburgh University Press 1998) 196–204.

a Scottish Assembly (CSA) was launched on 1 March 1980, on the first anniversary of the devolution referendum. In 1988 the CSA published the Claim of Right, which asserted the popular sovereignty of the Scottish people. While the document had no legal standing, it possessed moral and, arguably, constitutional force; certainly the echoes of the Claim of Right of the Scottish Revolution of 1689 and of the Kirk's Claim of Right of 1842 were deliberate.[47] After all, the publication of the Claim of Right followed successive general elections when Scotland had decisively rejected Thatcherism at the ballot box, only to find that its mandate at a UK level trumped the views of the Scottish electorate. In 1989 fifty-eight of Scotland's seventy-two MPs, that is all the Liberal Democrats and the entire Labour bloc, apart from the veteran anti-devolutionist Tam Dalyell, signed the Claim of Right. This endorsement paved the way for the establishment of a Scottish Constitutional Convention, supported by Labour, the Liberal Democrats, the Scottish Trades Unions, and the churches. The Conservatives would have no truck with the Convention. The SNP were in a quandary: should a pro-independence party support the unsatisfactory half-measure of devolution? After some initial engagement, the SNP too boycotted the process. The lineaments of the devolution plan eventually implemented after the Labour landslide election win of 1997 derived in large part from the schemes concocted in the Constitutional Convention during the early 1990s, and eventually published in its blueprint, *Scotland's Parliament, Scotland's Right* (1995).

Although the Conservatives under Thatcher's successor John Major did not budge in their rejection of legislative devolution, they quietly jettisoned unitarism, and embraced Scotland with greater empathy—though no greater electoral success—than Thatcher. At the 1992 general election, Major campaigned positively in defence of the Union.[48] Indeed, the results gave the Conservatives a mini-fillip and dented SNP hopes that the glaring defects of the 'democratic deficit' might unite the country against the Tories. Very little changed. Labour lost a seat, the Conservatives gained one, moving from ten to eleven seats, and the SNP remained marooned on a paltry three. Sillars—who lost his seat—complained that the Scots were 'ninety-minute patriots'.[49] Nevertheless, the democratic deficit remained. Ian Lang,[50] Major's Secretary of State for Scotland, introduced a Taking Stock exercise and produced a white paper punningly entitled *Scotland in the Union: A Partnership for Good* (1993).[51] However, the focus was largely on administrative devolution, something the Tories had long embraced, and on minor Scots-appeasing modifications of the 1707 settlement. Later, in 1996, Lang's dynamic, but less emollient successor, Michael Forsyth, repatriated the

[47] Cf. T. Brotherstone (ed.), *Covenant, Charter and Party: Traditions of Revolt and Protest in modern Scottish History* (Aberdeen University Press 1989); J. Hearn, *Claiming Scotland: National Identity and Liberal Culture* (Polygon 2000).

[48] John Major, *The Autobiography* (Harper Collins 2000) 415–30.

[49] C. Harvie, *Scotland and Nationalism* (Routledge 1994) 205.

[50] I. Lang, *Blue Remembered Years* (Politicos 2002).

[51] Scottish Office, *Scotland in the Union: A Partnership for Good* (Cm 2225, 1993).

Stone of Destiny from Westminster Abbey. But it was too little, too late. At the 1997 general election, the Conservatives lost all their seats in Scotland.

The efforts of parties, pressure groups, and the leaders of civil society are, however, only part of the story. In the aftermath of the 1979 referendum Scottish writers, artists, and musicians took up the cause of 'Scotland' as their own. Scotland in the 1980s went through a literary renaissance, which was highly politicized. Writers such as Alasdair Gray moved easily between high literature and polemic, promoting the idea that Scottish culture, both in its ethos and mode of expression, differed absolutely from the English literary tradition. The notion of a common British heritage gave way to neo-colonialist perspectives.[52] By the time of the referendum campaign, the arts in Scotland were ranged decidedly, if just short of unanimously, on the side of an independent future.[53]

IV. Implementing devolution

The return of the Labour Party to office in May 1997 under the leadership of Tony Blair, after eighteen years in opposition and with an unprecedented Commons majority, ensured that the question of devolution, and of Scotland's position within the Union, would be revisited. Labour campaigned on a platform of extensive constitutional renewal, seeking to address what was termed a 'national crisis of confidence': alongside devolution for Scotland and Wales, the House of Lords and the electoral system were to be reformed, and elected mayors and regional assemblies were proposed for England.[54] While some of these pledges were later abandoned, diluted, or defeated by public indifference, devolution was realized with remarkable efficiency. A White Paper, *Scotland's Parliament*, was published in July 1997, which recommended a unicameral Parliament of 129 Members, to be elected via the loosely proportional Additional Member system.[55] Moreover, this was devolution of a very different kind from that proposed in 1979. The 1997 version of devolution envisaged a powerful domestic Scottish Parliament, with only a limited number of policy matters reserved to Westminster. At the two-question referendum held two months later, voters were asked, first, whether they wanted a Scottish Parliament, and, second, whether that Parliament should have tax-varying powers of plus or minus three pence in the pound. Leading Labour figures canvassed in support of devolution in tandem with the Liberal Democrats

52 Influential, if controversial, was M. Hechter, *Internal Colonialism: The Celtic Fringe in British National Development, 1536–1966* (Routledge and Kegan Paul 1975). See also the Fanon-inspired approach to Scottish inferiorism of C. Beveridge and R. Turnbull, *The Eclipse of Scottish Culture* (Polygon 1989).

53 S. Hames (ed.), *Unstated: Writers on Scottish independence* (Word Power Books 2012); C. Kidd, 'Scottish Independence: Literature and Nationalism' *Guardian* (London, 19 July 2014) <http://www.theguardian.com/books/2014/jul/19/scottish-independence-literature-nationalism> accessed 21 May 2015.

54 *New Labour, New Life for Britain* (Labour Party 1996).

55 Scottish Office, *Scotland's Parliament* (Cm 3658, 1997).

and the SNP as part of 'Scotland FORward'. The opposition 'Think Twice' campaign was hampered by the absence of the support from business and academia that had marked the 1979 referendum, and by the fact that, of the major political parties, only the Conservatives, still reeling from their annihilation at the general election, were involved. The Scottish public voted three to one in support of a Scottish Parliament, and two to one in favour of granting the Parliament tax-varying powers.[56] (Ironically, these tax-varying powers were never deployed, notwithstanding the apparently growing demand over the following decade and a half for enhanced fiscal devolution.) Legislation was enacted the following year, and the first elections to the new Scottish Parliament were held in May 1999.

The confidence and conviction with which Labour implemented devolution, and the sweeping legislative powers conferred on the new body, contrasted with the timidity of earlier proposals. This stemmed from the revision in opinion which had taken place in the intervening years. Scottish Labour was now near-unanimously in favour of devolution, and if there were those who remained sceptical, they elected to keep their concerns private—with the exception of Tam Dalyell. The strength of this commitment was embodied in the formulation offered in March 1994 by John Smith, responsible for the ill-fated 1978 Scotland Act as a junior Minister and who assumed the Labour leadership after the Party's defeat at the 1992 general election. For Smith, speaking just two months before his untimely death, devolution was the 'settled will of the Scottish people', a dictum that countenanced little room for dissent.[57]

Beneath such vigorous constitutional innovation, however, there remained, if not an insincerity, then a contradiction within the Labour government's attitude towards devolution, and, more broadly, to Scotland's place within the United Kingdom. During the 1997 election campaign, Blair had reassured those in England concerned about the extent of the powers to be enjoyed by any Scottish Parliament by likening the new body to a Parish Council; nevertheless, he still felt that this Parish Council required the legitimation of a referendum, a buttress not envisaged by a literal reading of Smith's pronouncement.[58] Indeed, that the public were being asked to express their opinion prior to Parliament legislating represented a departure from the plebiscites of the 1970s. The decision to hold a referendum was received with unease in Scotland, where it gave the impression of backsliding, and hinted at Blair's indifference towards devolution.[59] Nor was there any eagerness to address systematically the wider implications of devolution. The West Lothian Question was dismissed via the rough expedient of reducing the number of Scottish MPs from seventy-two to fifty-nine ahead of the 2005

[56] The full results were 74.3 per cent in favour of a Scottish Parliament and 25.7 per cent opposed; 64.5 per cent supported that Parliament being granted tax-varying powers, with 36.5 per cent opposed.

[57] J. Mitchell, *The Scottish Question* (Oxford University Press 2014) 240.

[58] A. Marr, 'Blair Blunder Exposes Devolution Plan's Central Dilemma' *Independent* (London, 5 April 1997) <http://www.independent.co.uk/news/blair-blunder-exposes-devolution-plans-central-dilemma-of-devoution-plan-1265237.html> accessed 6 May 2015.

[59] Bagehot, 'Flattened by Blair' *Economist* (London, 6 July 1996) 37.

general election, lessening rather than removing the anomaly. For the Labour leadership, the devolution of power was a resolution, not a beginning.

Whatever the motivations underlying the decision to hold a referendum, the categorical nature of the results at least granted the new Parliament an authority and status that went beyond that conferred by mere statute. The poll revealed the extent to which Scottish public opinion had shifted in favour of devolution. In 1979 Orkney, Shetland, Tayside, Grampian, the Borders, and Dumfries and Galloway had all returned majorities opposed to a Scottish Assembly, reflecting concerns that any new body would discriminate in favour of central Scotland; in 1997, every single region supported a Parliament, and only Dumfries and Galloway and Orkney rejected tax-varying powers.[60] Thus, although the Scotland Act explicitly affirmed that the sovereignty of the Westminster Parliament remained undiminished, and in theory a future government could simply repeal the legislation and thereby reverse devolution, in reality such a drastic measure was, and remains, inconceivable.[61] The referendum implicitly recognized the validity of notions of popular sovereignty: the ultimate decision lay with the people.

Permanence aside, the question of purpose remained: what, precisely, was the new Parliament for? Was it intended to allow a new Scottish polity to flourish? To defend Scotland from the vagaries of Westminster rule? Or did it have a narrower partisan purpose? As George Robertson, then Labour's Shadow Scottish Secretary, remarked in 1996 in a pungent turn of phrase, devolution was expected to kill Scottish nationalism 'stone dead'.[62] In hindsight, the aphorism coined by Ron Davies, the Welsh Secretary, to the effect that devolution was a process rather than an event, was more accurate; it is, however, difficult to escape the conclusion that, in the years immediately after 1999, with the Party in office in London and Edinburgh, Labour lacked any vision for a distinctive Scottish politics.[63] At the 1999 Scottish elections Labour was returned as the largest party, and proceeded to form a coalition with the Liberal Democrats. At the opening ceremony Donald Dewar, the Labour First Minister and chief architect of the new Parliament, delivered an exceptional speech, one suffused with a potent cultural nationalism and a keen sense of the disparate elements which had helped forge Scottish identity.[64] But Labour's passion for devolution remained largely rhetorical, and much of the early drive within the coalition was provided by the Liberal Democrats. As a result of negotiations between the coalition partners, upfront university tuition fees were replaced with a graduate endowment in 2001; a year later free personal care for the elderly was introduced, and in 2003 the last vestiges of feudal tenure in Scotland were abolished.

[60] Cameron (n. 11) 349–55.

[61] See the assertion of Westminster's continued legislative supremacy: Scotland Act 1998, s. 28(7).

[62] Quoted in: C. Jeffrey, 'Where Stands the Union Now? Scottish-English Relations after Devolution' in Devine (ed.) (n. 23) 195.

[63] R. Davies, *Devolution: A Process not an Event* (Institute of Welsh Affairs 1999).

[64] The full speech can be found in: D. Torrance (ed.), *Great Scottish Speeches* (Luath 2011) 186–8.

These policy advances allowed the Holyrood administration gradually to differentiate itself from Westminster, a development not always welcomed by the latter. The nascent Parliament was nonetheless beset by intermittent controversies, not least the delays and overspends afflicting the Parliament building, finally completed in 2004.[65] In 2000 there was vocal, if futile, opposition to the decision to overturn the legislation prohibiting the 'promotion' of homosexuality in schools, which disturbed easy assumptions about a liberal consensus in Scotland. Further, in 2001 Henry McLeish, who had replaced Dewar as First Minister after the latter's death the previous year, was forced to resign after the emergence of financial irregularities relating to the subletting of his constituency office. His successor, Jack McConnell, proved a competent, albeit unimaginative, manager; under his leadership the coalition with the Liberal Democrats was renewed in 2003, an administration most notable for introducing the ban on smoking in public places in 2005.

While Labour complacently treated devolution as a promise delivered, it took the SNP longer to adjust to the new political landscape. Installed as the official opposition in 1999, the Party lost eight of its thirty-five seats four years later under the direction of John Swinney, as it struggled to offer a viable alternative to the coalition Executive, and the electorate returned a medley of Greens, Socialists, and Independents. At the 2007 elections, however, with Salmond having been reinstalled as leader three years earlier, the SNP emerged as the largest party by the narrowest of margins, securing forty-seven seats to Labour's forty-six. Lacking any willing coalition partners other than the two Green MSPs, the new Scottish Government, as the Executive was promptly relabelled, endured by negotiating a series of fleeting cross-party alliances. Despite some trying moments, the administration was a surprising success, and burnished its public image with a number of populist measures, including the freezing of council tax, and the abolition of bridge tolls and prescription charges.[66]

In the early months of the SNP government, Labour, now ably led by Wendy Alexander, offered the prospect of a robust opposition. It urged a review of the Parliament's remit, which resulted in the creation of the Calman Commission, a body supported by all the pro-Union parties. In May 2008 Alexander challenged Salmond to call a referendum on Scottish independence, but failed to clear this statement with the new Labour Prime Minister Gordon Brown. She resigned soon after, as details of an unlawful donation to her leadership campaign were leaked to the press, and she was replaced in September 2008 by Iain Gray.[67] More damaging was Labour's refusal to come to terms with its loss of power, which was regarded merely as a temporary aberration. Blair petulantly refused to phone Salmond to congratulate him on becoming First Minister. Such an interpretation appeared to be vindicated by the result of the 2010 general election, when, in the face of electoral failure in England, Labour's vote in Scotland increased, and the Party retained

[65] *Spitting Tacks: Lord Fraser's Report into the Building of the Scottish Parliament* (Tim Coates 2004).

[66] Hassan (ed.) (n. 30).

[67] I. MacWhirter, *Road to Referendum* (Cargo 2014) 287–97.

all forty-one of the seats won in 2005. But the SNP administration of 2007 was evidence of a deeper shift in Scottish politics, and of disillusionment with Labour on the political Left. This had two main foundations—first, opposition to the programme of public sector reform being pursued in England; and second, the decision to support the American invasion of Iraq. While opposition to the Iraq war was never as absolute as was later asserted, amongst the electorally vital liberal middle classes Iraq came to symbolize the hubris, delusions, and betrayals of the Blair years. Salmond's criticism of British intervention in Kosovo in 1999, which he termed an 'unpardonable folly', had been profoundly misjudged; by 2007 his anti-interventionist foreign policy was more attuned to the public mood.

Once the perils of a Nationalist government, central to the Labour campaign in 2007, proved to be imaginary, Scottish politics was transformed. The illusion of Labour ascendancy had been shattered, and the SNP proved competent in office, despite the limits imposed by minority government. At the 2011 elections the SNP was rewarded with the parliamentary majority that the electoral system had been designed to prevent. Under Salmond's leadership the SNP grasped that, in the years since 1999, the electorate had learned to distinguish between Westminster and Holyrood elections. In 2011 Labour mistakenly invited Scottish voters to use the Holyrood election to send a message to the deeply unpopular Conservative-Liberal Democrat coalition at Westminster. The public, it transpired, preferred to elect a government for Scotland. Labour's early lead in the opinion polls evaporated amid an abject campaign, and the SNP secured 69 of the 129 seats as they proved to be the chief beneficiaries of the Liberal Democrats' implosion.

After 2011, an independence referendum became probable, if far from inevitable, even if the SNP did not always seem entirely enthusiastic about such a prospect. Any attempt to explain why devolution produced such a dramatic outcome must include long-term structural shifts, including the economic transformation of Scotland between the 1960s and the 2000s, alongside the more immediate impact of events such as the Iraq War, and Cameron's miscalculation of the result the referendum might be expected to achieve. Fundamentally, however, the rise of Scottish nationalism has been a political phenomenon, and opponents of nationalism have been mistaken in attributing its rise to economic grievances. Thus, although the block grant to the Scottish Parliament rose by 60 per cent in real terms between 1999 and 2010, Labour received little electoral gratitude.[68]

V. Conclusion

It would be wrong to assume that nationalist sentiment determined Scotland's pathway to the referendum. Of course, as the ingenious Moreno Question,[69] a staple of Scottish polling surveys, has shown, Scots have become significantly

[68] Mitchell (n. 57) 260–1.

[69] A. Brown, D. McCrone, and L. Paterson, *Politics and Society in Scotland* (Macmillan 1996) 197.

more Scottish and less British in their identities over the past thirty years. In 1992 less than one in five Scots felt exclusively Scottish (not British at all) and a third of Scots self-identified as equally Scottish and British. By 2003, 31 per cent of Scots claimed an exclusively Scottish identity and only 22 per cent of Scots described themselves as equally Scottish and British. By 2003 the combined total of those asserting identities as either exclusively Scottish or 'more Scottish than British' was 65 per cent of the electorate. On the other hand, only 8 per cent felt either exclusively British or 'more British than Scottish'.[70] The problems of Unionism were already apparent; however, the Union itself was not under direct threat at this point. This was because until very recently strong pro-independence convictions were confined to a minority of the electorate. Devolution sufficed to assuage national longings. If nationalism has assumed a larger profile in Scottish politics since the referendum of 2014, it should not serve to obscure the more circumscribed role which it played in the preceding decades. Nationalism is only one among several themes which have made contemporary Scottish politics distinctive in its hues from politics south of the border. Arguably, the dominant element in Scottish politics from the 1960s until the first decade of the new millennium was Labourism, the ideology of a party which represented, variously, strands of authentic socialism, corporatism, and an entrenched non-ideological, time-serving municipal Establishment. Prior to 2014 and the stresses of the referendum campaign, the Labour Party was generally able to conceal the potential tensions inherent in this eclectic ideological mix. Of course, at certain points, the cracks in Scottish Labour were all too vividly on display; not least in the debates over devolution between 1974 and 1979. However intense electoral competition with the Conservatives at Westminster generally tamed nationalist aspirations.[71]

Sheer chance has played an unusually large part in the decline of Labour and the rise of the SNP. The premature death of John Smith served to open a chasm between pragmatic Old Labour and a deracinated New Labour-cum-Blairism. Other unexpected deaths, including the loss of Robin Cook, an opponent of the Iraq war, winnowed out the phalanx of Scots who led the British Labour movement in the 1990s and early 2000s. Most significant of all, perhaps, was the death of Donald Dewar, the 'Father of the Nation', who had brought devolution to Scotland, and who was succeeded by an unending churn of evanescent leaders—Henry McLeish, Jack McConnell, Wendy Alexander, Iain Gray, Johann Lamont, Jim Murphy. None of these succeeded in entrenching him- or herself in position, or in achieving the same level of name-recognition attained by the SNP's leaders,

[70] J. Curtice, 'Brought Together or Driven Apart?' in W. Miller (ed.), *Anglo-Scottish Relations from 1900 to Devolution and beyond* (Oxford University Press for British Academy 2005) 168. Intriguingly, however, recent surveys have shown a decline in those identifying as either wholly or predominantly Scottish, and a rise in those claiming to consider themselves equally Scottish and British: in 2014 these figures were 49 per cent and 32 per cent respectively. It is probable that the referendum campaign has politicized such questions, hardening attitudes. *Scottish Social Attitudes Survey 2014* <http://whatscotlandthinks.org/questions/moreno-national-identity-5#table> accessed 21 May 2015.

[71] Hassan and Shaw (n. 42).

Alex Salmond and Nicola Sturgeon. However, this phenomenon is thrown more clearly into relief when one recalls that during Salmond's first period of retirement, between 2000 and 2004, the SNP, led by the patently decent but uncharismatic John Swinney, also struggled to obtain media traction. Much as politicians themselves routinely deplore the press's seeming obsession with personality over policy, the perceived character and media profile of Scottish political leaders, especially since 1999, contributed enormously to the reorientation of political culture. The supplanting of Labour by the SNP is not just a reflection of changing values, though clearly there is a generational facet to this shift. Quirky intangibles, not least the projection of leadership in the media, are significant factors in the story.

Developments at the UK level—popular disenchantment with New Labour and Blairist foreign policy adventures, the collapse in Liberal Democrat support after the party's volte face on university tuition fees, ingrained distrust of Conservative plans for a slimmed-down state—had distinctive Scottish effects. The SNP was an established alternative to the mainstream parties, and since 2007 had governed Scotland in a responsible way. Voters drifted towards the SNP despite, not because of, its central policy objective of independence. Moreover, every false step by a *particular* British government—such as the bedroom tax—facilitated a critique of the British state in *general* as structurally unresponsive to Scottish needs. It did not require a political alchemist of the undoubted brilliance of Salmond to turn grievances with the main Westminster parties into a positive desire for an independent Scottish alternative. Hence, the predicament in which modern Scotland finds itself. Factors other than the direct appeal of nationalism have swollen the ranks of the pro-independence cause and contributed, indirectly, to the rise of nationalist sentiment. The SNP has displaced Labour as the principal vehicle of the social democratic Left in Scotland, but without quite convincing the electorate of the benefits of independence. The Scottish population is near-evenly divided between the attractions of independence and the continued security of the Union. Yet an emphasis on division is as unrevealing as a focus on the rise of nationalism. Polls in the spring of 2015 suggested that even those opposed to independence accepted its seeming inevitability, despite still being in a majority. Unionism seems to have shrivelled, but, for the moment, the Union itself endures.

PART II

THE REFERENDUM PROCESS

3

The Scottish Independence Referendum

A Model of Good Practice in Direct Democracy?

Stephen Tierney

I. Introduction

On 18 September 55 per cent of Scots voted No to the proposition: 'Should Scotland be an Independent Country?' Inevitably, during the campaign, attention was focused upon the outcome of the vote and major substantive issues of contention such as currency relations between an independent Scotland and the United Kingdom, and the ease or difficulty with which an independent Scotland would achieve membership of the European Union. What was often overlooked was the fact that the credibility of the outcome would ultimately depend upon the legitimacy of the referendum process itself. Given the heat which the debate generated in the last few weeks of campaigning, it was of the highest importance that the process of the referendum itself be fair and be seen to be so by both sides: in short, that the result was agreed *to*, even if it is not agreed *with*, by losers as well as winners.

In this chapter I will assess the referendum process. I will do so in light of the legislation passed by the Scottish Parliament to regulate the referendum but also against the broader context of UK-wide referendum law within which the Scottish law was made. I will begin by outlining broader work which considers whether referendums in general are capable of offering an environment within which ordinary citizens can make a reasoned and deliberative decision about matters of the highest constitutional importance. This will offer a theoretical framework with which to assess the Scottish referendum process. The ultimate question which the chapter poses is this: did the regulatory regime for the Scottish referendum help create a platform for the meaningful participation of citizens? In turn it is hoped that it will also inform the better delivery of referendums within the United Kingdom, where direct democracy is a growing trend.[1]

[1] This chapter was earlier published as S. Tierney, 'Direct Democracy in the United Kingdom: Reflections upon the Scottish Independence Referendum' [2015] *PL* 633. Research for this chapter was conducted with the help of an ESRC Senior Research Fellowship. See also S. Tierney, '"Popular Constitutional Amendment": Referendums and Constitutional Change in Canada and the United Kingdom' (2015) 41 *Queens Law Journal* 1.

II. The referendum pathology: Practice not principle?

Referendums are paradoxical. For some, they represent an ideal model of democracy. The voters are called upon to speak as one unified people, deciding on an issue directly without the mediation of politicians. The referendum gives a directly determining voice to the *demos* in a way that captures neatly both the people's popular sovereignty and the political equality of all citizens. What could be more democratic? For others, however, the referendum is a dangerous device because it in fact imperils democracy, which can only be properly effected through exclusively representative institutions; and, as a result, the referendum is best excluded from processes of constitutional change.

Elsewhere I have identified three main objections that inform the scepticism of the latter position: that referendums lend themselves by definition to elite control and hence manipulation by the organizers of the referendum ('the elite control syndrome'); that there is an inbuilt tendency of the referendum process merely to aggregate pre-formed opinions rather than to foster meaningful deliberation ('the deliberation deficit'); and that referendums consolidate and even reify simple majoritarian decision-making at the expense of minority and individual interests ('the majoritarian danger').[2] I have argued, however, that these are problems of practice, not principle, and that they can be overcome by good practice in the design and regulation of the referendum based upon principles of popular participation, public reasoning, and pluralism in decision-making. In particular, properly constructed electoral law and models of regulation can help construct a 'deliberative referendum'.[3]

The referendum in Scotland offers an ideal case study with which to test this hypothesis for the following reasons. First, it was organized within a healthy and fully functioning democracy. Secondly, it was long in the planning: the Scottish Government announced its intention to hold a referendum in January 2012,[4] some two and a half years before the vote itself, thus offering a lengthy span of time within which channels of deliberative participation might be fostered. Thirdly, the United Kingdom already had in place a model of detailed regulation of referendums (the Political Parties, Elections and Referendums Act 2000 (PPERA)) which, inter alia, created an independent Electoral Commission and invested it with a detailed oversight role in UK referendums; although this existing UK legal regime was not itself applicable to the independence referendum,[5] it was nevertheless very influential in the framing of the Scottish referendum process. Fourthly, the referendum process was framed against, and given additional legal

[2] S. Tierney, 'Constitutional Referendums: A Theoretical Enquiry' (2009) 72 *MLR* 360; S. Tierney, *Constitutional Referendums: The Theory and Practice of Republican Deliberation* (Oxford University Press 2012).

[3] S. Tierney, 'Using Electoral Law to Construct a Deliberative Referendum: Moving beyond the Democratic Paradox' (2013) *Election Law Journal* 1.

[4] Scottish Government, *Your Scotland—Your Referendum—A Consultation Document* (2012).

[5] Because it applies only to referendums authorized by the UK Parliament.

authority and political credibility by, the 'Edinburgh Agreement' between the UK and Scottish Governments, the aim of which was to ensure the referendum delivered 'a fair test and a decisive expression of the views of people in Scotland and a result that everyone will respect'.[6] And finally, the referendum was regulated by two statutes passed by the Scottish Parliament—the Scottish Independence Referendum (Franchise) Act 2013 ('the Scottish Franchise Act'), and the Scottish Independence Referendum Act ('the Scottish Referendum Act') 2013—which together offered a comprehensive framework of rules and constraints.

I will, therefore, assess how well this legislation served, first, to constrain elite control, and secondly, to help foster meaningful deliberation, particularly among citizens. Scotland is not a divided society with readily identifiable minorities whose interests are clearly imperilled by an exercise in majoritarian decision-making. Therefore, I will not discuss the third criticism of referendums ('the majoritarian danger') further here. In passing, though, it is notable that the referendum decision was reached upon the basis of a simple 50 per cent plus one majority rule. This has been a controversial issue elsewhere, particularly in Canada,[7] but was never a focus of debate in the Scottish context,[8] and again for this reason I will not address it further here.

III. The Scottish referendum: Constraining elite control?

The 'elite control syndrome' is generally the main objection to referendums. The charge is that referendums are organized by governments to effect political goals and are therefore only staged when the prospects of a successful outcome (from the government's viewpoint) are favourable. To this end an executive is able to shape—indeed manipulate—the various elements of process design to achieve this result. As well as the initiation power they can also set the question, choose the date, fix the franchise, decide whether and if so how the referendum will be regulated, and determine the funding and spending rules for the campaign.

How did the Scottish process measure up in response to this problem?

In a sense any referendum is 'elite-controlled', as indeed is any electoral process, if this is taken to mean organized by the established institutions of the state. The central issue is how this power is allocated among institutions. The feature that tends to set alarm bells ringing is when the organization power in a referendum,

[6] *Agreement Between the United Kingdom Government and the Scottish Government on a Referendum on Independence for Scotland*, 15 October 2012, available at: <http://www.scotland.gov.uk/About/Government/concordats/Referendum-on-independence>.

[7] S. Tierney, *Constitutional Law and National Pluralism* (Oxford University Press 2004) 320–2.

[8] A turnout threshold was used in the referendums on devolution for Scotland and Wales respectively, held in 1979. Of those who voted in the Scottish referendum, 52 per cent were in favour of devolution, but the turnout threshold, which required 40 per cent of registered voters to vote for this option, was not met. Nationalists claimed that the will of the majority of voters was thwarted, and perhaps in light of this controversy thresholds have never been applied in any subsequent devolution referendum in the United Kingdom.

or indeed any election, rests exclusively in the hands of the executive without a meaningful role for the legislature or for any level of independent oversight.

The first issue is the decision to set the referendum itself. Some countries, for example Australia and Ireland, offer constitutional regulation of the initiation power; a referendum is a legally required part of the constitutional amendment process. By contrast the United Kingdom leaves the initiation of referendums to the discretion of the central government as we have seen in the referendums of 1975, 1979, 1997, 1998, and 2011 (Table 3.1).

Table 3.1 Referendums in the United Kingdom

Place	Date	Issue	Turnout	Result
Northern Ireland	8 March 1973	Remain part of the United Kingdom	58.7	Approved: 98.9
Northern Ireland	22 May 1998	Belfast Agreement	81.1	Approved: 71.1
Scotland	1 March 1979	Creation of a Scottish Assembly	33	Approved: 52 (did not meet threshold)
Wales	1 March 1979	Creation of a Welsh Assembly	58.8	Not approved: 79.7
Scotland	11 September 1997	1. Creation of a Scottish Parliament. 2. Devolution of limited tax-varying powers	60.4	1. Approved: 74.3 2. Approved: 63.5
Wales	18 September 1997	Creation of a National Assembly	50.1	Approved: 50.3
England (London)	7 May 1998	GLA and Mayor	34.6	Approved: 72
England (North East)	4 November 2004	North East England regional assembly	47.8	Not approved: 78
Wales	3 March 2011	Devolution of further powers to the National Assembly	35.4	Approved: 63.5
Scotland	18 September 2014	Independence	84.7	Not approved: 55.3
United Kingdom	5 June 1975	Continued EC membership	64.5	Approved: 67.2
United Kingdom	5 May 2011	Electoral System: Alternative Vote	42.2	Not approved: 67.9

There is of course no explicit constitutional recognition of referendums in an unwritten constitutional system, although there has been some move towards making future referendums a legal requirement in the devolution context.[9] No such reference

[9] Northern Ireland Act 1998, s. 1; Government of Wales Act 2006, Part IV.

to referendums appears in the Scotland Act 1998 and indeed when the Scottish Government announced its intention to hold a referendum in January 2012 a dispute ensued as to whether the devolved institutions of government in Scotland had the power to stage a referendum on the issue of independence, given that 'the union' is a reserved matter under the Act.[10] There was an immediate rebuttal by the UK Government which challenged the legislative competence of the Scottish Parliament to pass this bill.[11] For a time the disagreement over the meaning of, in particular, section 29(3) of the Scotland Act, was intractable and it seemed as though this issue might find its way to the UK Supreme Court for adjudication.[12] But in the end, and to the surprise of many, on 15 October 2012 a deal was reached between the two governments.[13] This, and the associated 'memorandum of agreement', provided that the referendum should have a clear legal base; be legislated for by the Scottish Parliament; and be conducted so as to command the confidence of parliaments, governments, and people. This was formalized by an Order in Council (per Scotland Act 1998 s. 30) which devolved to the Scottish Parliament the competence to legislate for a referendum on independence which had to be held before the end of 2014.[14]

The result therefore was an intergovernmental agreement on the initiation power which also outlined further elements of the referendum process and the pathway by which these were to be drawn up. In this respect the Scottish referendum bears healthy comparison with other UK referendums that were instigated solely by the central government, on occasion for political purposes. For example, in the early 1970s the Labour Party feared that a damaging split could emerge over membership of the EEC and decided that a referendum would help avoid this by allowing a free vote for MPs, including ministers. James Callaghan described the referendum as a 'lifeboat' into which the party was climbing in order to see off the danger of fission.[15] Labour returned to the referendum in similar circumstances in relation to devolution. Proposals put forward in 1976 for assemblies for Scotland and Wales were widely opposed within the party. Vernon Bogdanor comments that the promise of a referendum which accompanied these proposals 'was a device that would enable Labour backbenchers opposed to devolution nevertheless to vote for it in the House of Commons while campaigning against it in the referendum'.[16] The bill was in the end withdrawn in March 1977. But when it was revived in 1977–8

[10] See eg A. Tomkins, 'The Scottish Parliament and the Independence Referendum' (*UK Constitutional Law Group blog*, 12 January 2012) <http://ukconstitutionallaw.org/2012/01/12/adam-tomkins-the-scottish-parliament-and-the-independence-referendum/>; and G. Anderson et al, 'The Independence Referendum, Legality and the Contested Constitution: Widening the Debate' (*UK Constitutional Law Group blog*, 31 January 2012) <http://ukconstitutionallaw.org/2012/01/31/gavin-anderson-et-al-the-independence-referendum-legality-and-the-contested-constitution-widening-the-debate/>.

[11] *Scotland's Constitutional Future* (Cm 8203, 2012).

[12] For further discussion see Tickell's Ch. 14 in this volume.

[13] *Your Scotland—Your Referendum* (n. 4).

[14] Scotland Act 1998 (Modification of Sched. 5) Order 2013, SI 2013/242, art. 3.

[15] D. Butler and U. Kitzinger, *The 1975 Referendum* (Macmillan Press 1976) 282.

[16] V. Bogdanor, *The People and the Party System The Referendum and Electoral Reform in British Politics* (Cambridge University Press 1981) 42.

referendums were again proposed and these were held in 1979. Again Bogdanor points to how the 1979 referendums were used 'to defuse an issue'.[17]

The Alternative Vote (AV) referendum in 2011 was also instigated for party political purposes. The decision to hold a referendum on this issue was the result of a political deal by the two parties forming the coalition government in 2010. One consequence of using a constitutional referendum as a political fix in this way (which also tightly circumscribed the model of electoral system which would be presented as an alternative to first past the post in the referendum) is that the issue to be put to the people is not subjected to wider deliberation; instead of a detailed discussion of electoral reform and the opportunity for all of the options to be fully aired, only one model, which proved to be difficult to understand and indeed to support, was put to the people.[18] This process came in for criticism from a number of people giving evidence to the House of Lords inquiry on referendums.[19] And again we must also see the prospective EU referendum in this light. The promise to hold an In/Out vote in 2017 is again a political device to confront the UKIP threat and to shore up a potential split in the Conservative party; in the latter respect this proposal bears parallels with the 1975 referendum.

The initiation power is, of course, not the only issue within the elite control criticism. A second charge is that, with this power, the executive also has carte blanche in framing the process for the referendum itself: determining the timing of the referendum, the setting of the question, defining the franchise, regulating the campaign and ballot procedure, setting funding and spending rules, and the like, and also determining the extent, if any, of independent oversight of these different components. But in fact when we look to the UK experience there is a growing body of legislation and good practice which now operates to regulate these various process components and in doing so to overcome the risks of elite manipulation.

For over a decade UK referendums have operated on the basis of a dedicated referendum law (PPERA), which emerged as a result of a report by the (Neill) Committee on Standards in Public Life.[20] In addition there tends also to be tailored legislation which sets further rules specific to a particular referendum.[21] As noted above, PPERA only applies to referendums organized by the Westminster Parliament and so did not regulate the proposed referendum in Scotland. However its terms acted as an important benchmark for the Scottish Government in drafting the Scottish Franchise Bill and the Scottish Referendum Bill,[22] and for the Scottish Parliament in deliberating upon these.

[17] Bogdanor (n. 16) 45.

[18] This can be contrasted with the elaborate way in which New Zealand used referendums to test the popularity of different electoral models: P. Aimer et al, *Toward Consensus?: The 1993 Election and Referendum in New Zealand* (Auckland University Press 1995) ch. 10.

[19] House of Lords Select Committee on the Constitution, *Referendums in the United Kingdom*, HL Paper 99, 2009–10, Minutes of Evidence.

[20] Committee on Standards in Public Life, *The Funding of Political Parties in the United Kingdom* (the Neill Report) (Cm 4057, HMSO 1998).

[21] eg Parliamentary Voting System and Constituencies Act 2011.

[22] The Edinburgh Agreement (n. 4) provided at para. 2: 'Both governments agree that the principles underpinning the existing framework for referendums held under Acts of the UK

PPERA also followed the recommendation of the Neill Committee in creating the Electoral Commission, and the Commission's supervisory and investigatory powers were extended by the Political Parties and Elections Act 2009. The Commission has various duties mostly related to funding and spending rules but also in relation to the intelligibility of the referendum question. This body is again central in the prevention of illegitimate elite control. As a creature of PPERA however, the Electoral Commission had no automatic role in relation to the Scottish referendum. Nonetheless such a role was agreed upon in the Edinburgh Agreement and was in time guaranteed by the Scottish Franchise Act and Scottish Referendum Act, and by the actions of the Scottish Government. The Commission's role will be discussed in detail in the next section of the chapter, and from this it will be clear that it played a hands-on role across a number of areas including the setting of the question, the provision of information to citizens, the regulation of funding and spending, and the management of the mechanics of registration and voting. For now it might be noted that early on in the process (September 2013) the Commission also conducted a full review to highlight any risks 'while there is still time to address them'. It concluded that 'preparations are on track to deliver a well-run poll'.[23]

And finally, in discussing the regulatory regime in broad terms we should also note that the Scottish Referendum Act included sanctions for violations of the referendum rules, both civil (Schedule 6) and criminal (Schedule 7) in relation to various categories of electoral malpractice; and once again the Electoral Commission was given an important role in enforcing the former.

In concluding this section we find that in general a great deal of discretion exists within the United Kingdom as to when and on what issues referendums should be held. But this is particularly the case in relation to the powers of the UK Government, as we saw with the AV referendum and are currently seeing in relation to a prospective referendum on EU membership. One of the recommendations of a House of Lords inquiry on referendums was that, if referendums are to be a feature of British democracy, there should be legal regulation of the types of issue that ought to be subject of referendums and of how and when these issues might be brought directly before the people.[24]

By dint of the limited competence of the Scottish Parliament and the subsequent uncertainty concerning its power to hold a referendum, the initiation power for the Scottish referendum was in fact regulated more fulsomely and by a more plural array of actors than would an equivalent process organized by the UK

Parliament—which aim to guarantee fairness—should apply to the Scottish independence referendum. Part 7 of the Political Parties, Elections and Referendums Act 2000 (PPERA) 2, provides a framework for referendums delivered through Acts of Parliament, including rules about campaign finance, referendum regulation, oversight and conduct.'

[23] Electoral Commission news release, 'Referendum Plans on Track to Deliver for Voters', 25 September 2013. <http://www.electoralcommission.org.uk/i-am-a/journalist/electoral-commission-media-centre/news-releases-referendums/referendum-plans-on-track-to-deliver-for-voters?>.

[24] *Referendums in the United Kingdom* (n. 19), Summary of Recommendations.

Government.[25] The result was a complex regime of regulation encompassing three distinct elements: the first was the primary role of the Scottish Government in initiating the proposal, and of the Scottish Parliament which was required to pass the key legislation. The second was the Scotland Act 1998 which delimits the powers of these two bodies, ensuring that each of these roles was circumscribed by the boundaries of devolved competence. And the third was a significant role for the UK Government and Parliament through a combination of the Edinburgh Agreement and the section 30 Order, with the latter, for the avoidance of any doubt, transferring any necessary powers to the Scottish Parliament to legislate for the holding of the referendum. As we will see in the next section, this combination of regulatory elements served significantly to constrain the powers of the Scottish Government.

A. Facilitating deliberation?

The second main criticism of referendums, by which they are often held in unflattering contrast to the purported merits of representative democracy, is that public reasoning which allows for the informed reflection and discussion of ideas before decisions are reached is absent from referendum processes. Various assumptions underpin this idea: referendums tend to be held quickly by way of a snap poll organized at the behest of the government;[26] voters are presented with an issue which is itself confusing and can be made worse by an unintelligible question; voters themselves lack the time, sufficient interest in the matter at stake, or the competence to understand or engage properly with the issue, and in effect turn up at the polling station, if indeed they bother to do so at all, in an unreflective manner, often following party cues in determining how to vote.

In this section I will consider a number of elements in the regulatory design of the Scottish referendum, assessing these against the benchmark of deliberative participation: the franchise (by which the inclusiveness of the poll can be assessed) and the participation of citizens in the referendum; the question, both its intelligibility and how the determination of this was overseen; the time and information available to voters to deliberate upon the issue; the sixteen-week 'referendum period' and twenty-eight-day purdah period within which the activities of political actors were regulated; and the spending and funding rules, designed to ensure that the campaign was not dominated by one campaign or powerful interests.

B. Franchise

In a mass popular engagement with democracy both participation and deliberation are vital. It is not enough that those who make the decision do so in a

[25] It is worth noting that the referendum franchise is not regulated by PPERA. It is therefore an issue to be determined in each case, with the possibility that this can be shaped to suit the government of the day.

[26] The referendum in Ukraine on 16 March 2014 is a recent, egregious example. See S. Tierney, 'Sovereignty and Crimea: How Referendum Democracy Complicates Constituent Power in Multinational Societies' (2015) 16 *German Law Journal* 523.

reflective and discursive way, it is also essential that the process should generate the widespread engagement of citizens across the polity if the exercise is to be truly legitimate. That the franchise is defined in a properly inclusive way is therefore the first step in achieving this goal. The body of voters in the Scottish referendum was largely uncontroversial. The franchise for the referendum was the same as for Scottish Parliament elections and local government elections,[27] mirroring the franchise used in the Scottish devolution referendum in 1997. One consequence was that EU citizens who are resident in Scotland were able to vote in the independence referendum.

One major difference from the 1997 franchise, however, was the provision in the Scottish Franchise Act extending the vote to those aged 16 and 17.[28] This was a radical departure; never before have people under the age of 18 been entitled to vote in a major British election or referendum.[29] It is not possible to determine why this decision was taken. On the one hand it could be seen as a cynical ploy to empower younger voters who would be more likely to vote Yes. On the other it has long been SNP policy that younger people should be allowed to vote and this was the first electoral event where this could be put into practice. In the end it did not arouse particular controversy within the Scottish Parliament's Referendum (Scotland) Bill Committee. Now that the Scottish Parliament has the power to set the franchise for the Scottish Parliament elections in May 2016,[30] it is using this to extend the vote to 16-year olds for this election.[31]

Another notable provision of the Scottish Franchise Act excluded convicted persons from voting in the referendum if they are detained in a penal institution.[32] This has been a controversial topic in the United Kingdom ever since the European Court of Human Rights ruled that the blanket ban on prisoner voting in UK elections violated Article 3 of Protocol 1 of the European Convention on Human Rights.[33] It seemed clear, however, that section 3 of the Franchise Act did not violate the Convention since A3P1 guarantees 'the free expression of the opinion of the people in *the choice of the legislature*' (emphasis added), which is generally taken to refer exclusively to parliamentary elections and to exclude referendums.[34] This view has been endorsed by Lord Glennie in the Outer House of the Court of Session,[35] and subsequently by the Inner House[36] and the UK Supreme Court.[37]

[27] Scottish Independence Referendum (Franchise) Act 2013, s. 2.
[28] Scottish Independence Referendum (Franchise) Act 2013, s. 2(1)(a).
[29] Representation of the People Act 1983, s. 1(d).
[30] Scotland Act 1998 (Modifications of Schedules 4 and 5 and Transfer of Functions to the Scottish Ministers, etc.) Order 2015, SI 2015/692.
[31] Scottish Elections (Reduction of Voting Age) Act 2015.
[32] Scottish Independence Referendum (Franchise) Act 2013, s. 3.
[33] *Hirst v the United Kingdom* (No. 2) [2005] ECHR 681.
[34] S. Tierney, *Possible Vires Issue in Relation to Section 3 of the Scottish Independence Referendum (Franchise) Bill*, Advice to the Scottish Parliament, Scottish Referendum Bill Committee Paper, 21 March 2013, available at <http://www.scottish.parliament.uk/S4_ReferendumScotlandBillCommittee/20130321_Letter_to_DFM_on_prisoners_voting_rights.pdf>.
[35] *Moohan and others, Petitioners* [2013] CSOH 199.
[36] *Moohan and others v Lord Advocate* [2014] CSIH 56.
[37] *Moohan and Another v Lord Advocate* [2014] UKSC 67.

Franchise is one thing, citizen engagement quite another. If citizens are simply not interested in the referendum then the very legitimacy of the process comes into question. It may simply be that the subject matter of the referendum is not an issue that most people think fit for an exercise in direct democracy. It is clear from the turnout and result in 2011 that many people did not view the AV proposition to be an important issue (turnout of 42.2 per cent; 68 per cent voted No and 32 per cent voted Yes). The referendum in Wales in 2011, with a turnout 35.4 per cent, also failed to mobilize public interest.

The level of debate and subsequent turnout demonstrate that the Scottish referendum did not suffer from this fate. Astonishingly 4,285,323 people (97 per cent of the electorate) registered to vote and in the end 84.7 per cent turned out, the highest figure for any UK electoral event since the introduction of universal suffrage, significantly trumping the 65.1 per cent who voted in the 2010 UK general election and the 50.6 per cent who bothered to turn out for the 2011 Scottish parliamentary elections. This is even more remarkable when we consider that the franchise was extended to 16- and 17-year olds, creating a significant logistical task for those registering new voters while taking care of data protection and other issues in relation to young people.[38]

Turnout is of course only one marker of participation. The story we now hear time and time again from voters and campaigners alike is that citizens felt greatly empowered by the referendum and the role they had in making such a huge decision. Evidence is emerging of the extent to which people sought out information about the issue at stake and engaged vociferously with one another at home, in the workplace, in pubs and public meetings, and, to an unprecedented degree in British politics, on social media through online newspaper comment sections, Twitter, Facebook, blogs, and other platforms.[39] My own evidence is merely anecdotal, but as someone who lived through the referendum campaign I can say that in the month before the vote I experienced a level of public engagement with a major political issue the like of which I have never known.[40]

C. Question: The intelligibility test

Do citizens understand the question? If not, then meaningful deliberation in any referendum is not possible. PPERA gives the Electoral Commission an important role in overseeing question-setting in referendum processes organized by the Westminster Parliament. Where a bill is introduced into Parliament which

[38] Scottish Independence Referendum (Franchise) Act 2013, s. 9.

[39] See A. Henderson et al, 'Risk and Attitudes to Constitutional Change', ESRC Scottish Centre on Constitutional Change Risk and Constitutional Attitudes Survey, 16 August 2014: <http://www.futureukandscotland.ac.uk/sites/default/files/news/Risk%20and%20Constitutional%20Attitudes%20Full%20Survey%2014%20Aug.pdf> and AQMen project <https://www.aqmen.ac.uk/project/socialmedia>.

[40] See also I. MacWhirter, *Disunited Kingdom: How Westminster Won A Referendum But Lost Scotland* (Cargo Publishing 2014) and James Mitchell's chapter in this volume.

provides for the holding of a referendum, and this Bill specifies the wording of the referendum question, the Commission 'shall consider the wording of the referendum question, and shall publish a statement of any views of the Commission as to the intelligibility of that question'.[41] Notably the Electoral Commission goes about its task of assessing intelligibility by addressing what people really understand by the question through convening focus groups, in other ways of testing the question empirically.[42]

Despite the fact that PPERA does not regulate the Scottish process, and therefore the Electoral Commission had no legally guaranteed role in relation to the 2014 referendum, the Edinburgh Agreement gave it such a role, leading the Scottish Government to send its proposed question for review by the Electoral Commission. This process was concluded quickly and the Commission reported back suggesting a minor change to the question.[43] This was accepted by the Scottish Government and this new question was included in the Scottish Referendum Act.[44]

The Electoral Commission also offered the view that the clarity of the question hinged not only on its syntax but upon the content of the independence proposal: 'clarity about how the terms of independence will be decided would help voters understand how the competing claims made by referendum campaigners before the referendum will be resolved.'[45] This is an interesting comment, reflecting as it does the requirement that a fully deliberative process is only possible if citizens know what they are voting for.[46] The Scottish Government published a White Paper in November 2013 which set out its vision of independence,[47] followed by a White Paper and draft Scottish Independence Bill which sought to

[41] Political Parties, Elections and Referendums Act, s. 104(2).

[42] Electoral Commission *Referendum on the UK Parliamentary Voting System: Report of Views of the Electoral Commission on the Proposed Referendum Question* (2010), <http://www.electoralcommission.org.uk/__data/assets/pdf_file/0006/102696/PVSC-Bill-QA-Report.pdf>; Electoral Commission *Referendum on Independence for Scotland: Advice of the Electoral Commission on the Proposed Referendum Question* (2013) <http://www.electoralcommission.org.uk/__data/assets/pdf_file/0007/153691/Referendum-on-independence-for-Scotland-our-advice-on-referendum-question.pdf>.

[43] The Scottish Government's proposed question was: 'Do you agree that Scotland should be an independent country? Yes/No.' The Electoral Commission took the view that 'based on our research and taking into account what we heard from people and organisations who submitted their views on the question, we consider that the proposed question is not neutral because the phrase "Do you agree ... ?" could lead people towards voting "yes".' They therefore recommended the following question: 'Should Scotland be an independent country? Yes/No.' Electoral Commission, 2013 (n. 42).

[44] Scottish Independence Referendum Act 2013, s. 1(2). See also, BBC News, 'Scottish independence: SNP accepts Call to Change Referendum Question' (30 January 2013) <http://www.bbc.co.uk/news/uk-scotland-scotland-politics-21245701>.

[45] Electoral Commission, 2013 (n. 42) at para. 5.41. See generally paras 5.41–5.44, eg 'We recommend that both Governments should agree a joint position, if possible, so that voters have access to agreed information about what would follow the referendum. The alternative—two different explanations—could cause confusion for voters rather than make things clearer' (para. 5.43).

[46] One of the main criticisms of the Quebec referendum in 1995 was that the proposal of sovereignty and partnership was not well understood by citizens: Tierney, *Constitutional Law and National Pluralism* (n. 7) at 293–9.

[47] Scottish Government, *Scotland's Future: Your Guide to an Independent Scotland* (2013).

lay out proposals for interim and permanent constitutions for an independent Scotland.[48] Each of these were of course heavily criticized by the UK Government and by the Better Together campaign. The November White Paper in particular led to a series of papers by the UK Government contesting many of the claims made in the White Paper. In the end, and surely inevitably, citizens were left with a debate fuelled by these competing claims in the context of the referendum campaign, rather than any agreed set of 'facts' about what independence would look like.

D. Time to understand the issue?

Another prerequisite of serious deliberation is that people have time to consider the issue upon which they are being asked to vote. An element of control which was left to the Scottish Government by the Edinburgh Agreement was the timing of the referendum and in January 2012 it set its course for a referendum some two and a half years hence. This timing was of course strategic. Correctly or not, the Scottish Government saw the autumn of 2014 as a propitious moment. It allowed the SNP sufficient time to make the case for independence and it would coincide with a number of significant events: the anniversary of the Battle of Bannockburn, the Commonwealth Games, and even the Ryder Cup in Gleneagles. It is difficult to argue that any of these events were of any significance at all to the result. It would also come shortly before a UK general election, which it was anticipated would distract the UK parties and perhaps make them less inclined to work together. But, from the perspective of deliberative participation, a beneficial side-effect of this procrastination was that the election debate was conducted over a very long period of time, allowing each side to make its case in full and giving citizens time and space to consider the issues.

A related issue is the fixedness of the date. One controversy which arose in the 1995 Quebec referendum was that the date was changed in the course of the campaign from June to October as opinion polls in the spring showed that the measure would probably fail.[49] In fact the date of 30 October was not fixed until 7 September, and not formally adopted by the National Assembly until 20 September. Similarly, the French referendum in 2005 on the EU Constitutional Treaty was brought forward as the government sensed support for the No side was growing.[50] Originally planned for the second half of 2005, on 4 March it was announced that the French referendum would be brought forward to 29 May. These are clear examples of how elites with too much power can manipulate the timing of the vote to their advantage.

[48] Scottish Government, *Scottish Independence Bill: A Consultation on an Interim Constitution for Scotland* (2014).

[49] R. A. Young, *The Struggle for Quebec: From Referendum to Referendum?* (McGill-Queen's University Press 1999) 13, 18, and 27.

[50] 'Chirac Accelerates EU Referendum after Gains for No Camp', *EU Business.com* 18 February 2005. <http://www.eubusiness.com/europe/france/050218132610.w1ahja90/> accessed 14 July 2011. See also S. Marthaler, 'The French Referendum on Ratification of the Constitutional Treaty', Referendum Briefing Paper No. 12, European Parties Elections and Referendums Network, 29 May 2005.

This issue did not arise in Scotland. The timing of the Scottish referendum was in part regulated by the Edinburgh Agreement and subsequent section 30 Order, which set a condition that the referendum must be held before the end of 2014. The actual date of 18 September 2014 was announced by the Scottish Government on 21 March 2013 and included in the Scottish Independence Referendum Bill. This was then passed into law and there was no suggestion at any stage that it might be changed. Other important timing issues included in the legislation are the sixteen-week 'referendum period'[51] and the four-week purdah period,[52] discussed below.

To conclude, one of the standard criticisms of referendums from the perspective of deliberation is that they are held too hastily without time for proper deliberation of the issues. This was clearly not a problem in the Scottish context where the referendum was proposed some thirty-three months before it was held and where both campaigns had almost two years from the conclusion of the Edinburgh Agreement to explain their respective cases to the voters. The timing was also regulated by both the Edinburgh Agreement and the subsequent legislation which fixed the date and gave certainty to both campaigns and citizens as to when the referendum would take place.

E. Information: Is there evidence that voters understood the issue?

Citizens cannot deliberate properly without access to sufficient, reliable information. In many ways such an environment depends more upon the health of a particular democracy and of its civil society than it does upon legal regulation. Indeed, excessive regulation can in fact serve to inhibit the free flow of ideas.

In the Scottish referendum there were many sources of information: both governments,[53] each campaign group, other registered participants in the referendum campaign, and various other sources in civil society,[54] including the media, and academia.[55] As noted above, a particularly prominent source of information was social media, with Twitter, Facebook, and blogs playing a major role in the dissemination of ideas and also in discussion and debate. The provision of information by the two campaigns has been touched upon in the context of the November White Paper and the assessment of the referendum question but other

[51] Scottish Independence Referendum Act 2013, Sched. 4, Part 3.

[52] Scottish Independence Referendum Act 2013, Sched. 4, para. 25.

[53] We have already noted the Scottish Government White Paper, *Scotland's Future* (n. 47). In June 2014 the UK Government sent a sixteen-page booklet entitled *What Staying in the UK Means for Scotland* to every household in Scotland, setting out the case for the No side. See 'UK "Fact Booklet" to be Sent to Scots Households' *Scotsman* (12 June 2014).

[54] See eg on the franchise and mechanics of voting issued by the Citizens Advice Bureau: <http://www.adviceguide.org.uk/scotland/law_s/law_civil_rights_s/law_government_and_voting_s/the_scottish_independence_referendum_s.htm>.

[55] eg see the major ESRC investment: *Future of the UK and Scotland*, <http://www.esrc.ac.uk/research/major-investments/future-of-uk-and-scotland/index.aspx>.

related issues include the provision, and indeed the very possibility, of providing independent or neutral information to voters through the Electoral Commission, and secondly, the provision of a state subsidy to the main referendum campaigns to provide a mailshot to households. In the United Kingdom both have become standard practice.

Taking the second issue first, PPERA contains the option of allowing each of the main campaign organizations in a referendum—if the campaigns register themselves as such—one free mailshot setting out their views; this can be adopted by the enabling legislation for a particular referendum.[56] The section 30 Order extended this power from PPERA, thereby allowing the Scottish Parliament to offer such a free mailing to each of the two main organizations.[57]

As regards the provision of neutral information, during the AV referendum campaign the Electoral Commission sent an information booklet to all 27.8 million households in the United Kingdom explaining what elections were taking place, the referendum question, how to take part in the referendum, and giving 'an independent explanation of the "first past the post" and "alternative vote" systems'. The booklet was also supported by a multimedia advertising campaign.[58] But this raises the question about how much the Commission can in fact say. The booklet set out briefly what the two models of voting on offer were but did not engage with the arguments for and against each. Instead it simply stated: 'Campaigners in the referendum will explain why they think you should vote "yes" (to use the "alternative vote" system) or "no" (to continue using the "first past the post" system). Look out for information from them.'[59]

The Scottish Referendum Act built upon this practice. Among a number of statutory duties, the Commission was given the task of promoting public awareness and understanding in Scotland about the referendum, the referendum question, and voting in the referendum.[60] This was always going to be a very challenging duty in light of the deep disagreement between the two campaigns about what was meant by independence.[61] It was always hard to see how the Electoral Commission could attempt to produce an objective account of a number of highly technical and fiercely contested issues, including not only international relations but also defence, economic relations, the question of a currency

[56] Political Parties, Elections and Referendums Act 2000, Sched. 12, para. 1.

[57] Scotland Act 1998 (Modification of Schedule 5) Order 2013, art. 4(1).

[58] 'Voting Referendum Confirmed', Electoral Commission News Release, 17 February 2011 <http://www.electoralcommission.org.uk/news-and-media/news-releases/electoral-commission-media-centre/news-releases-referendums/voting-referendum-confirmed>.

[59] Electoral Commission, *Local Elections and Referendum on the Voting System Used to Elect MPs to the House of Commons* (2011), <http://www.electoralcommission.org.uk/__data/assets/file/0005/109877/Eng-web.pdf>. This has been criticized for its lack of content: Richard Wyn Jones' evidence before the Referendum (Scotland) Bill Committee: Scottish Parliament Referendum (Scotland) Bill Committee, 9 May 2013, Official Report <http://www.scottish.parliament.uk/parliamentarybusiness/28862.aspx?r=8140&i=73882&c=1482666>.

[60] Scottish Independence Referendum Act, s. 21.

[61] S. Tierney, 'Why is Scottish Independence Unclear?' (*UK Constitutional Law blog*, 25 February 2014) available at: <http://ukconstitutionallaw.org/>.

union, the disentanglement of the welfare state, and the national debt etc, particularly when so many features of the post-referendum landscape would be contingent upon negotiations between the two governments in the event of a majority Yes vote. Indeed it was argued in evidence before the Scottish Parliament Referendum Bill Committee that it was simply not possible to perform such a role in a neutral way.[62]

In the end the Electoral Commission intimated that it would 'not seek to explain to voters what independence means' but would offer information 'aimed at ensuring that all eligible electors are registered and know how to cast their vote.'[63] The Electoral Commission also concluded that both governments had a duty here to help explain the implications of either a Yes or a No vote and that a joint position on this would benefit voters. This was a brave attempt to improve the deliberative environment for citizens, even if in political terms such a joint position was never likely to be achievable.

And so on 18 June the Commission announced the publication of a booklet that would go to all households with information on the voting mechanics. Rather than seek to explain the issue of independence the booklet instead contained campaign statements from both the designated lead campaigners, and a joint statement by the Scottish and UK Governments on the process that would follow the referendum.[64] The Electoral Commissioner for Scotland, John McCormick said about the booklet: '[it] provides important, factual information for voters in advance of polling day and we have tested it with the public to ensure it gives them the information they need.' With regard to the joint statement by the UK and Scottish Governments included in the booklet, McCormick noted:

> During our question assessment process people told us they wanted impartial information about the referendum before they voted. Although we said we did not expect the terms of independence to be agreed before the vote, we called for clarity from both governments about what would happen in the event of a yes or a no vote.

And in the end this is all that was achievable in the document launched on 11 August 2014.[65] The two-page joint statement at the end of the document did however set out a useful summary of what would happen following a Yes or a No vote. It did not try to explain what independence means but it did discuss the need

[62] William Norton evidence before the Referendum (Scotland) Bill Committee, 9 May 2013, Official Report <http://www.scottish.parliament.uk/parliamentarybusiness/28862.aspx?r=8140&i=73882&c=1482666>.

[63] John McCormick, the Electoral Commissioner for Scotland, evidence to: Scottish Parliament Referendum (Scotland) Bill Committee, 23 May 2013, Official Report, col. 431, <http://www.scottish.parliament.uk/parliamentarybusiness/28862.aspx?r=8326&mode=pdf>.

[64] 'Electoral Commission publishes its information booklet for the Scottish Independence Referendum', Electoral Commission news release, 18 June 2014, <http://www.electoralcommission.org.uk/i-am-a/journalist/electoral-commission-media-centre/news-releases-referendums/electoral-commission-publishes-its-information-booklet-for-the-scottish-independence-referendum>.

[65] 'Every Household in Scotland to get Impartial Voting Guide', Electoral Commission news release, 11 August 2014, <http://www.electoralcommission.org.uk/i-am-a/journalist/electoral-commission-media-centre/news-releases-campaigns/every-household-in-scotland-to-get-impartial-voting-guide>.

for negotiations in the event of a Yes vote, and the balance of devolved and reserved competences in the interim period.

F. Referendum period and purdah

The greatest threat to a deliberative referendum in which citizens can consider the issues calmly and without undue influence arises in the period immediately preceding the vote. Inevitably this is also the period of greatest intensity in campaigning, and so, just as voters are taking more interest in the issue, there is a particular risk of misinformation being fed to the public partly through distortions brought about by excessive, and potentially lop-sided, campaign spending.

The Scottish Referendum Act addressed this problem by two devices. First, it introduced a 'referendum period'[66] of sixteen weeks before the referendum within which the statutory regime of campaign regulation took effect, the main purpose of which was to impose limits on campaign expenditure.[67] The length of the period could perhaps be criticized on the grounds that it still left a substantial period of time following enactment of the legislation but before the referendum period began within which the two main referendum campaigns were not subject to these detailed provisions. And indeed PPERA offers flexibility here. It does not fix a specific length of time for every referendum period, provided it is more than ten weeks and less than six months.[68] The regulated period for the 1997 Scottish devolution referendum (held before PPERA was passed of course) was 119 days (seventeen weeks) and for the AV referendum in 2011 it was only eleven weeks. Sixteen weeks is therefore within the normal period for UK referendums. In addition, there was an additional practical concern. The sixteen-week period commenced shortly after the European parliamentary elections and it was considered by some that it would not have been practical to have two regulated periods operating at the same time in relation to different electoral processes.

Secondly, the Act also provided for what is commonly known as a 'purdah' period; called by the Act the 'relevant period'. This is common in UK elections. Again the Scottish Referendum Act reflected the existing UK legal regime. Under PPERA there is to be no promotional activity by government, local authorities, or public bodies during the twenty-eight day relevant period prior to an election poll.[69] This provision is largely replicated in the Scottish Referendum Act[70] in relation to the Scottish Government and a wide range of other public bodies which must not engage in promotional activity in the four weeks prior to the referendum. The UK Government also committed to be bound by equivalent restrictions in the Edinburgh Agreement.[71] In general the purdah period was well respected,

[66] Defined in Scottish Independence Referendum Act, Sched. 8.
[67] Scottish Independence Referendum Act, Sched. 4, Part 3.
[68] Political Parties, Elections and Referendums Act 2000, s. 102.
[69] Political Parties, Elections and Referendums Act 2000, s. 125.
[70] Section 10 and Sched. 4, para. 25.
[71] For comment on this by Deputy First Minister Nicola Sturgeon, see Scottish Parliament Referendum (Scotland) Bill Committee, 13 June 2013, Official Report, cols 554 and 560.

although it is open to debate whether the promise of more powers for Scotland in the event of a No vote, which was made repeatedly in the final weeks of the campaign, violated the UK Government's obligations.[72] The argument was that these promises came from the UK political parties, in the most prominent case presented by former Prime Minster Gordon Brown,[73] and not by the UK Government.

G. Funding and spending

Funding and spending is such a central part of any electoral event, and so potentially destabilizing to the deliberative participation of citizens, that it requires to be addressed as a separate category. The primary aim of the Scottish Referendum Act was to arrive at some degree of parity between the two campaigns. In this endeavour, as in its detailed provisions, the Scottish Referendum Act again largely reflected the PPERA regime.

PPERA is a serious attempt to address the funding and spending issue in detail with a view to a level playing field, while allowing for these rules to be tailored further from referendum to referendum. It contains a highly elaborate set of financial provisions (in fact the degree of elaboration has come in for some criticism).[74] The fact that the Electoral Commission oversees the setting and implementation of these spending and funding limits, as well as other aspects of the process, also goes a long way to satisfying crucial conditions for effective deliberation.

Building upon the UK regime, the Scottish Referendum Act sought to ensure equality of arms between the two campaign groups. Each side in the campaign was able to apply to the Electoral Commission to be appointed as one of two 'Designated Organizations', and both the Yes Scotland and Better Together campaign groups intimated their respective intention to do so. They were designated as such in April 2014.[75] Notably the Act sought to deal with a criticism of PPERA relating to designation. PPERA does not permit the Electoral Commission to designate only one campaign organization; either both (or more) must apply for designation or neither can.[76] In the referendum in Wales in 2011 the No campaign 'True Wales' did not apply, which led to a criticism that this was 'gaming', to prevent the Yes campaign from attracting public funding and the other benefits

[72] BBC News, 'Scottish Independence: Osborne's Further Powers Plan "Not Against Purdah Rules"' (7 September 2014) <http://www.bbc.co.uk/news/uk-scotland-29100372>.

[73] S. Johnson, 'Gordon Brown Unveils Cross-Party Deal on Scottish Powers' *Telegraph* (8 September 2014).

[74] N. S. Ghaleigh, 'Sledgehammers and Nuts?: Regulating Referendums in the UK' in K. Gilland Lutz and S. Hug (eds), *Financing Referendum Campaigns* (Palgrave Macmillan 2009).

[75] 'Electoral Commission Designates "Yes Scotland" and "Better Together" as Lead Campaigners at Scottish Independence Referendum', Electoral Commission news release, 23 April 2014, <http://www.electoralcommission.org.uk/i-am-a/journalist/electoral-commission-media-centre/news-releases-referendums/electoral-commission-designates-yes-scotland-and-better-together-as-lead-campaigners-at-scottish-independence-referendum?>.

[76] Political Parties, Elections and Referendums Act 2000, s. 108.

of designation.[77] By contrast, the Scottish Referendum Act allowed for designation by one side alone,[78] thereby avoiding this problem. In the end this was not an issue in practice as both campaigns applied for official status, but it does illustrate that the Scottish Parliament addressed PPERA in detail and was keen to adopt its advantages and tinker with its potential disadvantages. This might well be a lesson for future UK-wide referendums.

Another difference from the PPERA model is that the Scottish Referendum Act did not provide for any public funding for designated organizations. This again was a conscious departure from PPERA, which does offer grants to designated organizations.[79] The decision not to fund the 2014 referendum was a political one taken by the Scottish Government. It did not lead to any opposition within the Scottish Parliament, nor by either of the two main campaign groups—perhaps because both campaigns expected to be amply funded by private donors.

On a more detailed level, a 'Campaign Rules' provision within the Act created a regulatory regime through which funding, spending, and reporting were administered (s. 10 and Schedule 4). This is generally in line with standard PPERA rules. A 'Control of Donations' provision (Schedule 4, Part 5) indicates what types of donations were allowed and what constituted a 'permissible donor' (Schedule 4, para. 1(2)). Under these provisions an application must be made for this status. There are also reporting requirements which meant that reports on donations received required to be prepared every four weeks during the referendum period (Schedule 4, para. 41).

1. Spending limits

Within the Scottish Referendum Act there were four categories of actor entitled to spend money during the campaign period: 'designated organisations' (which could each spend up to £1,500,000) (Schedule 4, para. 18(1)); political parties as 'permitted participants' (see below) (Schedule 4, para. 18(1)); other 'permitted participants' who could spend up to £150,000 (Schedule 4, para. 18(1)); and any other participants spending less than £10,000, which means they did not require to register as permitted participants.

Political parties as 'permitted participants' had a spending limit of either £3,000,000 multiplied by their percentage share of the vote in the Scottish Parliament election of 2011, or £150,000 (whichever is greater). By this formula the spending limits for political parties represented in the Scottish Parliament were as follows:

Scottish National Party: £1,344,000
Scottish Labour Party: £834,000

[77] Richard Wyn Jones' evidence before the Referendum (Scotland) Bill Committee, 9 May 2013. See also S. Tierney and S. Suteu, *Towards a Democratic and Deliberative Referendum?: Analysing the Scottish Independence Referendum Bill and the Scottish Independence Referendum (Franchise) Bill* (ESRC Report, 21 August 2013).

[78] Scottish Independence Referendum Act, Sched. 4, para. 5(3).

[79] Political Parties, Elections and Referendums Act 2000, s. 110.

Scottish Conservative & Unionist Party: £396,000
Scottish Liberal Democrats: £201,000
Scottish Green Party: £150,000

The Referendum Act also defined 'campaign expenses'. These included campaign broadcasts, advertising, material addressed to voters, market research or canvassing, press conferences or media relations, transport, rallies, public meetings, or other events. This also extended to notional expenses such as use of/sum of property, services, or facilities (Schedule 4, paras 9 & 10). There were also detailed rules on reporting of expenditure (Referendum Act, Schedule 4, paras 20–4). The Electoral Commission had a power to issue guidance on the different kinds of expenses that qualify as campaign expenses: Schedule 4, para. 10.

It seems that these rules led to a generally level playing field in terms of expenditure within the referendum period (also called the regulated period). For example, the total spending limit for the two pro-independence parties (SNP and Greens) was almost equal to that for the three Unionist parties—Labour, Conservative, and Liberal Democrat. It should also be observed that these rules reflect the spending limits recommended by the Electoral Commission[80] by which they were overseen, and which issued statements on the four weekly reports.[81] Prior to the referendum there was some concern among commentators about 'splintering', whereby a larger group sets up a number of permitted participants to get round its own limited spending power.[82] There is no evidence that this was a significant issue in the Scottish referendum.[83]

An indication of the Electoral Commission's oversight can be seen from two interventions concerning the Confederation of Business Industry (CBI). In May 2013 the Electoral Commission did not permit this body to register as a permitted participant on the basis that the person signing the application form was not authorized to do so. The CBI director general John Cridland accepted that the attempt to register had been a mistake and no further attempt was made to do so.[84] Secondly, the Commission ruled that the CBI

[80] Electoral Commission, *Electoral Commission Advice on Spending Limits for the Referendum on Independence for Scotland* (2014), <http://www.electoralcommission.org.uk/__data/assets/pdf_file/0004/153697/Report-on-spending-limits-for-the-referendum-on-independence-for-Scotland.pdf>.

[81] 'First Pre-Poll Donations and Loans Report at Scottish Independence Referendum Published', Electoral Commission news release, 8 July 2014; 'Second Pre-Poll Donations and Loans Report at Scottish Independence Referendum published', Electoral Commission news release, 5 August 2014.

[82] BBC News, L. Adams, 'Scottish independence: Questions Raised Over Campaign Spending Rules' (1 May 2014) <http://www.bbc.co.uk/news/uk-scotland-scotland-politics-27228971>. And see B. Riley-Smith, 'Scottish Independence: Yes Campaign Accused of Using "Dummy" Organizations to Get Around Spending Rules' *Telegraph* (28 April 2014) <http://www.telegraph.co.uk/news/uknews/scottish-independence/10792157/Scottish-independence-Yes-campaign-accused-of-using-dummy-organisations-to-get-around-spending-rules.html>.

[83] Electoral Commission, *Scottish Independence Referendum: Report on the Referendum Held on 18 September 2014*, ELC/2014/02 (2014).

[84] 'Electoral Commission Voids CBI Listing as No Campaigner in Scotland Vote' *Guardian* (1 May 2014).

annual dinner held in August 2014 did constitute an election expense in part because it was to be addressed by the Prime Minister, but since it cost less than £10,000 it did not require the CBI to register as a campaigner in the referendum.[85]

IV. Conclusion

Law can only do so much. Deliberative participation depends primarily upon the interest of citizens in the issue before them, their civic education, the health of broader civil society, and the responsibility of the private media. Each of these elements will be assessed in retrospect as the referendum recedes. But law does have a role to play. The Scottish Referendum Act is an instrument which, in building upon the Edinburgh Agreement principles and in modifying the PPERA regime both to meet the specific needs of the Scottish process and to correct some of the negative side-effects of PPERA revealed by the two referendums of 2011, has helped set the conditions for a fair, lawful, and democratic referendum. A significant task for the Electoral Commission once the regulated period began was to monitor how well the legislation in the Scottish Referendum Act and Scottish Franchise Act was implemented and how responsibly all of those engaged in referendum campaigning behaved. The evidence is that it approached its regulatory role in a vigorous way.[86]

As we cast the Scottish process into wider perspective, we should take note of the view taken by the leading strategist from the Yes campaign in the Quebec referendum of 1995, a referendum which suffered from a rancorous relationship between the two campaigns and the absence of agreed and independently overseen process rules. He has commended the United Kingdom for the way in which the Edinburgh Agreement fostered a mutually acceptable referendum process, claiming this breakthrough to be of great significance for other countries facing similar referendum processes: 'Nations that have been through this wrenching debate recently or who, especially in Catalonia, will navigate these waters soon, need the British government to keep offering a template of fair play and respect for democracy.'[87] The Scottish referendum has indeed supplied an opportunity to provide a model of citizen engagement at a time when the referendum is proliferating around the world like never before.[88] In the end the quality of Scottish, and

[85] 'Electoral Commission Statement on the CBI Scotland's Annual Dinner', Electoral Commission, 27 August 2014, <http://www.electoralcommission.org.uk/i-am-a/journalist/electoral-commission-media-centre/news-releases-referendums/electoral-commission-statement-on-the-cbi-scotlands-annual-dinner>.

[86] See *Scottish Independence Referendum: Report* (n. 83).

[87] Jean-François Lisée, 'Well Done, Britain, for a Fair Referendum—it's a Shame Canada Didn't Manage It' *Guardian* (9 September 2014) <http://www.theguardian.com/commentisfree/2014/sep/09/britain-referendum-canada-scottish-independence-vote>.

[88] L. LeDuc, *The Politics of Direct Democracy: Referendums in Global Perspective* (Broadview Press 2003) 29.

indeed British, democracy could be gauged not only by how each side reacted to the outcome, but by the process through which that outcome was reached. The referendum was a site of deep disagreement in which the very existence of the country was at stake. The fact that the electoral system stood up to this stern test bears testament to the robustness of the democratic system within which the referendum was organized and contested.

4

The Referendum Campaign

James Mitchell

I. Introduction

Evidence from previous referendums suggests that campaigns can have an effect and it became clear from opinion-survey and polling evidence that the campaign affected the outcome of the Scottish independence referendum. What is clear is that the long intense campaign increased the amount of information available to voters and that the processing of this information by the electorate shifted opinion. The *long* campaign worked to the advantage of supporters of independence albeit not enough to close the gap. This does not mean that more time would have resulted in a different result. Opinion remained fairly stable for most of the campaign but shifted in the closing stages. A lengthier campaign might simply have seen a longer period of stability.

It is difficult to define when the intense campaign started. The 'Scottish Question' has had to be addressed by each generation though with varying levels of intensity and little consistency or agreement on what the question is, far less its answer.[1] Debate on Scotland's constitutional status and whether Scotland should be independent have been in the background, and occasionally foreground, of Scottish politics since the late 1960s. In this sense, there has been a long campaign dating back decades. Scholars of campaigns tend to define a campaign as the period of 'heightened intensity': this need not conform to the formal regulated period of the campaign period but is determined by protagonists and antagonists.[2] What became clear from early on was not only that there would be a lengthy campaign but that it would be intense from the start. Commentators as well as protagonists and antagonists agreed that this would be an 'historic' and 'important' event, as did most voters.[3] The BBC decided to spend an extra £5m covering the

[1] James Mitchell, *The Scottish Question* (Oxford University Press 2014).

[2] H. E. Brady, R. Johnston, and J. Sides, 'The Study of Political Campaigns' in H. E. Brady and R. Johnston (eds), *Capturing Campaign Effects* (University of Michigan Press 2006) 2.

[3] 'It is now up to the people of Scotland to make that historic decision. The very future of Scotland depends on their verdict. It is that important. This agreement delivers the people's referendum.' Prime Minister Cameron, October 2012. 'I'm honoured to announce that, on Thursday the 18th of September 2014, we will hold Scotland's referendum—a historic day when the people will decide Scotland's future.' First Minister Salmond, March 2013.

referendum.[4] Around 90 per cent of the electorate agreed or strongly agreed that the referendum was 'more important than any other vote in Scotland in the last fifty years'.[5] Only 3 per cent disagreed with this proposition and the remainder neither agreed nor disagreed. This view was most emphatic amongst supporters of independence with less than 2 per cent of their supporters disagreeing with it. The long campaign would resemble short elections campaigns in its intensity.

II. The road to the independence referendum

There are various reason for holding a referendum: constitutional necessity, legitimacy, and as a transfer of decision-making. There is no formal constitutional requirement to hold a referendum in the United Kingdom, and the increased use of referendums in UK politics has been marked by a lack of consistency. The SNP included a provision for the use of referendums prior to constitutional change in its draft constitution for an independent Scotland which was agreed at its 1977 conference, though at that time maintained that a majority of SNP MPs elected from Scotland would constitute a mandate for independence. The SNP shifted its position in favour of a referendum on independence in the late 1980s. The SNP had sought to reassure voters by stressing that independence would not be imposed without a clear mandate. It proposed to create a two-stage process involving both representative and direct democratic elements. First, a Parliamentary majority sanctioning a referendum would be required followed by a positive referendum vote in favour of independence. A further change occurred two decades later. The SNP's manifesto in 1997 proposed that the SNP would immediately begin negotiations for independence with the UK Government after the return of a majority of SNP MPs from Scotland. This was anticipated to take between six and twelve months after which time a 'simple one question referendum' would be held.[6]

The party changed its position again after the establishment of a Scottish Parliament. In its manifesto for the first Scottish Parliament in 1999, the SNP proposed to hold an independence referendum within the first four-year term of an SNP government. Independence was the tenth item in a list of ten 'priorities' in these elections, giving concern to some members that the leadership was diluting the party's commitment to independence. In the 2003 elections, the SNP proposed to hold a referendum within three years of coming to power. The emphasis was on winning power and demonstrating an ability to govern competently as a step towards building support for independence. There were some SNP members who questioned this strategy. In September 2003, SNP MSP Alex Neil asked whether the Scottish Parliament was empowered to legislate to hold a referendum. George Reid, Presiding Officer, refused to answer as there was no procedure for

4 <http://www.bbc.co.uk/news/uk-scotland-scotland-politics-22609982>.

5 ESRC Scottish Independence Referendum Study, ES/MOO3418/1.

6 SNP manifesto, *Yes We Can* (1997) 9.

making 'speculative rulings' and 'if a bill was submitted for introduction I would, as you know, offer a view on legislative competence as required under the Scotland Act'.[7] The referendum appeared a distant prospect and independence more so.

The commitment to a referendum allowed the SNP to insulate support for the party from opposition to independence. A similar situation was faced by the Parti Québécois (PQ) in the 1970s and the PQ's policy evolved much as the SNP's would a decade and more later.[8] The PQ had initially intended to declare Quebec independent on being elected to government but the party changed its policy in 1974 in favour of a referendum. This strategy of *étapisme*, or a step-by-step approach, was advocated by Claude Morin who became Minister for Intergovernmental Affairs when the PQ came to power in 1976.[9] It had two elements, each with parallels with the later SNP strategy: winning a majority to form a government then holding a referendum on independence. Decoupling support for independence from support for the PQ made it possible for the PQ to come to power.[10] During the 1976 election campaign, the PQ insisted that its objective was the election of a good (*vrai*) government rather than independence. It won a majority of seats with 41 per cent of the vote in 1976 but only 24 per cent supported independence.[11] The option proposed in the subsequent referendum, held in 1980, was a diluted form of independence. The PQ proposed sovereignty-association, an ambiguous idea that suggested continued association with the rest of Canada. A similar strategy was adopted by the Labour Party in the United Kingdom when it proposed to hold a referendum on devolution on returning to power in 1997. Labour was keen to dissociate its support for devolved government with tax-varying powers from any association with the 'tax-and-spend' image the party leadership believed undermined its prospects of winning the general election. A two question referendum—asking whether Scots wanted a Parliament and whether it should have tax-varying powers—was the device used to insulate Labour support from any doubts voters might have.

The SNP sought to do the same, making it possible to vote SNP in the knowledge that this would not automatically lead to independence. As SNP MSP Kenny MacAskill acknowledged prior to the party first coming to power,

> People vote on a multitude of factors—social and economic as well as constitutional. Support for a Party is usually given on a broad range of matters not simply one specific cause. An administration can be both won and formed on a minority of votes. To seek to impose a major constitutional change in these circumstances would be wrong. It would also be unsuccessful.'[12]

[7] *Herald* (29 September 2003).

[8] V. Murray, *Le Parti Québécois: de la Foundation à la Prise du Pouvoir* (Cahiers du Québéc 1976).

[9] G. Fraser, *René Lévesque & the Parti Québécois in Power* (Macmillan 1984) 191.

[10] M. Pinard and R. Hamilton, 'The Parti Québécois Comes to Power: An Analysis of the 1976 Quebec Election' (1978) 11 *Canadian Journal of Political Science* 739.

[11] Pinard and Hamilton (n. 10) at 743

[12] K. MacAskill, *Building a Nation: Post Devolution Nationalism in Scotland* (Luath Press 2004) 38.

The problem was that the electoral system appeared to militate against crossing the first hurdle of gaining an overall majority that would be required to gain a parliamentary majority to hold a referendum.

The SNP became the largest party in Holyrood in 2007 by one seat, well short of an overall majority. It had hoped to form a government in coalition with the Liberal Democrats but the LibDems refused to coalesce with the SNP because of the SNP's commitment to a referendum on independence. Support for independence in 2007 was at 23 per cent when voters were offered three choices—the status quo; more powers; and independence—and there was a 2:1 majority against independence on a simple independence vs the status quo choice. This suggested that those who advocated more powers would split emphatically in favour of the Union in any binary choice. While 83 per cent of SNP voters supported independence in 2007, only 5 per cent of Labour voters and 2 per cent of Conservative and Liberal Democrat voters did so.[13] The prospect of a referendum remained remote but the SNP would have struggled to win a referendum even had it been possible to construct a parliamentary majority. These figures highlighted the scale of the challenge for the SNP. First, it could not assume that all of its voters would support independence and even if they did this was far from enough to secure majority support for independence. Secondly, support for independence amongst voters for other parties offered little comfort. In the past, a much higher proportion of Labour voters supported independence. During elections in the 1980s, approaching 30 per cent of Labour voters supported independence.[14] But constitutional preferences and party support had become much more aligned with the result that there appeared to be fewer Labour voters who might be inclined to support independence.

Survey research offered a demographic and ideological profile of supporters and opponents of independence. Supporters of independence tended to be younger, male, working class, and more inclined to the left. Supporters of the Union were more broadly based demographically and socio-economically.

There was one glimmer of hope for the SNP. Survey data suggested that valence[15] considerations were important in determining constitutional preference; that is, voters' constitutional preferences were influenced by assessments of their expectations of the capacity of the constitutional order to deliver in public policy terms. If the SNP could prove itself competent it might not only became the 'natural party of government' in Edinburgh but that this would spill over into support for independence. However, even by the end of its first term in

[13] R. Johns, D. Denver, J. Mitchell, and C. Pattie, *Voting for a Scottish Government: The Scottish Parliament Election of 2007* (Manchester University Press 2010) 84–6.

[14] J. Brand, J. Mitchell, and P. Surridge, 'Will Scotland Come to the Aid of the Party?' in A. Heath, R. Jowell, and J. Curtice (eds), *Labour's Last Chance: The 1992 Election and Beyond* (Dartmouth Publishing Co Ltd 1994) 221.

[15] Valence issues are those on which parties and voters are in common agreement on objectives but differ as to which party is most capable of delivering eg economic prosperity. Position issues are those on which there are differences on objectives, eg nuclear disarmament. See D. Stokes, 'Spatial Models of Party Competition' (1963) 57 *American Political Science Review* 368–77.

government support for independence had not risen.[16] Shortly after coming to power in 2007, the SNP government launched a 'National Conversation' with a White Paper, *Choosing Scotland's Future: A National Conversation*. This document set out options, including independence and the status quo, but also 'redesigning devolution by adopting a specific range of extensions to the current powers of the Scottish Parliament and Scottish Government, possibly involving fiscal autonomy', with a chapter devoted to the case for 'Extending Scottish devolution'.[17] But the National Conversation was not the dominant concern of the Scottish Government, leading to criticisms from some SNP hardliners that the leadership preferred Ministerial office to making the case for independence. Jim Sillars, former deputy leader of the SNP—and a long-standing critic of what he saw as the SNP's failure to make the case for independence—wrote shortly before the 2011 election that 'the "I" word is on the back burner, shunted there, in the view of the leadership, by the superior tactic of gaining votes from all and sundry ... in order to reclaim those seats at the ministerial desks'.[18] The SNP may have been engaged in a fairly intense long campaign to get elected but not in making the case for independence.

Following the SNP's victory in 2007, the opposition parties in Holyrood established the Calman Commission to consider further devolution, with the support of the UK Government and serviced by UK civil servants. Calman's final report was published in June 2009 and set out a series of proposals to extend devolution.[19] This had the support of Labour, Conservatives, and Liberal Democrats. These twin developments—the National Conversation and Calman—did not dominate Scottish politics but were part of a backdrop in which the global financial crisis was dominant. The economy had become the main issue by the time of the 2011 election with a third of voters naming it as the single most important issue. Scotland's constitutional question had fallen from being named as the most important issue by 26 per cent in 2007 to 15 per cent four years later.[20]

The results of the 2011 elections suggested that the SNP might have been right with respect to the first part of its calculation but wrong in the second: the SNP was perceived to be highly competent and rewarded with an overall majority but support for independence remained stubbornly at the same level as in 2007. Support for the party may have doubled between 2003 and 2011 elections but

[16] C. Carman, R. Johns, and J. Mitchell, *More Scottish than British: the 2011 Scottish Parliament Election* (Palgrave Macmillan 2014) 99; A. Brown, D. McCrone, L. Paterson, and P. Surridge, *The Scottish Electorate* (Macmillan 1999) ch. 6; D. Denver, J. Mitchell, C. Pattie, and H. Bochel, *Scotland Decides: The Devolution Issue and the Scottish Referendum* (Frank Cass 2000) 159–68; L. Paterson A. Brown, J. Curtice, K. Hinds, D. McCrone, A. Park, K. Sproston, and P. Surridge, *New Scotland, New Politics?* (Polygon 2001) 112–13; P. Surridge, 'A Better Union?' in C. Bromley, J. Curtice, D. McCrone, and A. Park (eds), *Has Devolution Delivered?* (Edinburgh University Press 2006) 29–45.

[17] Scottish Government, *Choosing Scotland's Future: A National Conversation* (2007).

[18] *Scotsman* (13 April 2011).

[19] Report of the Calman Commission, *Serving Scotland Better: Scotland and the United Kingdom in the 21st century* (2009).

[20] Carman, Johns, and Mitchell, *More Scottish than British* (n. 16) 87.

support for independence remained stable.[21] There may have been a devolution bonus for the SNP, but there was no independence bonus from governing competently. Being competent seemed, if anything, to demonstrate the strength of devolution rather than a need for independence. Its overall majority meant there would be a referendum but the SNP faced the danger of prioritizing Scottish independence at a time when voters saw the economy as the single most important matter.

III. Rules of engagement as part of the campaign

Now that the SNP had an overall majority at Holyrood, the first matter to be addressed was whether the Scottish Parliament was empowered to legislate to hold a referendum. This divided legal opinion but ultimately the UK constitution remains a 'political constitution'. In Griffith's classic account, there are only 'political claims by individuals and groups'.[22] Disputes about the legality of any Holyrood legislation on a referendum gave way to the political imperative resulting from the Scottish election results. The UK Government conceded that the 'future of Scotland's place within the UK was for the people of Scotland to vote on'.[23] The Prime Minister insisted that this concession had a political rather than legal basis after the result of the referendum became known on 19 September 2014: 'The Scottish National Party (SNP) was elected in Scotland in 2011 and promised a referendum on independence. We could have blocked that; we could have put it off, but just as with other big issues, it was right to take—not duck—the big decision.'[24]

The SNP government's main objective over the months following the 2011 election was to win support to include a 'more powers' option on the ballot paper in the referendum. The idea of a 'multi-option referendum' had a long pedigree in Scottish politics and there were examples to be drawn upon from other polities.[25] Opponents of independence had advocated a second question on independence in the 1979 devolution referendum. Labour MP Norman Buchan had argued that it would be a 'disastrous error in proposing only one question' on devolution and warned against allowing devolution and 'separatism' to be conflated;[26] former Conservative Prime Minister Lord Home argued similarly in a speech in the Lords a year later.[27] At that time, the demand for a second question/third option came from opponents of independence. The idea of a multi-option referendum

[21] Carman, Johns, and Mitchell, *More Scottish than British* (n. 16) 99.

[22] J.A.G. Griffith, 'The Political Constitution' (1979) 42 *Modern Law Review* 1 at 17.

[23] UK Government, *Scotland's Constitutional Future* (Cm 8203, 2012), Preface.

[24] Scottish Independence Referendum. Statement by the Prime Minister, 19 September 2014, <https://www.gov.uk/government/news/scottish-independence-referendum-statement-by-the-prime-minister>.

[25] J. Mitchell, 'The Multi-Option Referendum: A Comparative Perspective' in A. MacCartney (ed.), *Asking the People: The Referendum and Constitutional Change* (Edinburgh University Press 1992) 7–19.

[26] *Glasgow Herald* (11 February 1977).

[27] HL Deb, Vol. 389, col. 1217, 14 March 1978.

was debated in the SNP, Labour, and Liberal Democrats before the 1992 election and had the support of each at some point. It was then supported by *Scotland United*, the cross-party campaign group for a Scottish Parliament formed following the 1992 election.[28] The motivation in each case was to maximize support for the preferred constitutional option of the advocate of the multi-option referendum. In 2011, the SNP supported a third option on the ballot paper as an insurance policy. It wanted to ensure that more powers would be won even if independence was defeated.

The Scottish Government offered the possibility of a second question in its consultation document on the proposed referendum.[29] It noted that two-question referendums had been held on the electoral system in New Zealand in 1992 and 2011 with a first 'gateway' question about whether the existing system should change and the second offering a choice of alternatives. It confronted a series of problems in advocating a third option on the ballot paper. It needed to define 'more powers' although it did not support this position itself; it needed to find a party or legitimate group that would back this position; and, crucially, it needed to convince the UK Government to agree to include a third option. There was much activity over the Summer of 2011 but by early Autumn it was clear that none of the other parties was willing to advocate this third option on the ballot paper. Polls consistently suggested that 'more powers', variously defined and vaguely understood,[30] commanded most support. The Liberal Democrats, as members of the UK Coalition and long-term advocates of federalism, might have been expected to use their position within the coalition to ensure that its preferred option was on the ballot paper, thereby claiming ownership of a popular measure in Scotland and distinguishing themselves from the Conservatives. But it was also clear that 'more powers' would be the SNP's second preference. Polls suggested that a straight contest between independence and the status quo would be an opportunity to defeat, possibly humiliate, the SNP. There was also a fear that having a third option on the ballot paper would split the anti-independence vote and that it was a ruse to win independence by default. Those whose first preference was neither independence nor the status quo would be pivotal in a two-option referendum. The agreement to have a simple binary choice ensured that the middle option would be the key battleground in the referendum: winning the support of supporters of more powers would be key to the final result. Bogdanor warns that referendums cannot resolve all conflicts but can allow for the 'articulation of a submerged consensus'.[31] But in the case of the Scottish referendum, a submerged consensus may have been blocked by omitting the 'more powers' option favoured by most Scots.

[28] J. Mitchell, *Strategies for Self-Government* (Polygon 1996) 165–6, 296.

[29] Scottish Government, *Your Scotland, Your referendum* (2012) 1.25–1.26.

[30] Different terms were used for a variety of different constitutional options lying somewhere beyond what was already envisaged under the Scotland Act, 2012 though still in the process of being implemented and independence: Devo-Max, Devo Plus, (Full) Fiscal Autonomy. Home Rule was a term that came to be used more often closer to polling day and after the referendum.

[31] V. Bogdanor, *The People and the Party System* (Cambridge University Press 1981) 91; V. Bogdanor, 'Western Europe' in D. Butler and A. Ranney (eds), *Referendums Around the World: the Growing Use of Direct Democracy* (American Enterprise Institute 1978) 45.

Another issue was the timing of the referendum. Some commentators imagined that the Scottish Government might prefer an early referendum to take advantage of the 'honeymoon' period following the SNP's 2011 election success, but this ignored evidence that support for the SNP did not equate with support for independence. The scale of the challenge, given the state of public opinion on independence, encouraged the SNP to propose a referendum in Autumn 2014 whereas the UK Government preferred a referendum 'sooner rather than later'.[32] The SNP was keen to buy time in order to challenge the strong lead in the polls against independence. The UK Government warned that 'continuing uncertainty about Scotland's future is damaging to Scotland and that whilst both the process and referendum remain unresolved this uncertainty will grow'.[33] The Scottish Government maintained that, 'Simple good sense, and a respect for due process, all point to the Autumn of 2014 as being the right time for the referendum. That will ensure that there is sufficient time for the fullest debate on what will be the most important decision in Scotland in 300 years.'[34]

Differences over the franchise to be used in the referendum were relatively easily resolved. The SNP was keen to expand the franchise for a mixture of principled and instrumental reasons. The franchise used for elections to Holyrood was wider than that for the Commons and included European Union citizens, and the SNP preferred this along with lowering the voting age to 16. The party had supported lowering the voting age since the 1980s. This had been in response to pressure from its youth wing combined with a belief that younger people were more inclined to vote for the SNP and independence. The UK Government agreed with the Holyrood franchise and accepted votes at 16 despite opposing such a franchise for elections to the House of Commons.

In October 2012, the two governments reached agreement on the ground rules. These rules had been agreed through negotiation and after public consultation. Each government would invoke its own public consultation in defence of its preferred position. While referendums have been criticized as 'weapons in the hands of government',[35] the process of determining the rules of the Scottish independence referendum involved two governments with opposing views on its outcome. This ensured the legitimacy of the referendum and limited the prospect of either side calling foul at the outcome.

IV. The role of the parties

Many scholars have noted that voters will overcome lack of knowledge about an issue with reference to 'information cues (endorsements) from like-minded

[32] HM Government, *Scotland's Constitutional Future* (Cm 8203, 2012) 18.

[33] *Scotland's Constitutional Future* (n. 32) 18.

[34] *Your Scotland, Your Referendum* (n. 29) 1.23.

[35] A. Lijphart, *Democracies: Patterns of Majoritarian and Consensus Government in Twenty-One Countries* (Yale University Press 1984) 204.

individuals or groups to identify if a ballot proposition is in their interest'.[36] The most obvious cues come from established political parties.[37] Kriesi has referred to party positions as the 'quintessential shortcut in direct democratic votes'.[38] Clear messages from political parties might mean that a referendum simply endorses the views of parties rather than offers an opportunity for deliberation. The views of the parties are usually given prominence in referendums. Analysis of the Norwegian referendum on EU accession in 1994 found that 'party endorsements received far more attention than the endorsements provided by interest organizations, nongovernmental organizations and public personas'.[39] There have been referendums in which all the mainstream parties have taken one side in a referendum thus ensuring victory for that position but there have also been occasions when this did not occur (for instance in the 1992 Danish and French referendums on Maastricht, the Canadian constitutional referendum of 1992, and the 1994 Swedish and Norwegian European referendums).[40] On these occasions, voters 'simply took their cues from sources other than the mainstream parties'.[41]

In the case of the Scottish independence referendum, the issues had been well rehearsed over many years. Nonetheless, this was the first occasion in which independence was on a ballot paper in a referendum and a sizeable element in the electorate found that their preference for 'more powers' was not available. There could be little doubt as to the views of Scotland's main parties on the issue of independence. Conservatives, Labour, and Liberal Democrats were emphatically opposed to independence. There had been occasional voices inside each of these parties, notably Labour and the Liberal Democrats, who supported independence over the years, but there was no Parliamentary representative of any of the main parties taking a position at variance with the party's official position on independence after 2011. The SNP had formally adopted independence as its objective when it revised its constitution in 2004. Previously, its aim was stated as 'self-government' but this came to be interpreted to mean independence even in the years prior to 2004. If the party was known for anything it was this commitment. While around one in ten SNP members gave further devolution rather than independence as their first preference on the constitutional issue in a survey of attitudes in 2007/08, the vast bulk of members preferred independence.[42]

When voters were asked in 2011 where they placed Scottish political parties on a scale indicating opposition to or support for more powers for Holyrood, the SNP

[36] J. Matsusaka, 'Direct Democracy' in C. K. Rowley and F. Schneider (eds), *Encyclopedia of Public Choice* (Kluwer Academic Publishers 2003) 151.

[37] R. R. Lau and D. P. Redlawsk, 'Advantages and Disadvantages of Cognitive Heuristics in Political Decision Making' (2001) 45 *American Journal of Political Science* 951–71; P. M. Sniderman, 'Taking Sides: A Fixed Choice Theory of Political Reasoning' in A. Lupia, M. D. McCubbins, and S. L. Popkin (eds), *Elements of Reason: Cognition, Choice and the Bounds of Rationality* (Cambridge University Press 2000).

[38] H. Kriesi, *Direct Democratic Choice: The Swiss Experience* (Lexington Books 2005) 139.

[39] S. Hobolt, 'Taking Cues on Europe? Voter Competence and Party Endorsements in Referendums on European Integration' (2007) 46 *European Journal of Political Research* 160.

[40] L. LeDuc, *The Politics of Direct Democracy* (Broadview Press 2003) 177.

[41] LeDuc (n. 40).

[42] J. Mitchell, L. Bennie, and R. Johns, *The Scottish National Party: Transition to Power* (Oxford University Press 2012) 118.

and Conservatives were perceived to lie at opposite ends of the spectrum and the perception of Labour had shifted since 2007 to incline more towards opposition. Around three-quarters of voters who supported independence voted SNP. Over three Scottish Parliament elections from 2003, the SNP had increasingly gained support amongst those who supported independence while also expanding its support beyond that base. The SNP won 15 per cent of those who supported the status quo and half of those who supported more powers in 2011. The Conservatives had almost no support amongst those who favoured independence, taking most of their support from amongst supporters of the constitutional status quo. Labour outpolled other parties amongst those who supported the status quo and only one in ten supporters of independence supported the Labour Party.[43] This suggested that opinion in favour of independence had polarized by party, though less so amongst those who preferred more powers or the status quo. The challenge for the SNP was to convert those who had voted SNP to the cause of independence but even that would be insufficient to win a majority. It would additionally need to convert voters who were both opposed to independence and who had voted for another party in 2011. If its opponents could convert those who had voted SNP in 2011 but were opposed to independence, then they could be assured of a very comfortable victory.

The Scottish Greens favoured independence but the electorate could be excused for being unaware of this during the 2011 election. Media coverage of the party's manifesto gave little prominence to its views on the constitution.[44] The party manifesto referred to the use of existing powers while arguing for a 'multi-option referendum' with three options—the status quo; a 'stronger Scottish Parliament; and independence—stating it would back the third.[45] The Scottish Green leader, Patrick Harvie, played a prominent part in the referendum (although his predecessor opposed independence). Nevertheless, the combined support for SNP and Greens would be insufficient to defeat the combined votes of Labour, Conservatives, and Liberal Democrats.

As the party that had dominated Scottish politics for half a century prior to the SNP coming to power, Labour had a central role in the referendum campaign. The Conservatives had anticipated that Labour would take charge of the 'ground war' with what was assumed to be a larger and more active membership. Labour played a full part in the umbrella *Better Together* campaign which was led by Alistair Darling, former Labour Chancellor of the Exchequer. In June 2013, he received a standing ovation after addressing a fringe meeting at the Scottish Conservative conference.[46] His approach was quite different from that of former Labour Prime Minister Gordon Brown. In May 2013, Gordon Brown launched Labour's *Vote NO* campaign alongside Johann Lamont, Labour's then Scottish

[43] ESRC Scottish Election Study 2011, RES-000-22-4539.
[44] <http://www.bbc.co.uk/news/uk-scotland-scotland-politics-13130985>.
[45] Scottish Greens, *Scottish Parliament Manifesto 2011* (2011) 24.
[46] BBC, 'Scottish Tory Party Conference: Labour's Darling Delivers Pro-Union Message' (8 June 2013) <http://www.bbc.co.uk/news/uk-scotland-scotland-politics-22810871>.

leader.[47] The former Prime Minister addressed a number of meetings especially towards the end of the campaign but never shared a platform with Conservatives. He invoked Keir Hardie, trade union leaders, and Fife miners, and criticized both the SNP and Conservatives at the launch. While both Messrs Brown and Darling focused on the dangers of independence and each emphasized pooling resources and sharing risk—a theme that was shared with the UK Government—Mr Brown's message was more explicitly calculated to appeal to traditional Labour voters even if this would not appeal to Conservative voters. Mr Brown may have believed that the best way forward was to 'pool and share resources' in the United Kingdom but not in *Better Together*.

The Conservatives had come to be seen as 'anti-Scottish' since the 1980s and it made sense for them to have a limited involvement in the campaign. Conservative commentators warned against any intervention that might prove counter-productive. In March 2013, Tim Montgomerie, of the *conservativehome* website, warned that the SNP would 'try and put the Tories on the ballot paper' and suggested that the reason the SNP preferred the referendum to be held close to the next UK election was to 'make it a vote about Tory rule from London versus SNP/Labour rule from Edinburgh'.[48] The SNP were keen to encourage senior Conservatives to play a prominent role in the campaign and First Minister Alex Salmond repeatedly challenged Prime Minister David Cameron to a debate. There was never much prospect of this happening but persistent demands for a debate were an attempt to maintain the impression that this was a contest between a Scottish First Minister elected by the Scottish people versus a Conservative Prime Minister with little support in Scotland. The Conservatives, having been marginalized in Scottish politics for almost a generation, were aware that the referendum offered an opportunity to appear alongside others. Ruth Davidson, Scottish Conservative leader, maintained that the referendum was 'revitalizing' her party in Scotland.[49] In March 2012, the party had established Conservative Friends of the Union (CFU), a body open to anyone. By September, it claimed to have 45,000 supporters. By September 2013, it was claimed to have 80,000 members and was being proposed as a 'possible future model for party membership'.[50] A year later, the party still claimed that 80,000 people had signed up to CFU.[51] In the event, the Conservatives were on the winning side in the referendum but went on to suffer their worst ever election result in Scotland in proportion of the vote in

[47] 'Gordon Brown Launches Labour "No" Campaign' *Scotsman* (14 May 2013).

[48] T. Montgomerie, 'Lots at Stake in Next September's Scottish Referendum' (*conservativehome*, 22 March 2013) <http://www.conservativehome.com/thetorydiary/2013/03/lots-at-stake-in-next-septembers-scottish-referendum.html>. See also, <http://www.conservativehome.com/thetorydiary/2012/10/vote-for-independence-or-scotland-will-be-ruled-by-the-lord-snooty-tories-forever.html>.

[49] R. Davidson, 'Scotland's Referendum Debate is Revitalizing Scotland's Conservatives' (*conservativehome*, 14 March 2014) <http://www.conservativehome.com/platform/2014/03/from-ruthdavidsonmsp-scotlands-referendum-debate-is-revitalising-scottories.html>.

[50] M. Wallace, 'The Scottish Tories Demonstrate a Possible Future Model for Party Membership' (*conservativehome*, 30 September 2013) <http://www.conservativehome.com/majority_conservatism/2013/09/the-scottish-tories-demonstrate-a-possible-future-model-for-party-membership.html>.

[51] BBC News, 'Conservative MP David Mundell Hails Surge in Pro-UK Activism' (28 September 2014) <http://www.bbc.co.uk/news/uk-scotland-scotland-politics-29399858>.

May 2015[52] and it was the SNP that saw its membership rise following the referendum to unprecedented levels. The Tories did not enjoy any positive association with other parties and Labour suffered from association with the Tories.

A key challenge for supporters of independence was to undermine strong party cues. While there was little doubt about Labour's official opposition to independence, there was an effort to blur this message or at least suggest that it was not disloyal to Labour to vote for independence and that independence was a means of progressing Labour's traditional values. A lesson could be learned from the devolution debates in the 1970s. In January 1978, Labour opponents of devolution established a distinct *Labour Vote No* (LVN) campaign. While Labour was officially in favour of devolution, the LVN campaign raised the possibility that it was possible to be loyal to Labour while opposing devolution.[53] LVN contributed to the shift amongst Labour voters towards opposition to devolution in the 1979 referendum. The challenge was greater in the independence referendum. LVN had the support of a number of prominent Labour figures including MPs. Its vice chairs were Labour MPs Tam Dalyell and Robin Cook and it included a number of prominent trade unionists as well as considerable grass-roots support.

Labour for Independence (LFI) was set up on Facebook in 2012 by Allan Grogan, a relatively unknown Labour Party member from Angus. Labour's Scottish deputy leader dismissed LFI as an 'SNP front'.[54] By August 2013, it had 'around 80–100 members of that around half are Labour members'.[55] LFI failed to attract any significant current Scottish Labour politician though a number from Labour's recent past publicly endorsed independence including a former Lord Provost of Glasgow, and former leaders of Lothian and Strathclyde Regional Councils as well as a few retired MPs. In April 2013, Mary Lockhart, chair of the Cooperative Party in Scotland, wrote an article supporting independence but stepped down from her party position a few days later. In her article she wrote that it was 'offensive' that Labour had joined 'forces in Better Together with parties who were taking a wrecking hammer to the NHS in England, demonizing the people whom their policies had left without work, perpetuating the myth of strivers and scroungers, and unpicking the fabric of the welfare state until there is no such thing as social security'.[56] This would be a key theme in the pro-independence campaign. It would be difficult to convince Labour voters that the party was at all sympathetic to independence but it might be possible to convince them that there was no threat to Labour ideals and values from independence. A number of other Yes campaign groups were formed, some essentially sponsored by *Yes Scotland* while others were more independent. *Women for Independence*, *Radical Independence Campaign (RIC)*, and *National Collective*

[52] The Conservatives won one seat with 14.9 per cent of the vote.

[53] A. Macartney, 'The Protagonists' in J. Bochel, D. Denver, and A. Macartney (eds), *The Referendum Experience: Scotland 1979* (Aberdeen University Press 1981) 20–4.

[54] BBC News, 'Scottish Independence: Labour attacks LFI group' (31 July 2013) <http://www.bbc.co.uk/news/uk-scotland-scotland-politics-23524348>.

[55] 'Labour for Independence: A Nationalist Sham or a Fresh Alliance of the Left?' *Guardian* (1 August 2013).

[56] M. Lockhart, 'Socialism Will Work Better in Independent Scotland' *Scotland on Sunday* (21 April 2013).

would continue to exist after the referendum, broadening out their activities and campaigns and each having a particular focus and approach.

V. Umbrella groups

Umbrella groups in referendum campaigns operate along a spectrum, from offering a loose-coordinating role, occasionally acting as mediators between different parties or other bodies and offering at least the appearance of a united campaign, to fully integrated campaign organizations, pooling resources and displacing political parties or other bodies. *Yes Scotland* was at the loose-coordinating end while *Better Together* was closer to the other end of this spectrum. Each differed in their main campaign focus with *Yes Scotland* more focused on the 'ground war' and *Better Together* on the 'air war'. Ground wars have been defined as '*projects*, distinct and temporary tasks defined by clear criteria for success—that is, victory—and an equally clear deadline: Election Day'[57] and are distinct from 'air wars', fought through the media. The SNP was by far the dominant campaign organization on the independence side but its leadership appreciated the value of *Yes Scotland* in broadening its appeal. *Yes Scotland* was launched in May 2012 and was chaired by Dennis Canavan, who had been a Labour Member of Parliament for 26 years before becoming an Independent Member of the Scottish Parliament until his retirement in 2007. It relied heavily on the SNP financially though its board consciously aimed to be broad-based. Its early activities during the long campaign focused on creating a network of activists across Scotland. The extent to which *Yes Scotland*'s local base was broader than the SNP is unclear, but in many parts of Scotland SNP activists dominated *Yes Scotland* local campaigns. *Yes Scotland* attempted to reach out beyond the core of SNP supporters with variable success locally. The SNP leadership dominated the air war on the pro-independence side of the debate but had to concede ground to the variety of local *Yes* campaigns. There was agreement within *Yes Scotland* in favour of independence but a range of different visions of the kind of Scotland desired. The Greens, radical left groups, and SNP may all have inclined to the left but that hid considerable differences. *Yes Scotland* was united in opposition to the Conservatives, a key defining feature of the Scottish party system and politics.

Better Together was formed to unite the various groups and individuals campaigning for the Union. This issue, though little else, united Labour and Conservatives. A wide range of political objectives may have existed under each umbrella group but *Better Together* suffered from having to unite two parties deemed by the electorate to be polar opposites. The role played by the Conservatives would be important. The *Telegraph*'s Scottish editor, Alan Cochrane, played an active role in the campaign for the Union, including advising the Prime Minister,[58] and described the nature of the pro-Union forces, 'it has become a bit of a truism that it would

[57] R. K. Nielsen, *Ground Wars: Personalized Communication in Political Campaigns* (Princeton University Press 2012) 19.

[58] A. Cochrane, *Alex Salmond: My Part in His Downfall* (Biteback 2014).

be principally fought by Labour's big names and its foot soldiers... but backed by Tory money.'[59] The registration of the campaign donations appeared to give credence to the latter part of this perception though there were concerns that Labour foot soldiers were rather thin on the ground. Some months after the referendum, Paul Sinclair, who had been Scottish Labour leader Johann Lamont's chief spokesperson, suggested that the 'real damage [to Labour] is that the Tories and the Liberal Democrats saw first hand that the "Labour machine" didn't exist'.[60] Acknowledging the unpopularity of the Conservatives (and Liberal Democrats following their coalition with the Conservatives), *Better Together* was keen to have Labour figures at the forefront of its campaign. After some prevarication, Alistair Darling agreed to be head of *Better Together*, giving both campaign groups figure heads with strong ties with Labour. *Better Together* and *Yes Scotland* both sought to emphasize links with the Labour Party.

The configuration of parties in the independence referendum differed from the devolution referendum of 1997. In the earlier referendum, the Conservative Party was the common enemy both in constitutional terms but also across a range of socio-economic policies for supporters of devolution. In 1997, the main challenge to this consensus came from the inclusion of the Labour Party and SNP under the *Yes for Scotland* umbrella. Labour saw devolution as the end of Scotland's constitutional journey whereas the SNP saw it as a stepping stone to independence, but the two parties were broadly agreed on a range of socio-economic policies. This proved important in the outcome of the 1997 referendum. Analysis of the results concluded that opposition to the Conservatives was key to explaining why Scotland had voted for devolution.[61] The Conservative Party might have been able to mobilize its support for the Union but would demotivate many Labour supporters sympathetic to the Union. Party cues tend to be seen only in terms of motivating and mobilizing support in favour of each party's formal position but may also have the opposite effect on supporters of other parties.

VI. The media and the public

While broadcast media are governed by regulations designed to ensure objectivity and fairness, the print media have no such limits. There was a perception amongst supporters of *Yes Scotland* that the BBC was biased in favour of the status quo at least in its network output produced by London-based staff.[62] The press was overwhelmingly against independence and while some papers formally adopted a position of neutrality,

[59] A. Cochrane, 'Labour is More Concerned about Itself than the Union' *Telegraph* (24 February 2012).

[60] P. Sinclair, 'Scottish Labour Took the People for Granted—and Now it's Set to Pay the Price' *The Times* (14 December 2014).

[61] D. Denver, J. Mitchell, C. Pattie, and H. Bochel, *Scotland Decides: the Devolution Issue and the Scottish Referendum* (Frank Cass 2000) 169.

[62] The role of the media in the referendum is dealt with in N. Blain, D. Hutchison, and G. Hassan (eds), *Scotland's Referendum and the Media* (Edinburgh University Press forthcoming).

the coverage was often heavily skewed in favour of the Union. No daily newspaper supported independence and only the Sunday Herald came out for independence (see Tables 4.1 and 4.2). However, over time the press has become less important in electoral politics partly due to a decline in newspaper circulation. Nonetheless, it still plays a part in setting the agenda followed by broadcast media. Research suggests that media organizations remain important in shaping messages not least with the decline of and changes in political parties. The decline of mass parties and rise of 'parties without partisans'[63] has altered the nature of campaigning. Supporters of independence feared what academic commentators have referred to as the 'mediatization' of politics—the process whereby the media dominate and distort politics.[64] Their response was to find an alternative way of subverting the media by identifying and mobilizing a pool of active partisans. The long campaign assisted them in this endeavour.

Table 4.1 Daily newspapers and the referendum

Newspaper	Circulation	Referendum position
Sun	246,066	Neutral
Daily Record	203,941	Neutral
Daily Mail	93,321	NO
Press & Journal	62,177	Neutral
Courier	48,955	Neutral
Daily Express	48,636	NO
Daily Star	41,799	Neutral
Herald	37,728	Neutral
Evening Express	34,894	Neutral
Evening Times	33,397	Neutral
Scotsman	27,208	NO
Evening News	25,908	Neutral
Times	20,402	NO
Evening Times	19,766	Neutral
I	18,712	Neutral
Daily Telegraph	18,599	NO
Daily Mirror	18.079	NO
Guardian	10,623	NO
Daily Express (Paisley)	6,477	Neutral
Independent	2,990	NO
Financial Times	2,312	NO

[63] D. Farrell and P. Webb, 'Political Parties as Campaign Organizations' in R. Dalton and M. Wattenburg (eds), *Parties Without Partisans: Political Change in Advanced Industrial Democracies* (Oxford University Press 2002).

[64] G. Mazzoleni and W. Schulz, '"Mediatization" of Politics: A Challenge for Democracy?' (1999) 16 *Political Communication* 247–61.

Table 4.2 Sunday newspapers and the referendum

Title	Circulation	Referendum position
Sunday Mail	231,821	Neutral
Sun on Sunday	175,525	Neutral
Sunday Post	146,940	NO
Mail on Sunday	83,079	NO
Sunday Times	46,927	NO
Scotland on Sunday	30,297	NO
Sunday Express	28,002	NO
Sunday Herald	25,000	YES
Daily Star Sunday	23,161	Neutral
Sunday Mirror	18,202	NO
Sunday Telegraph	16,543	NO
Observer	14,093	Neutral
Sunday People	9,678	Neutral
Independent on Sunday	5,896	Neutral

VII. Public participation

Beyond the media, the referendum saw a phenomenal increase in public participation. Interest in politics assumed unprecedented levels during the referendum. There has been no systematic analysis of levels of public engagement but interviews with key figures on both sides of the debate as well as journalists who covered the campaign confirm that this perception was widespread.[65] Turnout in referendums in the United Kingdom has tended to be lower than in general elections. Turnout in Scotland in the 1975 referendum on EEC membership was 63 per cent having been 75 per cent in the October 1974 election. In the 1979 Scottish devolution referendum, it was 64 per cent rising to 77 per cent two months later at the general election. In 1997, turnout at the general election in May was 71 per cent but only 60 per cent in the devolution referendum four months later. The turnout of 85 per cent in the independence referendum exceeded turnout in any general election in Scotland since the introduction of universal suffrage. Turnout was lowest in Glasgow, but at 75 per cent it was still higher than it was at any election in Scotland as a whole since 1992.

From early in the long campaign, grass-roots activists focused on registering voters in deprived communities and developing strategies to ensure turnout was higher in such areas than normal. This involved a very traditional form of canvassing by knocking on doors. *Radical Independence* campaigners were particularly active in this respect. The belief was that support for independence was greatest in the poorest sections of the community that were least likely to vote, if even registered to vote. The combination of a perception that the referendum was of great

[65] BBC News, 'The Rise of the Town Hall Meeting' (13 March 2014) <http://www.bbc.co.uk/news/uk-scotland-scotland-politics-26558087>.

importance and registration efforts resulted in a significant increase in the number of people who registered to vote. By the deadline to register on 2 September 2014, 4,285,323 people had registered. It had been officially estimated in 2012 that there were 4,410,288 people over 16 in Scotland, suggesting that 97 per cent of the eligible electorate had registered to vote in the referendum.

The degree of public engagement was partly accounted for by the length of the campaign but also reflected levels of political activism commentators agreed had not been previously witnessed in Scotland. Traditional forms of campaigning were supplemented by novel forms of engagement creating a carnival atmosphere with flash mobs, music and comedy events, and a *Yestival*—a rolling festival of creative artists for independence. Some of this activity had been supported by crowd funding, including paying for opinion polls. These alternative forms of campaigning were more evident on the pro-independence side of the debate. Although dismissed by opponents as amateurish agitprop, they had a 'Heineken quality', reaching the parts traditional campaigns failed to reach.[66]

Evidence of the intensity of the campaign, especially amongst supporters of independence, was acknowledged by both sides. Even opponents of independence conceded that pro-independence supporters were most active. The *New Statesman* reported that *Yes* supporters were 'winning the ground war' at the start of September as did the *Economist*.[67] The *New Statesman* published a table highlighting the different experiences voters had of campaign activity from each side of the debate (Figure 4.1).

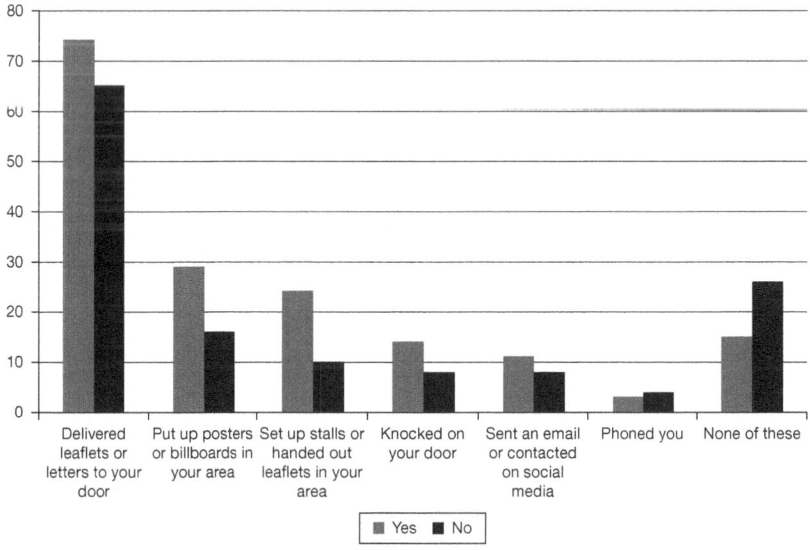

Figure 4.1 Different experiences of campaign activity

Source: New Statesman, 2 September 2014. 'The Yes campaign is winning the ground war in Scotland'

[66] A reference to a 1975 television advertisement for Heineken beer with the slogan, 'Heineken refreshes the parts other beers cannot reach'.

[67] 'The Yes campaign is Winning the Ground War in Scotland' *New Statesman* (2 September 2014); 'How Did it Come to This?' *Economist* (12 July 2014).

But it was not only that supporters of independence reached more voters; the messages were also perceived to be more positive. The SNP strategy in elections since 2007 had been to focus on positive campaigning, and especially to brand its campaigns as positive, in the belief that this paid electoral dividends. The evidence on the effect of negative campaigning is contradictory, suggesting variously that it encourages participation, demobilizes support, or has no effect.[68] Negative campaigning is usually thought to be the strategy of the underdog in any electoral contest but it was supporters of the Union that were perceived to have engaged in negative campaigning. While its connotations may themselves be negative, there is arguably an important place for negative campaigning. As Geer has suggested, negative campaigning can challenge misleading messages especially when presented robustly.[69] But, whether negative or positive, campaign messages require credibility to be successful.

The Director of Communications for *Better Together* had referred to its campaign as 'Project Fear', providing a campaign gift to opponents who were as relentless in referring to *Better Together* as 'Project Fear' as *Better Together* was relentlessly negative.[70] Being perceived to run a relentlessly negative campaign may undermine its impact and 'Project Fear' became an important—negative—campaign message from *Yes Scotland*. In as much as opponents of independence were arguing for a 'No' vote they would inevitably sound negative. The absence of agreement on whether more powers, and which powers, should be granted to Holyrood denied *Better Together* an agreed positive message. This was underscored by the diversity of opinion across a range of non-constitutional matters. The breadth of *Better Together* militated against a more positive campaign.

The adversarial nature of UK referendum politics meant that each side would avoid conceding ground to its opponents. In the classic formulation of adversarial politics, debate was conducted with 'bold' policy positions[71] that are then contested in the manner of an adversarial court in which the public act as the impartial judge. A more deliberative form resembling non-adversarial or inquisitorial judicial systems also operated with the public playing a fuller part in deliberation in order to gather information and reach a judgement (though the analogy breaks down in that

[68] S. Ansolabehere, S. Iyengar, A. Simon, and N. Valentino, 'Does Attack Advertising Demobilize the Electorate?' (1994) 88 *American Political Science Review* 829–38; S. Ansolabehere and S. Iyengar, *Going Negative: How Political Advertisements Shrink and Polarize the Electorate* (The Free Press 1995); P. Freedman and K. Goldstein, 'Measuring Media Exposure and the Effects of Negative Campaign Ads' (1999) 43 *American Journal of Political Science* 1189–208; K. Goldstein and P. Freedman, 'Campaign Advertising and Voter Turnout: New Evidence for a Stimulation Effect' (2002) 64 *The Journal of Politics* 721–40; R. R. Lau and G. M. Pomper, *Negative Campaigning: an Analysis of US Senate Elections* (Lanham, Rowman and Littlefield Publishers Ltd. 2004); L. Sigelman and M. Kugler, 'Why is Research on the Effects of Negative Campaigning so Inconclusive? Understanding Citizens' Perceptions of Negativity' (2003) 65 *The Journal of Politics* 142–60.

[69] J. G. Geer, *In Defense of Negativity: Attack Ads in Presidential Campaigns* (University of Chicago Press 2006).

[70] *Sunday Herald* (23 June 2013).

[71] S. E. Finer, 'Adversary Politics and Electoral Reform' in Finer (ed.), *Adversary Politics and Electoral Reform* (Anthony Wigram 1975).

the people, unlike judges, are under no obligation to explain their verdict). Even the most adversarial debates are likely to include some deliberative and inquisitorial elements. In the Scottish referendum, the debate in the media was generally adversarial but a more complex picture was evident on the ground. Social media played its part in the debate and research also suggested a 'mixed picture'.[72] While most of the print media was partisan and adopted an adversarial tone, other sections of the media, especially the broadcasters, higher education institutions, and a number of interest groups contributed to a more nuanced, inquisitorial form of debate.

VIII. Events, issues, and polls

The usual range of valence issues[73] from general elections was debated in the referendum but the focus was on the implications of alternative constitutional scenarios instead of which party would govern most competently. Position issues also played a part though the diversity of parties and opinions on each side of the debate limited the extent to which clear differences could emerge on position issues. Independence campaigners supported getting rid of the Trident nuclear weapons system from the Clyde. There were supporters of this position amongst opponents of independence but for the most part, the future of nuclear weapons was one of the key positional policy differences in the debate. Attitudes towards membership of the European Union cut across both sides but opposition to membership was rarely articulated by either side; instead the debate focused on whether independence would make EU membership more or less likely. While UKIP was vehemently opposed to independence, it was excluded from the *Better Together* umbrella. At the start of the long campaign, and indeed over many years before, opponents of independence had argued that Scotland would find itself outside the EU on becoming independent and would have difficulty gaining membership. Supporters of independence were on the defensive on this until the Prime Minister, in January 2013, committed his party to a referendum on the future of UK membership of the EU.[74] This raised the possibility that Scotland might find itself outside the EU after voting to remain a member because of opposition to membership elsewhere in the United Kingdom.

The dominant issues in the campaign were the economy and welfare. But the parameters of this debate were wider than during a general election. The Scottish Government had insisted that an independent Scotland would share the currency with the rest of the United Kingdom but UK Government insisted this would

[72] S. Quinlan, M. Shephard, and L. Paterson, 'Online Discussion and the 2014 Scottish Independence Referendum: Flaming Keyboards or Forums for Deliberation?' (2015) 38 *Electoral Studies* 193.

[73] See (n. 15).

[74] BBC News, 'David Cameron Promises In/Out EU Referendum' (23 January 2013) <http://www.bbc.co.uk/news/uk-politics-21148282>.

not be possible. Mark Carney, the Governor of the Bank of England, set out the options in a speech on the economics of currency unions in January 2014.[75] This was a reasoned outline of the issues, a model of public service balance and political neutrality. This was followed the next month with a speech by the Chancellor of the Exchequer who took what he described as the 'exceptional step' of publishing advice from Treasury Permanent Secretary Sir Nicholas MacPherson.[76] The Treasury official's statement caused controversy as it was in breach of the Civil Service Code and was subsequently criticized by the Commons' Public Administration Committee. The Committee, consisting entirely of MPs opposed to Scottish independence, concluded that the 'only purpose was to use the impartial status of a Permanent Secretary to give authority to the advocacy of a political argument.'[77] Four months after the referendum, he defended adopting a publicly partisan position during the referendum as the normal rules of civil service impartiality did not apply in such an 'extreme' case when 'people are seeking to destroy the fabric of the state' and 'impugn its territorial integrity'.[78] The intervention by the Chancellor and his Permanent Secretary had been preceded by a series of interventions from economists and business figures making similar points and was followed by coordinated supporting statements from Danny Alexander, Liberal Democrat Chief Secretary to the Treasury, and Ed Balls, Labour's Shadow Chancellor.[79] The message was that if Scotland voted for independence then the rest of the United Kingdom, regardless of which party was in power, would refuse to allow Scotland to share the currency. This was an attempt to further polarize the debate. The SNP's definition of independence had been refined over many years especially from the late 1980s when it launched its 'independence in Europe' campaign. This more pragmatic appeal had helped the SNP to win power.[80] Some *Yes Scotland* supporters including its chair Denis Canavan and Scottish Green Party leader preferred a separate currency but the SNP position dominated the message from supporters of independence.

It emphasized continuities and played down or denied any disruption or risk that might follow independence. This was evident in the White Paper issued by the Scottish Government and also policy statements made by senior Scottish Government Ministers. The purpose of the hardline position adopted by UK politicians on a currency union was an attempt to polarize debate and suggest that the Scottish Government retained a hardline position.

[75] M. Carney, 'The Economics of Currency Unions', Bank of England, <http://www.bankofengland.co.uk/publications/Documents/speeches/2014/speech706.pdf>.

[76] N. MacPherson, 'Scotland and a Currency Union' (HM Government, 11 February 2014) <https://www.gov.uk/government/uploads/system/uploads/attachment_data/file/279460/Sir_Nicholas_Macpherson_-_Scotland_and_a_currency_union.pdf>.

[77] Public Administration Committee, *Lessons for Civil Service Impartiality from the Scottish Independence Referendum*, Fifth Report of Session 2014–15, HC 111, para. 69.

[78] J. Rentoul, 'Why the Treasury Backed the "No" Vote in the Scottish Referendum: its Top Mandarin Speaks' *Independent* (20 January 2015).

[79] 'Party Big Guns to Rule out Currency Union with Scotland' *Guardian* (11 February 2014).

[80] J. Mitchell, 'Ever Looser Union' in Alan Trench (ed.), *The State of the Nations 2008* (Imprint Academic 2008).

Polls suggested that the intervention failed to undermine existing support for independence. Throughout the course of the long campaign, more voters thought Scotland would be worse off if independent but the gap started to narrow, though it never closed, over Summer 2014 and especially in the final weeks of the campaign. There was little change in how people expected their personal economic positions to be affected by independence over the course of the referendum. Around half the electorate tended to think they would be worse off, followed by a remarkably static figure of around 28 per cent who thought Scottish independence would make no difference to them personally, with those who thought they would be better off only rising to above one in four voters in the final stages of the campaign.[81] There may have been an increase over the long campaign in the proportion of people who thought Scotland would be better off but this was not reflected in assessments of personal economic fortunes.

Debates between the three main UK party leaders had taken place for the first time at the previous UK general election in 2010. Broadcasters were keen to hold debates between key figures in the referendum and there had been a long history of broadcast debates in Scottish politics including by-elections. In the first of a series of broadcast debates, SNP Deputy First Minister Nicola Sturgeon debated the economics of independence with Michael Moore, then Liberal Democrat Secretary of State for Scotland in May 2013 followed by an ill-tempered debate with Labour's Deputy Scottish leader four months later. In November, she took on Alistair Carmichael, who had replaced Mr Moore as Scottish Secretary because the latter was deemed to be insufficiently robust in debate. In February 2014, she debated with Johann Lamont, Scottish Labour leader. In addition, there were numerous televised round table debates and discussions involving a range of independence protagonists and antagonists as well as an unknown number of formal debates taking place across Scotland's communities. But the main debates were those held between SNP First Minister Alex Salmond and *Better Together* leader Alistair Darling. The first was held on August 5, 2014 and broadcast on Scottish Television and the second on 25 August on the BBC. The peak audience for the debate on STV debate was 920,000. The BBC debate attracted 843,000 viewers in Scotland plus a further 1.7 million across the United Kingdom. This was more than four times the number of Scottish viewers who had watched the Scottish party leaders' debate on BBC in the 2010 general election and twice as many as had watched the UK party leaders' debate in Scotland in 2010.

Key events during the long campaign had some impact on public opinion but not always in the direction anticipated. The Scottish Government issued its 670-page White Paper on independence in November 2013. This attracted considerable media and public attention and was followed by a weakening of support for the Union. Somewhat counterintuitively, there was little discernible impact from the Prime Minister's commitment to a European referendum but there was a

[81] See data from *What Scotland Thinks*, <http://whatscotlandthinks.org/questions/do-you-think-you-personally-would-be-financially-better-or-worse-off-if-scotlan#line>.

further weakening of support for the Union after the Chancellor's intervention on the currency. The leaders' debates appear to have had little impact. The European dimension recurred regularly throughout the referendum. The most notable tightening in the polls occurred in the final stages of the referendum. Less than two weeks before polling day, one opinion poll gave support for independence a 51–49 per cent lead.

While voters perceived different tones to the two campaigns, there was a significant negative aspect to *Yes Scotland*'s message. The message focused on the prospect of the Conservatives or New Labour dominance of British politics and a suggested threat to the welfare state. The National Health Service (NHS) and welfare in general had long been Labour's traditional electoral mainstay. Labour was always keen to put the NHS at the top of the agenda in electoral contests with the Conservatives. But in the referendum, Labour was in the uncomfortable position of attacking the Conservative government for undermining the NHS in England while sharing an umbrella with the Conservatives in Scotland. *Yes Scotland* shifted to a more negative message in the closing stages of the referendum. This discombobulated Labour and allowed *Yes Scotland* to take advantage of a traditional Labour campaign theme.

As polling day drew closer, it became clear that the massive advantage enjoyed by supporters of the Union at the start of the long campaign had been whittled away (See Figure 4.2 below). The poll showing *Yes* ahead forced leaders of the UK parties to finally concede what they had sought to exclude from the debate. Prime Minister David Cameron, Labour leader Ed Miliband, and Liberal Democrat leader Nick Clegg issued a joint statement in favour of more powers that was published on the front page of the *Daily Record* on Tuesday 16 September, three days before polling day. 'The Vow' committed each party to delivering 'extensive new powers' delivered to a tight timetable that would begin immediately after the referendum. They were committed to the continuity of the Barnett formula that allocated resources to Scotland, Wales, and Northern Ireland and that the 'final say on how much is spent on the NHS will be a matter for the Scottish Parliament'.[82] Former Labour Prime Minister Gordon Brown had outlined a timetable for the delivery of more powers the previous week. This would involve work starting on the day after the referendum, the UK Government outlining a timetable for its proposals by the end of October, a white paper by the end of November and draft new legislation by January.[83] The three UK party leaders were responding to pressure evident in polls. In so doing they were forced to acknowledge that it was no longer possible to avoid making a commitment to more powers. The absence of this option from the ballot paper had ensured that those who supported more powers would be pivotal. Support for the status quo proved insufficient and it was felt necessary to offer a firm timetable and explicitly refer to 'extensive new powers'.

[82] *Daily Record* (16 September 2014).

[83] BBC News, 'Scottish Independence: Brown Sets Out More Powers Timetable' (8 September 2014) <http://www.bbc.co.uk/news/uk-scotland-scotland-politics-29115556>.

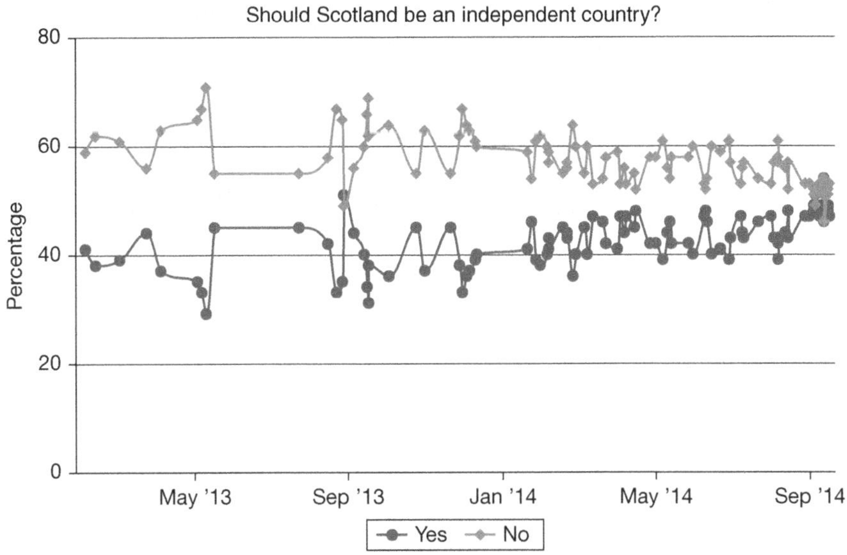

Figure 4.2 Attitudes towards independence

Source: John Curtice, What Scotland Thinks, <http://whatscotlandthinks.org/questions/should-scotland-be-an-independent-country-1#line>

IX. Conclusion

The result of the referendum was unambiguous. A clear majority voted to remain in the Union but that majority had been significantly reduced over the course of the campaign. The campaign had a number of effects. Its length and intensity were unusual and assisted in ensuring substantially higher levels of public engagement, voter registration, and turnout. Public engagement took on a much wider range of forms than in elections or indeed previous referendums creating a 'Heineken effect'. *Better Together* had the advantage of massive media support and a significant advantage having the UK Government on its side but this was offset by *Yes Scotland*'s advantage on the ground and the support of the Scottish Government. Spending by each side submitted to the Electoral Commission offers a very partial and thereby misleading sense of the resources of the two campaigns as this relates only to what is legally required and does not come close to an account of all resources used in a campaign.

The Yes campaign tilted to the left and succeeded in winning more support from amongst the poorer sections of the community and those inclining to the left of politics though, as ever, the picture that emerged was not clear-cut as that supporters of the Union included right-wingers and supporters of independence left-wingers. *Yes Scotland* incorporated more than the SNP and included parties, groups, and individuals who inclined to the left of the SNP with only a small, rather marginal set of right-of-centre supporters.[84] *Better Together* was impeded in appealing to Labour supporters in the normal way of Scottish politics of attacking the Conservatives. The *Labour Vote No* campaign launched by Gordon Brown was less inhibited but even it was limited in its message.

In the event, voters' predispositions won out over the impact of the campaign. But this needs to be set against the massive lead that predispositions gave to opponents of independence. The polarization of the debate meant that the option that received most support in opinion polls—that is, some form of further devolution—was formally not on offer. The ballot paper had submerged a potential consensus from emerging but the campaign forced this on supporters of the Union in the final stages of the referendum. The referendum had allowed for the 'articulation of a submerged consensus', in Bogdanor's terms, despite efforts to prevent this happening.

[84] The most notable was *Wealthy Nation*, <http://www.wealthynation.org>.

PART III

THE REFERENDUM DEBATE

5

The Constitutional Case for Independence

Aileen McHarg

I. Introduction

The 2014 independence referendum has been aptly described as an 'accidental referendum'.[1] It was accidental, first, in the sense that the condition that made the holding of a referendum possible—the election in 2011 of a majority Scottish National Party (SNP) government at Holyrood—was just not supposed to happen. The electoral system for the Scottish Parliament was designed deliberately to avoid single-party majority government. More fundamentally, by responding to Scottish demands for self-government, devolution itself was expected—by some at least—to kill off demand for independence.[2]

In fact, the SNP's election victory did not signal any strong public desire for independence. In 2011, popular support for independence was only around 25–30 per cent, which was relatively low by historical standards,[3] and the importance of the constitutional question compared to other electoral issues had also declined.[4] The SNP therefore won the election *in spite of* not *because of* its commitment to hold a referendum on independence; simply because 'most voters thought that the party would do a better job in office than its rivals'.[5] Indeed, the commitment to hold a referendum *before* commencing negotiations on independence, rather than after the conclusion of such negotiations, as had been party policy until 2000, was

[1] C. McCorkindale, 'An Accidental Referendum' (*Scottish Constitutional Futures Forum blog*, 16 August 2013).

[2] Former Secretary of State for Scotland, George Robertson, is famously said to have claimed that 'Devolution will kill nationalism stone dead'.

[3] Ipsos MORI, '35 Years of Scottish Attitudes Towards Independence', 15 March 2012, available at: <https://www.ipsos-mori.com/researchpublications/researcharchive/2935/35-years-of-Scottish-attitudes-towards-independence.aspx>. But NB support for a *referendum* on independence was higher: see *What Scotland Thinks* at <http://whatscotlandthinks.org/questions/do-you-support-or-oppose-a-referendum-on-scottish-independence#line>.

[4] C. Carman, R. Johns, and J. Mitchell, *More Scottish than British: the 2011 Scottish Parliament Election* (Palgrave Macmillan 2014) 87.

[5] R. Johns et al, 'Constitution or Competence? The SNP's Re-Election in 2011' (2013) 61 *Political Studies* 158 at 158.

a deliberate—and highly successful—tactic to decouple electoral support for the SNP from support for constitutional reform.[6]

The second sense in which the 2014 referendum was accidental, then, was that it took place without any clear evidence of dissatisfaction with the constitutional status quo.[7] This contrasted strongly with the 1997 referendum, when devolution was so clearly regarded as being (in John Smith's phrase) 'the settled will of the Scottish people' that many had argued that a referendum was unnecessary.[8] Admittedly, the question of Scotland's constitutional future had been on the political agenda since 2007, when the then minority SNP government launched its *National Conversation*[9] and the Unionist parties responded by setting up the Calman Commission to review the operation of devolution. But the Calman Commission found that devolution was popular, and considered that it had operated largely successfully.[10] Insofar as there was popular support for constitutional reform, therefore, it was for more devolution, rather than independence. However, the UK Government was unwilling to countenance a second referendum question on further devolution—ostensibly, inter alia, because independence and further devolution were distinct constitutional issues,[11] but also presumably because they thought that on a straightforward choice between independence and the status quo, independence would be comfortably defeated. In any case, as Unionists frequently pointed out, further devolution was *already* being delivered via the Scotland Act 2012, which had been enacted in response to the Calman Commission's recommendations.

If by 2011 there was no strongly-felt constitutional grievance to which independence was the answer, nor was the subsequent referendum debate conducted primarily in constitutional terms. As other chapters in this volume have noted,[12] once the debate moved beyond the early preoccupation with process issues, it was dominated by discussion of the substantive—and particularly the economic—effects of independence on public policy in Scotland and on the lives of its residents. This again contrasts sharply with devolution, which proceeded on a clearly articulated analysis of the defects in Scotland's then governance arrangements and of the constitutional right of the Scottish people to secure enhanced self-government.[13]

[6] D. Torrance, *The Battle for Britain: Scotland and the Independence Referendum* (Biteback Publishing 2013) 9–10.

[7] McCorkindale (n. 1).

[8] See A. King, *The British Constitution* (Oxford University Press 2007) 290.

[9] Scottish Government, *Choosing Scotland's Future: A National Conversation: Independence and Responsibility in the Modern World* (2007).

[10] Commission on Scottish Devolution, *Serving Scotland Better: Scotland and the United Kingdom in the 21st Century* (2009).

[11] See I. McLean, J. Gallagher, and G. Lodge, *Scotland's Choices: The Referendum and What Happens Afterwards* (Edinburgh University Press 2013) 9–14.

[12] See Gallagher, Ch. 6, and Scott, Ch. 7.

[13] See Campaign for a Scottish Assembly, *A Claim of Right for Scotland: Report of the Constitutional Steering Committee* (1988); Scottish Constitutional Convention, *Towards a Scottish Parliament: Consultation Document and Report to the Scottish People* (1989); Scottish Constitutional Convention, *Towards the Scottish Parliament: a Report to the Scottish People* (1990); Scottish Constitutional Convention, *Scotland's Parliament, Scotland's Right* (1995).

The substantive nature of the referendum debate is largely attributable to the fact that the Scottish Government chose to base its case for constitutional change not around an existentialist nationalist claim—that Scotland, being a nation, should also be a state (although such arguments undoubtedly were made by independence supporters, for instance in claims that independence would make Scotland a 'normal' country), or that independence was necessary to preserve Scottish identity. Rather, the appeal was to a utilitarian nationalism, which saw independence as a tool to achieve a better society.[14] This approach had the advantage of enabling many people who did not identify as Nationalists (at least with a capital N), and who continued to feel some degree of Britishness, to support the Yes campaign on the basis that an independent Scotland would better able to deliver progressive policy outcomes. Its disadvantage was that it was vulnerable to counterarguments that an independent Scotland would in fact be *less* able to achieve such policy outcomes,[15] and to claims—made particularly by Labour politicians—that the constitutional debate was a distraction from the real business of improving the lives of Scottish people.

However, what these counterarguments arguably failed fully to appreciate, and therefore adequately to address, was the fact that the instrumental case for independence was underpinned by a critique of Scotland's current governance arrangements. Except insofar as it was based on crude arguments about the assignment of tax revenues or the allocation of natural resources (arguments which were undoubtedly made, but which operated more as reasons why Scotland *could* be independent, rather why it *should*), the instrumental case necessarily assumed that an independent Scotland would be able to govern itself *differently* and *better* than would be possible if it were to remain part of the United Kingdom.

Thus, contrary to initial impressions, there *was* a constitutional case for independence, which was made with varying degrees of explicitness. Moreover, this was a case which strongly echoed the constitutional case that had been made for devolution a generation earlier.

The aim of this chapter is to elucidate that constitutional case, which, I contend, was based around four sets of (intertwined, but conceptually distinct) arguments: about a democratic deficit; about effective governance; about the place of Scotland in the United Kingdom's territorial constitution; and about the constitution of an independent Scotland. The chapter also seeks to evaluate the strength of these arguments, particularly in the light of the referendum itself and subsequent events. It is important to appreciate that the referendum was not merely an opportunity to pass judgment on Scotland's constitutional arrangements, but was itself a constitutionally significant event which shaped perceptions of those arrangements. Thus, the referendum debate has served to focus and intensify constitutional dissatisfaction, which subsequent opinion polls and

[14] See in particular N. Sturgeon, 'Bringing the Powers Home to Build a Better Nation', Speech at Strathclyde University, 3 December 2012.

[15] See Gallagher, Ch. 6 in this volume, and for a more optimistic assessment of the likely economic effects of independence, see Scott, Ch. 7 in this volume.

political developments suggest has certainly not weakened and may even have become stronger.[16] The argument advanced in this chapter is that while none of the four constitutional claims made by Yes campaigners individually amounts to a compelling case for independence, cumulatively they seem likely to become harder to resist, particularly if post-referendum political and constitutional trends continue.

II. A democratic deficit

The most frequently invoked constitutional argument in favour of independence was the idea of a democratic deficit; in other words, that independence is the only way to guarantee that Scotland always gets the government it votes for.[17] The claimed democratic deficit in Scotland's then system of government was of course one of the key justifications for the establishment of the Scottish Parliament. It was the election of four successive Conservative governments at Westminster between 1979 and 1997, during a period in which the party had only minority—and declining—electoral support in Scotland,[18] which provided a clear rationale for devolution[19] and persuaded a substantial majority of voters to support it. The ability of the government to impose unpopular policies (such as the poll tax) on Scotland came to be perceived not merely as 'the product of an occasional aberration by a particular British government [but as] a consequence of flaws in the system of government'.[20]

However, the Scottish Government argued, devolution 'has only been a partial solution to the democratic deficit'.[21] Significant policy issues, on which Scottish preferences might diverge from those of voters in the rest of the United Kingdom (rUK), continue to be dealt with at UK level, and this necessarily must be the case even under the most generous devolution arrangements. Moreover, Scottish policy-making in devolved areas continues to be constrained by policy preferences at UK level, most significantly to the extent that the funding of the devolved institutions remains tied to expenditure levels in England, but also through UK Government control of European Union (EU) and other international decision-making, and through the continued existence of GB-wide political party structures and policy communities. This was a point emphasized by the Scottish Government in the latter stages of the referendum campaign, when it highlighted the threat to the NHS in Scotland from the pursuit of privatization in England.

[16] See What Scotland Thinks at <http://whatscotlandthinks.org/questions/how-would-you-vote-in-the-in-the-scottish-independence-referendum-if-held-now-a#line>.

[17] See eg Scottish Government, *Scotland's Future: Your Guide to an Independent Scotland* (2013) xii, 41.

[18] Conservative representation in Scotland declined from twenty-two (out of seventy-one seats) at the 1979 general election to just eleven seats in 1992—House of Commons Library *UK Election Statistics 1918–2012*, Research Paper 12/43 (2012) 11.

[19] See Kidd and Petrie, Ch. 2 in this volume.

[20] *Claim of Right* (n. 13) at para. 8.4.

[21] *Scotland's Future* (n. 17) at 333.

Thus, independence was presented as a means of *completing* the democratic reform process begun by devolution.[22]

It is important to appreciate that the force of the democratic deficit argument—both as a justification for devolution and for independence—lies not merely in the *temporary divergence* of electoral majorities in Scotland and the United Kingdom as a whole (which could be resolved by a change of government at Westminster), but in the lack of *control* that Scottish voters have over the outcome of UK elections. The basic problem is the dominance of England, which has 84 per cent of the UK population.[23] As the independence White Paper pointed out, this means that constituency results for Scotland rarely affect the outcome of UK general elections; in only two general elections held since 1945 have Scottish votes made a difference, and those governments held office for less than twenty-six months in total.[24] This in turn means, it was claimed, that in order to win elections, parties have to present policies which appeal to voters in other parts of the United Kingdom whose voting patterns differ markedly from those in Scotland.[25]

According to the 1988 *Claim of Right*—the document which may be regarded as providing the political foundation for devolution—the constitutional flaw in Scotland's machinery of government was that it could only work within a limited range of election results.[26] As McCrone puts it 'so long as Scotland and England voted more or less the same way, the constitutional anomaly whereby the United Kingdom always got a government the English voted for did not matter.'[27] But the anomaly became unsustainable when, from the 1960s onwards, voting patterns began to diverge. This divergence shows no signs of diminishing and, indeed, became even more pronounced at the 2015 UK general election. The SNP's near-clean sweep of the Scottish seats, and the refusal of the Britain-wide parties to countenance coalition, or even some lesser support arrangement with it, effectively locked out the overwhelming majority of Scottish MPs from participation in government. For the first time, this meant that there would be a democratic deficit in Scotland *whichever* party won most seats at UK level.

The key assumption which underpins the democratic deficit argument is that Scotland is a distinct political unit, and indeed the primary political unit in which democratic majorities are to be calculated. This is turn rests upon an assumption that Scotland is a nation with a right to political self-determination. In this basic sense, the instrumentalist case for independence is as much a nationalist position as the existentialist one. In fact, the claim that Scotland is a nation is not controversial. Nationhood in general is a concept which is notoriously difficult to define, since it rests on subjective

[22] See, eg, Scottish Government, *Scotland's Future: from the Referendum to Independence and a Written Constitution* (2013) para. 1.1.

[23] Office for National Statistics 'Mid-Year Population Estimates for the UK 2014', <http://www.ons.gov.uk/ons/rel/pop-estimate/population-estimates-for-uk--england-and-wales--scotland-and-northern-ireland/mid-2014/mid-year-population-estimates-for-the-uk-2014.html>.

[24] *Scotland's Future* (n. 17) at 333–4.

[25] *Scotland's Future* (n. 17) at 334.

[26] *Claim of Right* (n. 13) at para. 3.6.

[27] D. McCrone, 'Scotland Out of the Union? The Rise and Rise of the Nationalist Agenda' (2012) 83 *Pol Q* 69 at 73.

perception rather than on purely objective criteria. But Scotland's claim to national identity is sufficiently well accepted, internally uncontested, and bolstered by sufficient historical, cultural, territorial, and institutional markers, that any questioning of Scotland's nationhood was confined to the fringes of the No campaign.[28]

However, the claim that Scotland, as a nation, should therefore enjoy political self-determination is more problematic. For some, the claim to national self-determination is inherently morally suspect. For instance, Joseph Weiler has argued that the secessionist claims of substate nations such as Scotland or Catalonia are 'ethically demoralizing'; they are, he claims, inherently associated with an atavistic, ethnic nationalism, and based on 'a seriously misdirected social and economic egotism, cultural and national hubris, and the naked ambition of local politicians'.[29] The United Kingdom—or Spain—as a multinational state therefore constitutes a morally superior site of political solidarity.

This kind of argument is arguably misconceived, at least in the Scottish case, because it misunderstands both the nature of the United Kingdom and the nature of Scottish nationalism. Keating argues that the United Kingdom is better understood as a 'plurinational' rather than a 'multinational' state. In other words, it is a state in which people have plural national identities, not merely one in which distinct national identities coexist.[30] 'Britishness' is therefore itself a national identity, albeit based on allegiance to a political order, rather than a common ethnic inheritance. However, the nationalism espoused by the SNP is equally a civic nationalism. It is not a claim based on the inherent distinctiveness of the Scots as a people, but on their allegiance to a distinct political system. The argument made by critics of independence[31] that there are only minor political differences between people in Scotland and the rUK is therefore broadly accurate,[32] but beside the point. What matters is the existence of a distinct Scottish *political system*. Institutionalized political communities take on their own dynamics; and it is undeniable that the terms of political debate in Scotland—for whatever reasons: different electoral systems; different voting patterns; different policy issues and/or policy contexts; different patterns of interest representation—have diverged from those which dominate at UK level.[33]

[28] See eg the British nationalist blogger, Effie Deans, 'We Must Attack the SNP at its Roots' (*Lily of St Leonards blog*, 18 April 2015); or mischievous suggestions that, if Scotland became independent, Orkney and Shetland should make their own claim to self-determination—eg Tavish Scott MSP, quoted in T. Gordon, 'Former Lib Dem Leader: "It's Shetland's Oil, Alex ..."' *Herald* (17 March 2013).

[29] J. H. H. Weiler, 'Editorial' (2012) 24 *European Journal of International Law* 909; 'Scotland and the EU: a Comment' (*Verfassungsblog*, 8 September 2014).

[30] M. Keating, *Plurinational Democracy: Stateless Nations in a Post-Sovereignty Era* (Oxford University Press 2001) 19, 26–7.

[31] See eg Gallagher, Ch. 6 in this volume.

[32] Successive British and Scottish social attitudes surveys suggest only slight attitudinal differences between Scotland and the rUK—see <http://www.natcen.ac.uk> and <http://www.scotcen.org.uk>.

[33] See M. Keating and M. Harvey, *Small Nations in a Big World: What Scotland Can Learn* (Luath Press 2014) 37 and ch. 9. However, the degree of divergence should not be exaggerated, and Jackson also points out that there is greater diversity in political cultures within the rUK than a focus on the UK level might suggest—B. Jackson, 'The Political Thought of Scottish Nationalism' (2014) 85 *Pol Q* 50 at 53–4.

The choice between the United Kingdom and an independent Scotland is therefore one between competing versions of civic nationalism, or competing sites of political identity.[34] In these circumstances, to prefer a priori the existing UK state to a putative Scottish state amounts simply to a bias in favour of the status quo, while to deny the relevance of nationhood to statehood altogether would be to ignore the reality of the existing state order.[35]

In fact, for liberal nationalist theorists, 'self-determination is part of the normative content of nationality itself'.[36] In other words, a claim to nationhood necessarily also entails an entitlement to collective self-government, arising from 'a respect for the freedom of individuals to choose their own lives and determine their political fate'.[37] Crucially, however, effective self-government does not necessarily require full statehood.[38] Nor is the claim an absolute one: particular self-determination claims may have to give way to competing principles.[39]

In the Scottish case, the ability of a distinct national identity to flourish without independent statehood is readily apparent. Until relatively recently, there was no serious questioning of the legitimacy of the Union in Scotland. However, what Kidd has called 'banal unionism'[40] did not mean the suppression of Scottish difference, nor the assimilation of Scottishness to Britishness. On the contrary, a commitment to the Union was consistent with the maintenance of substantial scope for Scottish self-government. The Union agreement itself preserved significant areas of autonomy in areas regarded as particularly important—in the law, the church, education, and social affairs;[41] while the later growth of a centralized state apparatus in the late nineteenth and twentieth centuries was accompanied by considerable institutional recognition of Scottish distinctiveness.[42]

From one perspective, therefore, the advent of legislative devolution in 1999 might be seen as a relatively minor development in the self-government of Scotland within the Union, and one which carries no implications for any further developments towards independence. It merely added a representative and legislative body to the existing institutions of Scottish self-government, and may be understood essentially as a defensive measure, aimed at protecting Scotland's distinct identity against perceived threats to its existence. The *Claim of Right* is in fact suffused with this kind of defensive language.[43] On this view, the

[34] Keating and Harvey, *Small Nations* (n. 33) at 18.

[35] Cf. N. Krisch, 'Catalonia's Independence: A Reply to Joseph Weiler' *EJIL: Talk!*, 18 January 2013.

[36] Keating, *Plurinational Democracy* (n. 30) at 4. See also N. MacCormick, *Questioning Sovereignty* (Oxford University Press 1999) ch. 11; N. Walker, 'Scottish Nationalism For and Against the Union State' in N. Walker (ed.), *MacCormick's Scotland* (Edinburgh University Press 2012) 168.

[37] Krisch (n. 35).

[38] Keating, *Plurinational Democracy* (n. 30) at 7–8.

[39] Keating, *Plurinational Democracy* (n. 30) at 28; MacCormick, *Questioning Sovereignty* (n. 36) at 174.

[40] C. Kidd, *Unions and Unionism* (Cambridge University Press 2008).

[41] See L. Paterson, *The Autonomy of Modern Scotland* (Edinburgh University Press 1994).

[42] See J. Mitchell, *The Scottish Question* (Oxford University Press 2014).

[43] See eg *Claim of Right* (n. 13) at paras 2.2, 3.2, 6.10 and Epilogue.

increased significance attached to separate political representation from the late 1960s onwards is explicable as a response to the relative decline of other carriers of national identity (due to processes of industrialization, urbanization, secularization, and the development of communications and democracy),[44] and as a necessary bulwark against interference in Scottish civic life by over-centralizing governments insensitive to Scottish difference.[45] But following devolution, with Scottish control over essential aspects of Scottish life now secured, and with no other obvious threats to Scottish identity or culture, a move to independence may be regarded as simply unnecessary.[46]

From another perspective, however, devolution in 1999 was indeed a constitutional turning point. Here, devolution may be understood, not as a defensive measure predicated on the insecurity of *Scottish* identity, but as a pure autonomy claim, deriving from a declining commitment to *British* identity, and a sense that distinct governmental institutions without a corresponding democratic base could no longer be seen as legitimate. On this alternative view, the case for self-government is not limited to areas of pre-existing Scottish difference or issues which are purely of concern to Scots. This was in any case always unconvincing as an explanation for the scope of devolution, and it becomes increasingly less persuasive as devolved competences expand. Instead, what is constitutionally significant about devolution is its basis in an explicit assertion of the sovereignty of the Scottish people (reinforced by popular consent through a referendum), and the platform it provides for the accentuation and proliferation of political, institutional, and policy difference, and the assertion of further autonomy claims.[47] If based upon a pure autonomy claim, it is of course much more difficult to set coherent and durable limits to Scottish self-government. Indeed, the Scottish Constitutional Convention in its 1989 consultation document, *Towards a Scottish Parliament*—a document which endorsed the *Claim of Right* but which was subtly different in its analysis—expressly acknowledged that it followed from the principle of popular sovereignty that the Scottish people could legitimately choose to be independent (although it did not necessarily follow that they would or should do so), and it also accepted that it could be difficult to draw a hard line between the legislative competences of the Scottish Parliament and matters to be reserved to Westminster.[48]

The democratic deficit argument therefore has considerable normative force as a justification for independence and not merely for devolution. However, it still cannot be regarded as conclusive. There are two further problems to be addressed. First, as Keating points out, 'it is a logical consequence of the doctrine of self-determination that its exercise may be limited by the equal rights of others',[49] in this case the rights of those who maintain a British national identity.

[44] Mitchell, *Scottish Question* (n. 42) at 11.
[45] Mitchell, *Scottish Question* (n. 42) at 257.
[46] See eg P. Jones, 'Existential and Utilitarian Nationalism in Scotland' in K. P. Müller (ed.), *Scotland 2014 and Beyond: Coming of Age and Loss of Innocence* (Peter Lang GmbH 2015) 152.
[47] S. Tierney, 'Federalism in a Unitary State: A Paradox Too Far?' (2009) 19 *Regional and Federal Studies* 237 at 246–9.
[48] (n. 33) at 18 and 62. [49] *Plurinational Democracy* (n. 30) 11.

This cannot be taken to mean that the desire of a majority of Scots to secede could be vetoed by a contrary desire of a British majority to maintain the territorial integrity of the United Kingdom, since that would be to subordinate the rights of a national minority to the wishes of the larger group. Indeed, it has never been seriously suggested in the UK context that issues of territorial self-determination are for anyone other than those living in the territory in question to determine (although the *interests* of the rUK in the process and consequences of such decisions have certainly been asserted).[50] Instead, it means that the continued British identity of people living in Scotland has to be taken into account.

In fact, this is potentially problematic for proponents of independence, since it is clear that many people living in Scotland have multiple national identities. Scottish Social Attitude Surveys continue to show that, if forced to choose between them, a clear majority will opt for a Scottish rather than a British identity (65 per cent and 23 per cent respectively in 2014).[51] But on the more subtle 'Moreno' scale, a similar majority (63 per cent in 2014) will opt for some degree of shared Scottish and British identity, with only a minority (23 per cent in 2014) choosing an exclusively Scottish identity.[52] Indeed, British identity seems to have become somewhat stronger in recent years, presumably as a direct result of the threat to that identity posed by the referendum itself.

To the extent that Britishness is still regarded as a relevant political identity, then the democratic deficit argument loses much of its force. If certain issues are regarded as being legitimately determined at UK level, then the fact that voters in Scottish constituencies sometimes end up with a UK Government they did not support is no more constitutionally relevant than similar regional disparities in voting patterns elsewhere in the United Kingdom.[53] Equally, if Scottish voters choose to support (regional) political parties which have no chance of forming a UK-wide government, then that is no more constitutionally problematic than a choice to support any other minority party.

However, one major difficulty with this argument is the assumption that Scottish and British national identities map unproblematically onto the distinction between devolved and reserved matters, or that they could ever do so. Political convergence and divergence between Scotland and the rUK is almost certain to cut across that boundary, wherever it is drawn, meaning that it is likely to be a continuing source of potential tension. Accordingly, unless territorial difference on reserved matters, as well as devolved matters, is handled carefully, there is an ongoing risk that policy difference on reserved matters may escalate into a

[50] See A. McHarg, 'The Independence Referendum, the Contested Constitution, and the Authorship of Constitutional Change' in Müller (ed.), *Scotland 2014 and Beyond* (n. 46) at 242–6.

[51] See *What Scotland Thinks* website at <http://whatscotlandthinks.org/questions/forced-choice-national-identity-5#line>.

[52] See *What Scotland Thinks* website at <http://whatscotlandthinks.org/questions/moreno-national-identity-5#line>.

[53] See eg K. Armstrong, 'Political Representation at Holyrood Would Suffer Under Independence' *Herald* (29 August 2014).

legitimacy deficit, particularly if the parties in power at UK and/or Scottish level have a political interest in provoking conflict.[54]

Another problem is that national (political) identity is clearly not fixed. While the independence referendum may have had the effect of strengthening British identity, it has also further embedded Scotland rather than the United Kingdom as the main political frame of reference. The referendum debate was emphatically a *Scottish* debate: it was a debate conducted *within* Scotland, with limited and largely unhelpful input from the rUK; and it was a debate *about* the future of Scotland, and the best interests of the Scottish people, not one about the United Kingdom.[55] As more power is devolved to Scotland in the wake of the referendum, the political salience of Scotland is likely to increase, and that of the United Kingdom to decrease, even further. Indeed, there are already signs that Scottish politics are beginning to trump UK politics—for instance, the willingness of a majority of Scottish voters at the 2015 general election to vote on Scottish rather than British lines,[56] and the prominence of devolved matters such as health in pre-election debates, or the fact that the Scottish Labour Party has felt the need to differentiate itself from the UK Party on a reserved matter such as the renewal of Trident ahead of the 2016 Holyrood election.

As the political relevance of Britishness declines, it also becomes vulnerable to the argument that there are ways of giving expression to it other than through continued common statehood. For instance, the Scottish Government during the referendum campaign sought to recast Britishness as a geographical and cultural rather than a political identity, and to stress the significant ties that would remain between Scotland and the rUK notwithstanding the ending of the political union between them.[57] Again, therefore, without careful attention to the continued supports for political solidarity across the United Kingdom, the democratic argument for independence is likely to become stronger.

However, the second reason why the democratic argument for independence cannot be regarded as compelling is because the empirical evidence suggests that perceptions of identity are not the sole factors determining people's constitutional preferences. Post-referendum survey evidence shows that, while people with a strong Scottish identity were more likely to vote Yes, and people with a strong British identity to vote No, a commitment to the Union was not

[54] See J. Mitchell, 'Devolution's Unfinished Business' (2007) 77 *Pol Q* 465 at 470.

[55] See A. McHarg, 'A Tale of Two Constitutions' (*Scottish Constitutional Futures Forum blog*, 16 December 2013); A. McHarg, 'Has the United Kingdom Had a Good Referendum?' (*Scottish Constitutional Futures Forum blog*, 14 June 2014).

[56] Whereas the contrasting results of the 2007 and 2011 Scottish Parliament elections, on the one hand, and 2010 UK general election, on the other, suggested a significantly greater willingness to vote for the SNP in Scottish rather than UK elections, the SNP's vote share at the 2015 UK general election (50 per cent) was its highest ever. Survey evidence suggests that the SNP are most trusted to work in the long-term interests of Scotland by supporters of all parties; and preliminary analysis of the 2015 election also suggests a spillover effect from the independence referendum. See: D. McCrone, *Changed Utterly* (2015), available at: <http://www.sps.ed.ac.uk/staff/sociology/mccrone_david>; E. Fieldhouse, *The British Electorate in 2015: the Fragmentation of Britain's Party System* (2015), available at: <www.britishelectionstudy.com>.

[57] See *Scotland's Future* (n. 17) at 213–16.

the decisive reason why independence was rejected. Instead, it was concerns about the risks and uncertainty of independence that were most important.[58] What this indicates is that while democratic arguments are clearly important, they are not the only relevant factor in the design of satisfactory constitutional arrangements.

III. Effective governance

In fact, the democratic argument for independence was combined with a second argument about effective governance. The claim was, as Alex Salmond put it during his first televised debate with Alistair Darling, that '[n]o one will do a better job of running Scotland than the people who live and work in Scotland.'[59]

Insofar as 'better government' means the pursuit of policies that the people of Scotland want, the claim that independence will lead to better decision-making may be regarded simply as a variant of the democratic deficit argument. However, understanding better government to be concerned, not only with the *ends* of public policy, but also with the *means* to those ends, it is conceptually separate: an argument about governmental *capacity*, rather than legitimate *authority*.

Once again, this echoed similar arguments made by advocates of devolution. For instance, the Scottish Constitutional Convention claimed that 'there is every reason to expect that the people of Scotland will tackle issues that confront them more effectively than Westminster acting remotely in their stead.'[60] The Scottish Government asserted—and the No campaign did not seek to deny—that devolution *had* been good for Scotland.[61] Once again, therefore, the independence case sought to build upon existing support for devolution, essentially to argue that 'completing' the powers of the Scottish Parliament would also be good for Scotland. In support of this claim, the Scottish Government made reference to the greater flexibility and policy coherence that would come from having access to a full set of legal competences and policy levers; the greater ability to tailor policy measures specifically to Scottish needs; and the advantages arising from the smaller scale of government in Scotland, such as greater agility, accessibility, and shorter lines of communication, the more manageable scale of policy challenges, and greater scrutiny of policy delivery.[62]

[58] See Lord Ashcroft's post-referendum poll—<http://lordashcroftpolls.com/2014/09/scotland-voted/>; and preliminary data from ESRC study post-referendum study—<http://centreonconstitutionalchange.ac.uk/sites/default/files/Scottish%20Referendum%20Study%2027%20March% 202015.pdf>.

[59] BBC News, 'Scottish Independence: Salmond and Darling Clash in TV Debate' (5 August 2014) <http://www.bbc.co.uk/news/uk-scotland-28649354>. See also *Scotland's Future* (n. 17) at ix, 40; N. Sturgeon, 'The Constitutional Future of an Independent Scotland', speech at the University of Edinburgh, 16 June 2014.

[60] *Scotland's Parliament, Scotland's Right* (n. 13) at 7.

[61] *Scotland's Future* (n. 17) at 40.

[62] See *National Conversation* (n. 9) at ix, 9; *Scotland's Future* (n. 17) at 48, 360.

In fact, academic analysis does support the view that small states can be more effective than larger ones,[63] although Keating and Harvey are careful to emphasize that their success is dependent not simply upon their size, but upon the adoption of modes of governance appropriate to their particular circumstances: 'small-state governments are not merely large-state ones at a reduced scale but need qualitatively different structures and skills.'[64]

However, the bigger problem for advocates of independence is that it is patently not *always* true that smaller governmental units are more effective. On the contrary, there are numerous reasons why the pooling of sovereignty in larger political units may lead to better policy outcomes. These include economies of scale—in particular, increased policy-making and regulatory capacities,[65] and a greater ability to manage physical and economic risks by pooling and sharing resources over a larger population base[66]—as well as policy spillovers and externalities, which create coordination and collective action problems in the absence of joint decision-making machinery. In addition, independent states face external constraints—through international law and the exposure to international markets—which bear particularly heavily on small states, and from which they may be more effectively shielded as a substate unit in a larger entity.[67] In short, *de jure* power does not always amount to *de facto* power.

In practice, the desirability of continued integration was accepted by the Scottish Government, which advocated a model of independence which assumed, not isolation, but substantial cooperation with other states, through membership of the European Union, NATO, and other international organizations, and particularly through close ongoing ties with the rUK on a transitional or more permanent basis. The latter included a currency union, a single energy market, a shared head of state, defence cooperation, shared financial regulation, a common travel area, reciprocal citizenship and voting rights, shared social security administration, coordinated transport networks, and shared scientific, technical, and research programmes.[68]

Though frequently derided by No campaigners as amounting to 'independence lite'—a mere tactic designed to reassure risk-averse voters that nothing much would change upon Scotland becoming independent[69]—and rejected by the UK Government as promising a greater degree of interstate cooperation than was to be found anywhere in the world,[70] this was arguably a sophisticated attempt to

[63] See Keating and Harvey, *Small Nations* (n. 33) at ch. 3.
[64] Keating and Harvey, *Small Nations* (n. 33) at 69.
[65] Keating and Harvey, *Small Nations* (n. 33) at 68.
[66] See Gallagher, Ch. 6 in this volume.
[67] The issue of whether an independent Scotland would be able to continue to charge university tuition fees to rUK students, but not to Scottish-domiciled students is a good example of this.
[68] *Scotland's Future* (n. 17).
[69] See Jackson, *Political Thought* (n. 33) at 55.
[70] HM Government, *United Kingdom, United Future: Conclusions of the Scotland Analysis Programme* (Cm 8869, 2014) para. 1.15.

come to terms with the conditions of 'post-sovereignty'.[71] In other words, the Scottish Government arguably had a far better understanding than their critics of the inevitable constraints upon the autonomy of states in an increasingly globalized world, and of the non-categorical nature of contemporary statehood.[72]

However, in its acceptance that sovereignty is not an absolute, but a matter of degree, the independence case inevitably became vulnerable to the argument that an appropriate blend of autonomy and interdependence could more satisfactorily be achieved through a constitutional arrangement short of full statehood[73]—and without the rupture and transitional costs that independence would necessarily entail.[74] Indeed, by the time of the referendum vote, it was just this sort of arrangement that the No campaign purported to be offering in the form of enhanced devolution within a reformed Union.

Two issues are particularly problematic for advocates of independence. The first is the argument that any sharing of sovereignty in the interests of effective decision-making would reintroduce a democratic deficit, because Scottish voters would be unable fully to control joint decision-making institutions. Indeed, the democratic problems associated with intergovernmental decision-making are arguably worse than any legitimacy deficit within the Union, insofar as joint decision-making is not subject to any direct parliamentary oversight (or in the case of the EU, only to weak parliamentary involvement), and executive decision-making in the field of intergovernmental relations is notoriously difficult to hold to account.[75]

There are several possible responses to this criticism. One is to accept that there are necessary trade-offs between democracy and effective government. However, just because *some* limits on sovereignty are acceptable, it does not follow that all are. It is not, therefore, a contradiction to choose to end one Union while maintaining others or entering into new cooperative arrangements. A second response is that any assessment of the implications of independence for democracy has to look at the *quality* of democratic engagement achievable under different constitutional scenarios and not merely at its formal *extent*.[76] For instance, for many supporters of independence, the loss of formal democratic control over, say, monetary policy, was a price worth paying for independence plus a currency union because they did not believe that Scottish voters currently exercise meaningful control in this area given both the general arguments about the democratic deficit

[71] SNP thinking on this issue was strongly influenced by Neil MacCormick—see *Questioning Sovereignty* (n. 36).

[72] See Walker, *Scottish Nationalism* (n. 36) at 187; Mitchell *Scottish Question* (n. 42) at 277, 279.

[73] See Walker, *Scottish Nationalism* (n. 36) and Ch. 11 in this volume.

[74] 'A constitutional rupture followed by agreement would be a very different matter politically from an internal constitutional reform. It would create antagonisms and polarize opinion forcing politicians to stress the dividing line between independence and less radical options rather than the continuum between them. This could hamper cooperation in building new forms of partnership'—M. Keating, *The Independence of Scotland: Self-Government and the Shifting Politics of Union* (Oxford University Press 2009) 140.

[75] See A. McHarg, 'Scotland and the United Kingdom' in G. Hassan and J. Mitchell (eds), *After Independence* (Luath Press Limited 2013).

[76] Cf. MacCormick, *Questioning Sovereignty* (n. 36) at 133–4.

in reserved decision-making, discussed above, and the fact that monetary policy is in any case subject to only limited political control.[77]

A final response is to point out that it is only independent statehood that places the choice in the hands of the Scottish people to decide when and to what extent they want to share power with others.[78] This may be argued to be an important democratic gain from independence because the relative advantages and disadvantages of autonomy and cooperation are likely to change, both over time and from issue to issue. While functional arguments can be made within a system of multi-level governance about the level at which particular powers are best exercised, these arguments are inherently contestable, both because conditions change and because functional arguments ultimately cannot be divorced from values: where powers are best exercised depends at least in part on what you want to do with them.[79] Thus, for example, the rationale for the Union has clearly changed over time, from an initial concern with trade and security, through a common commitment to empire and the Protestant religion, to a more recent concern to ensure a high standard of social protection through a common welfare state—a commitment which itself is now arguably on the wane.[80] Similarly, even those functions which, it is generally agreed, would have to be retained at UK level within any continuing Union—borders and citizenship; foreign affairs and defence; a common currency and single market—are subject to a range of external constraints and cooperative arrangements, which highlight the contingency of any territorial division of powers.[81] Accordingly, any attempt to fix the limits of autonomous Scottish decision-making may itself be regarded as undemocratic, with only independent statehood ensuring that the people of Scotland remain in control of decisions as to how their interests are best advanced.

This, however, leads to a different objection to the independence case, namely that a relationship based on self-interest is necessarily less satisfactory than one based on the solidarity that comes from membership of a common political unit.[82] This was an argument strongly advanced by the UK Government, which argued that '[c]o-operation between states is profoundly different from being part of one state'.[83] Any post-independence cooperation would, it stressed, require to be in the mutual interest of both Scotland and the rUK;[84] and, it suggested, it would in all likelihood *not* be in the interest of the rUK to cooperate to the degree proposed by the Scottish Government.

To some extent, the UK Government's attitude to post-independence cooperation might be thought to have lacked credibility;[85] a position adopted for tactical

[77] See eg R. McAlpine, 'Is Someone Offering Us a Democratic Monetary Policy' (*The Jimmy Reid Foundation*, 29 May 2012).

[78] *Scotland's Future* (n. 17) at 43.

[79] See Keating, *Independence* (n. 74) at ch. 7.

[80] T. Mullen, 'The Scottish Independence Referendum 2014' (2014) 41 *JLS* 627 at 637.

[81] See Scottish Government, *National Conversation* (n. 9) at 8.

[82] See in particular Gallagher, Ch. 6 in this volume; see also Jackson, *Political Thought* (n. 33) at 55–6.

[83] *Scotland Analysis: Conclusions* (n. 70) at para. 1.16.

[84] *Scotland Analysis: Conclusions* (n. 70) at paras 1.16–1.17.

[85] See Mitchell, *Scottish Question* (n. 42) at 278.

reasons which, as the history of British relations with the Republic of Ireland may suggest, might have changed once faced with the reality of independence.[86] However, the more serious underlying point is that a relationship based on self-interest, where either party may at any time choose to withdraw from it, is inherently unstable, and not therefore conducive to the making of necessary compromises. The acceptance of permanent restrictions on sovereignty—sacrificing the right to 'exit' in return for the exercise of 'voice' in a larger organization[87]—may therefore be a necessary price to pay for deeper and more meaningful cooperation.

Again, a number of responses are possible. Once again, the difficulty is to find a way of dividing powers that will prove to be stable and mutually acceptable. Approaching the issue from the perspective of what powers must be retained at the centre in order to maintain solidarity across the Union provides a decision-making criterion, but does not necessarily make it any easier to agree upon the answer. This is clearly illustrated by post-referendum disputes over the acceptable extent of fiscal and welfare devolution, and over the acceptable degree of variation in the provision and protection of fundamental rights. It also remains necessary to reassure Scots that they do have a meaningful voice in the exercise of reserved powers. This leads to the broader point that solidarity is not just a question of *where* powers are exercised, but also *how* they are exercised. Solidarity may be undermined *within* a political union by political behaviour which weakens common commitments—for instance, attacks on welfare provision, or erosion of citizenship rights—or which stokes resentment about perceived unfair treatment of certain territorial groups—such as more generous public spending in Scotland enabled by an unequal funding formula.[88] Finally, if the threat of exit is a destabilizing factor in relationships between states, it must also remain a problem in any UK constitutional order in which the right of the Scottish people (or other national groups) to self-determination is taken seriously.[89] This brings us to the third element of the constitutional case for independence, which is the problematic nature of the United Kingdom's territorial constitution.

IV. The United Kingdom's territorial constitution

The argument that aspirations for greater Scottish autonomy can be more satisfactorily accommodated within a reformed Union than through independence itself involves a constitutional claim. It must assume that a constitutional settlement can be reached which provides adequate recognition for Scottish autonomy and territorial diversity, yet which ensures sufficient constitutional cohesion to

[86] See McHarg, *Scotland and the UK* (n. 75).
[87] A. O. Hirschman, *Voice, Exit and Loyalty: Responses to Decline in Firms, Organizations and States* (Harvard University Press 1970).
[88] Cf. Mullen, *Independence Referendum* (n. 80) at 638.
[89] See further Tickell, Ch. 14 in this volume.

legitimate UK-level decision-making and hold the state together over the long term. Part of the case for independence, however, is that the United Kingdom's territorial constitution does *not* adequately recognize the plurinational character of the state.

In fact, in the wake of the referendum, there is substantial agreement amongst informed observers that reforms need to go beyond the transfer of additional powers to the Scottish Parliament and Scottish Government to include reforms to the territorial constitution more broadly.[90] In this sense, the constitutional discontents underpinning support for independence may again be seen as part of the 'unfinished business' of devolution.[91] Whilst devolution involved radical change at the peripheries, it left the central state apparatus largely unaltered and key constitutional assumptions—formally at least—intact. But where nationalists differ from Unionists is in their deep pessimism about the reformability of the UK constitution.[92]

There are three problems in particular with the current territorial constitution. The issue raised most frequently by nationalists is the *lack of security* for institutions of Scottish self-government, given the doctrine of Parliamentary sovereignty,[93] and the lack of legal recognition of Scotland's right to self-determination—constitutional defects which were also identified by the architects of devolution. For instance, according to the Scottish Constitutional Convention, '[w]e do not believe that the sovereignty of the Scottish people can be satisfactorily protected in a constitutional settlement which establishes a Scottish Parliament within the United Kingdom unless the provisions of that settlement are entrenched.'[94] Far from entrenching the Scottish Parliament, however, the Scotland Act 1998 included an explicit statement of the right of the UK Parliament to continue to legislate for Scotland on devolved matters (s. 28(7)), albeit subject to the understanding that, as a matter of convention, this power would not normally be exercised without the consent of the Scottish Parliament (the Sewel Convention).

In fact, the standard response to complaints about lack of constitutional recognition is to point to constitutional *practice* which, it is claimed, embodies a strong political commitment to the permanence of devolution, and clear acknowledgment of the fact that Scotland is in control of its own constitutional destiny. Indeed—as the Scottish Constitutional Convention eventually came to accept[95]—it can be argued that Scottish autonomy is just as well, if not better, protected under the United Kingdom's political constitution than in comparable written constitutional orders—the unusual (in comparative terms) willingness of

[90] See McEwen, Ch. 10 and Walker, Ch. 11 in this volume.

[91] See Mitchell, *Devolution's Unfinished Business* (n. 54).

[92] See eg Sturgeon, *Bringing the Powers Home* (n. 14); G. Hassan, 'The Making of the Modern SNP: From Protest to Power' in G. Hassan (ed.), *The Modern SNP: From Protest to Power* (Edinburgh University Press 2009) 14.

[93] See *Scotland's Future* (n. 17) at 336.

[94] *Towards a Scottish Parliament* (n. 13) at 19 (and 19–21); see also *Claim of Right* (n. 13) at para. 4.8 and Epilogue; *Scotland's Parliament, Scotland's Right* (n. 13) at 18–19.

[95] See *Scotland's Parliament, Scotland's Right* (n. 13) at 18.

the UK Government to concede a referendum on independence being a case in point.[96] Indeed, it might be argued that political commitment is *more important than* legal guarantees, since in the extreme and improbable political circumstances in which abolition of the Scottish Parliament might be contemplated, legal guarantees would be unlikely to save it.

All that accepted, however, political commitments lack the symbolic reassurance that legal entrenchment would deliver. In addition, the gap between the legal and political constitutions is not without practical significance.[97] The reality of the abolition of the devolved Northern Ireland Parliament and the repeated suspension of the Northern Ireland Assembly (albeit in very different political circumstances) stands in stark counterpoint to claims that abolition of the Scottish Parliament is unthinkable. Less dramatically, the lack of legal enforceability of constitutional conventions creates a structural bias in favour of the UK Government's preferred interpretation in cases where the scope of the Sewel Convention is in dispute—as for example, in relation to the right of the Scottish Parliament to veto any proposed repeal of the Human Rights Act.[98] And in relation to the independence referendum itself, while the UK Government accepted the Scottish Government's *political mandate* to hold a referendum, it nevertheless disputed its *legal right* to do so. The resulting legal uncertainty had practical consequences in enabling the UK Government to exert control over the terms on which the referendum took place, and makes the ability to hold a future referendum similarly uncertain.[99]

In fact, amongst the recommendations of the Smith Commission, which was set up to agree proposals for further devolution to Scotland following the referendum, were that the Scottish Parliament and Scottish Government should be made permanent, and the Sewel Convention placed on a statutory footing.[100] Provisions to give effect to these proposals have been included in the Scotland Bill which is, at the time of writing, being considered by the UK Parliament, and similar provisions are included in the draft Wales Bill.[101] However, implementation

[96] See A. Tomkins, 'Scotland's Choice, Britain's Future' (2014) 130 *LQR* 215 at 220.

[97] The resulting ambiguity over the constitutional status of devolution also has implications for the relationship between the Scottish Parliament and Government and the courts, in terms of how the latter approach questions concerning the scope of devolved competence, the review of devolved decision-making, and the validity of UK legislation encroaching upon devolved matters, all of which are important determinants of the extent of Scottish self-government in practice. For the difference that varying background assumptions about the constitutional status of devolution may make compare, eg, the speeches of Lord Rodger and Lord Hope in *Martin and Miller v Lord Advocate* [2010] UKSC 10; and the speeches of Lord Hope and Lord Reed in *AXA General Insurance Ltd v Lord Advocate* [2011] UKSC 46.

[98] On which see M. Elliott, 'Could the Devolved Nations Block the Repeal of the Human Rights Act and the Enactment of a New Bill of Rights?' (*Public Law for Everyone blog*, 12 May 2015); and 'The Scottish Parliament, the Sewel Convention and Repeal of the Human Rights Act: a Postscript' (*Public Law for Everyone blog*, 28 September 2015); and I. Jamieson, 'The Repeal of the Human Rights Act and the Sewel Convention in Scotland' (*Scottish Constitutional Futures Forum blog*, 12 June 2015).

[99] See further Tickell, Ch. 14 in this volume.

[100] *Report of the Smith Commission for Further Devolution of Powers to the Scottish Parliament* (2014) paras 21 and 22.

[101] Wales Office, *Draft Wales Bill* (Cm 9144, 2015).

has been accompanied by a narrative of impossibilism—that is, of the legal ineffectiveness of any attempt at entrenchment, given the doctrine of Parliamentary sovereignty—and, somewhat contradictorily, by reluctance on the part of the legislative drafters to use language which can be read as being unambiguously intended to have binding legal effect.[102] Moreover, although the Smith Commission report acknowledged 'the sovereign right of the people of Scotland to determine the form of government best suited to their needs', and 'that nothing in this report prevents Scotland becoming an independent country in the future should the people of Scotland so choose',[103] no attempt has been made to give this any legal expression. Indeed, an attempt by SNP MPs to amend the Scotland Bill to make it clear that the Scottish Parliament had the right to authorize another referendum was rejected.[104] In other words, the gap between the political and the legal constitutions will remain.

The second problem with the current territorial constitution is its *lack of attention to shared rule* as a counterbalance to the dispersal of power through devolution. Mechanisms for shared rule are important, both to deal with the inevitable policy spillovers, functional overlaps, and competence disputes that arise in any system of territorially-divided power, and also, as has been argued above, to take account of territorial differences on issues which remain reserved to the centre. However, as Nicola McEwen discusses in her chapter in this volume,[105] devolution was accompanied by only weak and largely informal mechanisms for intergovernmental relations (IGR), and no reorganization at the centre to enhance territorial representation.[106]

Despite recognition of the problem of shared rule—the IGR arrangements were criticized by both the Calman Commission and the Smith Commission[107]—there have only been limited attempts to address it. Following the recommendations of the Smith Commission, negotiations are ongoing between the UK and Scottish Governments to improve intergovernmental working, and in particular to improve Scottish Government input into EU decision-making. However, calls for the basic principles of the IGR system to be enshrined in statute[108] have so far gone unanswered. Reconstitution of the House of Lords as a territorial chamber has been mooted, but is not seriously in prospect, while the injection of an element of territorial representation into the House of Commons via the introduction of

[102] At the time of writing, the provisions in clause 1 of the Scotland Bill on the permanence of the Scottish Parliament and Government have been strengthened, but still, in my view, contain scope for ambiguity; the provisions in clause 2, 'recognizing' the Sewel Convention, still do not, in my view, create a legal rule.

[103] Smith Commission (n. 100) at paras 20 and 18.

[104] HC Deb, Vol. 602, cols 111–12, 9 November 2015.

[105] Ch. 10. See also N. McEwen and B. Petersohn, 'Between Autonomy and Interdependence: the Challenges of Shared Rule After the Scottish Referendum' (2015) 86 *Pol Q* 192.

[106] The only explicitly territorial mechanisms at UK level—the Scotland, Wales, and Northern Ireland Offices, and their corresponding parliamentary select committees—predate devolution.

[107] Calman Commission (n. 10) at Part 4; Smith Commission (n. 100) at Foreword and paras 28–31.

[108] See Scottish Parliament Devolution (Further Powers) Committee, *Changing Relationships: Parliamentary Scrutiny of Intergovernmental Relations*, 8th Report 2015 (Session 4), SP Paper 809.

English Votes for English Laws (EVEL) is actually aimed at *reducing* the influence of Scottish (and Welsh and Northern Irish) MPs over legislation (directly) affecting England only. Similarly, arguments that matters affecting the constitutional framework of the United Kingdom as a whole—such as withdrawal from the EU or reform of human rights law—should be subject to parallel consent in all four parts of the United Kingdom, rather than simply governed by a UK-wide majority, have been rejected.

The basic difficulty in responding adequately to the problem of shared rule is one of constitutional asymmetry. In part, this refers to the asymmetrical nature of the devolution arrangements (and in particular, the fact that England has no devolved government), which has allowed devolution to be regarded as a set of discrete and self-contained constitutional reforms, with no implications for the constitution as a whole. But the more fundamental problem is the asymmetry of the state itself: as MacCormick put it, 'there would be a severe democratic deficit in any blocking arrangement that enabled the two-elevenths [of the UK population] to protect their position against the nine.'[109]

The final problem with the current territorial constitution—and which is emphasized more by unionists than nationalists—is its *lack of reciprocity*. In part, this is also a problem of asymmetry and concerns the legitimacy problems and inherent instability caused by divergent devolution arrangements[110]—and in particular, the perceived injustice resulting from the lack of any separate political representation for England.[111] But it also refers to the absence of any explicit mechanisms to tie Scotland—and the other devolved nations—into the Union.[112] In the absence of any legally recognized right to self-determination, there is also no clear understanding of the limits to that right: for instance, how often and in what circumstances it might be legitimate to hold an independence referendum—nor any clear statement of the principles upon which the Union is based, which might be invoked to resolve disagreements about the appropriate territorial distribution of power.

This aspect of the territorial constitution has been almost entirely ignored post-referendum. Reforms to the devolution arrangements in Scotland, Wales, and Northern Ireland are proceeding through discrete and unconnected processes, while reforms in England—EVEL and the misleadingly-named 'city devolution' programme[113]—are in no way commensurate with the arrangements for self-government in the other parts of the United Kingdom. Any notion of an

[109] *Questioning Sovereignty* (n. 36) at 195.

[110] Mitchell, *Unfinished Business* (n. 54).

[111] See: A. Henderson et al, 'National Identity or National Interest? Scottish, English and Welsh Attitudes to the Constitutional Debate' (2015) 86 *Pol Q* 265 at 268.

[112] See G. Brown, *My Scotland, Our Britain: a Future Worth Sharing* (Simon & Schuster 2014) ch. 7; J. Gallagher, *The Day After Judgment: Scotland and the UK After the Referendum* (Policy Scotland 2014); Bingham Centre for the Rule of Law, *A Constitutional Crossroads: Ways Forward for the United Kingdom* (British Institute of International and Comparative Law 2015); Constitution Reform Group, *Towards a New Act of Union: a Discussion Paper* (2015), available at <www.constitutionreformgroup.co.uk>.

[113] See Cities and Local Government Devolution Act 2016.

overarching framework for devolution thus remains radically under-developed.[114] The essential problem here is the continued dominance of a political rather than a constitutional logic to devolution.[115] The problems of territorial governance being addressed through devolution have been viewed primarily through a political (and sometimes—as in the case of EVEL—a party political) lens, to be resolved as best suits local circumstances, with no concern for their overall coherence or long-term implications.

To adequately address these problems would require a root and branch overhaul of the territorial constitution probably including, as the Bingham Centre has argued, a written constitution.[116] Yet such a prospect seems wholly unrealistic. In the first place, there appears to be no political appetite for anything other than piecemeal reform. Any attempt to 'crystallize'[117] the territorial constitution would be a major change to the deep structure of the constitution, which values flexibility above all else. Such a radical departure would require some precipitating constitutional impetus, which simply does not appear to be present. As before the independence referendum,[118] the main focus of constitutional attention at UK level is now on issues other than the future of the Union—primarily, Britain's membership of the European Union and reform of human rights law—and the direction of travel is back towards, not away from, the traditional constitutional model.

Secondly, even if it were a realistic prospect, it is highly questionable whether a comprehensive constitutional resettlement would be desirable. The value of the political constitution lies not just in its flexibility but also in its (sometimes strategic) ambiguity, which allows competing understandings of the constitution to be maintained simultaneously without having to be finally resolved.[119] The territorial constitution above all has operated as an 'incompletely theorized agreement';[120] it has been 'a protean concept, taking different forms in different places'.[121] Any attempt to define and codify the Union therefore risks either being so bland and abstract as to be pointless,[122] or else exposing rather than resolving territorial disagreement. It may also act as an obstacle to further evolution at a time when understandings of the territorial character of the state are in flux.[123]

[114] The Bingham Centre argues that key principles can be derived from the devolution case law, including the principle that 'while there are differences of detail between the three devolution regimes, they are nonetheless best seen as a single body of legislative reform for the United Kingdom, accompanied by a single body of case law.' *Constitutional Crossroads* (n. 112) at 16. However, this is a highly contestable claim.

[115] See J. Mitchell, *Devolution in the UK* (Manchester University Press 2009) at 220–2.

[116] *Constitutional Crossroads* (n. 112) at 19.

[117] Gallagher, *Day After Judgment* (n. 112).

[118] McHarg, *A Tale of Two Constitutions* (n. 55).

[119] See M. Foley, *The Silence of Constitutions: Gaps, 'Abeyances', and Political Temperament in the Maintenance of Government* (Routledge 1989).

[120] C. R. Sunstein, 'Incompletely Theorized Agreements' (1995) 108 *Harvard Law Review* 1733.

[121] M. Keating, 'Can the Union Be Saved From Unionists?' (*Centre on Constitutional Change blog*, 18 September 2015).

[122] Brown, *My Scotland* (n. 112) at 195.

[123] On the value of constitutional 'unsettlement', see N. Walker, 'Our Constitutional Unsettlement' [2014] *PL* 529.

In these circumstances, evolutionary change—or 'muddling through'[124]—may be the best option on offer, and may eventually arrive at a stable equilibrium. For instance, the claimed impossibility of achieving legal entrenchment of the Scottish Parliament arguably underestimates the extent to which the doctrine of Parliamentary sovereignty has been qualified in recent years,[125] and may therefore be further qualified in future, including as a result of devolution. Nevertheless, in an evolutionary constitution, there can be no certainty that any statutory statement of the permanence of the devolved institutions would have that effect. The UK constitution is thus, by its nature, resistant to explicit steering, and in that sense the territorial constitution may accurately be described as unreformable. Moreover, in the meantime, the management of territorial relations must remain a fundamentally political matter. While attitudes to the future of the Union remain deeply polarized, there will be an ever-present risk that political disagreement may explode into constitutional crisis, whether over issues such as the scope or exercise of devolved powers, broader constitutional questions such as EU withdrawal, or merely the direction of public policy.

V. The constitution of an independent Scotland

The final element of the constitutional case for independence presented it not merely as a means of allowing Scotland to escape from an unsatisfactory constitutional position within the United Kingdom, but, more positively, as an opportunity for constitutional renewal. In other words, the constitutional discontents animating the desire for independence go beyond the territorial constitution to encompass a more comprehensive critique of the United Kingdom's political system: its inadequate democracy;[126] its lack of security for rights; and its overweening executive power.[127] Again, we see here a consistent thread between arguments for independence and arguments for devolution. According to the Claim of Right, 'the failure to provide good government for Scotland is a product not merely of faulty British policy in relation to Scotland, but of fundamental flaws in the British constitution.'[128] The Scottish Constitutional Convention thus sought not only decentralization of power from the United Kingdom to Scotland, but also to 'usher in a new way of politics that is radically different from the rituals of Westminster: more participative, more creative, less needlessly confrontational'.[129]

[124] See C.E. Lindblom, 'The Science of "Muddling Through"' (1959) 19 *Public Administration Review* 79.

[125] See eg *R v Secretary of State for Transport ex p Factortame (No 2)* [1991] 1 AC 603; *Thoburn v Sunderland CC* [2003] QB 151; *R (Jackson) v Attorney General* [2006] 1 AC 262; *R (HS2 Action Alliance Ltd) v Secretary of State for Transport* [2014] UKSC 3.

[126] Particular criticisms relate to the role of the unelected House of Lords, and the non-proportional nature of the House of Commons' electoral system.

[127] See eg Scottish Government, *Written Constitution* (n. 22) at paras 1.4–1.5.

[128] *Claim of Right* (n. 13) at para. 1.2. See also paras 4.2, 4.4, 4.5, and epilogue.

[129] *Scotland's Parliament, Scotland's Right* (n. 13) at 9. See also B. Crick and D. Miller, *To Make the Parliament of Scotland a Model for Democracy* (John Wheatley Centre 1995).

In the case of independence, the constitutional innovation was to be a written constitution, in contrast to the United Kingdom's 'unwritten' constitution, which would be developed through an inclusive and participatory process by an independent constitutional convention.[130] According to Nicola Sturgeon, 'the prospect of a Constitutional Convention and a written constitution are themselves positive reasons for voting Yes.'[131] This was particularly important as a way of emphasizing why the clean break entailed by independence would be more desirable than simply reforming the devolution settlement. It also served to underline the political differences between Scotland and the United Kingdom, being justified by reference both to the claimed existence of a distinct Scottish constitutional tradition (which could be more authentically realized in an independent state) and to the modernization and normalization of Scotland's governance arrangements.[132]

There are several possible responses to the constitutional renewal argument. One is to question the premise that independence is either a necessary or a sufficient condition for constitutional change. As to the former, Jackson argues that the nationalist critique of the shortcomings of the British state is ground in a New Left analysis[133] which

> does not seem to have been updated to take account of the large constitutional changes wrought by the Labour government of 1997–2010 ... These fundamental steps towards making Britain a more plural, inclusive and democratic state—regardless of whether they are ultimately far-reaching enough—suggest a flexibility and capacity for reform in British political institutions that is underrated by nationalist critics.[134]

In addition, as Page points out in his chapter in this volume, the devolved institutions in Scotland already enjoy considerable organizational autonomy, which is set to increase further once the Scotland Bill is enacted. Undeniably, though, Scottish voters are not currently fully in control of their governance arrangements, which leaves them at risk of constitutional reforms which the majority do not support—such as EU withdrawal or human rights reform.

Viewed simply as an argument about where formal powers to undertake constitutional reform are situated, the constitutional renewal argument seems simply to be an example of the broader democratic case for independence. In fact, however, the point is a different one, namely that a new constitutional beginning would provide an *opportunity* and *impetus* for radical and comprehensive reimagining of governance arrangements that *in practice* is unlikely to occur in a continuing constitutional order—particularly one like the United Kingdom which, as discussed above, combines flexibility with a fundamental constitutional conservatism. Thus, while the path to a constitutional convention and permanent written constitution was clearly marked if Scotland had voted Yes to independence,[135] it is

[130] Scottish Government, *Written Constitution* (n. 22).

[131] *Constitutional Future* (n. 59).

[132] See eg *Scotland's Future* (n. 17) at 332, 334–5.

[133] *Political Thought* (n. 33) at 50–2.

[134] *Political Thought* (n. 33) at 52.

[135] Section 33 of the draft interim constitution required the Scottish Parliament to make provision, as soon as possible after Independence Day, for the establishment of an independent constitutional

very difficult to identify a similar prospect in the UK context. Although proposals have been made for the establishment of a UK constitutional convention,[136] the issue is not, at least for the foreseeable future, seriously on the political agenda. In any case—and partly for the reasons discussed in the last section—it would be a much more complex and challenging undertaking in a UK context compared with an independent Scotland.[137]

However, if independence would provide greater opportunities for constitutional reform, it does not follow that it would in fact produce substantially different outcomes. For instance, while the formal design of the Scottish Parliament included some significant innovations—most importantly in relation to its voting system—the substantive implications for the conduct of government and politics in Scotland have been much more limited than expected.[138] This is because proponents of a new politics underestimated the degree of political continuity that devolution in fact entailed. Given that independence would itself build upon devolution, there would again be substantial continuity at the level of the day-to-day operation of the constitution which might blunt the radical edge of any formal constitutional changes.

In any case, there were considerable elements of continuity in the constitutional arrangements proposed by the Scottish Government. For instance, its draft interim constitution would clearly have involved an evolutionary development of Scotland's current constitutional framework, rather than a revolutionary change.[139] There were also some more surprising examples of constitutional conservatism, such as a commitment to retain the monarchy, and not to increase the size of the Scottish Parliament. Although these arrangements would all have been provisional, there was a clear danger of path dependency limiting the likelihood of more fundamental change being adopted in the permanent constitution.

Further, the idea that there is a distinctive Scottish constitutional tradition which could inform a new Scottish constitution is itself highly questionable.[140] Political actors in Scotland frequently appeal to a claimed Scottish tradition of popular sovereignty as opposed to Parliamentary sovereignty, and this principle

convention charged with the task of drawing up a written constitution—Scottish Government, *The Scottish Independence Bill: a Consultation on an Interim Constitution for Scotland* (2014).

[136] Most notably by the House of Commons Political and Constitutional Reform Committee, *Do We Need a Constitutional Convention for the UK?*, 4th Report 2012–13, HC 371.

[137] Though this is not to suggest that a Scottish Constitutional Convention would not be without its challenges too. See generally S. Suteu, 'Developing Democracy through Citizen Engagement: the Advent of Popular Participation in the United Kingdom's Constitution-Making' (2015) 4 *Cambridge Journal of International and Comparative Law* (forthcoming).

[138] See eg P. Cairney, 'Scotland's Future Political System' (2015) 86 *Pol Q* 217; and see Page, Ch. 12 in this volume.

[139] See A. McHarg, 'A Constitution for an Independent Scotland: the Draft Scottish Independence Bill' (*Scottish Constitutional Futures Forum blog*, 21 June 2014).

[140] For a contrary view see W.E. Bulmer, 'The Emergent Scottish Constitutional Tradition: Scottish, Nordic and Global Influences' in Müller (ed.), *Scotland 2014 and Beyond* (n. 46).

was to be enshrined in the interim constitution.[141] However such a claim is both of dubious historical accuracy[142] and of limited practical utility. Although it says something important about the location of constituent power within the state, it is not clear what further implications it has for the content of the constitution. Whilst the principle of popular sovereignty was invoked to justify the participatory constitution-making process that was envisaged,[143] it is clear that in reality these proposals owed more to comparative experience than to indigenous constitutional practice.

Nevertheless, the near-certainty that an independent Scotland would have ended up with an entrenched written constitution[144] would have been a significant departure from the UK constitutional tradition. In addition, the kind of constitution envisaged by the Scottish Government—not just 'a procedural framework for democratic participation' but one with 'an instrumental and transformative' role[145]—would have further accentuated the constitutional distance travelled. For Nicola Sturgeon, '[t]he constitution should ... set out the aspirations we have for our country and our vision for the future.'[146] The Scottish Government therefore proposed—albeit acknowledging that its voice would be only one amongst many—that the constitution should contain extensive rights guarantees, as well as various substantive commitments, for instance to a ban on nuclear weapons and the sustainable use of natural resources.[147]

In envisaging a heavily substantive constitution, though, the Scottish Government left itself open to charges of inappropriate politicization of the constitution, of over-judicialization, and of seeking illegitimately to bind future generations. It therefore sat uneasily with the claim that independence would enhance the democratic legitimacy of government in Scotland. The Scottish Government could also fairly be accused of complacency about the effectiveness of Scotland's existing democratic institutions, proposals for institutional and democratic reform being noticeably absent from its constitutional agenda.[148] However, there were voices during the referendum debate calling for more radical constitutional reforms,[149] and the constitutional convention would have provided an institutional platform for the articulation of such proposals—as well as for a broader debate about the appropriate form and content of the constitution.

[141] Draft Scottish Independence Bill, ss 2 and 3.

[142] See C. Kidd, 'Sovereignty and the Scottish Constitution before 1707' (2004) *Juridical Review* 225.

[143] Sturgeon, *Constitutional Future* (n. 59).

[144] The possibility that the process of drafting a permanent, written constitution would have failed cannot of course be excluded.

[145] Bulmer, *Scottish Constitutional Tradition* (n. 140) at 218.

[146] Sturgeon, *Constitutional Future* (n. 59).

[147] See Scottish Government, *Written Constitution* (n. 22) at para. 1.10. A number of substantive commitments were also included in the draft Interim Constitution—Scottish Government, *Interim Constitution* (n. 135).

[148] Cairney, *Scotland's Future Political System* (n. 138).

[149] See Bulmer, *Scottish Constitutional Tradition* (n. 140) at 218–19.

VI. Conclusion

The aim of this chapter has been to show that, despite the lack of clear evidence of constitutional discontent in Scotland ahead of the 2014 referendum, there was—and continues to be—a coherent constitutional case to be made for independence. However, certain tensions within the independence case, and the contestable nature of some of its assumptions, mean that it can be regarded as persuasive, but not incontrovertible. Independence may reasonably be considered to be *an* answer to the problems identifiable in Scotland's current constitutional position, but it cannot be regarded as *the* answer.

The constitutional case for independence is also inescapably a nationalist one—however uncomfortable some Yes supporters may have been with that idea. It is a nationalist case because it hinges on the acceptance of the relevance of Scotland as a self-determining political community. Paradoxically, however, what allowed the Yes campaign to play down its explicitly nationalist character is precisely the non-controversial nature of that claim in the Scottish context. That fundamental point was conceded when the Scottish Parliament was established in 1999. Indeed, as I have also sought to demonstrate, there is a striking similarity between the constitutional arguments used to justify devolution and those used in support of independence.

In part, this may have been a matter of attempting to piggyback support for independence upon the popularity of devolution. However, more fundamentally, I would argue that it also indicates that devolution did not fully answer the constitutional problems that its proponents identified. From this perspective, the apparent public satisfaction with Scotland's constitutional arrangements prior to 2011 may perhaps suggest quiescence rather than consent; in other words, it may have been attributable to the relatively favourable political and economic conditions during the first decade of devolution—political alignment between Westminster and Holyrood and generous public spending provision—rather than to a more fundamental resolution of the underlying constitutional discontents.[150]

In the wake of the independence referendum, political circumstances are very different and—when combined with evidence about voters' primarily instrumental reasons for rejecting independence—cannot give supporters of the Union much comfort. As I have sought to argue in this chapter, finding a satisfactory constitutional home for Scotland within the Union is not likely to be easy. At present the constitutional direction of travel therefore appears to be towards greater autonomy for Scotland rather than towards any stronger cleaving to the Union. Only time will tell whether Scottish voters are prepared to take the further step towards independence; whether their attitude becomes one of 'why not?' or rather 'why bother?'

[150] Cf. Mitchell, *Unfinished Business* (n. 54) at 470, although he is talking about constitutional dissatisfaction in England.

6

Making the Case for Union

Exactly Why Are We Better Together?

Jim Gallagher

This chapter looks at the arguments for Scotland's remaining part of the United Kingdom, mainly as made during the referendum campaign. It discusses how the issue was framed, as a positive case for the Union or a negative one against independence, and sets out the positive case, the three different aspects of union—political, economic, and social—defended during the campaign, and how they hang together. A core part of the argument is that these three aspects are mutually reinforcing. The United Kingdom is a union state, so Scotland is both Scottish and British, with separate Scottish institutions dealing with Scottish matters and expressing Scottish identity, as well as UK institutions shared with the other nations in the Union.

Political union makes economic integration possible. Integration with the UK economy provides Scotland with greater opportunity and less economic volatility, and has made Scotland one of the United Kingdom's richest regions.[1] Economic integration involves fiscal union, which supports a stable currency union, but sharing taxes and public spending also makes social solidarity effective across the whole territory. As a result, the United Kingdom has a common political, economic, and social citizenship, which in its turn bolsters political union. Such sharing and a sense of belonging go together, and most Scots feel both British and Scottish.[2] It is not possible, as proponents of independence claimed, to retain all these economic and social aspects of the Union while breaking up the political union which makes them possible. Finally, the chapter reviews the temptations of independence, how these arguments stand after the general election, and the further development of the United Kingdom's territorial constitution and Scotland's place in it.

[1] See eg Office for National Statistics (ONS), *Regional Gross Value Added (income approach)* (2013), available at <www.ons.gov.uk/ons/rel/regional-accounts/regional-gross-value-added—income-approach-/december-2013/stb-regional-gva-2012.html> accessed 14 November 2015.

[2] See eg David McCrone and Frank Bechhofer, *Understanding National Identity* (Cambridge University Press 2015).

I. Framing the question: Positives and negatives

The referendum framed the question addressed to the Scottish people in two important ways. Firstly, it was binary: independence or not? The potential range of Scotland–UK constitutional relationships was boiled down to a choice about separate statehood. This was SNP policy, and the only referendum which the UK Government (who had the legal powers)[3] were willing to enable. The SNP toyed with the idea of a third option, but did not pursue it. A multiple-choice referendum might have been technically possible, though the construction of the options and the vote-counting rules would have determined the outcome. (It would have had to consider voters' second preferences and a middle option, the second preference of most voters, would have won. So the authors of the middle option would have been writing the constitution.)[4]

Secondly, the question was 'Should Scotland be an independent country?' so supporters of independence became the Yes Campaign, and those campaigning to stay in the United Kingdom supported a No vote. Most UK referendums have asked voters to say yes or no to a proposed change. The first was different: voters were asked whether the United Kingdom should *stay* in the European Community, and that is how the UK Government wanted to frame the forthcoming EU referendum. The Electoral Commission however concluded a Yes/No question was the wrong approach there: instead voters will be asked to say which of two statements, one for remaining and one for leaving, they support. The Commission did not take that approach in Scotland.[5] It was clearly a political objective of the SNP, controlling the referendum process, to be seen as positive, and paint their opponents as negative. Negativity was indeed a persistent criticism of the Better Together campaign. Campaigning for No comes with a negative air, but much 'negativity' was criticism of the particular story of independence presented by the SNP. They sought to minimize its risks, claiming many things, for instance the currency, would remain unchanged. This is rhetorically clever: assert something superficially plausible and accuse your opponent of negativity—'talking Scotland down'—for challenging it. At a more profound level, however, independence has an emotional appeal, based on a patriotism most Scots will instinctively share. The case for union is not without emotion, but its reasoned arguments may seem negative when contrasted with a tug at patriotic heartstrings.

Nevertheless there was presented, if not always heard, a positive case for Scotland being in the United Kingdom. Many of the benefits of independence can be had within the United Kingdom, and the benefits of union are more or less

[3] But cf. Tickell's Ch. 14 in this volume.

[4] See I. McLean, J. Gallagher, and G. Lodge, *Scotland's Choices: The Referendum and What Happens After It* (Edinburgh University Press 2013; 2nd edn 2014) ch. 1 for more detail.

[5] The Electoral Commission argued that having two 'positive' words, 'yes' and 'remain', linked in the EU ballot slanted voters too far in one direction, but it was acceptable to have just the one 'positive' word on the Scottish paper. This has the air of a *post hoc* rationalization.

by definition the risks of independence: they are what would have been lost had Scotland left the United Kingdom. That case remains at least as strong today, not least because some of the forecast risks have crystallized very tangibly.

Supporters of independence were arguing for dramatic change. Better Together opposed it, but was not defending the constitutional status quo. The Scotland Act 2012 was already increasing the Scottish Parliament's tax powers, and the pro-Union political parties each proposed further increases in powers. Although the proposals were similar, they were not crystallized into a single offer until after the referendum. They now take the form of the legislation to implement the Smith Commission recommendations. Both sides in the referendum campaign were therefore arguing for change. The one option not available to Scots was the status quo, the Scottish Parliament of 1999, still less the pre-devolution world.

II. Making a positive case

The two main regulated campaigns were Yes Scotland and Better Together; others were peripheral. Both were dominated by political parties, and the campaign was like an election lasting over two years. Campaigning is ephemeral. Arguments that filled the headlines one day were replaced by others the next. Especially in a 24-hour news cycle, journalism relentlessly simplifies and exaggerates, emphasizing conflict and personality over analysis and reflection. But the referendum was unusual in having a government on each side, and most of the significant publications setting out the arguments were written in government. The Scottish Government's 'White Paper' *Scotland's Future*[6] described itself as a guide to an independent Scotland, and made the SNP's case for independence. It offered answers to 'frequently asked questions'. (Voters were reassured that, amongst other things, Scotland's time zone would not change, and Scotland would be in the Eurovision Song Contest.) *Scotland's Future* was a big document of 650 pages, strong on positivity, heavy with reassurance, but light on detailed analysis. The UK Government's *Scotland Analysis* programme[7] was literally and metaphorically weightier: thirteen documents, heavy with data and economic and fiscal analysis, but not readily accessible to ordinary voters. Other academic analysis, notably ESRC funded work, informed the debate.

In a little-reported lecture at Glasgow University in 2013 Alistair Darling set out Better Together's positive case at some length, under the title *We Belong Together: The Case for a United Kingdom*. This was subsequently published as a booklet.[8] Better Together, he said, wanted Scots to make a positive choice to remain part of the United Kingdom, not merely to reject the risks and

[6] Scottish Government, *Scotland's Future: Your Guide to an Independent Scotland* (2013).

[7] All the documents can be found at: <www.gov.uk/government/collections/scotland-analysis>.

[8] Better Together, *We Belong Together: The Case for a United Kingdom* (2013, 2014) available at <http://b.3cdn.net/better/8e048b7c5f09e96602_jem6bc28d.pdf> accessed 14 November 2015.

uncertainties of independence. While the onus was on those who wanted to break up the Union to justify the change, there was an obligation on those supporting the United Kingdom to explain the positive reasons why. There were first of all hardheaded reasons—Scotland's interests were best served by remaining in the United Kingdom; but there was also a choice about values and belonging, a matter as much of the heart as the head. This argument was built on a historical understanding of Scotland's political union, and moved on to consider its economic and social aspects.

A. A political union and its consequences

The Union between Scotland and the rest of the United Kingdom is a political union. It is the union of Parliaments negotiated in 1707, set out in the Treaty and Acts of Union. That is what a Yes vote would have ended. Most of the argument—and certainly the hardheaded or instrumental case for the Union—was however about the economic and social consequences that would have followed. The most obvious characteristic of political union is that the United Kingdom has a single international personality, dealing with foreign relations and defence. Armed conflict had been endemic pre-Union between Scotland and England, but ceased thereafter. The arguments for banding together for defence are strong, and accepted by most Scots. Scotland will be more secure, and have more influence in the world. Not all UK decisions may be popular, or even wise, but two thirds of Scots have consistently taken the view that Westminster should deal with defence and foreign affairs.[9] That means that Scotland is represented at the EU, on the UN Security Council, and in other international bodies by one of the world's largest nations, rather than being a small nation which has to be a price-taker in international relations.

Political union leads to economic integration. After peace, trade was one of the objectives of the Scottish negotiators of 1707—access to English-controlled markets. Political union also makes it possible to share resources to guarantee standards of welfare across the territory of the union, irrespective of the prosperity any one part. This can be described as a social union, and sharing resources is also needed to ensure the stability of an economic (and currency) union. This argument for the three interconnected aspects of union was made first in the Reports of the Calman Commission,[10] developed by Better Together, and reinforced in United Kingdom government publications. The comparison with the European

[9] See J. Curtice, *So Where Does Scotland Stand on More Devolution* (ScotCen Social Research 2013) available at <www.natcen.ac.uk/media/282285/ssa13-devo-max-briefing-report.pdf> accessed 14 November 2015. The one defence issue that was controversial in the campaign was renewal of the Trident deterrent. This appears to divide traditional SNP supporters (strongly opposed) from the Scottish population (evenly split).

[10] Calman Commission, *The Future of Scottish Devolution Within the Union: A First Report* (2009); Calman Commission, *Serving Scotland Better: Scotland and the United Kingdom in the 21st Century* (2009).

Union is instructive. It is a partial political union—neither a nation state, nor a federal institution. It has substantial, but not complete, economic union: trade is not wholly free, not all countries share the European single currency, and there is no fiscal union to underpin it (an argument very material in the referendum). It is not a social union as there is no resource sharing to guarantee public services or benefits in different countries. This has been most tellingly evident in Greece in recent years. Other EU taxpayers assume no obligation to support public spending in Greece, whose government cannot deal with its economic problems by currency devaluation, and hence is forced to make huge spending cuts. The Yes campaign argued economic union would continue without political union: the EU's travails are a telling counterexample of the difficulty of doing so.

Specifically, the Scottish Government argued that Sterling would remain an independent Scotland's currency, and that the UK Government's rejection of currency union was a deliberate untruth, intended to make independence look more risky than it really was. This is discussed in detail below; for now it is worth noting that Yes campaigners conspicuously avoided using the Eurozone as an example.

B. A political union, but a multinational state

It has become almost trite to describe the United Kingdom as a union state. The instruments which joined Scotland to England (and Wales) were the Treaty of 'Union' and the Acts of 'Union'. Legally, what would have been dissolved had Scotland seceded was the 'union of the kingdoms'. In the academic literature, a union state is rightly seen as one formed by the coming together of previous states but retaining some of the characteristics of the pre-union institutions.[11] J.P. Mackintosh[12] argued that this exactly described Scotland's relationship with England.

This is not just an interesting historical description of how the territory of the United Kingdom was consolidated as, say, France was consolidated into today's hexagon. It has political, legal, and constitutional implications. The most striking was that the UK state readily acknowledged the Scottish people could freely choose to leave.[13] This has been taken for granted. It contrasts markedly with the Spanish approach to the possibility of secession by Catalonia or the Basque country. The argument there is about whether the people in these places have the power to choose, on terms driven by their substate government. The Madrid Government regards the constitutional norm of the 'indissoluble unity' of the Spanish nation as overriding. Not so in the United Kingdom. The UK Government and Parliament acknowledged remarkably readily that membership of the United Kingdom was

[11] S. Rokkan and D. W. Unwin (eds), *The Politics of Territorial Identity: Studies in European Regionalism* (Sage Publications 1982).

[12] J. P. Mackintosh, *The Devolution of Power: Local Democracy, Regionalism and Nationalism* (Penguin Books 1968).

[13] The so-called Edinburgh Agreement committed both governments to 'respect' the result of the referendum, either way.

a choice, and that the sovereign entity for this purpose was the Scottish people. (There is an irony here: nationalism demands the Scottish people should become sovereign; it turns out they have been sovereign all along.) The UK state accepts Scotland is a nation, which could choose to be a separate nation.

So the Union state of the United Kingdom is a multinational state: a state consisting of more than one nation.[14] To assert this, however, is to deny one of the founding myths of Scottish nationalism. ('Myth' is not used offensively: myths are stories we tell ourselves to explain our nature and origins. All institutions have them. The question is how much truth and explanatory power they have.) The nationalist myth is of the sturdy Scottish nation, sharing a monarch with its aggressive, hegemonizing neighbour, being bullied into surrendering its sovereignty, sold out by its elite of the time, and absorbed into England. Only in the second half of the twentieth century did patriotic Scots rediscover Scotland's identity, leading to a Scottish Parliament and now the opportunity of independence.

This myth lacks both historical accuracy and explanatory power. As the historian Colin Kidd[15] has shown, union with England was contemplated in Scotland long before 1707. Scotland needed a strategy for dealing with a much more powerful neighbour. The 1707 Treaty was not the 'incorporating union' which the English had hoped for (and some thought they had achieved). The Scots' negotiating position was weak, but they were not powerless. They had leverage over the succession to the Crown, and secured things that mattered to them. At a time when religion mattered more than any political issue, Scotland and England had fought themselves to a standstill over which was the 'one true Protestant religion'; the Union recognized that there were two: Anglican and Erastian in England, Calvinist and proto-democratic in Scotland. It is easy to forget today how significant this was, to the whole population. Almost no one, save in the elite, had a voice in the old Scots Parliament. Almost everyone had some place in the church.

At the time of the Treaty, the domestic state consisted largely of the courts and legal system. Those were left unchanged and they remain today. As the powers of the state became wider, domestic institutions were created to discharge new functions—everything from education to agricultural improvement. Typically, these new bodies were Scottish boards, commissions, or government departments.[16] What they were not, in a pre-democratic age, was democratically accountable to Scots.

So it is easy to see from the eighteenth to the twentieth century Scotland retaining its own institutional identity, even as it became more and more economically integrated with the rest of the United Kingdom and its Empire.[17] But this

[14] Keating suggests a *plurinational* state, on the basis that there are competing claims to nationhood as well as different nations. See M. Keating, *Plurinational Democracy: Stateless Nations in a Post-Sovereignty Era* (Oxford University Press 2001).

[15] C. Kidd, *Union and Unionisms: Political Thought in Scotland 1500–2000* (Cambridge University Press 2008).

[16] For an insider's history, see J. S. Gibson, *The Thistle and the Crown: A History of the Scottish Office* (HMSO 1985).

[17] The economic benefits Scotland took from Empire are well documented. See eg T. M. Devine, *Scotland's Empire 1600–1815* (Allen Lane 2003).

historical description gives the lie to the notion that the creation of the Scottish Parliament in 1999 was a bolt from the blue, or (as in the tedious nationalist trope) the 'reconvening' of the late mediaeval institution which voted itself out of existence in 1707.

1999 was the democratization of existing Scottish governmental institutions: putting elected MSPs in charge of Scottish domestic policy; putting a Parliament on top of a legal system; and creating a democratic Scottish polity. It worked smoothly principally because the institutions of government were already there and did not have to be created from nothing. But they were domestic policy institutions, dealing with public services. Three significant policy areas were reserved to the United Kingdom: foreign affairs and defence, which in some senses define a nation state; macroeconomic policy and tax; and social security, the welfare state provided in cash rather than kind. This reflects how powers are allocated in most federal states. Typically, state, provincial, or land governments deal with most public services. Federal institutions deal with external relations, macroeconomics and most (but not all) tax, and social security.

C. Economic union: The benefits of economic integration

Most of the debate in the referendum campaign was not about constitutional principles. Economic issues dominated. This is not surprising. It took place in the aftermath of a global financial crisis, in which Scottish banks played a notorious role. The effects on the UK economy and public finances meant the debate was held against a background of falling living standards, high unemployment, cuts in public services, and reductions in welfare payments. So Yes campaigners could easily blame this on the present constitutional arrangements, and claim an independent Scotland would be free of such problems. The economic argument for the Union, nevertheless, is one of economic opportunity for individuals and businesses and greater certainty at a time of insecurity, through sharing risk.

Scotland has been part of the deep economic union for so long it is easy to take it for granted. The United Kingdom is an integrated economy, in terms of trade, labour, and capital markets. Trade was a Scottish objective in 1707, and Scotland's economy benefited hugely from the Union. In the second decade of the twenty-first century, the rest of the United Kingdom is overwhelmingly Scotland's biggest market. Scottish exports to it make up about a third of Scotland's economic output: roughly double those to the rest of the world combined; nearly four times as much as to the rest of the EU.[18] Their largest single component is services, notably finance and insurance, reflecting the significance of the Scottish financial services sector, which has around 90 per cent of its customers elsewhere in the United Kingdom, and directly or indirectly is said to account for 7 per cent of Scottish employment.[19]

[18] *Scotland's Future* (n. 6).
[19] HM Government, *Scotland Analysis: Financial Services and Banking* (Cm 8630, 2013).

The United Kingdom is a home market for Scottish businesses because there is a single business and regulatory framework, and (in the European jargon) no tariff or non-tariff barriers to trade. It is well established that international borders create barriers to trade. How significant depends on which sector: all exporting industries are affected but the more regulated the business, the greater the challenges to cross-border trade. Most businesses find it more difficult to trade with other countries than in the domestic market.[20] Financial services is an extreme case: there is very little cross-border selling of financial products, despite EU rules allowing for it, as businesses have to adapt to the complex regulatory framework in each jurisdiction. According to the UK Government,[21] 'international borders reduce economic integration, impeding flows of goods, capital and labour, even where countries are members of single markets without formal barriers to trade'. The overall effect of independence in creating trade barriers is hard to assess (being hypothetical) but HM Treasury estimated the potential impact of these so-called 'border effects' on Scotland's UK trade, and so economic growth. Over thirty years, a Treasury paper speculated, they might reduce trade by up to 80 per cent and Scottish household income by about £2,000 a year.[22] The size of the effect is arguable: that it exists is not—reducing border effects is what drives the creation of free trade areas everywhere.

These economic arguments go back to David Ricardo and Adam Smith: free trade allows individuals, firms, or even countries to specialize in what they are better at delivering than others. In practice Scotland has done this. As it happens, its trade with the United Kingdom is concentrated in sectors which are obviously vulnerable to border effects: warship building, financial services, or even higher education being notable examples. Any reduction in trade would be bad for the whole United Kingdom, but much more significant for Scotland than the rest of the country. Trade with Scotland is only about 3 per cent of the rest of the United Kingdom's exports.[23]

But that is to express a positive advantage as a negative risk. Benefiting from economic integration, Scotland is, even at a time of difficulty, one of the best-off regions of the United Kingdom. On the measure of Gross Value Added (GDP) Scotland is the third richest region of the country, at 94 per cent of the UK average per head, behind only London and the South East.[24] It has a similar showing on measures such as household income. One of the most striking statistics to emerge during the campaign[25] was that Scottish per capita economic growth had exceeded or equalled the UK average for every period since the statistics were first

[20] About one-third of businesses report legal and regulatory barriers to trade even within the EU. See UK Trade and Investment, *Business Strategies, Barriers and Awareness Monitoring Surveys* (2010–2013), quoted in HM Government *Scotland Analysis: Business and Microeconomic Framework* (Cm 8616, 2013).

[21] *Scotland Analysis: Business and Microeconomic Framework* (n. 20).

[22] HM Government, *Scotland Analysis: Macroeconomic and Fiscal Performance* (Cm 8694, 2013).

[23] *Scotland Analysis: Business and Microeconomic Framework* (n. 20).

[24] ONS (n. 1).

[25] *Scotland Analysis: Macroeconomic and Fiscal Performance* (n. 22).

collected in 1963. This is a benefit of economic integration and would be put at risk by the creation of a separate state.

Individual Scots benefit from economic integration too. The United Kingdom is a single labour market with complete freedom of movement for education, work, or retirement. As a result, 700,000 Scots live elsewhere in the United Kingdom, and each year about 1 per cent of the population moves either north or south across the border.[26]

D. Economic union: Risk sharing

Scotland is a small, open, country in a globalized economy, and one of the benefits of being part of a larger economic union is sharing risk. Risk comes in different forms. In recent years, the biggest economic risks that Scotland has faced stemmed from the financial crisis, in which the mismanagement of the Royal Bank of Scotland and Halifax Bank of Scotland, both headquartered in Scotland, played a leading role. The cost of dealing with this crisis was borne by the United Kingdom as a whole, and not by Scotland alone. As the assets of the Scottish banking sector were more than ten times Scotland's GDP,[27] it would not have been realistic for Scottish taxpayers to stand behind those banks as UK taxpayers did. The banking crisis was a recent example of an economic shock affecting Scotland more markedly than the rest of the United Kingdom. Historically, others have included the decline of traditional heavy engineering and coal mining. Today, the collapse in the price of oil and its effect on the North Sea industry and tax revenues is a shared risk, not one carried by Scotland alone.

The UK Government published a little noticed comparison[28] of Scotland and the small European countries the Scottish Government had chosen as comparators. It showed these small open economies had experienced much more severe effects in the global financial crisis. Scotland had been cushioned by being in the United Kingdom. But this was not obviously at the price of economic performance: overall Scotland's economic performance had been as good as typical comparator countries, just less volatile. Because they are carrying economic risks themselves, these countries typically follow cautious fiscal policies, and have higher tax rates. In Sweden, Finland, and Denmark, for example, taxes amount to 46 per cent of GDP rather than 38 per cent in Scotland.

The implication is that an independent Scotland would have to follow a markedly different economic model: more exposed to international than domestic trade; and self-insuring against volatility by following a cautious fiscal policy, with implications for taxation and spending. Whether in the very long run Scotland would be more or less successful economically as a result is

[26] *Scotland Analysis: Work and Pensions* (Cm 8849, 2014).

[27] *Scotland Analysis: Financial Services and Banking* (n. 19).

[28] *Scotland Analysis: Macroeconomic and Fiscal Performance* (n. 22) and *Scotland Analysis: Fiscal Policy and Sustainability* (Cm 8854, 2014).

impossible to say. But there is certainly no guaranteed 'independence bonus'. The SNP argued independence would give them tools to boost the economy and that *if* an additional 115,000 jobs were created, and *if* annual growth in labour productivity were boosted from 2.2 per cent to 2.5 per cent, and *if* net migration into Scotland rose from 16,000 to 24,000 per year, onshore tax receipts would go up £5 billion a year after 15 years, an 'independence bonus' of £2000 per household. This is ludicrously hypothetical. Two things are however guaranteed. In the long run, there would be less access to UK markets, via border effects; in the short run, inevitably, significant economic disruption caused by the necessity of moving to this markedly different economic model. Independence would have to deliver substantial long-run gains in order to offset these transitional losses. There is no evidence that it would do so, and good reason to think the opposite.

The economic case made for independence was surprisingly weak. It was argued, for example, that the fiscal decentralization consequent upon independence would lead to greater economic growth. There is a cottage industry of economists arguing whether fiscal decentralization does or does not promote growth. Some say it does, others that it might have the opposite effect.[29] At the very best this is an unproved conjecture, and hardly the basis for creating a new state. Most economists would probably subscribe to the view that it is not where economic decision-making powers are exercised that influences growth, but what choices are made: some small countries do well, others badly. Different proponents of independence, of course, argued for quite different economic approaches. Those on the left wanted Scandinavian levels of public spending; those on the right saw Scotland as another low tax jurisdiction like Luxembourg. Voters could project their economic vision, whatever it was, onto a state that did not yet exist. The only certainty is that at least some of them would have been disappointed.

E. Fiscal union

Being part of a larger state means sharing risks. The most obvious example is not in private economic activity economy but in tax and public spending. All states pool resources across their territories, redistributing from areas with more income to those with less, cushioning different parts of the country from falling receipts or increases in expenditure need. This is one of the defining characteristics of a state, and had Scotland become independent it would necessarily have ceased to share fiscal resources with the rest of the United Kingdom. Everyone except proponents of independence accepted that this would be substantially to Scotland's disadvantage.

[29] eg Baskaran and Feld conclude 'While initial estimations suggest that fiscal decentralization causes lower growth rates, we ... conclude that fiscal decentralization is unrelated to economic growth': T. Baskaran and L. P. Feld, 'Fiscal Decentralization and Economic Growth in OECD Countries: Is there a Relationship?' (2013) 41 *Public Finance Review* 421.

The basic arithmetic is well known, found in the long-standing series of Scottish Government publications, *Government Expenditure and Revenues in Scotland*.[30] Detailed comparative spending figures can be found in HM Treasury's *Public Expenditure Statistical Analysis*.[31] During the campaign the implications of this arithmetic were explained by independent bodies such as the Institute for Fiscal Studies[32] and by other academics and, in great detail with long term projections, by the UK Government.[33] The underlying fiscal reality is easy to understand. Scotland raises, per head of population, rather less in ordinary taxation than the UK average. This is not surprising: it is better off than most of the country but does not have the taxable capacity of London and the Southeast. But its expenditure is markedly higher, by about £1,300 per head a year. So, other things being equal, Scotland raises a bit less and spends a lot more, and so structurally has a deficit proportionately a lot bigger than that of the United Kingdom.

But other things might not be equal, because Scotland, if independent, would have access to most of the United Kingdom's offshore oil assets. Looking backwards, it is plain that Scotland's deficit would have been less than the United Kingdom's in many years, and in the 1980s, with oil revenues at their peak, Scotland would have run a surplus. But oil is in decline, and during the referendum campaign it became clear that Scotland had moved into a weaker fiscal position than the United Kingdom. This was a crossover moment: until the Scottish Government published the data for 2012–13 it was possible for them to claim Scotland with oil was in a stronger fiscal position than the United Kingdom. (The phrase used was 'relative surplus' concealing the fact that an oil economy was nevertheless running a substantial deficit.) The projections for oil revenue, almost whatever the oil price, were for further substantial falls, as oil became more expensive to extract and gradually ran out. Scotland's long-term fiscal position was correspondingly weaker. Every independent expert on fiscal policy agreed with this.[34]

Within the United Kingdom, this is not a fiscal problem for Scotland. Scottish public spending was (and is) supported by all UK taxes, of which North Sea oil is a small part. The risk of oil revenues falling does not fall on Scotland alone. A drop of £6 billion a year is around 10 per cent of Scottish public spending, but only

[30] Scottish Government, *Government Expenditure and Revenues in Scotland* (2014) at <www.gov.scot/Topics/Statistics/Browse/Economy/GERS> accessed 14 November 2015.

[31] HM Treasury, *Public Expenditure Statistical Analysis* (2014), available at <www.gov.uk/government/statistics/public-expenditure-statistical-analyses-2014> and HM Treasury, *Public Expenditure Statistical Analysis* (2015), available at <www.gov.uk/government/statistics/public-expenditure-statistical-analyses-2015> accessed 14 November 2015.

[32] D. Phillips, *Business as Usual? The Barnett Formula, Business Rates and Further Tax Devolution*, IFS Briefing Note BN155 (Institute for Fiscal Studies 2012).

[33] *Scotland Analysis: Fiscal Policy and Sustainability* (n. 28).

[34] eg IFS (n. 32); A. Armstrong, 'Commentary: Scotland's Currency and Fiscal Choices' (2012) 219 *National Institute Economic Review* F4; and R. Crawford and G. Tetlow, 'Fiscal Challenges and Opportunities for an Independent Scotland' (2014) 227 *National Institute Economic Review* R40. Apart from the structural problem of higher inherited spending and lower onshore taxes, economic analysts also suggested Scotland would have to pay higher interest rates on the international markets to fund its deficit, with consequent tax and spending implications (Armstrong, ibid).

1 per cent of the UK budget. For Scotland outside the United Kingdom such a drop would require fiscal retrenchment on a large scale. Seldom has a theoretical risk crystallized more swiftly than this one. Oil revenues have been falling for some years, but the collapse in the oil price shortly after the referendum has reduced them by an order of magnitude. The effect on Scotland's fiscal position has been dramatic. Recent estimates, by Fiscal Affairs Scotland,[35] are summarized in Table 6.1 below. Scotland's projected structural deficit compared to the United Kingdom is around £8 billion a year, about £1,500 per head greater than the United Kingdom's deficit. Since then, oil revenues have fallen even further.

These figures are easy to understand, but also subject to much obfuscation. So the table benefits from explanation. Scotland has higher public spending than the rest of the United Kingdom, by over 10 per cent per head. It raises in ordinary taxation ('onshore income') slightly less than the UK average. Its overall fiscal position, however, should take account of North Sea oil revenue ('offshore income'), which would accrue to Scotland if it were independent (or under fiscal autonomy). Now that oil revenues are very small compared to the past, Scotland's deficit is inevitably much larger than the UK deficit, by about £1,500 per head of population. So *just to be in the same position as the United Kingdom*, Scotland on its own would have to cut spending by 12 per cent or more, or raise taxes to yield the same amount.

Table 6.1 Scotland's structural deficit compared to the United Kingdom

	2014–15	2015–16	2016–17	2017–18	2018–19	2019–20
Scotland						
Spending £billion	68.4	68.9	68.7	69.0	70.4	74.0
Onshore income £billion	52.3	54.1	56.8	59.3	62.0	65.2
Offshore income £billion	2.3	0.6	0.5	0.6	0.7	0.6
Deficit £billion	-13.8	-14.1	-11.3	-9.1	-7.8	-8.1
Deficit per head £	-2583	-2643	-2103	-1687	-1429	-1599
UK						
UK deficit per head £	*-1398*	*-1158*	*-603*	*-193*	*+80*	*+105*
Difference						
Difference per head	-1186	-1485	-1501	-1494	-1509	-1599
Difference £billion	**-6.3**	**-8.0**	**-8.1**	**-8.1**	**-8.2**	**-8.7**

Source: Fiscal Affairs Scotland 2015, simplified[36]

[35] Fiscal Affairs Scotland, *Monthly Bulletin Supplement: Government Expenditure and Revenue Scotland (GERS) 2015*, available at <http://fiscalaffairsscotland.co.uk/wp-content/uploads/2015/03/Supplement-on-GERS-2015-rev-180315.pdf> accessed 14 November 2015.

[36] These calculations are based on the assumption that Scotland carries a *per capita* share of inherited debt; I argue below that this is reasonable. But they also assume that Scotland's deficit costs the same as the UK's to finance, which would be over-optimistic for an independent Scotland.

It is helpful to understand not only the basic arithmetic but the underlying reasons. Scotland's relative structural deficit is driven less by a shortfall in taxation, much more by high public spending. Here again the arithmetic is simple. Of the £8 billion a year additional deficit, £7 billion is higher spending. Where does this additional money go? Not on so-called 'non-identifiable' expenditure, like defence, foreign affairs, and debt interest. In calculating the fiscal balance the Scottish Government simply share this out *per capita*. Not much on UK reserved expenditure. This is almost all pensions and benefits. There is little extra expenditure here, about 2–3 per cent per head, amounting in total to perhaps £0.5 billion. It is almost all in devolved expenditure, calculated by the Barnett formula, and spent by the Scottish Government, where the 'excess' lies. That budget is around £30 billion a year, and Scotland enjoys devolved expenditure of roughly 20 per cent per head more than the UK average, and indeed compared with what it could fund if it relied on Scottish tax resources only.

1. Barnett

How has this come about? In short, through the Barnett formula. This simple piece of algebra has generated large amounts of spending and extraordinary amounts of comment.[37] When it was introduced in 1978, one Treasury objective, ironically enough, was to reduce the opportunities for Scottish Office special pleading and so restrain the growth of Scottish spending. Between 1978 and 1999, it was used to determine increasing proportions of the Scottish Office budget; and in 1999 this piece of administrative convenience became in effect part of the constitution of the United Kingdom, as it determined the new Scottish budget in a simple, depoliticized, way.[38]

Barnett works on a simple principle. Each year when additions are made to so-called comparable budgets in Whitehall departments, a population share of the change is added to the existing Scottish budget. Reductions are treated similarly, and both are colloquially referred to as 'Barnett consequentials'. The same system operates for Wales and Northern Ireland (though not for NI welfare spending). As a result, because expenditure in Scotland starts out higher, the percentage increase in the Scottish budget will be smaller than the percentage increase in comparable English budgets. Other things being equal, over time, devolved expenditure should tend to the same per capita level as comparable expenditure in England, as an increasing proportion of the budget will comprise the per capita consequentials added each year.

[37] For a summary see J. Gallagher and D. Hinze, *Financing Options for Devolved Government in the UK* (University of Glasgow 2005) available at <www.gla.ac.uk/media/media_22218_en.pdf> accessed 14 November 2015.

[38] Strictly, it is used to calculate the Scottish Government's so-called Departmental Expenditure Limit (DEL), by analogy with the DELs of UK Government departments. The items not in DEL are 'annually managed' expenditure (AME), which is much smaller. Leaving aside local government taxation, the most significant elements of AME are pensions in payment for teachers and NHS staff, whose associated pension contributions are found from within DEL. So it is reasonable to assume that Barnett determines virtually the whole Scottish budget other than devolved taxation.

Scottish expenditure has however not converged to English levels after nearly 40 years of Barnett. Much has been written about whether Barnett has been 'bypassed' to avoid convergence. There were some bypasses: for many years Barnett did not apply to the whole budget, excluding for example the financing requirements of nationalized industries. No studies have demonstrated whether this was to Scotland's advantage or not. Quite possibly not. In some respects the detail of the formula may have favoured Scotland,[39] but in each spending review the inexorable arithmetic means the percentage increase in the Scottish budget is smaller than in comparable budgets. But one other thing has changed: population. Over the period of the operation of Barnett, Scotland's population has declined relative to England's, by roughly 10 per cent. The English population grew; Scotland's was largely static. The existing budget in each spending review, the so-called 'baseline', was not adjusted for this change and was spread over a relatively smaller number of heads, tending to drive relative per capita expenditure up[40].

So additional spending in Scotland is a consequence of Barnett. Barnett is the main reason why Scotland, relying only on its own taxes and without big spending cuts, would run a very much larger deficit than the United Kingdom. So it is no surprise at all that the pro-Union campaign promised to retain Barnett. Much more puzzling is the SNP's policy of 'Full Fiscal Autonomy' under which Barnett would be abolished and Scotland would rely on its own resources. The inevitable consequence of this doctrine would be very big cuts in public services, much more than current austerity.

Whether these levels of public spending can be justified by some measure of need is a moot point. Scotland can argue some greater spending needs (population health and the cost of providing services in remote areas are often mentioned). And need is an elastic concept. Nevertheless, budgets 20 per cent above the UK average are hard to generate from any needs formula.[41] Some have suggested the high spending was unacknowledged compensation for Scotland's sharing North Sea oil revenues. There is no evidence of a direct connection, but the net effect has been that Scotland has banked oil revenues with the rest of the United Kingdom, and drawn them down in a steady flow, rather than in volatile amounts. In that sense, the United Kingdom has been Scotland's oil fund. One Scottish economist[42] made this assessment: 'I … can conclude not only has Scotland received a significant dividend from North Sea oil revenues, it has been almost fully compensated for these higher revenues by higher public

[39] One example, apparently gaining Scotland £600 million a year, is explained in Phillips (n. 32).

[40] The absence of Barnett 'convergence' may be down to other factors as well as population change: for a more detailed analysis, see J. D. Gallagher, 'Algebra and the Constitution: The Fiscal Framework of the Scotland Bill' (*A Gwilym Gibbon Centre Working Paper*, January 2016) available at <www.nuffield.ox.ac.uk/Research/Politics%20Group/Working%20papers/Documents/Gallagher%20WP%20-%20Algebra%20and%20the%20Constitution.pdf> accessed 13 February 2016.

[41] See eg House of Lords (2009), Select Committee on the Barnett Formula, *The Barnett Formula* 1st Report of 2008–9, HL Paper 139.

[42] B. Ashcroft, *Has Scotland Already Spent its Oil Fund?* (*Scottish Economy Watch*, July 2013) available at <www.scottisheconomywatch.com/brian-ashcrofts-scottish/2013/07/has-scotland-already-spent-its-oil-fund.html> accessed 14 November 2015.

spending.'[43] Two numbers illustrate this simply. In *Scotland's Future* the Scottish Government say that since 1980 Scotland has generated £1,350 per head additional tax each year at today's prices.[44] This is mostly from oil. Scottish public spending exceeds the UK average at today's prices by £1,339 per head. It looks as though the SNP's ancient slogan, 'It's Scotland's oil' turned out to be true after all. So it was.

2. *Arguing about the numbers*

Proponents of independence simply claim all these fiscal numbers are wrong, or deny the arithmetic is relevant. In the White Paper,[45] the Scottish Government referred to historical 'relative surpluses'[46] but dealt only with one year's spending, 2016–17, the supposed first year of independence. They made the numbers look good by assuming, first of all, large oil revenues—£6.8–7.9 billion, triple the £2.3 billion estimate made by the UK Office for Budget Responsibility at the time. OBR's estimates today are very much lower, at £0.5 billion.[47] (SNP ministers also proposed some cuts, mainly from dropping Trident, but these were small, and partly offset by promised increases.) In what must count as a truly heroic denial of the fiscal arithmetic, SNP ministers also said that Scotland could create an oil fund[48] as well as support present spending. Supporters of independence are still prone to claim that oil revenues are volatile and that this can be dealt with by creating an oil fund. Maybe this would have been a good idea in the past, though public spending in Scotland would have been much lower as a result over the last twenty-five years. But no fund exists today, and to create one even more spending cuts would be needed. Scotland would have to run a surplus in order to put money in the bank. As we have seen, major cuts would be needed even to get to a deficit proportionate to that of the United Kingdom. So this is nothing but an oil fantasy.

The fiscal arithmetic for Scotland in the United Kingdom assumes that Scotland carries a per capita share of government debt. So to generate a more favourable fiscal forecast the Scottish Government also suggested Scotland might not contribute a population share to the United Kingdom's inherited National Debt.[49] The

[43] This point is highly relevant to the argument made by the Scottish Government that an independent Scotland would pay less than a per capita share of the UK's inherited debt because Scottish oil revenues has swollen UK coffers in the past.

[44] *Scotland's Future* (n. 6) at 384. The White paper does not mention relative spending levels.

[45] *Scotland's Future* (n. 6) at 75—the only one of 650 pages to discuss fiscal issues, despite the argument that independence would end austerity.

[46] The White Paper also said that as a proportion of GDP Scottish public spending was lower than the UK's, and drew the misleading conclusion that it was therefore more affordable. The first statement is true if offshore GDP is included, but the conclusion follows only if around 40 per cent of offshore GDP can be taken as tax revenues. That is completely impossible.

[47] This persistent and surely deliberate over-estimation of potential oil revenues continued after the referendum. An *Oil and Gas Bulletin* (Scottish Government, 2015), one of a series issued intermittently at politically advantageous times, made new projections in June 2015. The lowest possible oil price it assumed was $70 a barrel. The price at that time was just over $60, and at the time of writing is $44.

[48] Actually, two oil funds: *Scotland's Future* (n. 6).

[49] The argument was that Scotland had contributed more in the way of revenues in past years, but additional spending did not seem to be acknowledged.

argument ran (and still runs in some quarters) that as the United Kingdom had made clear to the markets that it would honour all gilts issued, it was absolving Scotland of any liability. What's more, as Scotland had contributed oil revenues its historic share of debt should be less. The UK Government was having none of this. It argued that it was indeed the 'continuing state' in international law,[50] and so accepted that it retained the obligation to the lenders but the cost of repayments would be part of the overall allocation of assets and liabilities after separation. Debt costs the order of £5 billion a year, so even if it had all been written off, Scotland would still be facing an additional structural deficit a year compared to the United Kingdom (an additional cut of 5 per cent of public spending, say.) Why the United Kingdom would agree to anything other than a per capita share was never made clear. Indeed as Scotland would immediately become a borrowing nation a refusal to accept these liabilities might drive its interest rates higher.[51] Mr Salmond cheerfully muddied these waters by saying that Scotland would refuse to accept a share of debt if the United Kingdom refused to have a currency union. This made good headlines, but Scotland outside a monetary but trying to use Sterling anyway would face even worse fiscal problems: it would have to run a surplus to accumulate reserves to finance trade in its economy.

Overall, the evidence that fiscal union is in Scotland's interest is clear, and the arithmetic is largely incontrovertible. The case made for the Union included unequivocal commitments that it would continue, and explicitly that Barnett would remain for public service funding. This is a very tangible benefit of the Union, but willingness to share resources in this way is a sign of common citizenship, and a signal of belonging, which will take us into the argument for a social as well as economic union. But first it is helpful to look at the campaign's other main economic issue, the currency, and how it too connects to fiscal union.

F. Currency union

The connection between economic integration and fiscal sharing is that together they make for a successful single currency, in the jargon of the economists 'an optimal currency area'. Whether Scotland and the rest of the United Kingdom would share the pound after independence was a major dividing line in the referendum campaign. Opinion polls suggested that a substantial majority of Scots wanted to retain the pound. The position of the SNP government was that a currency union would remain, despite independence. This was part of their presentation of independence as only a small change. They argued the United Kingdom could not prevent Scotland from using the pound. By contrast, the UK Government argued that

[50] Something the Scottish Government was inclined to dispute, when it suited it to do so, but not in relation to debt. See further Bell, Ch. 9 in this volume.

[51] The Scottish Government also assumed that an independent Scotland would pay the same rates as the UK for its borrowing. This is implausible as smaller countries pay higher rates. They issue less debt and so it is less easy for lenders to sell on. So they pay a so-called liquidity premium, even if they are prudent borrowers. Various estimates of the size of this premium were made during the campaign but all were necessarily speculative.

in the absence of a fiscal union, and given that Scotland's economy would diverge from the United Kingdom's, a formal currency union would be in the interests of neither country.

The currency argument managed to combine technical complexity and emotional resonance in equal measure. The technical issues were extensively covered in the Scotland Analysis programme, notably the paper *Assessment of a Sterling Currency Union*,[52] and in the ESRC funded research.[53] An authoritative and dispassionate technical account was given by the Governor of the Bank of England in January 2014.[54] He explained that successful currency unions required first of all very similar economies, so that they reacted in the same way to external changes; secondly, they needed banking unions, so that the financial system could be managed as a whole; and finally they needed fiscal union, public resources shared across the whole territory of the currency union. Drawing on Canadian experience, he suggested that successful currency unions required a central authority controlling fiscal resources of approximately 25 per cent of GDP. These conditions are met in the United Kingdom today, though not, in contrast, by the Eurozone. As a result, the Eurozone is endeavouring to build a banking union and struggling with the consequences of the absence of fiscal union, for Greece especially. UK taxpayers pay for the pensions and public services for every part of the country, whatever the tax income raised in each. Not so in the European Union: German taxpayers do not pay Greek pensions.

The implications of the Governor's analysis were followed through by the UK Government, which concluded that a post-independence sterling currency union would not be stable. A banking union, and an effective deposit guarantee scheme, would be difficult to devise; and the absence of a fiscal union and the divergence of the economies would render a currency union unstable. History bears this out: the one recent example of a European country splitting into two was Czechoslovakia becoming Slovakia and the Czech Republic. The two countries shared a currency after separation, in a formal currency United Kingdom of the sort proposed by the SNP. It became clear within days this was unstable, and separate currencies were created within weeks.

The Scottish Government had no answer to these challenges, other than that their Fiscal Commission had recommended a currency United Kingdom. More emotionally, however, independence campaigners presented this as 'bullying'. They said that there was nothing to stop Scotland using the pound. This is in one sense absolutely true: countries with no currency of their own can use another currency without formal agreement, often the dollar (or in Montenegro the Euro). But such places have no effective central bank, no sophisticated financial system, and very restricted capacity for government borrowing as a result. The currency issue

[52] HM Government, *Scotland Analysis: Assessment of A Sterling Currency Union* (Cm 8815, 2014).

[53] Crawford and Tetlow (n. 34).

[54] M. Carney, 'The Economics of Currency Unions', lecture to the Scottish Council for Development and Industry, January 2014, available at <www.bankofengland.co.uk/publications/Documents/speeches/2014/speech706.pdf> accessed 14 November 2015.

became very much an emotional argument. But the positive case for remaining in the United Kingdom is that it guarantees Scotland can use the pound sterling in a stable currency United Kingdom, and in a banking United Kingdom which secures the stability of Scottish banks—something critically needed in the 2008 financial crisis.

It is still argued by campaigners that the UK Government was bluffing and that they would have agreed formal currency United Kingdom because it was in the United Kingdom's interest; and indeed that the whole exercise was a deliberate ploy to make independence seem risky, and to exaggerate the transitional disruption to frighten Scottish voters. Those who want to believe this will no doubt do so whatever the evidence. They would do well to consider the following. First, each UK political party had agreed this stance, and reversing it would have carried a serious political penalty. Secondly, it was consistent with the advice of HM Treasury officials and the analysis of the Bank of England. Thirdly, many in the UK economic establishment were (and are) convinced that staying out of the Eurozone had been a good decision as the single currency had unresolved structural weaknesses—exactly those they had identified in the Scottish Government plans. The United Kingdom would indeed have no interest in seeing an independent Scotland fail—but its response would more likely to have been to offer immediate and private help from the Bank of England and the Treasury to set up a new Scottish currency.

G. Social solidarity

The principal purpose of fiscal sharing, however, is not currency stability. It is to ensure that public services, pensions, and benefits are available across the territory of a state, irrespective of taxable capacity in different parts of it. In other words, it allows for social solidarity and common social citizenship. This is most directly seen in pensions and benefits. There is at present virtually no territorial variation in, and no requirement for local funding of, old-age pensions and social security benefits. This is a characteristic of most welfare states. It was hard won in the United Kingdom during the twentieth century when a failing local poor law was replaced by national social security. In this sense the United Kingdom is a social, or welfare, union as well as an economic and political union.

The funding of pensions and benefits is very obviously based on need, determined solely by individual eligibility for benefit or pension payments. It does not depend on Scottish taxable capacity. Under independence, of course, this would cease.[55] Pensions and benefits are the most obvious examples of risk sharing. State old-age pensions pool the risks of demography across the whole country. Working-age benefits pool the risks of economic shocks, notably

[55] A few nationalist campaigners argued quixotically that the United Kingdom would have to keep paying old-age pensions to Scots after independence. But this should not be taken seriously.

unemployment, across the entire territory of the union. One major piece of analysis by the UK Government looked at Scotland in the UK pension and benefit system.[56] This analysis makes a strong instrumental case for Scotland continuing to pool these risks in the United Kingdom. Demographic pressures mean demand for old-age pensions are likely to increase more in Scotland than in the United Kingdom as a whole, but this demand will be met by the whole country. This is in part a corollary of economic union: Scotland's demography will be influenced by the job opportunities for younger people elsewhere in the United Kingdom. Understandably, security of old-age pensions strongly appealed not merely to pensioners, but also to Scottish voters in general, as a tangible benefit of the union.

At a time of heavy cuts in welfare benefits (if not pensions), this is a hard sell. A UK Government with little support in Scotland can be confused with the Union itself and lower benefits do not feel much like social solidarity. The arguments of risk pooling nevertheless remain persuasive. This may suggest greater devolution if it can be squared with sharing risk, as discussed later.

H. Social union: Sharing and belonging

The arguments of economic and fiscal union make a strong instrumental case for Scotland remaining inside the United Kingdom. Opportunities are widened, and risks spread across a larger population. It is simply not possible, as SNP ministers argued, to retain these benefits while ending the political union. But the case for remaining in the United Kingdom is not based solely on what resources Scotland can draw from it. There are emotional bonds too. Some are personal, family or professional. Others reflect shared history. But the social union is a common endeavour to guarantee social and economic rights. These are most directly old-age pensions, but also the guarantee of sufficient resources to fund rights such as free healthcare and schooling everywhere in the United Kingdom, irrespective of economic differences. Scotland has shared resources with the United Kingdom for centuries. At a purely instrumental level, it would be an unwise choice to leave the United Kingdom, just at the time when Scotland will lose North Sea income. But this is not just an accounting calculation. Resources are shared within countries which share a common identity, so that sharing is unconditional: London taxpayers pay Liverpudlian pensions unquestioningly. Sharing across countries is unusual and difficult, as EU experience demonstrates.

The United Kingdom shares resources because its inhabitants do share an identity. Much has been written about whether there is a coherent idea of 'Britishness', or whether it is now in decline. But a common British identity does underlie a single welfare or social union across the United Kingdom. One of the paradoxes of the referendum is that Scots became more aware of their British identity: more

[56] *Scotland Analysis: Work and Pensions* (n. 26).

than three-quarters of Scots see themselves as wholly or partly British, up from two-thirds in 1999.[57] Belonging and sharing go together.

III. The temptations of nationalism

Other chapters in this volume may make a case for independence. But those who argue for the Union need to understand nationalism's attractions. Although this is hotly denied, nationalism is first and foremost a matter of identity, an expression of who people are, quite often defined by who they are not. English nationalism tends to the anti-European; Scottish nationalism defines itself by contrast to England, pejoratively referred to as 'London' or 'Westminster'. Identity clearly mattered during the referendum campaign. Those voters identifying themselves as purely Scottish were more likely to support independence. The majority of native-born Scottish residents voted Yes. Those who saw themselves as British, and those born outside Scotland, were more likely to vote No.[58] Scottish identity has always been powerful, whether expressed in church, legal system, culture, or even sport. But towards the end of the twentieth century it became more political. The syllogism runs: all nations should be states; Scotland is a nation; and so Scotland should be a state. The major premise is flawed. Not all nations need be states, and union is Scotland's way of sharing some of the functions of a state with other nations.

Others have argued that the issue is really a decline in British identity. In the absence of Empire, with the decline of Protestantism, and the passing of generations bound together by the experience of the Second World War and the creation of the welfare state, Scots lack a shared project with the rest of Britain, and feel a declining emotional attachment to it. There is something in this. The idea of 'Britishness' has proved hard to pin down: talk of shared values can dissipate into statements so general any civilized country would sign up to them. But the fact remains that even if British identity does not have the emotional resonance it had in 1945, three-quarters of Scots still feel it, and it is powerful enough to legitimate common rights and mutual obligations with real effects in terms of resource transfers and risks willingly shared.[59]

Any critical examination of the ideal of 'Scottishness' would swiftly reach the same conclusions about its content. The idea that Scotland is intrinsically an egalitarian, left-of-centre country shackled to a right-wing England is myth. Scotland's public opinion is very like England's, even if its political representatives are not. Avowedly right-wing parties may attract only a small share of the vote, but Scots favour present austerity, as Table 6.2 shows, in proportions very similar to England.

[57] See J. Eichhorn, 'There Was No Rise in Scottish Nationalism: Understanding the SNP Victory' (*British Politics and Policy blog*, 14 May 2015) available at <http://blogs.lse.ac.uk/politicsandpolicy/there-was-no-rise-in-scottish-nationalism-understanding-the-snp-victory/> accessed 14 November 2015, for a handy summary of the identity data.

[58] See J. Curtice, 'So Who voted Yes and No?' (*What Scotland Thinks blog*, 26 September 2014) available at <http://blog.whatscotlandthinks.org/2014/09/voted-yes-voted/2014> accessed 14 November 2015, for sources of who voted what way.

[59] McCrone and Bechhofer (n. 2) argue that British identity remains powerful for just these issues.

Table 6.2 Voter Support for Austerity

	UNITED KINGDOM	SCOTLAND
% VOTING FOR CON + UKIP	50%	17%
% 'SUPPORTIVE OF PRESENT AUSTERITY' (ie think present levels of public expenditure and taxation are about right or should be lower)	60%	52%

Sources: General Election result, British Social Attitudes survey, Scottish Social Attitudes survey.

The referendum vote and general election result were not solely about identity. One of the achievements of the SNP and the Yes campaign in the referendum was to equate being Scottish with anti-austerity political sentiments, but to do so without losing the support of right-of-centre nationalist voters. The correlation between deprivation and Yes voting was noticeable, and the areas of Scotland which recorded a majority of Yes votes included some of Scotland's poorest. Two-thirds of people in Scotland's most deprived neighbourhoods voted Yes.[60] The same pattern was evident in the general election. The temptations of independence are strongest for those who feel that they have the least stake in the present arrangements, and so feel they have the least to lose. The irony, of course, is that the poorest would have suffered most from the transition to independence: it is they who depend most on public services, which were bound to be badly affected, and who have the least to fall back on at a time of economic disruption, which is the inevitable consequence of change.

A. Developing the political union: Smith and the Scotland Bill

As we have seen, political union underlies the economic and social unions: it is however anything but unchanging. Even since 1999, there has been further devolution, notably the tax-raising powers to be exercised in 2016. The UK Government has 'vacated' ten pence in the pound of income tax, and the Scottish Government has to decide whether to levy the same or a different rate: it has voted for the same. During the referendum campaign, however, the three main pro-Union political parties each proposed developing devolution further.

Each party had a commission which produced recommendations covering the same territory, with different emphases.[61] The Liberal Democrats used the language of federalism; the Conservatives emphasized the single market; and the

[60] Curtice (n. 58).

[61] Scottish Conservative Party, *Commission on the Future Governance of Scotland* (2014), available at <http://www.scottishconservatives.com/wordpress/wp-content/uploads/2014/06/Strathclyde_Commission_14.pdf> accessed 14 November 2015; Scottish Labour Party, *Powers for a Purpose Strengthening Accountability and Empowering People* (2014), available at <http://www.scottishlabour.org.uk/page/-/resources/Powers%20for%20a%20Purpose.pdf> accessed 14 November 2015; Scottish Liberal Democrats, *Federalism: the Best Future for Scotland* (2012) available at <www.smith-commission.scot/wp-content/uploads/2014/10/Scottish-Liberal-Democrats-Submission-1.pdf> accessed 14 November 2015.

Labour party the strengths of social solidarity. All recommended more tax devolution, notably income tax, to give Holyrood greater fiscal autonomy; and all recommended devolving some aspects of welfare. No common position was produced before the referendum, but shortly before it the parties agreed how the proposals would be brought together in legislation afterwards, and in the so called 'Vow' promised substantial devolved powers. This led to the Smith Commission, reporting in November 2014, and a Scotland Bill, published in draft in January and introduced into Parliament in May 2015.

There is a crude sense in which devolution is simply a compromise between maintaining the Union and aspirations for independence. Both sides of this argument however want Scots to have their cake and eat as much of it as possible. So a more nuanced question is to ask how much further it is possible to increase Scottish autonomy while retaining the benefits of economic and social union. Any answer to this question has to begin by recognizing the extent of present devolution: most public spending, and virtually all domestic policy other than social security. Substantial tax powers come in 2016. The Scotland Bill will extend them further, to create a system which is more decentralized than almost all federal countries in terms of taxation and spending. Figure 6.1 compares the proportion of spending and revenue decentralized in a range of OECD countries, and shows that under the Scotland Bill the level of decentralization in Scotland will be comparable to that in Canada or Switzerland.

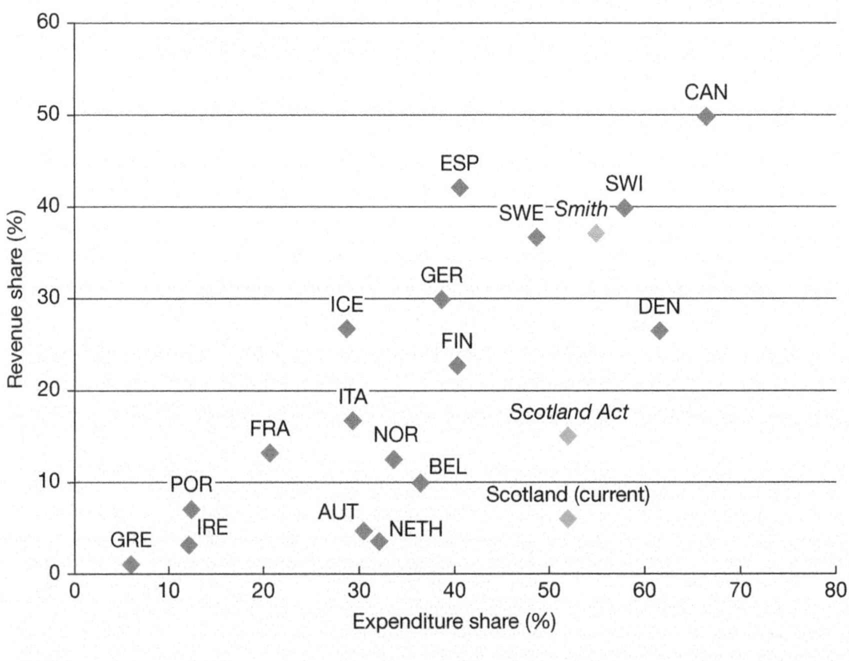

Figure 6.1 Proportion of Spending and Revenue Decentralized in OECD Countries

The tax devolution in the Scotland Bill is substantial. Virtually all income tax will be devolved, including the rates and the bands at which the different rates start. The yield of 10 percentage points of VAT (and 5 of the 10 points from the lower rated items) will be assigned to the Scottish Parliament. As a result around 40 per cent of devolved revenue will now be met from taxation belonging to the Scottish Parliament. The most radical addition to the Parliament's powers, however, relates to welfare. A number of benefits—totalling in value over £2.5 billion a year—will be completely devolved. They mostly relate to people who are sick or disabled, and will give Holyrood the power to refashion the welfare package offered. Attendance allowance, for example, is paid to pensioners, but many pensioners also receive care from local authorities: there will now be an opportunity to design a more integrated system. But in a significant move, the Government is proposing the Scottish Parliament should be able to top up UK benefits if it thinks they are inadequate. Subject to some relative details being sorted out (at the time of writing) this is a way of giving the Scottish Parliament the power to offer a more generous welfare package—higher benefit levels—while retaining most of the risk sharing with the rest of the United Kingdom. The cost of UK benefits will be borne by UK taxpayers, as now; if the Scottish people want to have a more generous welfare system they can do so: and Scottish taxpayers will have to cover the cost of the greater generosity, but only that. Politically, this makes the point that independence is not needed to have a more generous welfare state, and has been controversial in relation to cuts in tax credits.[62] Constitutionally, it says to Scotland that it can remain part of the UK social union, with UK social rights guaranteed, but operate a different (more, but not less, generous) social model if that is what Scottish opinion supports, provided Scots are willing to pay the additional taxation.[63]

B. The general election of 2015

The 2015 general election in Scotland was extraordinary. Labour support collapsed, and the SNP secured more than 50 per cent of the votes, and virtually all Scotland's MPs. So on the face of it, within less than 12 months Scottish people said two apparently contradictory things. They want to stay in the United Kingdom, and they want to be represented by the SNP. The SNP leadership however made clear this did not represent a vote for independence. Instead, they see it as a mandate to oppose UK austerity policies, and demand greater powers for the Scottish Parliament. So far as powers are concerned, the SNP manifesto

[62] These are a benefit, and are being reduced by the Conservative UK Government, against Labour opposition. Labour proposed that the Scottish Parliament should use the new powers to offset the reduction in Scotland. SNP Ministers initially resisted this idea, but now seem to have accepted it.

[63] For a fuller explanation of this, see J. D. Gallagher, *All Aboard the Constitutional Express? Where is the Scotland Bill Taking the UK* (Nuffield College Gwilym Gibbon Centre for Public Policy Working Paper 2015), available at <www.nuffield.ox.ac.uk/Research/Politics%20Group/Working%20papers/Documents/All%20aboard%20the%20Constitutional%20Express.pdf> accessed 14 November 2015.

called for 'full fiscal autonomy' or 'responsibility'. This is the notion of 'devo max', under which the Scottish Government would be responsible for all services except defence and foreign affairs, and would collect all the taxes, remitting a payment to Westminster to cover the cost of the army and any other common services.

It's not clear how seriously SNP leaders take this proposition. It is certainly not consistent with the union which was endorsed during the referendum campaign. The catastrophic fiscal consequences for Scotland are described above: balancing the books would require unsustainable expenditure cuts or tax rises. (The idea that the gap could be filled by additional economic growth resulting from fiscal autonomy is risible. As the arithmetic above shows, tax revenues would need to rise by about 15 per cent, and an additional 15 per cent growth in the economy is beyond even the unrealistic hypothetical scenarios set out by the Scottish Government during the referendum campaign.) That however is not the biggest objection to the idea of full fiscal autonomy. No substate government anywhere exercises powers like this. That is because it is not a form of devolution or decentralization, but a form of independence. It involves no fiscal sharing, other than contributing to common costs; it suffers from the same challenges to the maintenance of a currency union as independence; and it abandons any common UK economic or social citizenship. But most tellingly, it is not consistent with political union. It is inconceivable that Scottish MPs could sit in Parliament when Westminster decided no Scottish taxes, but UK taxes only. This is the West Lothian question, in a simply unanswerable form. Indeed it is the form of Irish home rule to which Parnell aspired in 1885: but the price he was willing to pay was the abolition of Irish MPs.[64] UK ministers must have been sorely tempted to give the SNP what they say they want, saving the Treasury large sums of money, enough to cut income tax by one or two pence in the pound. They must continue to resist the temptation in the interests of retaining the United Kingdom.

IV. Conclusion

The case for union between Scotland and the rest of the United Kingdom is as strong in the twenty-first century as it was in the eighteenth. Now as well as then, Scotland's political system is about safeguarding both and interest and identity, speaking to both head and heart. The instrumental arguments for where Scotland's interests lie are compelling. Economic union with England combines greater opportunity with risk sharing, and benefits both countries. On any measure of trade, job opportunity, or investment freedom, having a UK home market

[64] See J. Gallagher and I. Maclean, *Nationalists at Westminster Scotland and Ireland a Century Apart* (Nuffield College Gwilym Gibbon Centre for Public Policy Working Paper 2015) available at <www.nuffield.ox.ac.uk/News/Documents/Nationalists-at-Westminster-GG01-2015.pdf> accessed 14 November 2015.

is overwhelmingly in Scotland's interest. In an economically uncertain world, risk sharing provides security and reduces volatility. This applies in everything from international affairs to taxation and public spending, and the financial and banking system. Two collapses bookended the referendum: Scotland's banks, which had to be underwritten by the resources of the whole United Kingdom; and oil prices, which because of risk sharing did not affect Scotland's public services. Pooling those risks in the previous decades meant Scotland was entitled to expect the rest of the country to underwrite them when they crystallized. Independence of course would have ended that.

But politics is about the heart as well as the head, and most people in Scotland value and prioritize their Scottish identity. Scotland's political institutions must reflect that, and the Scottish Parliament must be as powerful as it can be without fatally undermining Scotland's interests. Here the pace of institutional change has to catch up with the public mood. Delivery of additional powers has lagged behind the demand, so that the reality of the devolution available has yet to be experienced. The powers of the Scottish Parliament must be wide enough to allow it to make real policy, fiscal, and welfare choices, so that if Scottish opinion does differ from the dominant view in England, Scotland has the tools to be able to do something about that—in public services, taxation, and welfare. Scotland must be able to put its money where its mouth is.

The institutional challenge is, as it has always been, how to reconcile wide Scottish discretion with the pooling of risk. Social union too is undeniably in Scotland's interest, even at a time when UK Governments are cutting benefits, because the demographic and economic risks continue to be underwritten by the wider risk pool. For public services, funding is already to be partly on a UK and partly on a Scottish basis. The Scotland Bill will take this markedly further, but it is of critical importance that shared UK resources remain available so that if Scotland's income decreases, the key elements of the welfare state, notably free healthcare and schooling, are not threatened. If Scotland does well, of course, it can enhance this provision. For pensions and benefits, because these are paid directly to individuals, a different approach is needed. UK pensions and benefits must be seen as an entitlement, guaranteed by UK citizenship, and supported by taxes paid across the whole United Kingdom, including Scotland. The Scotland Bill now provides a mechanism for Scotland to be able to supplement these, from its own resources, if that is where Scottish opinion truly lies.

This is a development not merely for Scotland, but the whole territorial constitution of the United Kingdom. Since the Union, the United Kingdom has allowed itself to carry a degree of ambiguity about its own nature: Scots generally understood themselves to be distinct within a union, whereas the English were traditionally confused about the difference between being English and British. England now understands its separateness more, and wants a separate expression of it. Scots, who can legitimately demand decentralization of power in a way that is consistent with the maintenance of the Union, can hardly deny the same to England. The mechanisms however will differ markedly for the dominant partner in the United Kingdom: Westminster will remain England's Parliament as well as the United Kingdom's[65] and the United Kingdom will not survive if it is simply a locus for competing nationalisms. Much thought has been given to how something which is more like the functional equivalent of a federal system might be developed, and there is merit in that. The Scotland Bill will legislate to declare the permanence of devolution within the Union, rather as in a federal constitution. But the lesson of the referendum debate is that political union is intimately connected with both economic integration and social solidarity. Economic integration is not under substantial threat, but the United Kingdom will need to have a clearer understanding of the nature of its social solidarity, perhaps through defining more explicitly the social rights which are guaranteed across its territory, and the mechanisms by which they are delivered. Given such guarantees, Scotland, and perhaps Wales and Northern Ireland too, can have the option of pursuing a more generous social model from England while retaining the benefits of union for which it has voted.[66]

Hugh MacDiarmid famously referred to the Caledonian antisyzygy,[67] a supposed kind of bipolarity in Scotland's character. As with so much of MacDiarmid, it does not do to take him too seriously, but Scots are both British and Scottish, and Scotland's political institutions must reflect that in a way which is compatible with the needs of the time. Independence can never do that, but the right form of union can. No similar term has been coined to describe the United Kingdom's multipolar nature, but its complex and untidy political institutions are beginning to evolve in a way that reflects its nature as a multinational state.

[65] For the options, see J. Gallagher, *England and the Union: How and Why to Answer the West Lothian Question* (Institute for Public Policy Research 2012), available at <www.ippr.org/publications/england-and-the-union-how-and-why-to-answer-the-west-lothian-question> accessed 14 November 2015.

[66] See Gallagher (n. 63) for how this might be done.

[67] The phrase was coined by a literary critic, C. Gregory Smith, but the idea was elaborated by MacDiarmid in two famous essays in the magazine *The Modern Scot* in the early 1930s.

7

Economics and National Autonomy

Andrew Scott

I. Setting the scene

From the outset it was clear that the economic dimension would play a central, and quite possibly decisive, role in the independence debate. That this turned out to be the case suggested that, at least in large measure, the debate was engaged on a broadly utilitarian agenda rather than on issues commonly associated with conventional nationalist political movements—culture, language, identity, and so forth. This is not to suggest non-economic issues did not surface. As examined elsewhere in this volume debates relating to broader issues of democratic accountability and governance were extensively engaged by both sides in the run-up to the referendum.[1] But it was the potential economic consequences of independence that dominated the debate, accounting for more newspaper column inches and official publication pages than any other issue. Politicians from both sides campaigned relentlessly on the implications of independence for the economy, each side offering competing estimates of the per capita income benefits from—or costs of—independence distilled and presented throughout the latter stages of the campaign. Academics, expert commentators, think tanks, business groups, and representatives of civil society across the United Kingdom offered a range of predictions (positive and negative) of the likely future states of health for the Scottish economy in the event of a Yes vote.[2] Notably few conducted a similar exercise should the status quo prevail.[3] And both the Scottish and United Kingdom Governments published an array of analytical and policy papers addressing a range of issues

[1] See McHarg, Ch. 5, and Page, Ch. 12 in this volume.

[2] Outside of the many government publications, both the National Institute of Economic and Social Research (NIESR) and the Institute for Fiscal Studies (IFS) produced a number of reports analysing various aspects of the economic implications of independence. The Economic and Social Research Council (ESRC) also funded a range of research projects on the economic and wider consequences of independence.

[3] An issue that takes on a new significance following the return of a Conservative majority government at the general election of 7 May and, at the same time, the resounding success of the SNP across Scotland.

central to Scotland's future economic prospects under competing constitutional scenarios.[4]

That economic issues took centre stage in the constitutional debate is unsurprising. For the vast majority of the public it is the economic health of the country that determines not only the prosperity and wellbeing of individuals and families, but which largely determines the quantity and quality of public services available to society as a whole. In turn this focus on the provision of public services became a proxy for a wider debate around the broad themes of social justice and social inclusion that were likely to be delivered under alternative constitutional futures. By suggesting that the essentially social democratic traditions of Scottish society were being undermined by an increasingly libertarian Westminster consensus (evidenced by austerity-driven public spending cuts that were hitting the most vulnerable in society hardest), the Yes campaign were tapping into a rich vein of political tradition in Scotland from which historically the Scottish Labour Party had benefitted, and which was to benefit the SNP in the aftermath of the referendum. Unsurprisingly the prospect of greater social justice and social inclusion under independence triggered an intense debate around the prospective state of public finances in an independent Scotland—and of the potential costs of exiting a union in which fiscal deficits in one area could be compensated by fiscal transfers from more prosperous parts of that union.[5]

Consequently, the economic segment of the constitutional debate, technical as often it was, tended to become a proxy for a much wider social and indeed philosophical discussion of Scotland's prospects under the competing constitutional scenarios. In the course of the campaign this was distilled into the 'two futures' strapline of the pro-independence movement—the choice (presented) being between remaining in a Union in which Scotland's social democratic ethos was being compromised at best, and undermined at worst, and independent statehood where policies would not only ensure adequate social protection to Scotland's citizens but where the greater social cohesion that would result would, itself, become an added source of strength for the economy.

Attractive as this prospect may have been to many voters, questions remained about the immediate economic prospects facing an independent Scotland. Would taxes—or borrowing—have to rise to support Scotland's higher (than UK average) per capita public spending? Or would these be funded by Scotland's higher (than UK average) per capita tax contributions? Would businesses (actual and potential) take fright at the prospect of independence and move their activities south of the border? Or would business prosper under a different economic policy regime? What would independence mean for the integrity of the UK internal market? Would an independent Scotland remain inside the EU? Were there reasons to believe economic growth and employment would be higher under independence? And what would be the currency in an independent Scotland? These

[4] The UK Government alone produced 16 'research and analysis' papers examining the impact of Scottish independence, the majority of which addressed aspects of the economics of independence.

[5] In a sense this was the essence of the 'Better Together' campaign.

were among the main economic questions asked ahead of the referendum and on which various expert opinions were provided.

This chapter reviews a number of these issues, although no attempt is made to offer any firm conclusions. These questions could not, and cannot, be answered in the counterfactual. Instead they would only be answered definitively in the wake of the negotiations that would have followed an affirmative vote for independence. The more modest aim is to set out and comment upon the main issues engaged in the debate; to consider how the issues raised during the constitutional debate may shape the development and implementation of future economic and social policies in Scotland; and to assess the economic implications of the proposals to reform the current devolution settlement that were made immediately after the referendum.

Two principal conjectures underpin this chapter. The first is that if the result of the 2011 Scottish Parliamentary election—which gave the SNP an absolute majority in the Scottish Parliament—meant that a referendum on independence was virtually inevitable, the economic context in which the campaign unfolded almost certainly made the 2014 referendum unwinnable for the pro-independence side. For a society reeling from the post-2008 near-death experience of its banking sector and thereafter enduring the worst recession in living memory—and only now experiencing, some five years later, the beginnings of a fragile economic recovery—it would be surprising if the average voter was not averse to exposure to the further economic risks that many claimed were unavoidable in the event of independence.

The second, and related, contention is that the decision by the UK Government (and the leaders of the main UK political parties) to adopt a 'hard exit' strategy to prospective independence negotiations meant that in the event of independence, and assuming that strategy was implemented, it appeared to many that Scotland's economy would face potentially significant and damaging short term discontinuities and disruptions. A hard exit describes the situation where the Scottish Government would receive minimal—if any—cooperation from the UK Government in managing the transition to independence. By the time of the referendum the UK Government had essentially ruled out sharing existing—or establishing new (cross-border)—institutions or agencies to implement common economic policies or facilitate economic policy coordination if Scotland become independent.[6] Under a hard exit a very inflexible definition of economic self-interest would be applied by the UK Government in its negotiations with the Scottish Government, mediated perhaps only by international (especially EU-related internal market) obligations to which the United Kingdom was bound.[7] A hard exit strategy is one that, in this context, discounts the benefits of future economic and social policy coordination. It is a strategy likely to be preferred if

[6] As we discuss below this most obviously applied to the UK Government refusal to countenance establishing a formal monetary union with an independent Scotland. However it also seemed unlikely the UK Government would agree to any proposal for the common regulation of financial services or utilities which would have adverse consequences for the unity of the UK internal market.

[7] The issue of an independent Scotland's putative status under EU law is dealt with in Ch. 8 of this volume. The Scottish Government worked on the assumption that Scotland would have

one of the negotiating parties considers its interests cannot be adversely affected to any significant extent by the effects of policy decisions taken by the other party.

A 'soft exit', which was readily identified as the Scottish Government's preference, describes a process in which both parties cooperate over economic policy to minimize the shared economic costs of Scotland's transition to independence.[8] Both governments would seek to minimize the potential disruption to either economy, and agree to future policy coordination over matters of common concern including, where appropriate, establishing shared institutions. A soft exit strategy would be rational where significant negative externalities (economic or social) occur to both parties as a result of policy decisions made by either party in isolation (ie there is a high degree of economic interdependence).

The suggestion here is not only that the UK Government adopted a hard exit position in the run-up to the referendum, but that by doing so it sought—and arguably was able—to demonstrate that the discontinuity and disruption costs of independence (the transition costs) would both be significant and would outweigh not only any prospective gains from independence, but indeed the putative costs of remaining within the Union.

Finally it is worth stressing that by the time of the referendum few experts doubted that an independent Scotland could become a successful and prosperous independent economy. This was best captured perhaps in a Financial Times op-ed penned by the highly respected economist John Kay the day before the Scottish referendum appropriately entitled 'Scotland can prosper whether yes or no'.[9] However, as we discuss later in this chapter, there was no such consensus over the immediate transition costs of a Yes vote.

II. The key economic issues

The constitutional debate unfolded against the backdrop of the most ruinous global financial crisis on record followed by a recession of a severity and duration without parallel in living memory.[10] This raises the question how significant the economic context was to the debate in shaping the narratives, and ultimate fortunes, of both anti- and pro-independence campaigns. Three issues directly linked to the economic context dominated the debate: first, the implications of

'continuity of effect' with regard to the privileges and obligations of full EU membership, notwithstanding the formal Treaty procedure that may be required to normalize its position as an independent EU member state. See Scottish Government, *Scotland in the European Union* (2014).

[8] In a series of speeches leading up to the referendum First Minister Alex Salmond implicitly identified with a soft exit strategy when he described Scotland as belonging to 'six unions', of which it only sought to exit one—the political union with the rest of the UK (rUK). An independent Scotland would remain in the other five unions: the (UK) currency union, (UK) social union, (UK) defence union, Nato, and EU.

[9] *Financial Times* (17 September 2014).

[10] For a useful review of the comparative severity of the post-2007 recession see IMF World Economic Outlook 2009, ch. 3.

the 2008–10 financial crash for the regulation and stability of the domestic financial services (especially banking) sector in an independent Scotland; second, the sovereign debt crisis that was afflicting a number of countries in the Eurozone monetary union and which critics claimed demonstrated why a future sterling monetary union would not work; third, the ongoing consequences for Scotland's public finances of the economic recession (and subsequent sluggish recovery) triggered by the crash and in which the UK economy remained trapped throughout the referendum campaign. Fourth was the issue of an independent Scotland's future in the global economy. Each of these issues will be reviewed.

A. The domestic implications of the financial crisis

The crisis in world financial markets that began in September 2008 when Lehman Brothers filed for bankruptcy quickly revealed the UK banking sector (and that of many other countries) to be exposed to unprecedented levels of risk and financial losses which, if not tackled by immediate Government action, would have presaged bankruptcies across the sector and—in all likelihood—the collapse of the entire financial system. At root, the financial crisis was the result of the conjunction of a number of inter-related factors that characterized US and European banking practices: inadequate regulation, imprudent and highly leveraged holdings by the sector of what turned out to be very high risk securitized investment products (especially sub-prime mortgage backed securities and linked collateralized debt obligations); and, more immediately, the end of the long boom in property prices in the USA and a number of European countries leading to a collapse in the value of bank assets linked to sub-prime mortgages.[11] Few events have the capacity to fundamentally shake public confidence in the entire economic system more than the risk of a collapse of the banking sector and the consequences this would have for ordinary individuals and families.

In the United Kingdom the government response to the financial crisis was three-fold. First, in early October 2008, the government announced that the Bank of England would increase the funds available under the Special Liquidity Scheme (SLS) to ensure sufficient liquidity was available to the financial system (thus stemming any putative bank run). This was augmented in January 2009 by the creation of an Asset Purchase Facility at the Bank effectively heralding the onset of quantitative easing. Second, the Government opted to part-nationalize the weakest banks to maintain their on-going viability as solvent institutions.[12] In the case of the Royal Bank of Scotland (RBS) the government ultimately acquired over 80 per cent of its shares at a cost of £46 billion—a less costly intervention was also

[11] Other than the case of Greece, it is now generally recognized that the 2008 banking crisis created the sovereign debt crisis across the EU, rather than the other way around. The popular narrative that profligate government spending created the currently high levels of public deficits and debt—and to which the appropriate response is austerity measures—commands little support among economists: P. Krugman, *End This Depression Now* (W.W. Norton & Company 2012).

[12] By so doing the Government ensured the Bank of England was not providing liquidity support to insolvent institutions—which it was not permitted to do.

necessary to save the Bank of Scotland (BoS). Third, and in conjunction with reforms implemented at EU level, the government introduced a series of major changes to the regulation of UK financial services, particularly the banking sector, intended to rectify deficiencies in the regulatory system that had created the conditions that made possible the 2008 crisis.[13] And while these measures undoubtedly saved the UK financial system from collapse, the entire episode reminded the public that even in the twenty-first century it was possible for banks to find themselves in need of direct government support on a massive scale to assure their survival.[14]

The immediate relevance of the financial crash (and subsequent policy response) to the Scottish constitutional debate was clear, if hypothetical. For the general public the collapse and government rescue of the RBS and BoS raised the question of whether an independent Scottish Government could have 'saved the banks' and, more pertinently, protected the publics' savings and other investments, not least non-state pensions. And what regulatory regime would an independent Scottish Government put in place to prevent a rerun of the events of 2008? Similar questions were also posed by the industry. The financial services sector is a major employer in Scotland, and Edinburgh is widely regarded as one of the principal 'off-centre' financial centres in the world. Outside the embattled banking sector, Scotland's financial services industry retained a high business reputation, part of which—as is true for most service providers—reflected the reputation of the UK-wide regulatory regime that ensured the rigorous standards were met both in the financial products being sold and the firms providing of these products. As the sector's main market lay in England, providers argued it was important that independence did not result in Scotland and the rest of the United Kingdom (rUK) having divergent regulatory regimes that would make UK-wide trading more costly.

Doubtless these questions would have arisen in any event. However that they played such a central part in the debate reflects the post-crisis context in which it unfolded. The difficulty for advocates of independence was that, in practice, the institutional and regulatory future of Scotland's financial services sector under independence would only be decided once exit negotiations had commenced. In theory there was no technical obstacle to designing a single (common) regulatory architecture that would continue to allow continuity in cross-border trade in financial services between an independent Scotland and rUK.[15] And while the specific issue of bank supervision in an independent Scotland attracted much comment, in principle the Bank of England could continue to provide 'lender of

[13] Maintaining the integrity of the single EU market in financial services meant that regulatory reforms in non-banking financial services were legislated principally at EU level, and implemented domestically under revised supervisory arrangements.

[14] In 2008 total UK bank assets exceeded 450 per cent of GDP, a significant share of which was accounted for by what became toxic instruments. For Ireland the comparable figure exceeded 700 per cent of GDP. This indicates the scale of the bailout required in order to rescue the financial system from collapse.

[15] The emerging EU financial services regulatory regime offered a template whereupon ultimate authority for macro-prudential and micro-prudential regulation would reside with the Bank of England, supported by newly established financial services agencies in Scotland responsible for implementing common rules and monitoring compliance.

last resort' (LOLR) liquidity provision to solvent Scottish banks, underwritten by the Scottish Government.[16] Implicitly this scenario required sterling to remain the currency in an independent Scotland and, almost certainly, within the framework of a formal monetary union with rUK.[17]

In principle, therefore, the post-independence integrity of the UK single market for financial services could be maintained by establishing the necessary cross-border institutions and agreements to maintain intact the present regulatory regime including, where necessary, creating any required adjunct supervisory authorities in Scotland.[18] However this could only be achieved if the UK Government agreed to pursue a soft exit negotiating strategy—that is, one that recognized the benefits of retaining the existing supervisory coherence of the United Kingdom. If the UK Government pursued a hard exit strategy the transition to independence would be more complex albeit feasible, not least because the regulation of financial services is almost entirely prescribed by EU regulations that are designed to achieve free movement of services. Although viable alternatives did exist to the Scottish Government's preferred approach to the joint (with rUK authorities) regulation of financial services in an independent Scotland, the absence of a detailed architecture for an alternative (to the current) regulatory regime—including market perceptions regarding the credibility of any new regime—raised concerns about the stability of the sector during a transition period.

B. The currency question: A UK monetary union and the Eurozone crisis

From the outset of the referendum campaign the Scottish Government advocated retaining sterling as the currency of an independent Scotland within the context of a formal monetary with the rUK.[19] Here the Scottish Government was following the recommendations of its Fiscal Commission Working Group (FCWG):

> ... the preferred model would be for Scotland to enter a formal monetary union with the rest of the UK with the Bank of England (the Bank) operating as central bank for the common monetary area (the 'Sterling Zone').[20]

[16] In the course of the debate considerable confusion arose between the LOLR liquidity-provider function of the central bank, and LOLR solvency-underwriting function of governments. Central banks cannot lend to insolvent banks.

[17] Cross-border trade in financial services requires a common currency regime. Exposure to exchange rate risk would deter consumers in one currency area from purchasing financial assets denominated in another currency. Of course this does not necessitate providers of financial services to be located in the currency area of their main market.

[18] As may be required under EU rules.

[19] The currency issue was addressed in a number of articles. See: A. Armstrong and M. Ebell, 'The Scottish Currency Question' in Bell et al (eds), *The Economic Consequences of Scottish Independence* (Helmut Schmidt Universitat 2014); A. Armstrong, 'Scotland's Currency and Fiscal Choices' (NIESR 2012) 219; Fiscal Commission Working Group, First Report—Annex, 'Assessment of key currency options' (Scottish Government 2013); HM Government, *Scotland Analysis: Currency and Monetary Policy* (Cm 8594, 2013).

[20] FCWG First Report (n. 19) para. 3.29.

It was acknowledged this would necessarily mean an independent government forgoing control over domestic monetary policy[21] as well as (almost certainly) obliging the government to adhere to jointly agreed rules concerning public finances (deficit and debt ceilings).[22] Underpinning the FCWG recommendation was recognition that retaining sterling within the current UK-wide monetary framework would be the best option for ensuring a stable macroeconomic framework in an independent Scotland. First, it would ensure continuity in the integrity of the UK internal market for goods, services, capital, and labour to the benefit of both Scotland and rUK. Second, it would deliver financial stability for both Scotland and rUK by ensuring consistency and coherence in the regulatory arrangements for the highly integrated UK-wide financial services sector. Third, the fiscal rules attached to the monetary union would enhance the credibility of a newly independent state in global capital markets.

The FCWG advice also reflected the view that Scotland and rUK satisfied the conditions of an 'optimal currency area' (OCA)—that is an area within which it is practicable to have a single, common currency and a single central bank responsible for conducting monetary policy for the area as a whole. The criteria for an OCA are highly open and interdependent economies, convergent business cycles, near-perfect mobility of labour, and relatively flexible wages. These criteria ensure the presence of mechanisms through which the economies within the currency area can adjust to an asymmetric economic shock without requiring income and employment stabilizing fiscal transfers from other members of the OCA.[23] And, as noted earlier, currency area agreements also include rules that restricted the fiscal policies of member governments (ceilings on government deficits and net borrowing) to ensure the fiscal activities of any one government did not destabilize economic conditions across the area as a whole. Moreover by adhering to sound public finance rules in normal times, individual governments would have sufficient fiscal headroom to implement fiscal policy responses to asymmetric shocks if required without breaching the ceilings.

One of the more dubious 'lessons' presented by the UK Government from the Eurozone crisis was that single currency areas (monetary unions) that were not also fiscal unions—that is where governments also ceded authority over national fiscal policy to collective oversight and control—were inherently unstable.[24] Certainly

[21] Since 1997 the Bank of England had been independent of the UK Government, and its Monetary Policy Committee (MPC) was mandated to use monetary policy instruments to deliver a UK annual rate of inflation no higher than 2 per cent. The Scottish Government agreed that central bank independence was a necessary for a stable macroeconomic framework in an independent Scotland, and would seek to input to the MPC appointment process. That a currency union was inconsistent with fiscal sovereignty was the central message delivered by Mark Carney, Governor of the Bank of England, in a speech just before the referendum.

[22] The Eurozone's Stability and Growth Pact provisions (budget deficit not to exceed 3 per cent of GDP and total debt below 60 per cent of GDP) were generally regarded as appropriate benchmarks. This did not imply any constraints on the rates at which particular taxes were levied, the government's public spending preferences or on government borrowing subject to an agreed upper ceiling.

[23] Where the shock hits the entire currency area some part of the adjustment could involve changes to the common monetary policy—the interest rate or the exchange rate.

[24] See HM Government, *Scotland Analysis: Currency and Monetary Policy* (n. 19).

there were lessons to be drawn from that crisis, although that Scotland and rUK would necessarily be subject to the type of crisis that afflicted the Eurozone was not one. The Eurozone does not meet the OCA criteria, comprising as it does wildly divergent economies.[25] Moreover, and with the singular exception of Greece, the sovereign debt crisis that lies at the heart of the Eurozone's troubles was not caused by fiscal profligacy on the part of member governments. Rather that crisis was a product of the commercial bank failures that swept the EU and necessitated high levels of government borrowing to bail out Europe's insolvent banking sector.[26]

While the UK Government's analysis suggested that a formal sterling monetary union would restrict the scope for fiscal policy activism in an independent Scotland, and might lead to a situation in which (BoE-controlled) monetary policy was less suitable for Scotland's economic circumstances than under the present arrangements, it did not rule this out. However in February 2014 Chancellor George Osborne announced that the UK Government would not enter into a monetary union with an independent Scotland, citing direct advice from Sir Nicholas Macpherson, then Chief Secretary to the Treasury: advice that was—in a virtually unprecedented move—made public. It was clear that Macpherson's doubts were based on political reasons:

> And so to sum up, I would advise you [Chancellor] against entering into a currency union with an independent Scotland. There is no evidence that adequate proposals or policy changes to enable the formation of a currency union could be devised, agreed and implemented by both governments in the foreseeable future.[27]

Macpherson's advice—which was that the UK Government should not contemplate a formal monetary union under *any* circumstances—seemed to confirm the UK Government had settled on pursuing a hard exit in any forthcoming independence negotiations. In response, the Scottish Government restated its position that if the UK Government refused to participate in a sterling monetary union, then Scotland would refuse to accept a share of UK debt. At the same time Scotland's First Minister accused the UK parties of 'bluff, bluster and bullying' in their currency stance, claiming it was not in the rUK interest to adhere to this position in the event of a Yes vote.

What would have transpired in the event of independence is unknowable. Certainly an independent Scottish Government did not need UK Government approval to adopt sterling as its currency (a policy of 'sterlingization'). However, although this would release the Scottish Government's fiscal policy from the constraints likely under a formal monetary union, it would also transfer to a Scottish central bank responsibility for providing sterling liquidity to the domestic banking

[25] There are very few common features between the economies of Greece and Portugal on the one hand, and Germany and the Netherlands on the other hand.

[26] Other than Greece, that the significant sovereign-debt crises occurred in Spain and Ireland reflected the strength of the (bank-financed) leveraged property booms that occurred in both countries.

[27] <https://www.gov.uk/.../Sir_Nicholas_Macpherson_-_Scotland_and_a_currency_union.pdf>.

system—sterling that would need to be earned or borrowed. Other options existed—introducing a new Scottish currency pegged to sterling or freely floating, or perhaps joining the Eurozone. However each option implied a potentially more disruptive transition to independence at least over the very short term. In a debate that was firmly focused on the economic benefits of the competing constitutional scenarios, the UK Government ruling out a formal monetary union dealt the pro-independence campaign a heavy blow.

C. Independence and Scotland's public finances

In his letter to the Chancellor advising against creating a sterling monetary union, Macpherson had alluded to the prospective state of public finances in an independent Scotland in support of his recommendation. And this emerged as the third key battleground in the debate.

The commonly used indicators of the state of health of a country's public finances are its annual budget deficit (ie the difference between annual revenues accruing to, and public spending undertaken by, a government) and the total stock of outstanding public debt, both expressed as a percentage of GDP. Budget deficits tend to arise (or increase) during economic downswings when tax revenues fall and welfare spending increases and typically are financed by government borrowing, adding—at least in the short term—to the total government debt. This poses no problems for the government assuming it repays debt when the economy recovers and government revenues exceed spending. Failure to manage the level of public debt prudently, however, will result in the level of debt increasing as a share of GDP and higher interest rates being charged by lenders on future government borrowing, with a greater share of annual government spending being spent servicing the debt.[28]

How would the public finances of an independent Scotland compare with the status quo?[29] Would independence result in a deterioration in Scotland's public finances, putting in jeopardy payments to pensioners or funding for essential public services? If independence left Scotland's government in a worse fiscal position than the status quo (ie higher deficit-to-GDP and/or higher debt-to-GDP ratios), this implied either higher taxes, lower public spending, or more government borrowing (or a combination thereof) would be required. But if the public finances in an independent Scotland were healthier than for the United Kingdom as a whole, independence would release a fiscal bonus to Scotland's taxpayers to be used to cut taxes, increase public spending, or redeem outstanding debt (or a combination thereof), or indeed launch a sovereign wealth fund in which to invest part of the

[28] This would manifest itself in a downgrading in the country's credit rating. In extreme cases, for example Greece in recent years, the government may simply be unable to borrow (sell its sovereign debt instruments) on the international capital market at any price.

[29] This was, arguably, the most contested issue in the referendum debate. See: D. Phillips and G. Tetlow, *Taxation, Government Spending and the Public Finances of Scotland; Updating the Medium-Term Outlook* (IFS 2014): Scottish Government, *Government Expenditure and Revenue* (2014); A. Armstrong and M. Ebell, 'Real Devolution: the Power to Borrow', NIESR Discussion Paper No. 437 (2014); D. Eiser and M. McGoldrick, 'Fiscal Position on Independence' in Bell et al (n. 19).

proceeds of North Sea oil revenues (and provide a financial buffer against future dips in oil revenues) as the SNP had long claimed desirable.[30]

Official data showed that over the period since the financial crash (2008–9) Scotland's public finances had fared somewhat better than for the United Kingdom as a whole. Including a geographic share of North Sea revenues (it was widely assumed that the assignment rule would prevail post-independence), Scotland's current budget deficit had been below the UK level for each post-crisis year and—notwithstanding per capita public spending in Scotland being higher than the UK average—only in the latest year (2012–13) had it risen slightly above the UK level (GERS, 2014; IFS, 2014).[31] No data was available for the debt-to-GDP ratio in an independent Scotland, although assuming the Scottish Government accepted a population-based share (8.4 per cent) of UK debt there would be no significant change in the debt burden (as a percentage of GDP) under independence to that which Scotland implicitly held if it remained in the Union.

As matters stood there seemed little reason to believe independence would, in itself, result in any significant deterioration in Scotland's public finances: indeed they could marginally improve. However if there was no doubting about the facts of Scotland's public finances before independence, their possible trajectories thereafter became a matter of the most intense debate. Three issues dominated that debate: anticipated revenues from North Sea oil, the cost of borrowing on the international capital market, and the prospects for an economic growth dividend under independence.[32] Taken together these factors would determine an independent Scotland's public finance prospects.

According to 2012–13 data, North Sea revenue would constitute around 15 per cent of total government revenues in an independent Scotland.[33] However—as recent events have demonstrated—these revenues are dependent on the rate of extraction, the tax regime, and, critically, the prevailing market price of oil. There was no consensus on either the likely movement of the oil price or future North Sea extraction rates with different authorities providing conflicting estimates on anticipated price movements[34] and likely extraction rates.[35] Critics argued that

[30] An option supported by the Fiscal Commission Working Group. See Fiscal Commission Working Group, 'Stabilization and Savings Funds for Scotland' 53–71 (Scottish Government 2013).

[31] In 2009–10 the UK deficit reached 7.6 per cent GDP before declining to 5.7 per cent in 2011–12. The comparable figures for Scotland were 7.1 per cent and 3.1 per cent respectively. In 2012–13 the UK ch deficit was 5.8 per cent GDP and in Scotland was marginally higher at 5.9 per cent GDP.

[32] A fourth but essentially long-term issue was the implications for public finances under independence of Scotland's demographic trends.

[33] Although significant, in Norway oil and gas revenues account for closer to 30 per cent of government revenues.

[34] The UK Government extensively cited OBR estimates, which forecast an ongoing decline in oil prices, while the Scottish Government pointed to a range of forecasts that contradicted the OBR to a lesser or greater extent. In the event no forecasting body anticipated the dramatic decline in oil prices that occurred early in 2015. The Scottish Government's forecasts were set out in the May 2014 *Oil and Gas Analytical Bulletin*, available at <http://www.gov.scot/resource/0045/00451335.pdf>.

[35] The Scottish Government did note that, in 2012–13, record levels of investment were being made in the North Sea which Oil & Gas UK expected to result in a significant increase in oil production from that sector.

because oil prices could be volatile, public spending plans under independence would be subject to derailment by a sudden fall in the oil price—a situation that would not arise if Scotland remained within the union.[36] Of course as the FCWG pointed out, the effects of unanticipated (oil price) shocks that temporarily reduce government revenues can be 'smoothed' by increasing the short-term borrowing or, indeed, by using reserves that had been assigned to an oil revenue-financed sovereign wealth fund.[37]

Second was the prospective cost of borrowing by a newly independent Scottish Government. Although this attracted much press comment, there is little reason to suppose the credit rating assigned to Scottish debt over the medium term would be significantly different from that assigned to UK debt.[38] The issue did become more complex when the UK Government adopted a hard exit stance by ruling out a formal monetary union with an independent Scotland and, as noted earlier, the First Minister's response by refusing to assume a share of the UK national debt.[39] Had this hard exit scenario unfolded it is not clear how the capital markets would have reacted. On the one hand any suggestion that Scotland had defaulted on its debt obligations would have damaged her reputation and tended to push down her credit rating. On the other hand Scotland would not, at least in a legal sense, have defaulted on her obligations and would henceforth be seeking to borrow on international capital markets free from any outstanding debt—a factor that almost certainly would have boosted her credit rating.

Third, the state of health of public finances in an independent Scotland would depend on future rates of economic growth and employment. A central plank in the pro-independence campaign was that transferring control over key levers of economic policy to the Scottish Government would allow it to introduce measures that would raise the economy's underlying rate of growth and, by doing so, narrow the gap between Scotland's performance and that of other small EU countries:[40]

> It is the view of the Scottish Government that this growth gap is due to the fact that, in a competitive globalized economy, targeted policies designed to capture the unique strengths and address the relative weaknesses of an economy are vital. The current

[36] See HM Government, *Scotland Analysis: Fiscal Policy and Sustainability* (Cm 8854, 2014) especially ch. 1.

[37] Coping with day-to-day volatility in oil prices is quite a different challenge than coping with the long-run implications of declining levels of oil reserves. The former can be managed by using accumulated assets (oil fund) as proposed by the Fiscal Commission Working Group (n. 19). The latter requires the government to support the emergence of alternative tax bases capable of providing a (tax) revenue source sufficient to compensate for the permanent exhaustion of Scotland's oil reserves.

[38] In May 2014 Moody's predicted that new Scottish debt would initially be assigned an investment grade A rating (two notches below the then UK credit rating), with the prospect of upward rating over time as Scotland made a successful transition to full independence.

[39] By then the UK Government had made clear that it would assume liability for the total amount of UK debt in the event Scotland opted for independence. Strictly speaking an independent Scotland could not be forced to assume any part of UK debt.

[40] For a comprehensive statement of the prospective gains from 'key levers' control see the Fiscal Commission Working Group, 'First Report, Macroeconomic Framework' (Scottish Government 2013).

constitution arrangements do not allow economic policies to be tailored to the challenges faced in Scotland. This puts Scotland at a disadvantage ... [41]

Of course not all policy levers would be fully available under the Scottish Government proposals. As long as sterling remained the currency of an independent Scotland, interest rates would continue to be set by the Bank of England Monetary Policy Committee (MPC). Moreover if Scotland and rUK did agree to create a formal monetary union, it was accepted this would require the Scottish Government to adhere to agreed fiscal rules limiting the size of annual budget deficits and the total stock of government debt.[42] While critics claimed these arrangements undermined economic policy autonomy in an independent Scotland, in practice it demonstrated the Scottish Government's recognition that maintaining a stable macroeconomic (monetary and fiscal policy) framework was essential to an independent Scotland's future prospects.[43]

However, that access to the fullest practicable range of economic policy levers would better equip a Scottish Government to tackle Scotland's underlying economic problems accorded with a fundamental tenet of fiscal federalism; that ' ... *in multilevel governments, each level of government (including the central government) will maximize social and economic welfare within its own jurisdiction*'.[44] Accordingly the availability of additional policy levers would enable the government to develop bespoke policies that boosted growth and raised economic welfare. Crucially, perhaps, independence could enable a Scottish Government to escape the austerity policies of the current government which, a range of experts contended, were undermining (rather than promoting) a return to sound public finances by lowering the economies' immediate and longer term growth prospects.[45]

One policy proposal in particular grabbed the headlines—cutting the rate of corporation tax in an independent Scotland to three pence below the rUK rate (at the time from 23 per cent to 20 per cent), a policy government analysis suggested would increase GDP by 1.4 per cent and employment by 27,000 by year 2020.[46] However the potential for an independent government to improve Scotland's rate of economic growth went beyond headline tax measures, important as these could be. The Scottish Government argued that in addition to giving it competence over the fiscal

[41] Scottish Government, *Scotland's Economy: the Case for Independence* (2013) 28.

[42] Armstrong and Ebell (n. 19) contested the necessity for the need for fiscal rules in a putative UK monetary union insofar as the externality argument that Scotland's fiscal decisions could impact on rUK stability was incorrect, given the relative sizes of the two countries.

[43] Some aspects of the debate seemed to suggest, oddly in an interdependent world, that in pursuing continuity rather than change in specific economic policy areas the Scottish Government was seeking a diluted form of independence.

[44] W. E. Oates (1972) as quoted in A. H. Hallett, 'The Scottish Economy under Independence' in Bell et al (n. 19) 45–50.

[45] In the short term public spending cuts were harming growth-generating capital investment while over the longer term the impact of unemployment resulting from austerity policies could lead to an erosion in human capital and labour productivity.

[46] See Scottish Government, *The Impact of a Reduction in Corporation Tax on the Scottish Economy* (2011). This would work by encouraging investment (both domestic and inward FDI) and output, thereby raising the tax base and increasing government revenues.

levers of growth, independence would allow it to target a range of non-fiscal policy levers on raising productivity and investment, and boost economic growth. These included industry regulation, energy markets, international trade, public procurement, and, perhaps most significant over the longer term, immigration[47]—policies that could impact positively on every sector in the economy. In setting out its vision for a successful independent Scottish economy, the Scottish Government (and the SNP) clearly saw Scotland's future as an enterprise-friendly, innovative, and socially cohesive society. This rhetoric reflected an approach to economic and social policies that emphasized partnership and cooperation between stakeholders, provided an appropriate social policy 'safety-net' and was resonant of an older 'corporatist' tradition for managing industrial relations that many regarded as underpinning the economic success of the similarly sized Scandinavian countries—the so-called 'third way' between capitalism and socialism.[48] At the same time the Scottish Government recognized that economic success was not only a matter of fostering partnership and cooperation in the workplace. It also required action to address a range of wider challenges facing Scotland's society, action that would foster closer cohesion and provide the necessary social foundations for economic success.

Independence, it was claimed, would allow the Scottish Government to introduce the reforms to Scotland's social welfare policies needed to narrow societal inequalities and deliver greater social justice. In part this would be achieved through the stronger growth and higher employment that would result from economic policies implemented after independence. But an independent government would also reform national welfare policies to strengthen social cohesion across the country—cohesion that would, in itself, act as an independent driver of economic growth and employment.[49] At one level this proposition is disarmingly simple, resting as it does on the established proposition that 'inequality effectively redistributes income from those with a high marginal propensity to consume to those with a low propensity to consume',[50] with a consequential negative effect on aggregate demand.

[47] It is well known that the principal challenge to Scotland's public finances over the longer term lies in her ageing population. Attracting migrant labour is widely recognized as a key mechanism in tackling this demographic challenge. The Scottish Government argued that the rising tide of anti-immigration in parts of the United Kingdom is leading to lower immigration that will worsen public finances and stifle growth.

[48] This approach is often associated with the tagline 'the third way' recognizing the contribution of A. Giddens, *The Third Way: The Renewal of Social Democracy* (Wiley 1998). See also C. Green-Pedersen et al, 'Neo-liberalism, the "Third Way" or What? Recent Social Democratic Welfare Policies in Denmark and the Netherlands' (2001) 8 *Journal of European Public Policy* 307–25.

[49] This rests on the proposition that social cohesion creates a pool of social capital that can be exploited to raise productivity and growth rates. The relationship between income inequality and economic growth was addressed by the Fiscal Commission Working Group, *Macroeconomic Framework* (n. 40) at 55–9.

[50] J. Stiglitz, 'Macroeconomic Fluctuations, Inequality and Human Development' (2012) 13 *Journal of Human Development and Capabilities: A Multi-Disciplinary Journal For People-Centred Development* 31–58. Stiglitz also demonstrates the mechanisms through which inequality can be a source of economic volatility that, in turn, generates further inequality—producing a downward vicious circle. For a more recent review of the relationship between inequality and economic growth see E. Dabla-Norris et al, *Causes and Consequences of Income Inequality: A Global Perspective* (IMF Staff Discussion Note 2015).

However the proposition also rests on non-traditional concepts of 'capital' that can be exploited as sources of economic growth and which augment the conventional physical and human capitals typical of growth theory. Chief amongst these is social capital, although a comprehensive audit would include both natural capital and cultural capital.[51] Although enjoying an uneasy relationship with conventional economics, the concept and components of social capital and social cohesion are increasingly regarded as key building blocks of a successful economy.[52] The civic sense of common purpose, trust, and collective commitment that underscores the notion of social capital is perhaps best captured in the clichéd expression that 'we are all in this together'. The more economic and social institutions, norms, and public policies embody this collective sense of civic responsibility and purpose, the stronger will be their overall contribution to social cohesion and the greater the value of social capital available to be invested in furthering collective social and economic goals, including growth.[53] The proposition can also be framed in the negative—that increasing inequalities in income and wealth serve to exacerbate divisions in society and undermine the sense of trust and common purpose that is essential to replenishing the stock of social capital. And although the economic (or political) consequences of depleting the quantity (or quality) of social capital are unlikely to be immediate or easily observed, ultimately they will adversely impact on growth and employment.

That the United Kingdom is one of the most unequal countries in the OECD in terms of income distribution was not disputed.[54] Moreover it was self-evident to supporters that independence would provide the Scottish Government with the necessary economic and social policy levers to reverse this trend and, by doing so, reduce economic volatility and promote social cohesion and growth. However, compelling as they were, the propositions that greater social cohesion could be achieved under independence and would positively contribute to higher growth and employment would only be tested over the long run. The nature of the constitutional debate, focused as it was primarily on the short-term prospects of an independent Scotland, meant that these propositions failed to gain much, if any, traction in the run-up to the referendum.

[51] See J. Coleman, 'Social Capital in the Creation of Human Capital' (1988) 94 *American Journal of Sociology*, Supplement: Organizations and Institutions: Sociological and Economic Approaches to the Analysis of Social Structure S95–S120. Here Coleman identifies three distinct forms of social capital: obligations and expectations, information channels, and social norms.

[52] For a review of the literature see P. F. Whitley, 'Economic Growth and Social Capital' (2000) 48 *Political Studies* 443–66.

[53] The World Bank defines social capital as referring 'to the institutions, relationships, and norms that shape the quality and quantity of a society's interactions ... Social capital is not just the sum of the institutions which underpin a society—it is the glue that holds them together'. See <http://web.worldbank.org/WBSITE/EXTERNAL/TOPICS/EXTSOCIALDEVELOPMENT/EXTTSOCIALCAPITAL/0,,print:Y~isCURL:Y~contentMDK:20185164~menuPK:418217~pagePK:148956~piPK:216618~theSitePK:401015,00.html>.

[54] In February 2015 the OECD *Income Equality Update* reported 'The level of income inequality among the total population in the United Kingdom has been well above the OECD average in the last three decades' and that 'The share of the top 1 per cent of income earners increased from 6.7 per cent in 1981 to 12.9 per cent in 2011'.

D. Scotland's future in the global economy

As a small, open economy part of the debate revolved around the consequences of independence for Scotland's position in the global economy. Considerable attention was given to the EU dimension of Scotland's external relations. In economic terms EU membership is central to Scotland's economic prospects—independent or not. The EU accounts for approximately one-half of total Scottish imports and exports. Moreover Scotland hosts a significant level of inward investment, a large part of which produces goods and services sold across the EU internal market. The EU membership question under independence is fully addressed elsewhere in this volume.[55] Suffice it to say here that such was the scale of the potential economic disruption involved that any suggestion that independence would lead to Scotland being required to exit the EU was bound to have a significant impact on the constitutional debate. And it did.

The wider global setting posed fewer uncertainties, and indeed advocates of independence provided a number of reasons why an independent Scotland could prosper in the global economic setting. For instance Skilling argues small, developed economies are better placed to adapt to the challenges of globalization in the modern context than are large economies. He attributes this to three factors: the tendency for them to have a higher level of social capital and trust than larger counterparts; a capacity to develop a coherent strategic focus in response to global challenges; and a competitive discipline linked to their relatively greater exposure to global developments than larger economies.[56] The intuitive plausibility of these explanations, along with the empirical data that demonstrated many of the 'older' smaller countries had—in the course of the financial and economic crisis—outperformed their larger neighbours,[57] added credibility to the Scottish Government's views that with independence Scotland would emerge as a successful global economy.

No consensus had formed around the second question as to whether an independent Scotland would be more successful than would be the case if it remained part of the United Kingdom. As we have already noted, this would depend, in part, on the exit conditions Scotland could negotiate ahead of formal independence. That the UK Government had, it seemed, settled on a hard exit approach to prospective negotiations implied that the transition to independence would not be straightforward. There are very good analytical reasons for criticizing the UK Government's stance in this regard. First by publicly setting out red lines (eg on currency) that potentially raised the costs of independence, it disregarded the potentially adverse consequences for the rUK of a non-cooperative series of exit negotiations with the Scottish Government.[58] Second the degree of economic

[55] See Douglas-Scott, Ch. 8 in this volume.

[56] D. Skilling, 'Centrifugal World: Why the Future is Small' (2013) *Global Brief* Spring/Summer.

[57] See eg Credit Suisse, *The Success of Small Countries* (2014). For possible lessons for Scotland see J. Rae and S. Westlake, *When Small is Beautiful: Lessons from Highly-Innovative Smaller Countries* (NESTA 2014).

[58] eg on tax competition or immigration policy, or indeed on non-economic issues such as the future of the Trident missile system based in Scotland.

interdependence between Scotland and rUK suggested that, over time, policy responses that had the effect of disrupting Scotland's economy would adversely impact on the rUK economy—not least perhaps in the external value of sterling.

III. The post referendum situation: Towards fiscal autonomy?

In the days immediately preceding the referendum the UK Government—along with leaders of the main UK political parties—announced that in the event of a 'No' vote new legislation would be enacted that would strengthen the powers of the Scottish Parliament.[59] The new arrangements subsequently unveiled proposed to increase the fiscal autonomy of the Scottish parliament by devolving complete power to set income tax in Scotland, including competence to set rates within—and create new—tax bands. Further the Scottish Parliament will receive a share of VAT receipts raised in Scotland, and have increased borrowing powers to support capital investment and to smooth temporary shortfalls in government receipts. Elements of welfare policy will also be devolved to the Scottish Parliament, enabling the Scottish Parliament to provide additional support in specific cases and where public finances permitted.[60]

These proposals, like those which informed the 2012 Scotland Act, will change the basis on which public spending on devolved issues in Scotland is financed. Until the 2012 legislation, virtually all spending by the Scottish Parliament on devolved matters was financed by a block grant from Westminster, the size of the grant being adjusted from year to year according to a formula devised in 1978 by Joel Barnett, then Chief Secretary to the Treasury. Essentially the Barnett formula provided for the Scottish Government to receive a pro rata (to its population share) increase (decrease) in its block grant to match increases (decreases) in UK Government spending on devolved policies. The 2012 legislation had provided for the Scottish Parliament to levy a new Scottish rate of income tax of one-half of the UK basic rate—the UK basic rate levied in Scotland being reduced accordingly.[61] This would mean the Scottish Parliament would be responsible for raising an additional 15 per cent of its income from taxes it directly levies in Scotland.

Both the UK Government's proposal to devolve greater authority over income tax in the wake of the referendum, and the Scottish Government's response by

[59] For a critique of the Commission's proposals, see D. Phillips, *The Smith Commission's Proposals—how big a change do they represent? And what questions remain to be addressed?* (IFS 2014).

[60] Whether the legislative proposals go as far as the Smith Commission recommended, especially regarding the devolution of welfare powers, is a matter of intense debate. After scrutinizing the UK Government proposals the Devolution (Further Powers) Committee of the Scottish Parliament concluded these fell short of what the Smith Commission had proposed. See *New Powers for Scotland: An Interim Report on the Smith Commission and the UK Government's Proposals*, 3rd Report, Session 4 (2015), SP Paper 270. For a critique of the Commission's fiscal proposals see J. Cuthbert and M. Cuthbert, *Smith Commission: Why the Economic and Fiscal Arrangements Need to be Changed* (The Jimmy Reid Foundation 2015).

[61] Two relatively minor taxes were also devolved under the 2012 legislation—stamp duty and landfill tax.

renewing its call for fiscal autonomy, has reignited the debate about 'how much' fiscal authority should be devolved to the Scottish Parliament. The financing of devolved government within a unitary state can take a variety of forms ranging from a wholly grant-based model where all devolved spending is funded by a central government grant at one extreme, to fiscal autonomy (FA) where responsibility for all fiscal functions (ie the complete array of taxes *and* (devolved) spending) are assigned to the devolved government at the other extreme.[62] Ensuring some part of revenues is raised by taxes levied directly by the devolved administration establishes a direct line of accountability between the taxpayer and elected members and should encourage government to ensure public spending is efficient. However there is no consensus about what the appropriate share of total spending raised by 'local' taxes versus central government transfers should be. Advocates of FA, on the other hand, point to two economic benefits likely to occur if public spending in the devolved jurisdiction is funded entirely by taxes levied by the devolved administration. First, and building on the previous point, this can be expected to maximize the efficiency of public spending. Second, and arguably more significantly, assigning authority for all taxes levied in the devolved jurisdiction to the devolved administration, including decisions over the tax mix (ie balance between different taxes), FA would provide the government with the fiscal levers necessary to improve the country's underlying economic performance.[63]

Critics of FA contend that the devolved government's spending plans will be vulnerable to derailment as a result of unanticipated shortfalls in revenues that no longer can be 'smoothed' by (discretionary or automatic) fiscal transfers from central government. And that this will be particularly problematic where a significant share of revenue accrues from a tax base that is unpredictable, if not volatile. In the case of Scotland this issue arises because, as already noted, around 15 per cent of revenues have typically accrued from North Sea oil taxes whose yield is directly linked to the price of oil which, as experience shows, can be volatile over relatively short time periods.[64] If public spending is to be maintained in the face of temporary revenue volatility, one or both of two conditions must be met. First the devolved administration must have competence to borrow to cover a revenue shortfall by issuing its own debt instruments on international capital markets. Debt incurred during a temporary revenue shortfall can be redeemed

[62] For a comprehensive discussion of the case for fiscal autonomy for Scotland see P. Hallwood and R. MacDonald, *The Political Economy of Financing Scottish Government* (Edward Elgar 2009). For a review of how fiscal autonomy would enhance Scotland's economic performance see A. Hughes Hallett and A. Scott, *Scotland: A New Fiscal Settlement*, GMU School of Public Policy Research Paper No. 2010–15 (2010).

[63] That there is a positive relationship between greater fiscal decentralization and improved economic performance is confirmed in three OECD Working Papers on Fiscal Federalism. See: H. Blöchliger, *Decentralization and Economic Growth—Part 1: How Fiscal Federalism Affects Long-Term Development*, WP No. 14 (OECD 2013); H. Blöchliger and B. Égert, *Decentralization and Economic Growth—Part 2: The Impact on Economic Activity, Productivity and Investment*, WP No. 15 (OECD 2013); K. Fredriksen, *Decentralization and Economic Growth—Part 3: Decentralization, Infrastructure Investment and Educational Performance*, WP No. 16 (OECD 2013).

[64] In the twelve months from June 2014 to June 2015 world oil prices fell from about $110 per barrel to around $60 per barrel.

later when prices (and so revenues) recover. Second, and closely related, the devolved administration should adhere to a medium term budget rule of 'close to balance or in surplus' in order to access international capital market at reasonable cost. Such a rule is also consistent with having available revenues from budget surpluses earned in previous years when the tax yield from North Sea oil activities was unexpectedly high.[65]

On the other hand, under FA a decline in oil prices (and so tax yield) that is expected to persist requires a different response. If taxes are not to rise—or public spending curtailed—over the medium-term, economic (including fiscal) policy must be oriented towards augmenting existing, or promoting new, sources of tax revenue (ie widening and/or deepening the tax base). Greater FA enables the devolved administration to deploy tax policy in a strategic manner, and in conjunction with other levers of economic policy, to achieve this result.

There is an unfortunate tendency for the economic debate around greater fiscal autonomy for Scotland to be conflated with the political debate over Scotland's constitutional future. From an economic perspective the aim in discussing FA is to determine the 'best' (in economic terms) assignment of fiscal policies between the United Kingdom and the devolved Scottish Government *and* the most appropriate process of moving towards that outcome. In discussions about FA, Scotland's *constitutional* status is not being questioned. Moreover *if* it is in the long-term interests of the Scottish economy for the (greater) control over (potentially all) fiscal and economic policy levers (excepting VAT for reasons of EU law) to be assigned to the Scottish Parliament, this does *not* mean an immediate move to this position is either necessary or desirable. Indeed there are a number of reasons for suggesting a sudden transition would be destabilizing and jeopardize the long-run objective of the exercise. And while critics may contest the economic benefits of FA, it is quite misleading to base criticisms of FA on the spurious proposition that there is only one feasible transition path. A range of possible transitions to (full) fiscal autonomy exists, distinguished by both the timescale of the process and sequence in which relevant tax powers and spending obligations are transferred. Furthermore a shift to FA does *not* imply (as independence might) a comprehensive de-linking of fiscal policy in Scotland from wider UK macro-economic policy considerations. Among other aspects, one might expect a comprehensive FA agreement to include provisions covering tax competition, public finances (deficit and debt), and broader matters of economic policy coordination—*including* adjusting to asymmetric shocks and other exceptional events.[66]

As noted earlier, under current proposals the fiscal powers of the devolved Scottish administration will increase, and the revenue accruing from the block grant will diminish. At the same time it is expected that borrowing powers

[65] The SNP has long advocated creating a Norwegian-style sovereign wealth fund where oil-related surpluses can be invested to be used as a revenue buffer in those years when revenues unexpectedly declined.

[66] This could be achieved by the further development of the Joint Ministerial Committee architecture established in the wake of the 1999 devolution legislation.

assigned to the Scottish Government will increase, though it remains unclear by how much.[67] However because a greater percentage of total public spending will be funded by devolved taxation, it will be necessary for borrowing powers to increase commensurately to ensure the Scottish Government is able to 'smooth' public spending in the face of an unexpected shortfall on tax revenues. Because the new legislation is set to increase the share of devolved spending funded by taxes levied by the Scottish Parliament, we would expect modest efficiency gains to accrue as a result. However under the legislation only competence over income tax is being devolved and that poses a number of problems for the devolved administration. First, although manipulating rates and structure of income tax is an effective lever to change the distribution of income within the population, and may have some—though very limited (in a UK-wide open economy context)—utility in managing the level of aggregate demand, it is of little use in effecting changes in the supply-side of the economy (ie levels of investment and rates of productivity). Second, because Scotland has fewer tax payers who pay the top marginal rate of taxation than the UK average, income tax receipts in Scotland are likely to grow slower than in the remainder of the United Kingdom—putting additional pressure on public spending in Scotland. Third, the Scottish Government will be permitted limited borrowing powers both for capital and (anti-cyclical) current spending but repayments must be financed only from income tax receipts and an assigned share of VAT receipts. While the addition of VAT receipts is an improvement on the 2012 provisions, it continues to exclude national insurance contributions and corporation tax revenues—both of which can be expected to be positively correlated with capital and current account government spending.

IV. Conclusion

Although it is clear that the 'economics' of Scottish independence came to dominate the debate in the run up to the referendum, it is difficult to know how significant these questions ultimately were in determining the way individuals voted. Certainly by September 2014 it was clear that some of Scotland's most significant sectoral interests opposed independence on economic grounds. And it was also clear that the UK Government—and the main UK opposition parties—were determined to stress the scale of the challenges that would confront an independent Scotland, at least during a transition period. By pursuing a hard exit strategy in this manner the UK Government was able to present the alternative to the status quo as immensely risky. In a perceptive piece in the *Financial Times*, Janan Ganesh wrote:

> Many Scots voted against separation out of pragmatism rather than sentiment. According to YouGov's analysis of the campaign, the hard unionist questions about an independent

[67] Any new powers will build on the limited borrowing powers assigned under the 2012 Scotland Act.

Scotland's economy—its currency, its banking sector, its oil revenues—were the only way of winning over the many voters who had no visceral feeling for the union.

As prime minister, Tony Blair liked to say that he favoured Britain's adoption of the euro 'in principle', subject to the economic conditions falling into place. Scotland's judgment on independence resembled that formulation. The ideal was independence; practical realities did not allow for it.[68]

This is not, of course, to suggest independence would be risk-free. Independence would have placed unprecedented challenges before Scotland's elected politicians and tasked them with reshaping the institutions of governance, and the policies these delivered, to unlock the economic benefits they insisted would follow from independence. That Scotland could be a successful and prosperous independent country was not contested—even Prime Minister David Cameron conceded that point. Yet the transition to independence was uncertain, and the threat of a hard exit approach by the UK Government—had it been carried through and in the context of what was a fragile economic recovery—doubtless would have made that transition more difficult than otherwise. The alternative transition scenarios that would be triggered by a soft exit strategy were never fully considered despite the fact pursuing a soft exit was almost certainly in the best interests of both countries had a majority in Scotland voted for independence.

It remains unclear what impact the pre-referendum promise that more economic powers would be devolved to the Scottish Parliament had on the referendum result. However that new powers will be devolved is certain, albeit perhaps not on the scale initially promised. These new powers over income tax and elements of welfare spending have yet to be finalized, as have the mechanisms by which they will be implemented, but the Smith Commission and the consequential Scotland Bill are unlikely to be the final word in the ongoing process of revising Scotland's constitutional position in the United Kingdom. This is because the new (fiscal) powers assigned to the Scottish Parliament are unlikely to assist the Scottish Government achieve its twin objectives of raising the Scottish economy's rate of economic growth and delivering a greater degree of social justice—an ambition that recognizes that social inequality may well represent a distinct and significant drag on growth.

[68] See <http://www.ft.com/cms/s/0/37fc4da4-86f4-11e4-982e-00144feabdc0.html#ixzz3eFeYC75Y>.

8

Scotland, Secession, and the European Union

Sionaidh Douglas-Scott

This chapter discusses Scotland's relationship with the EU in the context of two different secession events. The first concerns the question of an independent Scotland's EU membership in the event of Scotland's secession from the United Kingdom. The second discusses the position of Scotland in the context of a UK in-out referendum on EU membership. This chapter concludes that in neither case should Scotland be forced to leave the EU against its will.

The context of both of these secession movements is a sense of shifting constitutional loyalties, and a concern about the nature and bounds of the political community and locus of ultimate authority. In some cases, this results in a claim for statehood, in others, for self-government. In investigating this context, there are interesting insights to be had as to the nature of the EU and the British constitution.

I. An independent Scotland in the EU

During the Scottish independence debates leading to the 2014 referendum, the Scottish Government made clear that an independent Scotland would seek to remain within the EU. Secession from one union, the United Kingdom, was not seen as entailing secession from the larger European Union. However, it soon became clear that not everyone shared this view, and that, for some, Scottish independence was not consistent with EU membership. This chapter disagrees with this contrary view and argues that it should be possible for a future independent Scotland to maintain its EU membership. This argument is made on the basis of EU law itself, which, it is argued, provides the resources necessary to assure an independent Scotland's EU membership through EU treaty amendment, rather than the cumbersome accession process as a new member state.

A. Disagreement before the 2014 referendum

First, let us look back to the 2014 referendum, during which there existed a polarization of the debate as to if and how an independent Scotland could become part of the EU.

The UK Government and 'Better Together' view may be roughly summarized as arguing that international law would govern the process of an independent Scotland's EU membership, and that Scotland would have to apply through the standard accession provision in the Treaty, Article 49 TEU, in the same way that totally new applicants, such as Croatia, have done. In the run-up to the Scottish referendum, several Westminster Parliamentary Select committees pronounced on the perceived difficulties of an independent Scotland remaining in the EU. The UK Government also produced a series of reports,[1] one of which, *Devolution and the Implications of Scottish Independence*, appended a specifically commissioned *Opinion* from two senior international lawyers, James Crawford and Alan Boyle, which considered the effect of independence on Scotland's membership of international organizations.[2] While finding it 'not inconceivable' that Scotland could automatically become a member of the EU, the jurists' *Opinion* was that Scotland would have to apply for membership of the EU through the standard accession provision in the Treaty, Article 49 TEU.

In contrast, the Scottish Government argued that an independent Scotland's EU membership could take the form of an 'internal enlargement' of the EU, using the procedure for treaty amendment in Article 48 TEU. Alex Salmond's characteristically trenchant response to arguments that emphasized the difficulties of Scotland's EU membership was to argue that, 'The only threat to Scotland's place in Europe comes from David Cameron's in-out referendum as Westminster dances to a UKIP tune and flirts with the exit door of the EU'.[3] The reports produced by the Scottish Parliament were also more optimistic than those of the Westminster Parliament about an independent Scotland's place in the EU.[4]

Nor have public international lawyers brought only bad news for Scottish separatists. Commenting specifically on the Crawford and Boyle *HMG Opinion*, international lawyer David Scheffer wrote:

> One cannot help but observe a political objective at work in HMG opinion, namely to make the legal implications appear so burdensome and traumatic for Scotland and its people, ... that voters will decide it is not worth the effort and vote 'no' on the independence referendum.[5]

The conclusion that might be drawn is that the issue of Scotland's future in Europe has hardened into two adversarial approaches, one separatist and one unionist. Yet

[1] For the collection of these papers, see the UK Government's Scotland Analysis webpage at <https://www.gov.uk/government/collections/scotland-analysis>.

[2] A. Boyle and J. Crawford, 'Opinion: Referendum on the Independence of Scotland—International Law Aspects' appended to HM Government, *Scotland Analysis: Devolution and the Implications of Scottish Independence* (Cm 8554, 2013).

[3] See 'Scotland warned of Three Years in Wilderness' *Scotsman* (3 June 2014).

[4] eg contrast House of Commons Scottish Affairs Committee, *The Referendum on Separation for Scotland: Scotland's Membership of the EU* 12th Report, 2013–14, HC 1241; with Scottish Parliament European and External Relations Committee, *Report on the Scottish Government's Proposals for an Independent Scotland: Membership of the European Union*, 2nd Report, Session 4 (2014), SP Paper 530.

[5] D. Scheffer, *International Political and Legal Implications of Scottish Independence*, University of Glasgow, Adam Smith Research Foundation, WP 2013/01 at 16.

to this we should add the view of the EU *itself* on Scottish independence. This chapter argues that a strong case can be made for an independent Scotland's continued EU membership on the basis of EU law. The significance of this point is that most of the arguments that follow should be applicable in the event of any future referendum on Scottish independence.

B. An EU approach to an independent Scotland

1. The issue of a newly independent Scotland's EU membership is not addressed explicitly by EU law

The first point to note is that, within EU law, there exists no specific precedent for what happens when a territory of an existing Member State becomes independent, and wishes to retain EU membership. While Article 49 TEU deals with the situation of new applicant countries, Article 48 TEU deals with amendments to the treaties by existing members, but neither deal with the potential Scottish situation directly or explicitly. The process by which a separate Scotland may become a member of the EU is therefore subject to speculation.

2. The Barroso and UK Government view ignores the distinctive nature of EU law

Notwithstanding the lack of specific EU sources on secession, the UK Government took the view that an independent Scotland would have to reapply for EU membership using the Art. 49 procedure. This is also the view taken by former Commission President Barroso, and some academics and practitioners. However, this view is not inevitable, and may not even be well reasoned.

Notably, the former Commission President, José Manuel Barroso stated: 'if part of the territory of a Member State would cease to be part of that state because it were to become a new independent state, the Treaties would no longer apply to that territory'.[6] The problem is that this view misconstrues both the EU itself and EU law. In making this assertion, Barroso was looking to international law, rather than the more specific and singular concepts that EU law has built up over its near 60-year history.

The EU is a *sui generis* organization and the European Court of Justice (ECJ) has long held that, while a creation of international law, the EU constitutes a distinctive new legal order. As the Court famously stated in *van Gend en Loos*, 'the Treaty is more than an agreement which merely creates mutual obligations between the contracting parties'.[7] Perhaps the most striking way in which EU law early on distinguished itself was by its focus on individual rights (not traditionally

[6] Available at: <http://www.parliament.uk/documents/lords-committees/economic-affairs/ScottishIndependence/EA68_Scotland_and_the_EU_Barroso's_reply_to_Lord_Tugendhat_101212.pdf>.

[7] Case 26/62 *van Gend en Loos* [1963] ECR 1.

a concern of international law). Moreover, EU law does not have a straightforward relationship with international law, in which international law always takes priority. Indeed the European Court has on occasion refused to apply international law measures on grounds of their incompatibility with EU law, such as UN Security Council Resolutions in the 2008 *Kadi* case.[8]

EU law therefore manifests itself as a new and singular legal order that goes beyond the traditional state-based concerns of international law, differentiating itself from other international organizations. EU law also characteristically takes a pragmatic and purposive approach to pressing issues that are not dealt with by specific treaty provisions. There was no explicit provision in the treaties capable of dealing with the situation of German unification in the 1990s. But the (then) EEC Institutions responded to this event in a practical and expedient manner, enabling a united Germany to become a member of the EU without long drawn-out negotiations, accession proceedings or legal wranglings. This is evidence of the capacity of EU Institutions and member states to reach a pragmatic agreement in the absence of a specific treaty article governing the situation at hand.

Further, the Barroso view is clearly not the only view ever presented by EU Commission officials. For example, Graham Avery, honorary Director-General of the EU Commission, has written the following:

> The idea in London was that, on independence, Scotland would have to leave the EU, apply for membership from outside, and spend years trying to join ... This kind of argument struck me as absurd. It seemed to me that depicting the EU as a major handicap to Scottish independence was incorrect. To use it as a 'weapon of mass dissuasion' would be wrong.[9]

Avery has argued persuasively that Art. 48 TEU may be used to ensure Scotland's membership continues on independence.

3. EU law rather than international law governs the issue of an independent Scotland's membership

In any case, those who provide support for the UK Government's view, such as Alan Boyle and James Crawford, acknowledge that membership of international organizations, such as the EU, 'depend on the particular constitution or rules of each organization',[10] rather than deriving from one comprehensive rule of international law. It all depends on the rules and practice of each organization and

[8] Joined Cases C-402/05P & C-415/05P *Kadi v Council of the European Union* [2008] ECR 1225.

[9] Quoted in G. Avery, 'Scotland's Independence and the EU: What's the Problem?' (*Centre on Constitutional Change blog*, 12 June 2014) <http://www.centreonconstitutionalchange.ac.uk/blog/scotland%E2%80%99s-independence-eu-what%E2%80%99s-problem>.

[10] Boyle and Crawford, in their *Opinion* (n. 2) at para. 184, refer to Art. 4, Vienna Convention on the Succession of States in Respect of Treaties 1978, which expressly states that succession to constituent instruments of an international organization is: 'without prejudice to the rules concerning acquisition of membership and without prejudice to any other relevant rules of the organization'.

is often determined by negotiation and agreement rather than law. And many international organizations automatically recognize secession states as members.

However, in spite of acknowledging that even under international law, the practice is to look to the distinct rules of the specific organization, Boyle and Crawford do not consider that EU law provides an affirmative answer to the continuation of Scottish membership. In contrast, this chapter argues that the particular constitution and rules of the EU provide sufficient resources for an independent Scotland to continue EU membership through the treaty amendment route in Art. 48 TEU. This argument will now be pursued in more detail.

C. EU law provides the resources for an independent Scotland's continued EU membership

There are sufficient resources in EU law to deal with an independent Scotland's continued EU membership. The relevant provisions in particular are Arts 4(3) and 50 TEU, but EU citizenship and EU values and principles also provide further compelling reasons.

1. The principle of sincere cooperation and the relevance of Article 50 TEU[11]

Article 4(3) TEU sets out a 'principle of sincere cooperation'. As a recent Common Market Law Review editorial states, Art. 4(3)

> refers to the Union as a special ethos: Member States are bound to adopt a certain attitude towards the other actors. It mainly consists of a principle of sincere cooperation, full mutual respect, and a duty of mutual assistance. It also means that Member States must have due regard to the Union system as a whole.[12]

According to Art. 4(3), the EU and Member States shall, 'assist each other in carrying out the tasks which flow from the Treaties'. It is clear that one of the most significant tasks that flows from the EU Treaties is the promotion of the EU's Single Market, so much so that the very term, 'Common Market' formerly acted as a metonym for the EEC itself. A salient objection to the Barroso and UK Government position is that it would foster immediate discontinuity within the Single Market. For, according to this view, on becoming independent, Scotland would, as a non-EU state, be ejected from the EU. Its exodus would be automatic. Yet it is not clear from which treaty basis such an automatic ejection derives.

Automatic ejection certainly stands in contrast to the formal procedure for withdrawal from the EU in Article 50 TEU. Indeed, Article 50 is the only provision in the EU treaties for withdrawal from the EU, and it sets out procedures and obligations that apply to both the withdrawing Member State and the EU

[11] This section follows closely along the lines of the persuasive arguments made by Professor Sir David Edward on these points, eg D. Edward, 'EU Law and the Separation of Member States' (2013) 36 *Fordham Int'l LJ* 1151.

[12] Editorial comments: 'Union Membership in Times of Crisis' (2014) 51 *CMLR* 1–12.

institutions, with the aim of minimizing dislocation and disorder. It obliges them to negotiate and to conclude an agreement, providing a two-year period to do so, thus confirming that withdrawal is not to be automatic. The example of Greenland, which took well over three years to withdraw from the EEC as then was, illustrates just how long it can take for a territory to withdraw.[13] So, for example, if the United Kingdom decided to withdraw from the EU, it could use Article 50 to give notification of that intention to the European Council, and then would have a period of time in which to conclude negotiations.[14] However, Article 50 would not be a procedure that Scotland would follow, as the Scottish Government has asserted that it would not withdraw Scotland's EU membership following independence.[15]

The existence of Article 50 acknowledges that acquired EU rights and mutual dependencies cannot be immediately extinguished. For example, nationals of other EU member states have directly enforceable EU law rights in Scotland regarding free movement of workers, free movement of goods, and freedom of establishment. Scottish nationals possess corresponding rights in other Member States. If Scotland's membership were automatically terminated they would become illegal immigrants. Such acquired rights under EU law would have to be respected. The European Court of Justice stated as long ago as 1963 that these rights are part of individuals' 'legal heritage'.[16] The existence of Article 50 evidences the lack of any capacity in EU law automatically to terminate such rights,[17] and Article 4(3) illustrates the obligation of EU institutions and states to recognize acquired rights and obligations through a duty of sincere cooperation.

Moreover, international law also recognizes the status of acquired rights. Sir Gerald Fitzmaurice has written that:

> It is an accepted rule of treaty law that the termination of a treaty ... cannot per se affect or prejudice any right already definitively and finally acquired under it, or undo or reverse anything effected by any clause of an executed character in the treaty.[18]

Thus, any rights acquired prior to any termination, or withdrawal, would continue to be effective. This is particularly so, considering the mutual obligations of loyalty and good faith of the member states and EU Institutions under Article 4(3) TEU.

[13] See eg *Status of Greenland: Commission Opinion*, COM (83) 66 final, 2 February 1983, 12.

[14] See eg *Leaving the EU*, House of Commons Research Paper 13/42 1 July 2013, at 12. See also M. Nash, 'Could Britain Leave the European Union? The Greenland Option' 46 *NLJ* 6752.

[15] See The Scottish Government, *Scotland in the European Union* (November 2013) at 14 (available at <www.gov.scot/Resource/0043/00439166.pdf>).

[16] Case C-26/62, *van Gend en Loos* [1963] ECR 1.

[17] Neil MacCormick recognized this point. He wrote: 'the Treaties ... remain in force for the whole territory or territories in question, until such time as any variation of this or derogation from it is determined by an Intergovernmental Conference and enshrined in an appropriate treaty.' N. MacCormick, 'Is There a Constitutional path to Scottish Independence?' (2000) 53 *Parliamentary Affairs* 734.

[18] G. Fitzmaurice, *The Law and Procedures of the International Court of Justice*, vol. I (Cambridge University Press 1986).

2. *EU citizenship*

A separate but related argument relies on the privileged position of individuals as subjects of EU law, to emphasize the crucial importance of EU citizenship. According to Article 9 TEU and Article 20 TFEU, 'Every national of a Member State shall be a citizen of the Union. Citizenship of the Union shall be additional to national citizenship and shall not replace it'. However, in the 2001 *Grzelczyk* case, the European Court famously declared that 'Union citizenship is destined to be the fundamental status of nationals of the Member States',[19] and has shown itself willing to overlook, or look beyond, the rule that matters of citizenship and nationality are internal matters for the Member States only. From the relatively humble roots of EU citizenship in the Treaty of Maastricht, the European Court has added flesh to the bones of this concept through a series of cases, notably *Rottmann* and *Zambrano*.[20]

Rottmann is relevant as it concerns the loss of an individual's EU Citizenship as a result of the revocation of nationality. The European Court held that an Austrian man who moved to Germany to avoid criminal prosecution could not have his German naturalization revoked if that would leave him stateless and deprive him of his EU citizenship. *Rottmann* makes it clear that the withdrawal of EU Citizenship (in contrast to its acquisition) will fall within the scope of EU law, if the withdrawal of member state nationality deprives an individual of EU citizenship (and allied rights such as free movement, establishment, and equal treatment).

Ruiz Zambrano is also relevant in this context. In this case, the CJEU held that national measures cannot deprive citizens of 'the genuine enjoyment of the substance of the rights conferred by virtue of their status as citizens of the EU'.[21] Therefore, a Colombian father of two Belgian children was able to use EU law, and specifically his children's rights to EU citizenship (the children having been born in Belgium) to regularize his stay in the country. The Court decided that the children would be deprived of the enjoyment of their citizenship rights if their father were to be deported.

In sum, there is clear case law to the effect that EU law can restrain national law in situations which are capable of causing individuals to lose their status as EU citizens and rights attaching thereto.

Boyle and Crawford nevertheless dismiss arguments based on citizenship. Stressing the derivative nature of EU citizenship, they argue that citizens of an independent Scotland would no longer possess the basic citizenship status to benefit from EU citizenship. They rely on Articles 24 and 25 of the 2000 ILC Articles on the Nationality of Natural Persons in Relation to the Succession of States which provide that persons having their place of habitual residence in the

[19] Case 184/99 *Grzelczyk* [2001] ECR 1-6193.

[20] Case C-135/08 *Rottmann v Freistaat Bayern* [2010] ECR I-1449; Case C-34/09 *Gerardo Ruiz Zambrano v Office National de l'Emploi* [2011] ECR I-1177.

[21] Case 34/09 *Ruiz-Zambrano* at para. 42.

successor state will receive the nationality of that state while the predecessor state 'shall withdraw its nationality from persons concerned qualified to acquire the nationality of the successor State'. Therefore, on this argument, persons acquiring Scottish nationality would no longer be UK citizens and could no longer avail themselves of the protections of Union citizenship.[22]

However, since the British Nationality Act of 1948, there exists in general no restriction in UK law on a British national being a citizen of another country. The UK Government Home Office, in its January 2014 analysis of the consequences of independence (focusing on borders and citizenship), stated: 'The UK has ... been tolerant of plural nationalities, and it is likely there would be no barriers to holding both British and independent Scottish citizenships'.[23] Individuals who had, or were entitled to, British citizenship on the date of independence should therefore have that right protected, and Scots would in any case remain EU citizens by virtue of retaining UK nationality. The question is how best to ensure that they maintain the attendant rights.

To be sure, the doctrine of EU citizenship cannot by itself engender automatic membership of the EU for an independent Scotland. It would be necessary for the treaties to be amended. However, we should not underestimate the central importance of EU citizenship to the issue of an independent Scotland's EU membership, which requires that, as Aidan O'Neill argues, 'rather than analyze the matter from the classic viewpoint of public international law ... EU law requires one to look at the issue from the viewpoint of the individual EU citizen'.[24] Given the importance accorded by the Court to the primacy of EU law, and EU citizenship as being 'the fundamental status of nationals of the Member States', it is unlikely that the European Court would consider that Scottish independence deprived Scots of their acquired rights as EU citizens. So the citizenship argument is a strong one.

D. An EU of values

1. What sort of organization is the EU?

The economic nature of the EU is sometimes over-emphasized, while the traditional premise of the EU is sometimes forgotten. The focus on the Single Market should not eclipse the fundamental issues that inspired the original EEC in the post-war period, namely a search for peace and stability in Europe and the protection of democratic values. Scottish self-determination is part of this democratic development, as it has evolved over the decades through the devolution process. Neil MacCormick found an apt description when he described the EU as a 'commonwealth' whose members have certain vital interest of peace and prosperity in

[22] Boyle and Crawford, *Opinion* (n. 2) at 114.

[23] HM Government, *Scotland Analysis: Borders and Citizenship* (Cm 8724, 2014) para. 4.71.

[24] A. O'Neill, 'A Quarrel in a Faraway Country? Scotland, Independence and the EU', available at <http://eutopialaw.com/2011/11/14/685/#more-685>.

common.[25] This too, is part of the EU's raison d'être, a feature recognized by the award to the EU of the Nobel Peace Prize in 2012, an award that looked beyond the economic achievements of the EU.

So the nature of Scottish independence within the EU must be understood in the context of the EU's wider mission to pursue peace and democratic values. This requires a closer look at the values espoused by the EU, particularly democracy and fundamental rights. Article 2 TEU provides a basis, setting out the values on which the EU is said to be founded, and was specifically amended by the Treaty of Lisbon to replace the term 'principle' with the more morally suggestive term 'value'. Article 3 TEU adds to this that the EU shall promote the well-being of its people. Article 2 TEU reads as follows:

Article 2

The Union is founded on the values of respect for human dignity, freedom, democracy, equality, the rule of law and respect for human rights, including the rights of persons belonging to minorities. These values are common to the Member States in a society in which pluralism, non-discrimination, tolerance, justice, solidarity and equality between women and men prevail.

2. *Democracy*

If Scotland had voted for independence in September 2014, this would have been a vote to dissolve the constitutional union in the United Kingdom. However, the legitimacy of such a vote would not have been in doubt, being the result of a fully constitutional process, conducted on a democratic basis. The referendum and processes leading up to it were conducted under the rule of law, with the full consent of the UK Government, and represented the democratic will of those eligible to vote in Scotland. It would therefore have been entirely incompatible with EU general principles and values to eject Scotland from the territory of the EU, (with also the possible consequent loss of EU citizenship, and acquired rights) as a result of the exercise of the Scottish peoples' democratic right to self-governance.

Democracy is proclaimed as one of the EU's values in Article 2 TEU and is also one of the principles set out in the Preamble of the EU Charter of Fundamental Rights. The EU is eager to vaunt its adherence to the values proclaimed in Article 2, and also seeks to promote democracy outside of the EU. While actual achievement in the pursuit of democracy overseas may sometimes have been lacking, and the EU's statements may have the appearance of a rhetorical puff, the EU's commitment to democracy as such cannot be faulted.

Therefore, the EU's very raison d'être is at issue here. It would be ironic, at the very least, if an institution such as the EU, that has promoted the cause of democracy at home and abroad, proclaimed it in its post-Lisbon headline statement of values in the treaty, were to act in such a way as to dispossess Scots of their

[25] N. MacCormick, *Questioning Sovereignty* (Oxford University Press 1999) 143.

acquired rights and EU citizenship as a result of Scotland using the democratic right to vote for independence. This would seriously undermine the EU's credibility and its claim to be a promoter of democracy.

3. Democracy and self-determination

Self-determination is not mentioned as a value in Article 2 but it is closely linked to the principle of democracy and has given rise to much argument in the context of Scottish independence. Robert Lane has argued that: 'A Scotland bent upon independence grounded in the clear democratic support of the Scottish people would create a moral and, given the international law principle of self-determination, probably a legal obligation for all member states to negotiate in good faith in order to produce such a result'.[26]

However, for some, arguments based on self-determination are of little relevance. Boyle and Crawford, for example, argue:

> Outside the colonial context, the principle of self-determination is controversial. The Canadian Supreme Court has held that 'a right to secession only arises under the principle of self-determination of peoples at international law where "a people" is governed as part of a colonial empire'. In metropolitan territories such as Scotland, 'peoples are expected to achieve self-determination within the framework of their existing state'.[27]

Yet, in return it might equally be argued that one should interpret the right to self-determination 'using a modern frame of reference and not the decolonization theories and practices of the past century ... grounded in the primacy of sustaining national cohesion following decolonization'.[28] One might also dispute the relevance of the *Quebec* case in the context of the 2014 Scotland referendum, given that it involved issues of potential unilateral self-determination by the Quebec government, and the attempt to use international law to ground a right to self-determination in the absence of legality under the Canadian Constitution. The Scottish referendum was an entirely different case, involving a constitutionally approved process within the framework of UK Constitutional law. Therefore, the Scots had no need to rely on a legal principle of self-determination to make their argument.

However, in different circumstances (ie those in which the UK Government did not accept the legitimacy of a Scottish independence referendum) Scotland might wish to make use of a right to self-determination, and the *Quebec Secession* case could be of relevance. Although the Supreme Court of Canada found the Quebecois to have no right to unilateral secession, the Court nonetheless affirmed a right to self-determination under the condition that the other Canadian provinces agreed to the secession. The Court stated that the Constitution was 'not

[26] R. Lane, 'Scotland in Europe: an Independent Scotland in the European Community' in W. Finnie et al (eds), *Edinburgh Essays in Public Law* (Edinburgh University Press 1991) 143, 154–5.

[27] Boyle and Crawford (n. 2) at para. 175, citing *Reference re Secession of Quebec* (1998) 115 *ILR* 536, 594–5.

[28] Scheffer (n. 5).

a straightjacket', thus, 'a clear majority vote in Quebec ... in favour of secession would confer *democratic legitimacy* which all of the other participants in Confederation would have to recognize'.[29]

Such an analysis of 'negotiated' self-determination has important implications, as it opens the way to a concept of self-determination as the right to negotiate one's position within the state and international order, rather than as limited to the action of secession. It is also in tune with an evolving practice of acknowledging self-determination as a question of *democracy* rather than a question of nationality or ethnicity.

However, Joseph Weiler has made an opposing argument (in the context of the case for Catalan independence)[30] based around international law and the *Quebec Secession* case. He reasons that because international law recognizes no automatic right to secede in the case of national minorities who enjoy extensive individual and collective freedom, therefore the EU should not be expected to indulge the independence claims of these unoppressed sub-state nations in its accession policy:

> Europe should not seem like a Nirvana for that form of irredentist Eurotribalism which contradicts the deep values and needs of the Union. The assumption of automatic membership in the Union should be decisively squelched by the countries from whom secession is threatened ...[31]

But Weiler's analysis is inapplicable to the case of Scotland for a number of reasons.

The first is that no parallel can be drawn between the cases of Scotland in 2014 and Catalonia. As already discussed, the 2014 Scottish referendum was not a unilateral act, but one crafted within the aegis of UK Constitutional law. The Edinburgh Agreement stated that a referendum would 'deliver a fair test and a decisive expression of the views of people in Scotland and a result that everyone will respect'.[32] Any decision by the Scots on independence in the context of the 2014 referendum would have possessed a legitimacy that it would have been impossible for the EU to ignore.

Secondly, even if the legitimacy of a future Scottish independence referendum were less clear than in 2014, it is in any case hard to argue, as Weiler does, that separatism (or in Weiler's terms 'irredentist Euro-tribalism') contradicts the 'deep values and needs of the Union'. Is it atavistic or incoherent for Scots (or Catalans) to look for independence when the EU forges its way towards ever greater union? It is hard to place Scotland in the mould of nationalism and tribalism. Contemporary Scottish nationalism reveals a lack of essentialist thinking, exhibiting a non-tribalist nationalism as its dominant strand.

[29] *Reference re Secession of Quebec* (1998) 115 ILR 536, 594–5.

[30] J. Weiler, 'Catalonian Independence and the European Union' (2012) 23 *EJIL* 4.

[31] Weiler, 'Catalonian Independence' (n. 30).

[32] Edinburgh Agreement, or *Agreement between the United Kingdom Government and the Scottish Government on a Referendum on Independence for Scotland* (HM Government/Scottish Government 2012).

There are other ways of understanding the desire for independence than as a nationalist impulse to disintegration and economic self-interest, fuelled by a 'what's in it for us' mentality. An alternative is to notice the ways in which the desire for self-governance is linked to decentralization, localism, but also interconnectedness, and *subsidiarity*—another principle that looms large in the EU treaties—as well as a concern for the boundaries of political community. These issues cannot be resolved within monist structures premised on the basis that there can be only one nation and only one form of sovereignty.

The very values on which the EU is founded are precisely those intended to disrupt the post Great War tribalist mentality, but this does not mean that they must be unfriendly to self-determination movements. The Scots are seeking to escape the sovereignty of the UK Government, but the EU itself changes the significance of national sovereignty, recasting it as something less absolute, something sometimes pooled, voluntarily ceded for principled reasons. The rejection of membership of one union (the United Kingdom) need not be inimical to participation in another (the EU). The existence of the EU recasts and reforms traditional ideas of sovereignty and belonging into something more impalpable.

Furthermore, the way in which the EU manages self-determination claims may well have important ramifications beyond Europe. To be sure, the EU's level of supranational integration goes beyond anything adopted in other parts of the world. However, the context in which the EU's separatist disputes are worked out provides a secure location in which to achieve unique solutions to self-determination claims that may be of value in less stable areas.

4. Fundamental rights

Lastly, fundamental rights present an interesting case. There exists a compelling school of thought in international law that human rights treaties automatically bind successor states. Such a view is evidenced by the UN Human Rights Committee's General Comment No. 26 on the continuity of obligations. Further, many years ago, Wilfred Jenks vehemently argued that there could be no clean slate in respect of multilateral treaties of a legislative or universal character, most particularly those that vest rights in individuals or organizations.[33] Most human rights treaties have no termination clauses (nor did EU law until the Treaty of Lisbon). In the *German Settlers* case,[34] the Permanent Court of International Justice held that private rights, including rights or property, might be invoked against successor states. In present times, human rights are the most important rights that may be invoked against the state. The doctrine of acquired rights recognized in international law certainly applies to human rights.[35]

The European Convention on Human Rights (ECHR) is a salient example of this. Although it is a 'condition precedent' of membership of the Council of Europe,

[33] W. Jenks, 'State Succession in Respect of Law-Making Treaties' (1952) 29 *BYIL* 105 at 142.
[34] *German Settlers in Poland* (Advisory Opinion) 10 September 1923, PCLJ Series B, No. 6, at 36.
[35] R. Mullerson, *International Law, Rights and Politics* (Routledge 1994) 154–7.

governed by Article 4 of its Statute,[36] that a new state deposit an instrument of accession with the Secretary General, membership of the ECHR itself, however, is a different matter. In the 2009 case of *Bijelic v Montenegro and Serbia*[37] the European Court of Human Rights held that the ECHR remained in force over the territory of a successor state (in this case, Montenegro) at all times, despite independence. It explained:

> given…the principle that fundamental rights protected by international human rights treaties should indeed belong to individuals living in the territory of the State party concerned, notwithstanding its subsequent dissolution or succession … the Court considers that both the Convention and Protocol No. 1 should be deemed as having continuously been in force in respect of Montenegro as of [the date it entered into force in respect of Serbia and Montenegro through to the date of Montenegrin independence] as well as thereafter. …[38]

This is in keeping with the school of thought that human rights treaties will *automatically bind* successor states and therefore, it would appear that the ECHR will continue to apply to Scotland uninterrupted.

The ECJ in *van Gend* stressed the importance of rights. The TEU and TFEU may not be predominantly human rights treaties, but the EU Charter of Fundamental Rights is most certainly one, and it now has the same legal value as the Treaties (Article 6(1) Treaty on European Union). The opening recitals to the Charter's preamble are in the following terms:

> … the Union is founded on the indivisible, universal values of human dignity, freedom, equality and solidarity; it is based on the principles of democracy and the rule of law. It places the individual at the heart of its activities, by establishing the citizenship of the Union and by creating an area of freedom, security and justice.

Moreover, Advocate General Maduro in the *Centro Europa 7* case, asserted that, 'Protection of the common code of fundamental rights accordingly constitutes an existential requirement for the EU legal order'.[39] In the *Kadi* case,[40] the ECJ proclaimed the constitutional autonomy and hegemony of the EU legal order, stating that the EU is a community based on the rule of law, and that respect for fundamental rights is an integral part of the EU legal order. So there is a strong argument to be made that, as a Union based on human rights, EU law requires the recognition of EU fundamental rights by Scottish citizens, rather than their termination by independence.

In any case, at the very time that members of the UK Parliament are trying to pass legislation to disapply the Charter of Fundamental Rights in the United Kingdom,[41] there is a dignity, if not an irony, in calling on fundamental rights as an added ground for Scotland's continuing membership of the EU.

[36] Article 4, Statute of the Council of Europe.
[37] *Bijelić v Montenegro and Serbia*, no. 11890/05, §§ 67–70, 28 April 2009. 39.
[38] *Bijelić v Montenegro and Serbia* (n. 37).
[39] Case C-380/05 *Centro Europa 7* [2008] ECR I-349 at para. 19.
[40] Joined Cases C-402 & 415/05P *Kadi & Al Barakaat Int'l Found. v Council & Commission* [2008] ECR I-6351.
[41] House of Commons European Scrutiny Committee, *The Application of the EU Charter of Fundamental Rights in the UK: a State of Confusion*', 43rd Report of Session 2013–14, HC 979.

Therefore the argument is that the Commission, and indeed the EU and its member states more generally, should have regard to the values, principles, and basis of the EU, indeed to its very reason for existence, instead of making statements that counter and undermine the character of the EU. The case of Scottish independence makes very clear the need for the EU to self-interrogate as to its values, and to use arguments with a public reason character that take it beyond an instrumental economic rationale or a grounding in international law.

E. Conclusion

In conclusion, it is argued that the principled and practical route to take, should Scotland ever elect to become independent of the rest of the United Kingdom, is that of Article 48 TEU, which deals with Treaty amendment. Proceeding by way of Article 48, as opposed to using Article 49 TEU, which would require a full Accession Treaty, would avoid the risk that a newly independent Scotland would be cast into the wilderness, its ties with the EU cut on the date of independence. This would be a form of internal enlargement for the EU, and in this way, Scotland's uninterrupted membership of the EU could be preserved. (It would, however, be necessary for negotiations to commence immediately upon a Yes vote in the independence referendum so that messy contingency arrangements between the EU and a new Scottish state could be avoided.) Such a route takes account of both member states' and EU institutions' obligations under Article 4 TEU, as well as taking seriously the EU's proclaimed statement of values, which include democracy and fundamental rights.

In a recent editorial, the *Common Market Law Review* referred to 'the birth of a distinctive form of legal discourse that departs from the traditional law of integration' and which implies a 'major conceptual shift' by understanding that

> EU law is not addressed to Member States [alone] ... but also their peoples and communities are involved in the European project. This resonates in a textual change introduced by the Lisbon Treaty: Article 1(3) TEU, focusing on the organization of Member States' relations, is substituted by Article 2 TEU that puts forward a model of 'society of societies' heavily interconnected and relying on values.[42]

It is this interconnected 'society of societies' and its reliance on values that should predominate over the notion of an EU either as a state-like framework of integration or as a mere contract of independent states.

II. The position of Scotland in a UK referendum on continued EU membership

The issue of an independent Scotland's EU membership continues to be salient, notwithstanding the No vote in the independence referendum in September

[42] *CMLR* editorial comments (n. 12) at 12.

2014. Perhaps the most obvious way in which the issue might resurface would be in the event of a UK vote to leave the EU in an in-out referendum on EU membership. Following the 2015 general election, an EU Referendum Act 2015 was legislated. This chapter was, however, written before 23 June 2016, the planned date for the referendum. A vote in favour of the United Kingdom leaving the EU could trigger a bid for another Scottish independence referendum, and so lead to the end of the United Kingdom. Yet the consequences on devolution tend to be little considered in any discussion of 'Brexit'.

A. Different approaches to the EU among the nations of the United Kingdom

The devolved nations tend to be less eurosceptic than most of England (although we should not forget London, which bucks England's eurosceptic trend[43]) and thus most likely to vote for the United Kingdom's continued EU membership. How each constituent part of the United Kingdom would vote in an exit referendum is not certain, but in the 2015 UK general election, UKIP gained a 14.1 per cent share of the vote in England, but in Scotland only 1.6 per cent.[44]

EU regional funding tends to benefit Scotland, Wales, and Northern Ireland more than it does England. Furthermore, Scottish, Welsh, and Northern Ireland governments have expressed opposition to the prospect of leaving the EU. For example, the Scottish Government's *Agenda for EU Reform* paper[45] disagreed with the proposed renegotiation of Britain's EU membership, did not support any potential subsequent referendum, and asserted that EU reform could be delivered without major treaty change. So the UK central government could be on a path of EU renegotiation and referendum without the support of devolved administrations.

Initially, it might seem that Scotland's No vote for independence would lessen the chance of EU secession, given the greater pro-EU vote in Scotland. However, the relatively lower eurosceptic vote in the devolved nations would not make a great impact on an EU in-out referendum overall, given that the population of the devolved nations is small compared to that of England. According to the Office for National Statistics, England has about 82 per cent of the UK population.[46] This is significant if the vote in the devolved nations is of a less eurosceptic complexion than the English vote in an EU in-out referendum.

B. An EU exit and the devolution settlement

An EU exit could wreak havoc with the devolution settlement, risking a constitutional crisis. Both the ECHR and EU law are incorporated directly into

[43] See eg T. Oliver, 'Londoners are Not Little Englanders' (*British Policy and Politics blog*, 2014).

[44] UK general election results 2015, viewable at <http://www.bbc.co.uk/news/election/2015/results>.

[45] Available at <http://www.gov.scot/Publications/2014/08/5067>.

[46] See Office for National Statistics, Electoral Statistics for UK—2012, available at <http://www.ons.gov.uk/ons/rel/pop-estimate/electoral-statistics-for-uk/2012/stb---2012-electoral-statistics.html#tab-Parliamentary-Electors>.

the devolution statutes in Scotland, Wales, and Northern Ireland. For example, section 29(2)(d) of the Scotland Act 1998 provides that Acts of the Scottish Parliament that are incompatible with EU law or with ECHR rights are 'not law'. Section 108(6) Government of Wales Act 2006 states that any act of the Welsh Assembly incompatible with EU law or the ECHR falls outside its competence. Section 24 of the Northern Ireland Act prohibits any legislation contrary to EU or ECHR law.

Therefore, although the Westminster Parliament may repeal the European Communities Act 1972, this would not bring an end to the impact of EU law in the devolved nations. It would still be necessary to amend the relevant parts of devolution legislation. But this would be no simple matter and could lead to a constitutional crisis.

This is because, although, as a sovereign parliament, the UK Parliament retains the power to amend the devolution Acts, the UK Government has stated that it will not normally legislate on a devolved matter, or on any change to the powers of the devolved nations, without the consent of the devolved legislature.[47] This requires a Legislative Consent Motion under the Sewel Convention.[48] However, the devolved legislatures might be reluctant to grant assent, especially as the Scotland Bill 2015, working its way through the UK Parliament at time of writing, contains a commitment to entrench the Scottish Parliament's powers, thus, at least arguably giving legal force to the Sewel Convention.[49] So the need to amend devolution legislation renders a UK EU exit constitutionally highly problematic.

Should the UK Parliament press ahead with legislation in the absence of legislative consent we would be entering difficult (and uncharted) constitutional territory. So far, legislative consent has only very rarely been refused, and to date, Westminster has not legislated on devolved matters in the absence of consent.[50] However, what would be the consequences of Westminster ignoring the requirements of the Sewel Convention?

Conventions have been traditionally defined as 'a binding rule, a rule of behaviour accepted as obligatory by those concerned in the working of the constitution'.[51] Whether or not they are legally enforceable is debatable, as they are not embodied

[47] Scotland Office policy paper, *2010 to 2015 Government Policy: Scottish Devolution* available at <https://www.gov.uk/government/publications/2010-to-2015-government-policy-scottish-devolution/2010-to-2015-government-policy-scottish-devolution> states that the Sewel Convention is triggered not just by substantive Westminster legislation on devolved matters, but also by constitutional change which 'alters the legislative competence of the Scottish Parliament.'

[48] See on the Sewel Convention, eg P. Bowers, *The Sewel Convention* (House of Commons Library SN/PC/2084, 2005).

[49] This clause was inserted to give effect to the Smith Commission proposals which in turn considered the 'Vow' made to the Scottish nation, immediately before the 2014 Scottish independence referendum: *Report of the Smith Commission for Further Devolution of Powers to the Scottish Parliament* (2014), available at: <http://www.smith-commission.scot/wp-content/uploads/2014/11/The_Smith_Commission_Report-1.pdf>.

[50] In Scotland, consent was refused for parts of the UK Welfare Reform Bill in 2011. In Wales, consent has been refused on four occasions.

[51] K. Wheare, *Modern Constitutions* (Oxford University Press 1951) 179, quoted in G. Marshall, *Constitutional Conventions* (Oxford University Press 1984) 7.

in hard law. In the United Kingdom, they have traditionally not been enforced by the courts, although courts have acknowledged their existence as aids to judicial interpretation.[52] So it is unclear whether a challenge mounted to UK legislation adopted in the absence of legislative consent would be justiciable. However, Conventions do trigger soft legal commitments—Sewel is subject to a Memorandum of Understanding and a supplementary agreement between the UK Government and devolved authorities.[53]

Furthermore, any attempt to disregard the legislative consent of devolved legislatures in a subsequent UK statute might infringe *H v Lord Advocate*[54] in which the UK Supreme Court held that the Scotland Act 1998, as a 'constitutional statute' cannot be impliedly but only expressly repealed. This would imply that a subsequent UK Parliament could legislate for Scotland without consent but only explicitly, in which case it would have to take the political consequences, which could be considerable.

But there may be further obstacles along the way to any repeal of the European Communities Act 1972 and amendment of the devolution Acts. In October 2014, Scottish First Minister Nicola Sturgeon stated that, if a Bill were proposed in the House of Commons for a referendum on EU membership, the SNP 'would table an amendment, requiring that for the United Kingdom to leave the EU, each of the four constituent nations—England, Scotland, Wales, and Northern Ireland—would have to vote to do so, not just the UK as a whole',[55] and she has since confirmed this call for a 'double majority lock' on a number of occasions. In making this point, Sturgeon was aiming to ensure that none of the UK nations would be removed from the EU against their will. However, she was also emphasizing a point made by Westminster leaders during the Scottish referendum campaign—that the United Kingdom is a 'family of nations',[56] with equal status for each of the family members. Sturgeon's point was that to withdraw the United Kingdom from the EU, against Scotland's will, would be 'democratically indefensible'. In making this case Sturgeon drew some comparisons:

> If you look at states like Australia and Canada there are some circumstances where changes to their constitution requires not just a majority across the country but in each of the provinces as well ... Germany requires its Länder to sign-off on changes to the Basic Law, through a two-thirds vote in the *Bundesrat*. So you can see that such double majorities do exist.[57]

[52] *Att.-Gen. v Jonathan Cape Ltd* [1976] QB 752 and *Re Amendment of the Constitution of Canada* [1983] AC 394, HL.

[53] Cabinet Office, *Devolution: Memorandum of Understanding and Supplementary Agreement* (2012).

[54] *H v Lord Advocate* [2012] UKSC 24.

[55] See I. MacWhirter, 'A Federal Bomb is Dropped into More-Powers Debate' *Herald* (30 October 2014). In fact, SNP attempts to table such an amendment in the course of the European Referendum Bill in 2015, failed.

[56] eg 'PM begs Scots not to break up "Family of Nations"' *Reuters* (10 September 2014).

[57] N. Sturgeon, speech, 29 October 2014, discussed at <http://www.heraldscotland.com/comment/columnists/a-federal-bomb-is-dropped-into-more-powers-debate.25721371>.

C. A 'family of nations'

Is Sturgeon's argument plausible? Would it be possible for the devolved nations to set a threshold for withdrawal from the EU that required a majority of votes in each of the devolved nations? Although, in the frantic last days before the Scottish independence referendum, there was talk of moves towards a 'federal' United Kingdom, we do not have a federal system in the United Kingdom, which currently lacks institutional protections for regional government of the sort that Sturgeon's examples of Australia, Canada, or Germany possess. The present UK devolution settlement is an asymmetric one, in which England is dominant (in spite of calls for English votes for English legislation). A move to federalism might seem unlikely (in the short term at least) and however the Smith Commission[58] provisions on further devolution to Scotland are implemented, they are unlikely to include greater autonomy for devolved nations in foreign affairs (which is taken to include the EU), or the UK constitution as a whole, which are reserved matters under Schedule 5 Scotland Act 1998. In the absence of any federal-type settlement, it is challenging to create institutional arrangements on a regional basis to accommodate the particular needs of devolved nations regarding the EU, and indeed, the attempted SNP amendment to insert a 'double majority lock' into the EU Referendum Bill failed in 2015.

However, as many areas of EU competence relate to devolved matters,[59] and continued Scottish membership of the EU is a concern in the event of Scottish independence, EU membership is likely to be of great interest in Scotland and probably Wales and Northern Ireland. The prospect of an EU exit could therefore provoke the demand for another independence referendum in Scotland. It is likely that the Scottish independence debate would be reopened in the event of such a fundamental constitutional change as a forced EU exit, and the removal of Scottish citizens' EU rights, without their consent.

In this context, Sturgeon's reminder that the United Kingdom is 'a family of nations' highlights existing problems of the United Kingdom's constitutional structures, as well as requiring those who have urged federalism[60] to take seriously the consequences of federalist principles. Failing this, 'Brexit' may spark another Scottish independence referendum.

D. Sovereignty and exiting the EU

Therefore an exit from the EU, or the threat of one, is likely to provoke substantial constitutional disruption. This is significant because those who wish

[58] (n. 49).

[59] For example many EU fields, such as agriculture, relate to devolved Scottish competences, even if the UK's relationship with the EU overall is a matter of foreign affairs, and thus reserved.

[60] See eg 'Independence Referendum: UK Should Adopt Federal System in Event of No-Vote, Says Lib Dem Commission' *Telegraph* (16 October 2012).

to exit the EU often argue that such an exit would fully restore parliamentary sovereignty[61]—a projected return to some Diceyan traditionalist constitution with the supremacy of the UK Parliament as its apogee. However, it is far from clear that an EU exit would repair any alleged loss of parliamentary sovereignty. There is of course the fact that alternative arrangements would have to be made by the United Kingdom to join other regional, international, and trading groups—whether it be EEA, EFTA, or a lonely world of bilateral trading arrangements within the overall aegis of the WTO. Such arrangements would undoubtedly have a major impact on UK sovereignty, although their discussion is beyond the remit of this chapter. But let us look a little more closely at this 'sovereignty' that supposedly could be restored.

As stated, a British exit from the EU is sometimes justified in terms of the maintenance of parliamentary sovereignty, which presently must concede the supremacy of EU law (acknowledged both in CJEU case law such as *Costa v ENEL*,[62] and s. 2(4) of the European Communities Act). However, the Diceyan orthodoxy of parliamentary sovereignty has never been as powerful north of the border. In the 1953 case of *MacCormick v Lord Advocate* in the Court of Session, the Lord President, Lord Cooper, (a former Conservative and Unionist politician and eminent legal historian) contested the Diceyan orthodoxy thus:

> The principle of the unlimited sovereignty of parliament is a distinctively English principle which has no counterpart in Scottish constitutional law ...[63]

In her well-known work, *Britons: Forging the Nation*[64] Linda Colley reminds us that both the British state and the British national identity were 'forged' by the Acts of Union of 1707. The United Kingdom is only 300 years old, not an ancient natural phenomenon, and it may be undone. Given that the Union of 1707 brought into being the British state, ought we not give this historical event of the Acts of Union its due as a keystone of the British constitution, rather than the Diceyan mantra of parliamentary sovereignty? In which case, perhaps we should recognize that the British constitution is not simply the English constitution, and that Scottish constitutional principles (and Northern Irish, and even now nascent Welsh[65]) play their part in a multiple constitutional order, and may be of particular salience at times of crisis or 'constitutional' moments, such as the issue of whether to withdraw from the EU. Scottish intellectuals, lawyers, and politicians of many different political persuasions stand by an indigenous Scottish tradition of popular sovereignty that is claimed to date back to the Declaration of Arbroath in 1320. They hold that, before the 1707 Act of Union, sovereignty resided in the

[61] eg John Redwood, 'Is Parliament Still Sovereign?' 23 November 2012, available at: <http://johnredwoodsdiary.com/2012/11/23/is-parliament-still-sovereign/>.

[62] Case 6/64, *Flaminio Costa v ENEL* [1964] ECR 585.

[63] *MacCormick v Lord Advocate* 1953 SC 396, 1953 SLT 255.

[64] L. Colley, *Britons: Forging the Nation, 1707–1837* (Vintage 1996).

[65] See eg the 'Welsh Byelaws' case: *Attorney General v National Assembly for Wales Commission and others* [2012] UKSC 53.

Scottish people—and that it still does so, in spite of the claims of Diceyan parliamentary sovereignty.[66]

Many Scottish politicians accept the doctrine of Scottish popular sovereignty. It was this doctrine that pervaded the Claim of Right for Scotland in 1989. The draft interim Constitution for an independent Scotland, published in 2014, sets out as a fundamental principle that 'the people are sovereign' and that 'the people have the sovereign right to self-determination and to choose freely the form in which their State is to be constituted and how they are to be governed'.[67]

Therefore, reflection on the entirety of the Union, and its constitutional basis, poses the question of whether, at least in Scotland, the doctrine of popular sovereignty might form the basis of Scotland's own right to determine whether or not it exits the EU.

E. Towards a different (federal?) constitution?

If we recognize that a UK exit from the EU should be seen through not just an English, but also Scottish, Northern Irish, and Welsh constitutional lens, where does this perception lead?

We live in uncertain constitutional times. At time of writing, a Scotland Bill, building on the Smith Commission recommendations, is passing through the UK Parliament[68] at the same time as an EU Referendum Bill.[69] These two Bills may well be in tension with one another—as, while an EU Bill would seek to regain for Parliament sovereignty transferred to the EU, a Scottish Bill might have constitutional implications of a very different sort. The Smith report recommended a guarantee that a Scottish Parliament be made permanent, and that the Sewel Convention be placed on a statutory footing. As the doctrine of parliamentary sovereignty currently stands, it would be difficult to provide such permanence by way of legal guarantee. However, even if the permanence of a Scottish Parliament cannot be ironclad in law, it would possess the strength of political commitment, shedding a federal light on constitutional arrangements, and no doubt other demands would follow on from an appreciably strengthened Scottish Parliament. There could be calls for greater regional powers in England, more radical reform of the House of Lords, and for constitutional reform more generally. The demand for, and process of, devolution may have an irresistible momentum of its own.

However, if we accept that the British constitution may have to adapt to cope with momentous constitutional upheavals in the coming years, then we should face this prospect with an open mind, and realize that not all demands for recognition

[66] On this see further eg N. MacCormick, 'On Sovereignty and Post-Sovereignty' in *Questioning Sovereignty* (n. 25); C. Kidd, *Union and Unionisms: Political Thought in Scotland, 1500–2000* (Cambridge University Press 2008). And see Kidd and Petrie, Ch. 2 in the present volume.

[67] *Scottish Draft Independence Bill: A Consultation on an Interim Constitution for Scotland* (The Scottish Government 2014) ss 2 and 3.

[68] Scotland Bill (HC Bill 48) introduced to the UK Parliament on 28 May 2015.

[69] European Union Referendum Bill (HC Bill 6) introduced to the UK Parliament on 28 May 2015.

of status may come from Britain's devolved areas. At present it is England that is most desirous of leaving the EU. If it is undemocratic for Scotland to be forced out of the EU on the back of a majority vote from England, then would it not be undemocratic for England to be forced to remain in the EU, if the majority of its people wished to leave but the votes of devolved nations prevented exit? In such a case, it may be England that wishes to turn to federal precedents or seek to distinguish itself by greater autonomy while remaining in the United Kingdom. Might it be possible for England to exit the EU within the aegis of a 'federal' United Kingdom in which Scotland, Wales, and Northern Ireland remained EU members?[70]

In 1985 the then EEC lost half of its land area when Greenland withdrew from the EEC, following opposition to the EEC common fisheries policy, an event already discussed earlier in this chapter. Greenland however continued to be part of part of the kingdom of Denmark (albeit with a high level of internal autonomy) and Denmark continued to be a member state of the EEC. Following withdrawal, Greenland became associated with the EU as an Overseas Country and Territory through the Greenland Treaty.

The Greenland example sets a precedent for the fact that *part* of a member state may leave the EU. Of course England and Greenland are very different cases. Greenland has only a population of 56,000 and was not the dominant territorial component of Denmark. There would undoubtedly be very difficult questions concerning the relations between component parts of the United Kingdom if its largest part were not an EU member. Perhaps such an arrangement would simply not be possible. However, the varied arrangements of autonomous, or semi-independent, former UK colonies within the Commonwealth, and present day examples of substate entities, such as federacies, suggest that there already exist a wealth of prototypes that could be useful role models.[71] Without such (admittedly) adventurous arrangements, the breakup of the United Kingdom may be likely.

However, the Greenland analogy is only one further step down the path of a thought experiment set in motion by the very realistic prospect of an EU exit referendum. The second part of this chapter has tried to analyse this issue from the perspective not only of the British constitution, but of the component parts of that constitution, without assuming that England will necessarily carry the other nations with it wherever it wishes to go.

In conclusion, it is to be stressed that a British exit from the EU could imperil the very national sovereignty and self-determination that its advocates believe it will bring about. These issues will not wither away. Euroscepticism will bubble

[70] See also on this point E. Hepburn, 'Scotland: if Not Independence Then a Federacy?' (*British Politics and Policy blog*, 16 December 2014).

[71] For a sample see eg: Y. Ghai and S. Woodman (eds), *Practising Self-Government: A Comparative Study of Autonomous Regions* (Cambridge University Press 2013); R. Watts, 'Federalism, Federal Political Systems and Federations' (1998) *Annual Review of Political Science* 117; E. Hepburn, 'Recrafting Sovereignty: Lessons from Small Island Autonomies?' in A. Gagnon and M. Keating (eds), *Political Autonomy and Divided Societies* (Palgrave Macmillan 2012).

on, especially within parts of England, even if there were to be an affirmative vote to stay in the EU in an in-out referendum. Therefore the British constitution will need to adapt to take account of these pressures.

III. Conclusion

Reflection on these two referenda, and on the prospect of two different secession events, has required us to look deeply at the law supporting the current legal situation—the EU legal system and the British constitution—and indeed to interpret and interrogate them beyond their face value. In both cases, I have argued for an interpretation that acknowledges these legal systems' capacity for heterogeneity, and for their recognition of the importance of rights—fundamental and acquired. I also argue for an analysis of the rights of these Unions' component parts that go beyond the legalistic and formalistic.

The notions of secession from the EU, or secession within the EU, present novel twenty-first century challenges. It is to be hoped that participants will rise to these challenges. As Neil Walker reminds us, when writing about MacCormick's legal and political theory, such political nationalism may be characterized as that of 'the *unsettled state*, one ill-defined within our existing political and constitutional vocabulary', and for some, this will be 'an unsettling conclusion'.[72] But, in this context, we might do well to conclude with the words of the late Neil MacCormick himself, who was an enthusiastic supporter of an independent Scotland within the EU, and who wrote of the EU in the following words:

> For this is a new form of political order, a new kind of 'commonwealth', which offers the hope of transcending the sovereign state rather than simply replicating it in some new super-state ... It creates new possibilities of imagining, and thus of subsequently realizing, political order on the basis of a pluralistic rather than a monolithic conception of the exercise of political power and legal authority.[73]

[72] N. Walker, 'Scottish Nationalism: For and against the Union State' in Walker (ed.), *MacCormick's Scotland* (Edinburgh University Press 2012) 190.

[73] MacCormick (n. 25) at 191.

9

International Law, the Independence Debate, and Political Settlement in the UK

*Christine Bell**

I. Introduction

This chapter examines the role that international law played in the Scottish independence debates. I argue that international law—perhaps surprisingly—played a central role. International law was used by both Yes and No campaigns in strategically instrumental ways, to bolster their political claims as to the consequences of independence.

However, contrary to the view that appeals to 'the international' are more the terrain of Nationalists than Unionists, reliance on international law was much greater by the No campaign than the Yes campaign.[1] The international legal characterization of post-independence Scotland as a 'successor state', and the remaining United Kingdom (rUK) as the 'continuing state', became central to UK Government/Better Together/No arguments relating to the economic, physical, and social security of an independent Scotland. These arguments were central to the UK Government's campaign strategy, and in consequence international law also became important to Scottish Government/Yes campaign rebuttals.

In this chapter I examine how the UK and Scottish Governments used international law as a tool to engage in domestic politics. I suggest that the central place accorded international legal argument constituted a departure from the United Kingdom's traditional treatment of the revision of its central political settlement as an exclusively domestic political matter, so bringing it into line with what is normally considered the *sui generis* case of Northern Ireland. The centrality of international law to domestic political argument signals just how important

* This chapter has benefited from thinking from the Political Settlements Research Programme <www.politicalsettlements.org>, funded by the Department for International Development, but views represent the author's own and not the views of the programme or the funder.

[1] See eg W. Lord, 'Scotland, Independence, and Internationalism' Carnegie Council for Ethics in International Affairs (25 February 2013) <http://www.carnegiecouncil.org/publications/ethics_online/0079.html> accessed 19 October 2015.

international law has become with respect to processes of political settlement globally—the creation of an international law of polity formation is itself a fast-moving international legal development.

I further argue that these global legal developments illustrate a dynamic whereby the attempt to regulate polity formation by reference to international legal argument carries an extraordinary capacity to reshape international law. I suggest that this was the case with the Scottish independence referendum. Arguments as to how international law applied that relied on an incomplete and inapposite international legal framework, point to the ways in which international legal doctrine relating to secession needs 'completed' and so have a capacity to reshape the law. I therefore consider the ways in which Scottish independence arguments themselves became or could become constitutive of international law.

II. International law and political settlement in the United Kingdom

Traditionally, as a strong state and one of the five permanent members of the UN Security Council, the United Kingdom has resisted and been able to resist internationalization of internal challenges to its political settlement and constitutional order. Most notably in Northern Ireland, any notion that international law had anything to say about resolution of the conflict, or that international law regulated how the United Kingdom could reconfigure the political settlement in that part of its jurisdiction was strongly resisted right up until the months before the Belfast/Good Friday Agreement was signed.[2]

Resistance to international legal interference in internal affairs is bolstered by the United Kingdom's constitution's capacity to deny and accommodate challenges to the United Kingdom's political settlement through pragmatic accommodation.[3] Famously the UK constitution 'evolves' rather than is made: its political settlement slowly mutates to accommodate challenges from within the state's boundaries. This has enabled internal processes of change to evade the clutch of international law: international law comes more easily into play in moments of extraordinary transition in which the state's territorial boundaries and self-definition are up for grabs. The idea that international law should have any regulatory hold over the United Kingdom's internal political settlement processes is often seen as itself unconstitutional, and therefore a non-unionist and radical position. Legally, those who challenge the United Kingdom's political settlement run up against the orthodox Diceyan mantra concerning Parliamentary sovereignty over all other internal or external law. Politically, they run up against a

[2] C. Bell, *Peace Agreements and Human Rights* (Oxford University Press 2000) 56–60.

[3] See: C. McCrudden, 'Using Comparative Constitutionalism in Human Rights Discourse: Ireland's Past and Scotland's Future' [2013] *EdinLR* 314; C. Bell, 'Constitutional Transitions: The Peculiarities of the British Constitution and the Politics of Comparison' [2014] *PL* 446.

fairly conservative form of constitutional patriotism that views all outside interference with suspicion.

In contrast, Nationalist challenges to the United Kingdom's constitution have often sought to ground their claims in the language of 'internationalism', forming transnational alliances, appealing to cosmopolitan identities, lobbying international organizations, and using international legal argument. Although they have done it in very different ways, both Irish and Scottish Nationalists have often self-consciously located arguments for change in 'the international', in contrast to their Unionist counterparts who defend the Union in domestic terms.[4] This Unionist/Nationalist difference is not a matter of different national psychologies or cultural politics (although no doubt some will make arguments that these form a part of the picture), but can be understood in terms of the political dynamics that accompany first-order political challenges to states. These challenges involve the suggestion that the political settlement that underpins the status quo should be radically reworked, and in so doing shape a political economy (as in a pattern of public choice rational self-interest) of how international law is accessed and by whom.

These first-order challenges must contest not just the substance of that order, but the underlying constitutional and political rules that prevent such challenge. International law is often resorted to as a way of confronting from outside the state's internal default responses to any challenge. To put it more prosaically: for any state, if those in power have what they want and seek to keep it, they will use the internal constitutional order to stave off internal assertions of change. Conversely, contenders will reach outside that political order to try to challenge the legitimacy of its default political and constitutional positions. And so, particularly in stable liberal democracies, 'the international', including international law, tends to be a tool of the contender and resisted by those in favour of the status quo.

The Scottish referendum campaign, however, indicates the ways in which international law also can be used in more conservative ways to bolster the prevailing system of states. As is often said: 'international law is not a suicide club for states'.[5] Even in this globalized world international law remains at heart an interstate body of law, and in so a positivist concept of international law was useful to the UK Government as a key campaign tool for reinforcing the status quo of the United Kingdom. A form of 'internationalization reversal' occurred whereby the state used positivist conceptions of international law to shore up its sovereignty, while it

[4] On internationalist dimensions of Scottish Nationalism see N. Walker, 'Scottish Nationalism For and Against the Union State: The Vision of N. MacCormick' in N. Walker (ed.), *MacCormick's Scotland* (Edinburgh University Press 2012) 163. On internationalist dimensions of Irish Nationalism (and others in the conflict) see A. Guelke, 'Comparatively Peaceful: The Role of Analogy in Northern Ireland's Peace Process' [1997] *Camb Rev Int Aff* 28.

[5] The phrase is used by a range of international lawyers when talking of self-determination, often with quotation marks but not attributed. The best attribution may be to H. L. A. Hart, who stated that '... our concern is with social arrangements for continued existence, not with those of a suicide club.' H. L. A. Hart, *The Concept of Law* (Clarendon Press 1961) 188.

proved difficult for nationalists to engage with international law, whether in relation to the EU, or state succession. This dynamic has precursors elsewhere: strong liberal states are particularly able to use international law to underline the lack of availability of secession. Similar recourse to international law was made by the Federal Government in Canada, as part of its opposition to Quebec secession in 1997, asking the Canadian Supreme Court to determine, among other things, whether Quebec had a right to secession under international law.[6] As a result, the Canadian Supreme Court found itself reworking key understandings of Canada's constitution, but also needing to engage with the self-determination doctrine of international law.

III. The use of international law in the referendum campaign

International law played three key roles in the Scottish referendum campaign. First, it formed a silent 'shadow' against which self-determination claims and modalities played out. Second, international law intermingled with European law, in arguments over whether Scotland would be admitted (or enabled to continue) as a member of the EU after a vote in favour of independence. Third, the law on state succession played a crucial political role in underpinning arguments about the currency and division of assets and liabilities. I will address each of these in turn; however, the last of these three roles was most significant and will be most centrally addressed in this chapter.

IV. International law and the entitlement to a referendum

International law was relevant to the idea that Scotland was entitled to a referendum in several ways, but indirectly rather than directly. Here it ensured that key battles over how independence could be achieved were pushed into the domestic constitutional frame of reference.

The move to hold a referendum took place in the shadow of international self-determination law. The United Kingdom quickly accepted that Scotland could hold a referendum and could leave the United Kingdom, if that referendum was successful. It is worth noting that it was not entirely predetermined that the UK Government's position would be to immediately concede a referendum when the SNP gained a majority in the Scottish Parliament in 2011 and announced their intention to hold one. This concession was fairly unusual for a western, liberal state. International law does not support a right to Scottish secession. Scottish people are not 'a people' as defined by that law—because they do not comprise the whole of the people in the territory.[7] Arguably, they are not even a 'national

[6] *Reference Re Secession of Quebec* [1998] 2 SCR 217.

[7] H. Gros Espiell, *The Right to Self-Determination: Implementation of the United Nations Resolutions* (United Nations 1980).

minority' as defined in international minority rights standards, because those standards understand the term 'minority' in identity terms that closely ally with status equality categories, such as race or ethnicity, because they imply that identity is not a political choice.[8] While historically 'Scottishness' could have sustained such an identity claim, interestingly, contemporaneously the SNP itself has reframed 'Scottishness' in terms of a chosen 'civic' identity rather than in 'status equality' terms such as ethnicity or national origin.

Neither was there any positive constitutional law imperative to concede a referendum. Unlike Section 1 of the Northern Ireland Act 1998, the Scotland Act 1998 did not mention referendums much less provide a procedure for one. From a domestic constitutional law perspective the idea that Scotland could have a referendum on independence was backed up only by the fact that devolution required a vote of the people of the jurisdiction, and ongoing arguments that subjecting major constitutional change to a referendum is gaining the status of constitutional convention.[9]

However, another shadow of international law played a role in reinforcing what could be understood as a domestic constitutional imperative to accommodate the demand for a referendum. A 'Union state' narrative of the UK constitution has always underwritten arguments for understanding the Union as based on ongoing consent.[10] The notion that the Acts of Union 1707, whereby the Scottish and English Kingdoms were united, remained in some sense a treaty between sovereign nations played a role in underwriting the constitutional commitment to Scottish choice. Long-standing Nationalist arguments claimed that they continued to operate as in some sense international treaties providing for a new foundational constitutional understanding of the united kingdoms of Scotland and England, that depended not just on the consent of that moment but on the consent of the Scottish people on a continuing basis.[11] These arguments were used to push for Scottish devolution in the 1970s, and to achieve Scottish devolution in 1997–8 (through the assertion of a 'Claim of Right' and a

[8] For example, the United Nations Minorities Declaration, adopted by consensus in 1992, refers in its article 1 to minorities as based on national or ethnic, cultural, religious, and linguistic identity, and provides that States should protect their existence. As the Office of the United Nations High Commissioner for Human Rights points out, there is no internationally agreed definition as to which groups constitute minorities, and it is often stressed that the existence of a minority is a question of fact. However, any definition must include both objective factors (such as the existence of a shared ethnicity, language, or religion) and subjective factors (including that individuals must identify themselves as members of a minority). Similarly, in the foundational study by Francesco Capotorti, a minority is: 'A group numerically inferior to the rest of the population of a State, in a non-dominant position, whose members—being nationals of the State—possess ethnic, religious or linguistic characteristics differing from those of the rest of the population and show, if only implicitly, a sense of solidarity, directed towards preserving their culture, traditions, religion or language.' F. Capotorti, *Study on the Rights of Persons Belonging to Ethnic, Religious and Linguistic Minorities* (United Nations 1979) at 5–15. While historically 'Scottishness' may have been able to be articulated in these terms the contemporary concept of Scottishness has a much more complex political dimension.

[9] V. Bognador, *The New British Constitution* (Hart 2009) ch. 7.

[10] See Kidd and Petrie, Ch. 2 in this volume.

[11] See eg *MacCormick v Lord Advocate* 1953 SC 396, 1953 SLT 255.

'constitutional convention'), and in turn were reinforced by those devolution referendums. The use of a referendum to confirm devolution contributed to the sense that devolution itself was a 'constituent moment' propelled and underwritten by the consent of the people and in continuity with historic notions of the Scottish Parliament and the 'Union state' narrative of the United Kingdom.

Unlike Spain, therefore, where the constitutional claims of 'unity' are used to deny a referendum, the United Kingdom's unwritten constitution can be argued to permit and even require that referenda are supported where the majority of a historic national minority appears to support it. In global terms, the United Kingdom's constitutional commitment to a right to secession places the United Kingdom in an exclusive constitutional club of which the other members are Bougainville Papua New Guinea, Ethiopia, Saint Kitts and Nevis, Lichtenstein, and Slovakia, and arguably with fewer procedural hurdles than in those jurisdictions.[12]

The UK concession at the outset of Scotland's 'right to decide', meant that struggles over the referendum played out in the domestic constitutional terrain and over questions of who could hold it, frame the question, and set the process, rather than the question of whether a referendum was permitted. These struggles are dealt with elsewhere in this collection, and were resolved by the provision of a Section 30 Order under the terms of the Scotland Act 1998, which devolved power to hold a referendum to the Scottish Government as part of a UK–Scotland intergovernmental agreement.[13]

Although international law on self-determination did not ostensibly drive the United Kingdom's approach to the referendum, the approach of the United Kingdom was progressive and in line with new understandings of international law. A number of academics, myself included, have pointed out that international self-determination law is currently being reinterpreted to push more towards 'a right to be heard' and even accommodated, rather than towards an outright right to secession.[14] Indeed, the Quebec Secession case in some senses helped establish and bolster this understanding of how self-determination might work where arguments of colonization or gross injustice do not apply. In that sense, the United Kingdom's support for the referendum bolsters support for this trajectory of international law as a procedural rather than a substantive right. However, the concept of a 'right to be heard' has its own ambiguities, and here the Scottish case may point the way to their resolution. It is unclear which groups have 'a right to be

[12] See Constitute <https://www.constituteproject.org> accessed 19 October 2015. Neil Walker also argues that the UK constitution today is unusually facilitative of secession in comparison to these constitutions which have substantial procedural safeguards before a referendum is held, see N. Walker, 'Beyond Secession? Law in the Framing of National Polity' in S. Tierney (ed.), *Nationalism and Globalization* (Hart 2015).

[13] See in particular Mitchell, Ch. 4 and McEwen, Ch. 10 this volume.

[14] See in particular Wellers, Kymlicka, and Klabbers, respectively, in M. Wellers, 'Settling Self-Determination Conflicts: Recent Developments' [2009] *EJIL* 112; W. Kymlicka, *Multi-Cultural Odysseys: Navigating the New International Politics of Diversity* (Oxford University Press 2007); C. Bell, *On the Law of Peace: Peace Agreements and the Lex Pacificatoria* (Oxford University Press 2008); and J. Klabbers, 'The Right to be Taken Seriously: Self-Determination in International Law' [2006] *HRQ* 186.

heard', or the extent to which this right imposes a corresponding duty to respond, and if so—how far: to a right to secession or something else?

As regards these ambiguities, the example of the United Kingdom is interesting because it suggests an approach to group accommodation that is contingent on the domestic constitutional order and national status of the group in question. Even after the Scottish referendum, it does not seem entirely certain that the United Kingdom would take the same view as regards Welsh demands to secede as it did with Scotland, and it would be entirely unlikely to allow referenda for secession of Cornwall, or parts of North England. The United Kingdom's accommodation of self-determination challenges could be understood to depend on historic notions of 'relevant political and national' communities that have their roots in the different processes of state formation by which the United Kingdom was formed out of constituent nations.

This approach can usefully contribute to a better international understanding of 'who' exactly has a right to be heard, and how far they should be listened to and accommodated. The United Kingdom's answer to the question of 'who' has the right to be heard and 'to what end' is effectively that groups who have strong historical arguments that they should be included in first-order decisions of the state's political form should be responded to, to the extent that their ongoing consent is necessary to the state's on-going stability and legitimacy—something that depends on the resonance of their claim as regards the state's foundational political settlement.

This approach can perhaps be viewed as a logic of political bargaining as much as a legal approach—those who have capacity to fundamentally disrupt the state's stability should be accommodated. However, it is facilitated legally by the 'Union state' narrative that understands the United Kingdom as based on an on-going union of states.[15] Nonetheless, the approach could well operate as a useful normative rule of thumb elsewhere, and a contribution to emerging international legal reworking of self-determination law. Ironically, the close-run nature of the referendum may undermine 'take up' of this new approach by more risk averse governments.

V. Scotland and membership of the European Union

Although it is beyond the scope of this chapter, it is worth noting for the sake of completeness that public international law also came to the fore with questions over whether Scotland would be able to join the EU. The situation, not provided for in the EU treaties, of a region which was, as part of the state in which it belonged, within the EU, wanting to remain in the EU but seceding from the parent state, caused much discussion and debate over whether Scotland would remain a member of the EU, or have to reapply, and what the implication for negotiations

[15] See further Kidd and Petrie, Ch. 2 this volume.

and EU treaty revision would be. While the central arguments revolved around interpretation of the EU treaties as a matter of EU law, these arguments were underwritten by public international law. Article 31(1) of the Vienna Convention on the Law of Treaties provides that: 'A treaty shall be interpreted in good faith in accordance with the ordinary meaning to be given to the terms of the treaty in their context and in light of its object and purpose.'[16] This question was of course crucial politically, as for many years the Scottish National Party (SNP) had tied its commitment to independence to a concept of 'Scotland in Europe', that was able to present independence as becoming a more central part of a larger entity, rather than becoming a smaller 'ourselves alone' state-let. International law on state succession also played a role in this debate as it implicated ongoing membership of Scotland in all the international organizations of which the United Kingdom is a part, as will be discussed further below.

VI. International law and the disentanglement of a union

While international law was the shadow under which the entitlement to a referendum was negotiated, and debates around Scotland's EU membership unfolded, questions of how the Scottish and rUK might be disentangled and broken up post any Yes vote saw international law take centre stage.

The United Kingdom used its first formal intervention into the referendum debate—the first of a series of 'Scotland Analysis' papers—to make a strong claim that in the event of a Yes vote and Scottish independence, the United Kingdom would remain intact as a state (in legal terms a 'continuing state'), with Scotland leaving and becoming a new state (in legal terms 'a successor state').[17] Most of the key UK arguments in the referendum flowed from this relatively unchallenged assertion that in the event of Scottish secession the rUK would be a continuing state with full legal and political continuity, while Scotland would become a new and separate 'successor' state. The Scotland Analysis paper was bolstered by a legal opinion commissioned by the UK Government. This legal advice was appended to the paper, and was provided by international lawyers Alan Boyle, Professor of Public International Law, University of Edinburgh and James Crawford SC, Whewell Professor of International Law, University of Cambridge. Publication of legal advice to the government is itself fairly unusual—the convention is that the existence of legal advice does not have to be revealed let alone published, and publication is often only conceded in moments

[16] See D. Edwards, 'Scotland and the European Union' (*Scottish Constitutional Futures Forum*, 17 December 2012) <http://www.scottishconstitutionalfutures.org/OpinionandAnalysis/ViewBlogPost/tabid/1767/articleType/ArticleView/articleId/852/David-Edward-Scotland-and-the-European-Union.aspx> accessed 19 October 2015.

[17] See HM Government, *Scotland Analysis: Devolution and the Implications of Scottish Independence* 2013 (Cm 8554, February 2013), and Annex A's legal opinion by Boyle and Crawford <https://www.gov.uk/government/uploads/system/uploads/attachment_data/file/79417/Scotland_analysis_Devolution_and_the_implications_of_Scottish_Independan...__1_.pdf>.

of extreme political pressure. Skilfully, however, this move swiftly pulled the 'internationalist' rug from under Nationalists' feet and lent legal gravitas to the UK Government's No campaign.

In rebuttal, the Scottish Government and the Yes campaign did very little. The Scottish Government was careful not to confirm acceptance of the UK position, but there is no evidence that a legal opinion was sought, and no strong alternative legal or other argument was mounted. The Scottish Government's failure to set out an alternative legal narrative perhaps reflected a political judgment that legal arguments would not win the day, as well as a legal judgment that the rebuttal legal arguments would be fairly weak.[18] It is difficult to tell how much the approach of responding to law with politics was a gut campaign reaction or a thought-through strategy.

However, arguably their approach underestimated the close interrelationship the UK Government was weaving as regards legal positions and core campaign messages. The Unionists' key campaign strategy was to focus on underlining the political, international, and financial security brought by the United Kingdom, mostly articulated in negative terms as a message of what people in Scotland had to fear from leaving the United Kingdom (hence the label 'Project Fear' ascribed by the Yes campaign). The complexity of nationality and identity claims in the United Kingdom meant that there was almost no Unionist defence of the Union in ideological or identity terms, and the incapacity to fight for the Union in these terms pushed the defence onto a pragmatic and ostensibly simple message of what materially would be lost to Scotland and its people. This move can be understood to have in a sense forced Unionists towards international law as a key resource because the sovereignty card handed control over Scotland's material future to the status quo state.

The recourse to international law by the Unionist campaign, while logical in hindsight, at the time was surprising. Few would have predicted that the United Kingdom's opening gambit in the referendum debate would be to set out the rather dry and dusty argument that what was at play was 'secession' rather than 'dissolution'.

VII. On the use of law and lawyers

A short digression on the role of lawyers in the debate is warranted, because the approach to lawyers and legal advice itself can be understood to be a key Unionist/nationalist campaign distinction. The UK Government located its primary 'thinking' in the Scotland Office, headed up by the Secretary of State for Scotland, with a particularly important role ascribed to the Advocate General of Scotland (a UK Government position), Lord Wallace of Tankerness QC, former MP for Shetland

[18] A. Carty and M. Clyde, 'Scotland and England: From a Union of Parliaments to Two Independent Kingdoms' (2014) 2 *London Review of International Law* 299.

and Orkney, MSP for Orkney, deputy First Minister of Scotland (the first one) and leader of the Liberal Democrats in Scotland. In common with other parts of the campaign, Scottish members of the government and Liberal Democrats were put at the forefront of the campaign, as being less 'toxic' than English Tories, more available than Scottish ones (who were in short supply), and also because it strongly signalled 'Unionism' as also a genuinely 'Scottish' position. However, the situating of the key analysis unit in the Scotland Office with Lord Wallace meant that important UK Government formal interventions in the debate were made by lawyers with legal emphases.[19] However, the Scotland Office (UK Government) legal capacity was also significantly boosted by access to lawyers from across the civil service. The UK Government had at its disposal international lawyers from the Foreign and Commonwealth Office, and constitutional lawyers involved in central constitutional projects.

The lawyers chosen for the legal opinion were independently contracted barristers: Alan Boyle, and James Crawford—one of the world's most renowned international lawyers on self-determination and secession. Boyle is originally from Northern Ireland, and Crawford from Australia, although both have been academics in the UK 'mainland' for a long time. Professionally they were beyond challenge. Crawford had given legal expert opinion in the Canadian Secession case,[20] and such is his status that his view of the law is likely to even be viewed as in some sense constitutive of the law (as 'the teachings of the most highly qualified publicists' are one of the sources of international law[21]). Whatever their own political positions, they were acting in the British legal tradition as lawyers for hire: properly acquired, briefed, and presumably paid. Unusually however, Crawford at least gave media interviews arguing for his opinion, although he also went 'off script' in terms of UK Government positions (for example, on the feasibility of the Scottish Government's post-referendum negotiation timelines).[22]

In an early move the Scotland Office and Lord Wallace also set up a 'Forum of Independent Legal Experts' with representation from the Law Society and Faculty of Advocates, and legal academics, established to 'inform' the Government as regards its legal positions.[23] While many if not all of the lawyers agreed to

[19] Interestingly, the one Government Legal Service for Scotland provides legal advice both to the Scottish Government and the Lord Advocate on Scottish Law <http://www.gov.scot/About/People/Directorates/LPS/glss/glsslsla>. In practice many of the civil service lawyers in the UK Scotland Office working on UK law were seconded from jobs with the Scottish Government. So there were complex networks and relationships between the civil service lawyers working for the different governments and campaign positions.

[20] Interestingly, the mode of Crawford's intervention here was very similar to that in the Quebec case: the Attorney General of Canada filed a factum with the Supreme Court as to how he thought the questions to the court should be answered, and to that factum was appended a supplement entitled 'Expert's Report' by Professor Crawford which gave a formal legal opinion on international law on self-determination and unilateral secession which coincided with the Attorney General's factum.

[21] Article 38(1)(d) Statute of the International Court of Justice, 1946 at <http://www.icj-cij.org/documents/?p1=4&p2=2>.

[22] See BBC News, 'Scottish independence: Experts say a 'yes vote' Scotland would need new powers' (11 February 2013) at <http://www.bbc.co.uk/news/uk-scotland-scotland-politics-21408823>.

[23] In the interests of disclosure, this included the author. See generally, <https://www.gov.uk/government/groups/forum-of-independent-legal-experts>.

participate on the grounds that participation did not require taking a position on the referendum or being part of the campaign, the establishment of the group was a smart move in co-option of legal thinking in Scotland, in a sense operating also as a 'wooing' of the legal community. So, for the UK Government, international and constitutional lawyers were at the forefront of the intellectual underpinning of the UK Government's campaign thinking.

This move was not mirrored by the Scottish Government, members of whom criticized the United Kingdom's legal expert forum as 'a kangaroo court'.[24] In fact, it is fairly difficult to ascertain how the Scottish Government obtained and used independent legal advice. There was no public group of independent lawyers recruited to advise, although individual 'external' lawyers were given particular advice roles. While clearly the Scottish Government had the support of civil service lawyers and party members and allies who were lawyers, the use of lawyers played a less public and structured role and legal argument appeared to play a more subsidiary role in relation to formulating and underwriting campaign strategy that focused on political rather than legal argument. The Scottish Government did not initially commission formal legal advice on EU membership issue to much pillorying, whereupon it commissioned but did not publish advice. Whether or not they commissioned advice on Scotland's post-referendum status is not known. In the Scottish Parliament and other public statements, in response to British legal positions on Scotland's status and currency issues, the First Minister relied on unsolicited published papers and blogs.[25] By virtue of their nature, these materials were framed not as formal legal advice but more discursively and in that sense appeared more tentative than the opinions of Boyle and Crawford.

Finally, the House of Lords Constitution Committee made interventions that largely mirrored the Better Together/UK Government legal analysis, informed by a legal advisor, at that time Adam Tomkins, John Millar Professor of Public Law at the University of Glasgow, who was also an ardent political supporter of the Union in a personal capacity and has since been selected as a Conservative candidate for the 2016 Holyrood elections.[26] On the Yes side, around a month before the referendum a group of lawyers signed a statement that there was no international legal impediment to Scotland's independence, and that none of the legal issues was irresolvable.[27]

[24] See 'Mike Russell calls Legal Academics a Kangaroo Court' *Telegraph* (22 August 2012) <http://www.telegraph.co.uk/news/uknews/scotland/9490872/Mike-Russell-calls-legal-academics-a-kangaroo-court.html>.

[25] See BBC News, 'Scottish independence: Salmond warns over cost of currency union block' (17 February 2014) at <http://www.bbc.co.uk/news/uk-scotland-26226061> (citing Alex Salmond citing the author's blog); see further Alex Salmond's New Statesman Lecture, (Alex Salmond citing Scheffer's Glasgow lecture—see (n. 30), at <http://www.newstatesman.com/politics/2014/03/alex-salmonds-new-statesman-lecture-full-text>.

[26] For his personal views on the referendum see archived blog, *Notes from North Britain*, at <https://notesfromnorthbritain.wordpress.com/author/conlawforum/>.

[27] In the interests of disclosure the present author signed this statement, which is available at <http://www.lawyersforyes.org/declaration/>.

VIII. Was there a credible counter-argument to the rUK assertion of continuing state status?

But were there better counter-international legal arguments to make? It would certainly be possible to mount an argument that the break-up of the United Kingdom would amount to a dissolution rather than secession. Given that the UK constitution contemplates itself as being rooted in the on-going consent of its nations, it can be argued—most strongly in the case of Scotland of all the devolved regions—that should it withdraw from the Union, the United Kingdom in some fundamental sense ceases to be. To some extent this argument is backed up by what can be understood as a constitutional right to secession provided by the United Kingdom's unwritten constitution, as argued above. In the admittedly very different case of Yugoslavia, the Badinter Commission based their analysis that 'dissolution rather than secession' was at play, in part on the basis that the Constitution of the Socialist Federal Republic of Yugoslavia permitted secession.[28] Boyle and Crawford cite copious converse examples. However, they also note that other possibilities are possible with the consent of both states. Crucially, they note that their advice was ascertained with respect to confirming (or denying) the legal basis for a clear prior UK Government position that the United Kingdom would be a continuing state and Scotland a successor state. Critically, Boyle and Crawford's core opinion is carefully nuanced, coming down to the position stated in paragraph 93, that:

> The state practice on the dissolution of predecessor states into two or more entirely new states thus does not cast doubt on the preliminary conclusion drawn above: that the rUK would be considered the continuator state of the UK. On the contrary: assuming that the UK would be in a position to negotiate the terms of Scottish independence and that Scotland and other states would probably accept the rUK's claim to be the continuator of the UK, it strengthens that conclusion.[29]

In other words, the UK position was not untenable and had some support in international law, and provided the UK Government could negotiate it with Scotland would be likely to be accepted by other states. This is difficult to quarrel with, in part because it is very soft: it does not answer the rather more difficult question of how that position would be negotiated, or how law might help to determine the outcome of any political impasse.

In contrast, David Scheffer's international legal arguments made in a lecture in Glasgow and later relied on publicly by Alex Salmond, challenged that position and provided an interesting alternative view.[30] This view did not assert a 'dissolution'/'two successor states' alternative, rather Scheffer suggested that some sort of half-way house would need to be achieved. He suggested that the lack of violence

[28] Opinion 1, 29 November 1991, 92 ILR 162, 162–3.

[29] *Scotland Analysis: Devolution and the Implications of Scottish Independence* (n. 17) at Annex A.

[30] D. Scheffer, 'International Political and Legal Implications of Scottish Independence' (Adam Smith Research Foundation, University of Glasgow, Working Paper Series 2013:1) at <http://www.gla.ac.uk/media/media_270495_en.pdf>.

and consent of the United Kingdom made the Scottish situation *sui generis* all other secessions, and that a continuing consensual approach to questions of succession and continuity in terms of international organizations should be the political imperative. Noting that the United Kingdom was strongly advancing a position of its own continuing state status, Scheffer argued:

that posture would prove needlessly disruptive of a transition to Scottish independence. But if that remains London's position, then Scotland could issue a unilateral declaration of interpretation of its treaty relations and wait for any objections from other governments. Provided the diplomatic work is carefully undertaken in advance, such objections may not be delivered.

In fact, he went further and argued:

From this exercise a new precedent for international law may emerge: Where a State resurrects its former nationhood and sovereignty through peaceful referendum in accordance with democratic principles, the restored nation may sustain existing treaty relations where practical and provided there are no explicit objections from relevant State Parties that cannot be overcome.[31]

In other words rather than working between secession/dissolution poles, Scheffer suggested that some sort of way of dealing with both the need for continuity and for independent statehood would require to be worked out, to the benefit of both sides. This approach has some support in more general accounts of how international law on state succession needs to be approached in the contemporary context. In a review of this law in 1998, Matthew Craven pointed out how international law's apparently rigid distinction between secession and dissolution is no longer apposite to the types of guidance needed in times of transition in which the most important need of both parts of the (former) state, and of their international partners, is for continuity and smooth transfer of sovereignty. He argued that the law currently leaves a lot to political technique, and suggested that:

a far more gradated approach needs to be taken whilst dealing with questions of succession. No longer is it simply a case of determining the applicability of different rules according to a simple bifurcation between continuity and discontinuity, but rather of justifying changes to legal relations by reference to degrees of changes in the identity of the subject [that is the identity of the state].[32]

The problem for the Yes campaign was that it was difficult to articulate a single conceptual 'model' for independence that did not give away too much: secession put Scotland at a clear disadvantage vis-à-vis the rUK; while dissolution meant that everything would be up for grabs with little basis for any kind of continuity (for example in relation to EU membership); co-continuing states would only work so long as no one else in the wider world was too bothered about the identity of the state they had a relationship with—something that seemed unlikely if one

[31] Scheffer (n. 30) 10.

[32] M. Craven, 'The Problem of State Succession and the Identity of States Under International Law' [1998] *EJIL* 142.

thinks even just of UN Security Council membership or EU membership.[33] This difficulty was part of the imbalance of appeals to international law.

IX. Arguments flowing from the 'secession not dissolution' premise

The question of the security of Scotland's future was inevitably central to voter concerns as to the standing and military and financial viability of Scotland post-independence. For Scotland the question of what future resources it would have was central to its ability to survive and flourish post-independence, and therefore to the case it was presenting to voters. A range of crucial questions in which the public were very interested concerned what assets it could expect to inherit and what goods (for example embassies) it might have to go out and 'buy'; and what debt it would inherit, and to whom it would owe the debt. These questions affected not just the finances of any new state but also the size of the task facing an independent Scotland in getting its institutional infrastructure up and running.

Questions of military and financial security were, of course, similarly vital to the UK Government—the calculation of what the United Kingdom had to lose can be read between the lines of the Scotland Analysis reports, although neither campaign side had an interest in articulating it. The potential losses were financial, both in terms of the costs of unwinding the United Kingdom, the loss of Scottish wealth, and the risk of sending out a message to creditors of the national debt that the United Kingdom was unstable. Critical questions were at stake: would the rUK lose oil revenues, of which 93 per cent or so came from Scotland, or end up carrying the national debt alone? There were also significant security issues for the United Kingdom in assets and liabilities: nuclear submarines and substantial military hardware were located in Scotland—if these became Scotland's there were security implications for the United Kingdom.

Although receiving much less attention, it is worth noting that the questions were also crucially important to external third parties, most notably creditors to whom the current UK national debt is owed. Recent practice has seen creditors and international financial organizations play a key role where they see uncertainties over how debt will be repaid, as will be considered below. External states also needed to know what the status of Scotland and the United Kingdom would be, as it affected their continuity of treaty relationship. This had implications for big issues such as membership of international organizations—including notably—the Security Council (for the United Kingdom) and the EU (for Scotland). But it also had a bearing on important but less visible issues, such as the need for bilateral treaties to underwrite air traffic control operations.

[33] I am indebted to discussions with Mathew Craven for this point.

X. How each side employed international legal argumentation

Most of the most critical arguments in the Unionist armoury flowed from their central argument that 'secession' rather than 'dissolution' was at play. Notably, Unionist arguments as to the financial settlement post-separation—who would get what, and who would owe what to whom—were all claimed to flow inexorably from the assertion that the United Kingdom would be the continuing state.

However, interestingly in all these areas international law was much less favourable to the Unionist claim than their reliance on it suggested. Crucially, the press to remain the continuing state left them likely to saddle all of the international debt. The approach to international law was therefore to use the 'big gun' of a clear and authoritative legal opinion on continuing state status, and to nuance and even obscure the international legal consequences of what would flow from that premise.

The Scottish Government response on division of assets and liabilities was to set out what were in essence negotiating positions, and to try to provide reassurances to the public as to how these matters might be resolved. This was in line with international law's main emphasis on negotiated agreement, but the difficulty from a campaigning point of view was that this emphasis worked to reinforce the 'status quo bias' that tends to accompany major new political propositions: the referendum would not automatically bring independence but a negotiation between the United Kingdom and Scottish Government negotiating teams.[34] This created a fundamental campaigning problem for the Scottish Government that none of the critical contours of post-independence Scotland could be firmly guaranteed in advance.

XI. Assets and liabilities

Let us look in turn at how each government approached the division of assets and liabilities.

The Scottish Government in its White Paper on independence, *Scotland's Future*, claimed that it would support an 'equitable division of assets and liabilities'.

In detail, the Scottish Government contemplated that assets would be dealt with in the following way. As regards movable and immovable assets located in Scotland, they claimed:

Assets already used to deliver devolved public services in Scotland, such as schools, hospitals and roads, would remain in Scottish hands. Physical assets located in Scotland and needed to deliver currently reserved services, such as defence bases and equipment, and

[34] D. Kahneman, J. L. Knetsch, and R. H. Thaler, 'Anomalies: The Endowment Effect, Loss Aversion, and Status Quo Bias' [1991] *J of Econ Perspectives* 193.

buildings to support administration of welfare, tax and immigration, will transfer to the Scottish Government.[35]

This statement left the scope of Scotland's claim rather undetermined: it could have been as broad as nuclear submarines, military helicopters, or only those things essential for the delivery of public services, for example ambulances. As regards movable and immovable assets outside Scotland, the Scottish Government suggested that negotiations should take place to produce equitable division. The Scottish Government asserted that '[d]efence and overseas assets transferred as part of these negotiations will form a basis for Scotland's defence forces and overseas representation following independence.'[36] And that, Scotland will also negotiate how to 'share assets such as bespoke IT software' used to deliver current services.[37]

Two specific key assets were particularly in contention: oil and currency (if currency can be understood as an asset, as will be discussed; itself a key contention between the governments). As regards oil, the Scottish Government contemplated 'that oil and gas within Scotland's territory (which includes its waters) will become the full responsibility' of the Scottish Government, and they set out plans for how oil revenues would be dealt with;[38] although, again, what exactly would be recognized as being in 'Scottish territory' could have been contentious. As regards currency, the Scottish Government's White Paper stated 'The pound is Scotland's currency just as much as it is the UK's' and set out its preferred option as being a monetary union between Scotland and the United Kingdom and continued Scottish use of the pound.[39] This statement as to 'ownership' of the pound was taken up and rebutted by the Better Together Campaign as a statement of claim to an equitable share of currency compelling a currency union between Scotland and the United Kingdom.[40]

As regards the national debt, the Scottish Government claimed that UK national debt (then expected to be £1.6 billion in 2015/16) would be 'negotiated' and an agreement reached on Scotland's fair share. The Scottish Government suggested some possible formulae for deciding what would be 'equitable'.[41]

Interestingly, for its part the UK Government avoided explicit discussion of assets and liabilities. There was no 'Scotland Analysis' paper stating a UK view on the issue and no legal opinion was made public although one would suspect one was sought.[42] One could surmise that there were several reasons for this relative legal silence. First, that any legal opinion would have been likely to state that the position on the national debt that flowed from their claim to be a continuing state

[35] *Scotland's Future* 345. [36] *Scotland's Future* 346. [37] *Scotland's Future* 346.
[38] *Scotland's Future* ch. 8. [39] *Scotland's Future* 7.
[40] See HM Government, *Scotland Analysis: Assessment of a Sterling Currency Union* (Cm 8815, February 2014) Annex A <https://www.gov.uk/government/uploads/system/uploads/attachment_data/file/279454/CM8815_2901849_SA_SterlingUnion_acc.pdf> accessed 19 October 2015.
[41] *Scotland's Future* 347–8.
[42] For full Scotland Analysis papers see <https://www.gov.uk/government/collections/scotland-analysis> accessed 19 October 2015.

was potentially much less favourable than the 'equitable division' formula offered by the Scottish Government. In the only remotely relevant precedent, Russia had maintained continuing state status in the event of the departure of its Republics but had as a consequence—under creditor pressure—assumed all of the national debt; while Ireland's departure for the United Kingdom in the early part of last century saw the United Kingdom absorb all of that debt, despite negotiations to the contrary. Of course both these examples turned on their particular facts. Second, the UK Government was concerned not to be seen to be 'pre-negotiating' independence as this would have been a campaign victory for the Yes campaign.

Despite this silence, issues relating to division of assets and liabilities were touched on by the UK Government when addressing other issues, such as EU and International Relations, or currency, or continuation of UK institutions, and gave some idea of their position. Arguments were also made by academics and bodies such as the House of Lords Constitution Committee, which challenged the Scottish Government's positions as set out above and operated as No arguments. They viewed the United Kingdom's status as 'continuing state' to be crucial as to how assets and liabilities would be distributed, and seemed to view international law as dictating how certain assets would be distributed.[43]

Insofar as it can be ascertained from their own documents and statements, the UK Government position with regard to assets and liabilities understood division in the following way.

As regards movable and immovable assets inside Scotland, the UK Government, while not stating any general position, seemed to contemplate that Scotland would inherit assets on Scottish territory in relation to defence—and so by implication it seemed to accept the Scottish Government position that movable assets inside Scotland would pass to any newly independent Scotland.[44]

As regards movable and immovable assets outside Scotland, the United Kingdom asserted that, as a 'continuing state', institutions of the current United Kingdom would become institutions of rUK. The UK Government argued that:

> the bodies that support the UK now, for example the Bank of England, would continue to operate on behalf of the remainder of the UK on the same basis as before Scottish independence. If an independent Scottish state wanted to continue to receive services from UK institutions or utilise them to carry out functions in relation to Scotland, that would be a matter for negotiation and would have to be agreed with the continuing UK.[45]

Here a complication enters the picture. While one side (Yes) talked of 'assets and liabilities', the other (No) talked of 'institutions'. From one point of view,

[43] See House of Lords, Select Committee on the Constitution, *Scottish Independence: Constitutional Implications of the Referendum* (HL Paper 188, 8th Report of Session 2013–14) <http://www.publications.parliament.uk/pa/ld201314/ldselect/ldconst/188/188.pdf> accessed 19 October 2015; see also submissions to that committee.

[44] See HM Government, *Scotland Analysis: Defence* (Cm 8714, October 2013) <https://www.gov.uk/government/publications/scotland-analysis-defence> accessed 19 October 2015.

[45] HM Government, *EU and International Issues* (Cm 8765, January 2014), at 43, <https://www.gov.uk/government/publications/scotland-analysis-eu-and-international-issues>.

the UK Government's statement neither responded to nor contradicted Scottish Government claims with regard to assets and liabilities: asserting that the UK institutions will continue as rUK institutions neither addressed nor determined how the value of their assets, or indeed their liabilities, would be accounted for and equitably divided as per international law. Some commentators, however, went further. Notably Adam Tomkins presented robust international legal opinions without citing any underlying international legal authority to draw a distinction between 'assets' and 'institutions' as absolute and of international legal consequence.[46] He appeared to assert that anything that could be defined as an 'institution' would be kept by the rUK as a matter of right rather than negotiation, and that this included embassies, banks, military, and even currency. There is no clear authority in international legal sources for this view, but little attempt was made by the Scottish Government to rebut it. In fact, institutions such as these are not something quite distinct from assets and liabilities; rather, they all involve complicated combinations of assets and liabilities in ways that are difficult to untangle. These matters would have had to be untangled post-independence and international law gives very little guidance which could assist the untangling beyond affirming that negotiated agreement is the preferred option.

With regard to embassies, the UK Government stated that '[a]n independent Scottish state would not be entitled by right to any UK diplomatic premises, equipment or staff'.[47] This appeared to contradict the Scottish Government position of equitable division of immovable assets outside the United Kingdom, such as embassies in other countries. Adam Tomkins again went further, and asserted in evidence to the Scottish Parliament's EU and External Relations Committee that international law without more determined the issue of diplomatic premises and that the White Paper therefore misstated international law.[48] This view is difficult to sustain as a reasonable legal position. As will be explained, there is no clear customary law in this area, the relevant Vienna Convention is not binding law, and is unclear on the issue in any case.

In contrast to Tomkins' assertions, one could take the view that the UK Government's statement as quoted above was deliberately finely nuanced precisely because the legal position is unclear. There is an ambiguity (one might surmise intentional) in whether the assertion of 'no right' to diplomatic premises was a denial of any Scottish international legal entitlement to equitable division, or merely reinforced that, as a matter of pure practical access, any use of embassies would have to be negotiated by Scotland rather than being something that could be automatic.

As regards oil, the UK Government stated that: 'In the event of independence, the allocation of North Sea oil and gas revenues would be subject to negotiation.'[49]

[46] See A. Tomkins, 'Unanswered Questions' (*Notes from North Britain blog*) at <https://notesfromnorthbritain.wordpress.com/2014/05/>.

[47] HM Government, *Scotland Analysis: Defence* (n. 44).

[48] See 'White Paper is Wrong in International Law' *Scotsman* (12 June 2014) at <http://www.scotsman.com/news/politics/top-stories/white-paper-is-wrong-in-international-law-1-3442059>.

[49] HM Government, *Scotland Analysis, Fiscal Policy and Sustainability* (Cm 8854, May 2014) at 5, <https://www.gov.uk/government/publications/scotland-analysis-fiscal-policy-and-sustainability>.

This statement again was nuanced and ambiguous. It could have been read as a statement that the United Kingdom would seek some equitable distribution of all oil and gas revenues, or that the question of what oil and gas revenues belong to 'the territory of Scotland' required to be negotiated, although here too international law on maritime boundaries would have played some role.

It was, however, on currency that the United Kingdom made its biggest claim and took its biggest political risk. The UK Government stated clearly that they did not view the pound as 'an asset', and rejected what they viewed as a Scottish Government position that equitable division of assets and liabilities established in international law required the United Kingdom to enter a currency union:

> it is wrong to say that an independent Scotland would be entitled to share the continuing UK's currency, the UK pound, as part of a formal currency union. There is no rule or principle in international law that would require the continuing UK to share its currency with an independent Scottish state. The system of currency used by a country is not part of its assets.[50]

This again was clearly a nuanced statement that used the language of law to argue against what had not been explicitly claimed by the Scottish Government or the Yes campaign. Technically the UK Government's statement was correct—there is nothing in international law to require a particular negotiated outcome. However, currency—as the UK Government also pointed out—is not a simple 'thing' but rather is a broader 'system', and as a system it depends on the backing of reserves which are clearly assets and subject to division.

As regards national debt again, surprisingly it might seem, the UK Government did not produce a clear position paper. Publicly the Better Together campaign castigated Alex Salmond for suggesting that winner takes all 'hard-ball' negotiating positions by the UK Government would lead to the United Kingdom carrying all the debt (a position that has some international legal precedent as we have noted) as amounting to a 'refusal' to take Scotland's share of the debt. However, this approach belied the weakness of the UK position on national debt—a much trickier position than the public might have perceived.

The United Kingdom was in the grips of the global financial crisis during the referendum campaign and any dip in creditor confidence would have had a direct impact on interest rate rises for government borrowing. The big political risk for the United Kingdom was that by bringing debt and currency into the campaign frame they would undermine creditor confidence and worsen the financial crisis. In the precedent of the dissolution of the USSR into Russia and the Balkan Republics, as the UK Government would have been only too aware, the creditors played a crucial role in making sure that those who could pay retained all of the liability for the debt.

The United Kingdom therefore played a high game of poker with the country's finances as it triggered the currency argument as a campaign tactic. It walked a line

[50] HM Government, *Scotland Analysis: Currency and Monetary Policy* (Cm 8594, April 2014), at 52, <https://www.gov.uk/government/publications/scotland-analysis-currency-and-monetary-policy>.

between scaring the Scottish public with a currency wilderness, and making sure that the United Kingdom's international creditors remained confident in its commitment and capacity to repay debt. To ensure the latter, around a week before it detonated its 'no shared currency' bomb, the United Kingdom made its position clear in a public statement to creditors that largely went unnoticed and unpublicized to the general public.[51] This statement confirmed that as continuing state they would continue to take responsibility for the entire debt. Although they would negotiate that Scotland pay an equitable share, this would be done by way of transfer from Scotland to the United Kingdom, who would continue to pay creditors throughout.

It is worth noting, however, that there was also a serious debt risk for the Scottish Government in pushing any 'dissolution' analysis—and this may have informed their reticence to mount a strong 'dissolution' case. If the break-up of the United Kingdom was seen as more akin to dissolution than secession, international creditors could well have stepped in, as they had in the Balkans, and insisted on both rUK and independent Scotland being jointly and severally liable for the United Kingdom's national debt until the issue was resolved: that is—both remaining liable for all of the debt.

Interestingly, neither side had an incentive to bring the international debt uncertainties of the other side transparently to the forefront of their campaign. There was no incentive for the Scottish Government to suggest that the rUK might face financial instability post-independence—their campaign was premised on winning confidence on the basis that 'nothing significant would change about people's lives either side of the border'. Pointing out rUK post-secession financial instability would have undermined rather than supported the independence claim. For the United Kingdom, similarly, suggesting that Scotland might be jointly and severally liable for UK debt would have been to suggest that the rUK would be in a weak situation politically and financially as a 'rump state' rather than a continuing state.

XII. What was the international legal position (or who was right)?

In fact, the international legal position underlying all these assertions on division of assets and liability was uncertain. There is very little clear international law on how assets and liabilities are to be divided, although conventions not yet in force provide some basis for understanding what the international community views as the relevant principles. Such international law as exists comes from 'customary international law' established by past practice of states which act in the belief that international law applies. International legal experts are agreed that while the content of international customary law is often difficult to determine categorically, there is greater difficulty in this area because secessions are relatively

[51] UK Debt and the Scotland Independence Referendum available at <https://www.gov.uk/government/publications/uk-debt-and-the-scotland-independence-referendum>.

rare, and each one proceeds within a very specific political context (many against a backdrop of violence). It is therefore particularly difficult to establish routine state practice undertaken in the belief that it is required by law—each secession works out its own context-specific negotiation to its own conclusion. While a wealth of practice exists with regards to de-colonization, this is viewed as distinct from contemporary state secession practice. A Vienna Convention on Succession of States in Respect of State Property, Archives and Debts, Vienna, 8 August 1983, attempted to set out legal rules for division of assets and liabilities, but never came into force, and is neither signed nor ratified by the United Kingdom.[52] Nonetheless it provides some indication of customary law in the area.

The only really clear international legal position is that division of assets and liabilities should be on the basis of agreement grounded in the concept of equity. Customary law, the Vienna Convention, and opinions of international bodies most clearly establish a principle of division by 'equitable agreement' as the overriding legal obligation. In other words, international law itself places division of assets and liabilities into the realm of good faith political negotiations.

Notions of territoriality, reflected in the Vienna Convention, suggest that should the parties fail to agree, then:

- Immovable state property in the successor state passes to that state (so Scotland would inherit all immovable state property within its borders);
- Movable state property connected with the predecessor's activities in the territory of the successor state passes to the successor state (so Scotland would inherit all movable state assets of the United Kingdom connected with its territory);
- Movable state property elsewhere should be allocated in equitable proportion (so movable property elsewhere in the United Kingdom would be subject to 'equitable' division—something that Scotland never claimed).

The position as regards immovable property in third states—such as embassies—is less clear. The Vienna Convention which codifies the above principles does not explicitly mention such property, although one could argue that the relevant section 17 dealing with continuing and successor states implies that the continuing state keeps the embassies. This position is backed up by the fact that in the case of dissolution, the treaty does make explicit provision that assets in third countries should be equitably divided.

However, the treaty is not clear on the matter and, as noted, is of debatable legal status, and neither is customary law clear. In recent cases of secession involving a continuing state and a successor state, embassies have been viewed as a matter for negotiation on the basis of equity (notably with regard to the break-up of the USSR, and North and South Sudan). Moreover, while historically the disposition of property according to rules such as those laid out in the Vienna Convention was understood not to involve compensation either way, the treaty in fact provides

[52] See <http://legal.un.org/ilc/texts/instruments/english/conventions/3_3_1983.pdf>.

that these rules 'are without prejudice to any question of equitable compensation as between the predecessor state and the successor state that may arise as a result of the succession of states' (Article 17 2(b)). A later draft treaty trying to fill out the gaps in this treaty—while never adopted—provides for equitable division of assets outside of both states, even in the case of a continuing state existing.[53]

Beyond the primacy placed on agreement and equity, international law provides little or no guidance as to what equitable division should look like—it is completely silent as to what the principles of 'equity' are. Both principles and their application would therefore have to be negotiated between the parties in negotiations where assets and liabilities are linked—the more of the assets the more of the liabilities and vice versa. Neither does international law provide definitions of the distinction between 'assets' and 'institutions', or indeed the distinction between 'assets' and 'natural resources'—natural resources also being understood in human rights treaties as a part of a right to self-determination.[54]

Surprisingly, perhaps, it can be argued that the issue of whether the United Kingdom would be a continuing state or not had *marginal relevance* to the division of assets and liabilities. The United Kingdom's continuing state status was important with regard to when property required to be formally transferred to new states or could simply remain with continuing states. It was important, as the UK Government argued, with regard to the legal continuity of the institutions and international obligations of the predecessor (and continuing) state. However, the rules as to division of assets insofar as they are clear are not terribly different in a case of dissolution than secession: arguably only with relation to division of immovable assets overseas. It is also worth noting that with regard to liabilities or debt, although the concept of 'equitable division' prevails, creditors are also likely to enter into negotiations to preserve their interest.

There was much talk from both sides of law, legal rights, or assets and liabilities being 'apportioned according to legal principles'.[55] In their striving to sound certain, both sides underplayed that international law's clearest rule is that the parties must negotiate in good faith for an equitable solution, and that good-faith agreed apportionment overrides 'legal principles', which are only meant to apply when such agreement cannot be reached. Interestingly, both sides underplayed the uncertainty that would follow. They failed to point out that in practice, the still relatively undeveloped 'default rules' of international law have been radically altered by agreements between the negotiating states. The capacity of negotiations to alter any rules held risks for each side. So for example, Russia secured a 'long lease' on nuclear facilities in one departing territory, rather than see them automatically transfer to the break-away state as 'immoveable property'. South Sudan as part

[53] State Succession in the Matter of Property and Debt, Institute of International Law, Seventh Commission Rapporteur Geog Ress, 2001 at <http://www.idi-iil.org/idiE/resolutionsE/2001_van_01_en.PDF#page=7&zoom=auto,-101,565>.

[54] See common article 1, International Covenant of Civil and Political Rights 1966, and International Covenant of Economic, Social and Cultural Rights 1966.

[55] See *Scottish Independence: Constitutional Implications of the Referendum* (n. 43) Executive Summary.

of the overall negotiations over debt and liabilities agreed to make time-limited payments (or 'Transitional Financial Assistance') of £3.028 billion, to compensate (North) Sudan from the 'shock' of losing its oil revenues, even though the oil in South Sudan was clearly agreed by both parties to belong to South Sudan as a matter of national sovereignty.[56]

Neither side wanted to talk about the uncertainties of the negotiation ahead as they both had something important to lose. The United Kingdom would have had to admit that it could well end up unilaterally shouldering the national debt as a matter of obligation. While both states accepted 'equitable division' of national debt, eminent international lawyers view the 'default' position in the case of a continuing state to be that the continuing state keeps all the debt.[57] However, Scotland also may have found political and financial pressures that were not publicly discussed to assume some of the debt. As political, legal, and economic experts on division of assets and liabilities note, law aside, there can be powerful political and economic reasons for new countries to 'volunteer' to take on a portion of the predecessor state's debt. In one of the few informed interventions on the issue it was suggested that the pressure of negotiations and the need for Scotland to establish its credibility would lead to incentives to negotiate quickly following any successful referendum.[58] This, it was argued, would lead to Scotland having a relatively weak negotiating position.[59]

Moreover, had it become unclear whether there was a 'continuing state' which would continue to owe the debt, for example because Scottish independence was considered to be part of a process of 'dissolution' of the United Kingdom, then creditors and international financial institutions would have been likely to increasingly intervene in the negotiations to protect their financial positions. The UK statement to creditors constituted an attempt to ensure that creditors viewed their situation as secure come what may.

In the event that the UK and Scotland could not agree to a sensible division of assets and liabilities there would have been no easy legal solutions. While it would be possible to agree to refer the matter to some form of binding arbitration process, neither side would have been likely to want to hand over the decisions to a third party, no matter how reputable and independent.

[56] See Agreement between the Republic of South Sudan and the Government of Sudan on Oil and Related Economic Matters, 12 December 2012 at <http://sites.tufts.edu/reinventingpeace/files/2012/09/Oil-Agreement-between-SudanSouth-Sudan0001.pdf>. (Although payment was agreed in a context of ongoing conflict over oil in disputed border regions, and the fact that South Sudan needed the pipes and ports of (North) Sudan to be able to export its oil.)

[57] See M. Shaw, *International Law* (Cambridge University Press, 7th edn 2014) ch. 17.

[58] J. Pryce, *Debt and Destiny: An Assessment of an Independent Scotland's Fair Share of the United Kingdom's National Debt and the Impact it Could Have on Scotland's Future* (The Scotland Institute June 2014).

[59] See also A. Armstrong and M. Ebell, 'Assets and Liabilities and Scottish Independence' [2014] *Ox Rev of Pub Plcy* 297, who argued that Scotland would begin its independence with a substantial debt burden and less scope for risk sharing, while the rUK would see its debt burden rise substantially (above Scotland's burden), and would be likely to attract the attention of credit agencies. For a collection of essays and perspectives on assets and liabilities and Scottish independence see D. Bell, D. Eiser, and K. Beckmann, *The Economic Consequences of Scottish Independence* (Helmut-Schmidt-Universität/Universität der Bundeswehr Hamburg 2014), at <http://www.scotecon.org/pdf/SES-Indy-ebook.pdf>.

XIII. Dogs that did not bark

Two further matters might have come up as international legal issues as regards division of assets and liabilities but did not and these silences perhaps deserve a mention. The first was the UK's nuclear submarines. Strict application of the legal principles that the parties appeared to contemplate as relevant would have meant that Scotland would own nuclear-armed vessels in its territory on the day of independence, even though it did not want them and had stated that it would seek to relocate them. While the issue of Trident was raised in the campaign, it was not debated as a matter of assets and liabilities because the Scottish Government stated clearly that they did not want nuclear submarines. However, moving the submarines is difficult. Even had Scotland negotiated a more nuanced provision—for example a long-term lease, as a new state they would have been under immense pressure to sign the nuclear non-proliferation treaty (which presumably they would also have wanted to sign).

The second issue which—surprisingly perhaps—did not come up was cultural heritage: maybe it was something that was viewed as being for the negotiation period rather than the campaign. International law on state succession has tended to deal with issues of cultural heritage and archives differently than other property, in an attempt to ensure that the new state inherits those objects and documents that relate to its history and heritage.[60] This could have ended up becoming relevant to the negotiations and perhaps future treaty relations but was not the subject of public discussion or intergovernmental legal positions. In practice these issues can be fraught: think of the Stone of Scone—hugely important to the cultural heritage of both nations. By comparison, it was only in very recent years that Britain and Ireland finally reached an agreement on the Lane pictures enabling their temporary return to Ireland, after a dispute which had run continuously since independence and remains somewhat unresolved.[61]

XIV. Conclusion: The role of international law in political settlement

The Scottish referendum debate should be of interest to international lawyers and public lawyers for the degree to which international law was important to the attempt to renegotiate the current political settlement, and the ways in which

[60] See further A. Jakubowski, *State Succession in Cultural Property (Cultural Heritage Law and Policy)* (Oxford University Press 2015).

[61] Hugh Lane's extensive art collection including paintings by Renoir, Magret, and Monnet, was left to Ireland on the condition that there was a national gallery to house them. However, after partition they were taken to London and when Ireland built a national gallery to house them, not returned. A special agreement between the Dublin City Gallery and the National Gallery London in 1993 established a rotating loan agreement for the key pictures. See further R. Foster, 'How Ireland was Robbed of Hugh Lane's Great Art Collection' *Guardian* (30 May 2015) <http://www.theguardian.com/artanddesign/2015/may/30/how-ireland-was-robbed-hugh-lanes-great-art-collection>.

it began to sketch the contours of any post-Yes vote negotiation. What perhaps worried voters most about the UK Government's legal position was less what they were, and more what those positions signified: less important than specific threats as regards particular legal claims was the underlying message from the UK Government that while it had conceded the referendum in a soft bargaining dynamic that characterizes relationships between family and friends, once Scotland decided to leave it would find itself in a very hard ball game in which it would be the rather weaker party, and likely to come off worse. There was a hint of a 'we'll wreck the place' tactic in which the unwanted divorce was presented as potentially much less velvet than the Scottish Government were promising. Yet in practice 'wrecking the place' would have been very unlikely to be the UK tactic. The history of other 'departures' shows a consistent approach—based in self-interest—of pragmatically trying to leave in place as many ties and modes of influence as possible in the departing territory, and to have as financially sound and politically stable a neighbour as possible.

The use of international law by the United Kingdom to assert that 'we will be a tough and self-interested negotiating partner' is difficult to assess in terms of effectiveness. To the extent that it worked, it undercut the opposite tactic of emphasizing togetherness and even UK 'love' for Scotland. Yet, as the referendum campaigning neared its finish the United Kingdom's 'Project Fear' and particularly its economic ramifications seemed to weigh heavily with those who voted No. However, support for independence only really began to rise in the polls when the currency grenade was lobbed into the debate in the first place. Was this just a coincidence, reflecting the arrival of the 'end stage' of the campaign game when nationalists might be most expected to gain ground anyway? Or Scottish stubbornness at being told 'No'? Or a sense by those in Scotland that they were no longer being engaged with by rules of fair play and good neighbourliness? Others have surmised but there is insufficient evidence to judge. Undoubtedly, however, the currency issue had both intuitive and counter-intuitive campaign effects.[62] Perhaps more interesting from a political point of view was how legalistic arguments and associated political manoeuvring relating to the international law position of rUK and any seceding Scotland were predominant, largely eclipsing any attempt to articulate (or rebut) a more principled or visionary reason for the Union.

The decision of Scottish people became caricatured as a decision between 'head' (for the remaining in the United Kingdom) and 'heart' (for independent Scotland). To some extent this characterization mirrored the campaign strategies: one was focused on pragmatic arguments and short on vision, the other long on vision and short on the pragmatics of achieving it. These strategies in turn were mirrored in different approaches to the use of international law: a positivist and categorical approach (from the UK Government side), and a more discursive and experimental assertion of the *sui generis* nature of Scottish independence (from the Scottish Government side).

[62] See further Mitchell, Ch. 4 in this volume.

Since the referendum wider political interest has focused on the extent to which post-referendum the SNP appears to have lost the battle but won the war. As a result, the political settlement that was fought for by Unionists continues post-referendum to be reworked. This reworking can be viewed as consistent with the developing direction of international law on self-determination—because if 50 per cent plus one triggers a 'requirement to negotiate', then so must 45 per cent, even though the latter rules out independence as the conclusion. While there is much talk of a second vote, the referendum exposed the difficulty of selling to voters a decision that will lead not to a defined outcome, but to a negotiation process the outcome of which cannot be certain. This dynamic would not go away second time around: it is just how things are—the exact contours and consequences of independence would indeed need to be negotiated. There is therefore no easy way for independence campaigners to have better answers to issues like the currency for a public concerned to keep the pound, or stay in the EU, second time around.

If other matters stay the same, what therefore seems likely to proceed are moves such as the Smith Commission proposals, and an ongoing pragmatically-defined Union, governed and held together not by any common political vision, but by the management of issues and relationships between Scotland and the United Kingdom as a form of ongoing technocratic negotiation to be left in the domain of the legal and technical experts of each government. In one final nod to international law this is a domestic constitutional development that parallels the reshaping of international law in the era of globalization, from a law of states to a law of regimes[63] rooted not in any new global constitutional vision—because such is impossible to get agreement on—but rather in technical conversations and turf wars between legal experts operating as specialists within different regimes.

[63] See M. Koskenniemi, 'The Fate of Public International Law: Between Technique and Politics' [2007] 70 *MLR* 1.

PART IV

TERRITORIAL POLITICS AND THE UK CONSTITUTION AFTER THE REFERENDUM

10

A Constitution in Flux

The Dynamics of Constitutional Change after the Referendum

Nicola McEwen

The United Kingdom is in a state of constitutional flux. Less than a year after Scottish independence was defeated in the referendum, proposals were in train to increase the power and responsibility of the Scottish Parliament, the constitutional autonomy of the National Assembly for Wales, and the fiscal autonomy of the Northern Ireland Assembly. Even England has been brought into play, with English Votes on English Laws at Westminster running alongside plans to create so-called 'regional powerhouses' by devolving power and responsibilities to combined local authorities and elected mayors on the model of the Greater Manchester agreement. Nationally and internationally, commentators have been asking whether these latest reform proposals put the United Kingdom on a path towards federalism.

Although reform proposals across the United Kingdom have their own dynamic, changes to the territorial structure of the state were given added impetus by the Scottish referendum. The defeat of Scottish independence in the referendum may have preserved the territorial integrity of the UK state, for now at least, but pre-referendum promises kick-started the 'constitutional chain reaction' now unfolding.[1] Though based largely on short-term thinking, these changes in the territorial structure of government and representation have the potential to reshape fundamentally the UK constitution in the longer term. Moreover, both the strength of the Yes vote in the referendum, which viewed historically was rather high, as well as the electoral dominance of the SNP since then, suggest that the long-term unity of the United Kingdom cannot be taken for granted. Certainly, the Prime Minister's declaration that the new Scottish devolution settlement emerging from the post-referendum Smith Commission would be 'built to last' seems rather optimistic.

[1] C. Jeffery, 'Constitution-Making on the Hoof that Could End in Meltdown' *Herald* (27 December 2014).

This chapter examines the constitutional direction of travel in the United Kingdom. It first considers whether the United Kingdom is heading towards federalism by evaluating ongoing constitutional and political developments against the features of federalism. Although the United Kingdom is far from being a federation in the formal sense, and unlikely to become one in the foreseeable future, the measures to strengthen devolution, at least with respect to Scotland, Wales, and Northern Ireland, can be expected to enhance some of the United Kingdom's federal features. However, some core features of federal systems are notable for their absence in the United Kingdom, including: the absence of a constitutional division of sovereignty between a 'federal' level and the nations and regions of the United Kingdom; the absence of a system, or mechanisms, to facilitate the sharing of power between the two levels; the continued lack of meaningful devolution within England; and the lack of a federal mindset at the heart of government. The chapter then examines the substance, implications, and sustainability of the proposals for Scotland, and considers the political dynamics likely to fuel further demands for a change to the territorial governing arrangements of the United Kingdom. At the time of writing, the Scotland Bill 2015 is making rapid progress towards the Statute Book. The enhanced presence of the Scottish National Party in the House of Commons—electing fifty-six out of fifty-nine Scottish MPs in the 2015 UK general election—has ensured that the Bill's provisions have been contested at every stage of the legislative process in the House of Commons. That contestation has taken place not just in the public glare of the parliamentary chamber, but in the privacy of the intergovernmental arena, where the SNP government sought to use the party's electoral strength to push for additional powers in employment policy, social security, equalities law, and taxation. The Scottish Parliament, whose consent is required by convention before the Bill is passed at Westminster, had its own scrutiny process and its Devolution (Further Powers) Committee published an often critical interim report of the draft clauses and Command paper which preceded the Scotland Bill.[2] However, the Conservative UK Government enjoys a parliamentary majority and the speed of the legislative process alongside the rhetoric of government ministers suggest it is not inclined to reopen significantly the devolution package on offer—a package it has frequently suggested would make Scotland one of the most powerful devolved parliaments in the world.[3] This chapter evaluates the claim by examining the new devolution settlement from a comparative perspective, as well as reflecting on the particular features of the Scotland Bill which may affect the durability of this most recent of several attempts to achieve a lasting constitutional settlement between Scotland and the rest of the United Kingdom. It suggests that while the new powers will increase the decision-making autonomy and responsibility of the Scottish Parliament and Government, the new devolution settlement also seems set to

[2] Scottish Parliament, Devolution (Further Powers) Committee, *New Powers for Scotland: An Interim Report on the Smith Commission and the UK Government's Proposals*, 3rd Report Session 4 (2015), SP Paper 720.

[3] HM Government, *Scotland in the United Kingdom: An Enduring Settlement* (Cm 8990, 2015).

heighten the extent to which the scope for action of the devolved government and parliament will be shaped by decisions taken at Westminster over which they have little influence. These interdependencies, alongside broader political developments, suggest that the latest Scotland Bill, like its predecessors, is unlikely to secure a lasting constitutional settlement.

I. Towards a federal United Kingdom?

Before evaluating the extent to which the United Kingdom is heading towards federalism, one must reflect on what that would entail. The federalism literature usually draws a distinction between federalism as a political principle and federalism as a description of the territorial structure and organization of the state.

As a normative principle, federalism relates to the advocacy of a territorial structure of government which values the diffusion of power 'among many centers'.[4] Federalism can unite people, societies, and polities in common-purpose government while recognizing their separateness and distinctiveness in constituent territorial governments. It is thus a means of achieving 'unity in diversity', and is often seen as a route to preserving the territorial integrity and very survival of a state in the face of the territorial diversity of its population.[5] Federalism creates the conditions under which 'different political units can live together yet apart since they share a government while at the same time having their own'.[6] For advocates of the federal principle, the value of federalism is its capacity to accommodate, preserve, and promote distinctive territorial identities within a larger political system, thus creating a form of government which is more responsive to the needs of citizens and collectivities, while maintaining the perceived benefits of shared government. For federalists, such a system of government also offers the possibility of finding a balance between unity and diversity, independence and dependence, and coordination and subordination.[7] Multinational federations, in particular, are intended to provide a territorial and constitutional framework 'that can accommodate and as far as possible resolve some of the most intractable political conflicts of our time: those that stem from competing national visions, whether within or between established states'.[8]

A *federation*, then, is the structure of government which most embodies the federal principle. In federations, power is divided between two or more territorial layers of government, whose existence and authority is constitutionally

[4] D. J. Elazar, *Exploring Federalism* (University of Alabama Press 1987) 34.

[5] Elazar (n. 4) at 33; M. Burgess, *In Search of the Federal Spirit: New Theoretical and Empirical Perspectives in Comparative Federalism* (Oxford University Press 2012) 188–9.

[6] A. Lecours and G. Nootens, *Dominant Nationalism, Dominant Ethnicity: Identity, Federalism, and Democracy* (Peter Lang 2009) 19.

[7] F. Lépine, 'A Journey through the History of Federalism' (2012) 363 *L'Europe en Formation* 21–62.

[8] J. Pinder, 'Multinational Federations: Introduction' in M. Burgess and J. Pinder (eds), *Multinational Federations* (Taylor & Francis 2007) 1.

guaranteed. In a federation, neither the federal level nor the constituent units are constitutionally subordinate to the other. Each has an independent source of authority with recognized sovereignty within its sphere of jurisdiction, exercising legislative, fiscal, and executive powers directly on behalf of their population, and directly elected by and accountable to them.[9] Early categorizations of federations placed considerable emphasis on the division of powers into clear, 'watertight' compartments, within which the constituent units and the federal government had independent authority. In a classic legalistic definition inspired by the US model, Wheare defined a federation as a political system which embodies the federal principle, which for him meant the 'method of dividing powers so that the general and regional governments are each within a sphere, coordinate and independent'.[10] In practice, especially within the post-war period, the development and expansion of government meant that neither level of government could ever be wholly independent of the other. Decisions at one level have spill-over effects for the other and the constituent units are often dependent upon the federal level for a large proportion of their revenues. Thus more recent conceptions of federalism place as much emphasis on how sovereignty and authority is *shared* between the different levels of government as on the autonomy a federation guarantees its constituent parts.[11]

Federations come in many shapes and sizes, though broadly share some core institutional features which emphasize the combination of self-rule and shared rule. These include: having two (or more) orders of territorial government acting directly on their citizens; a formal constitutional distribution of legislative and executive authority, including an allocation of revenues between the two orders of government 'ensuring some areas of genuine autonomy for each order'; representation of regional views within federal policy-making institutions, often within a territorial second chamber; a supreme written constitution which is not unilaterally amendable by any one level; a formal mechanism for dispute resolution with an independent umpire (in the form of the courts or through popular referenda); and an institutionalized process of intergovernmental relations to facilitate cooperation and coordination between the levels of government in areas of mutual and overlapping interests.[12]

The balance between self-rule and shared rule is influenced by the way in which powers are allocated to different levels of government. Models of power allocation conform to two ideal types—dual and cooperative—and most federal systems will lean towards one or other. Dual models place emphasis upon the autonomy and exclusive jurisdiction of each level of government over legislation and executive decision-making, and so have less institutional mechanisms for sharing power. Cooperative models incorporate an institutional design in which the powers and responsibilities of each are interlocked. In some cases, the regional unit

[9] R. L. Watts, *Comparing Federal Systems* (McGill Queen's Press, 2nd edn 1999) 8.
[10] K. Wheare, *Federal Government* (Oxford University Press 1963) 10.
[11] M. Burgess, *Comparative Federalism: Theory and Practice* (Routledge 2006).
[12] Watts (n. 9) at 6–7.

implements decisions made at the federal level. In others, both levels of government operate in the same jurisdictional sphere with shared or concurrent powers. Such systems have built-in incentives and institutional mechanisms facilitating a high degree of collaboration and 'shared rule' to coordinate and co-decide legislation and policy-making.[13]

The term federalism has also been applied to political systems which adopt elements of the federal idea without necessarily matching the criteria of a federation. Elazar draws a distinction between federalism in its broadest sense 'as a genus involving combinations of self-rule and shared rule rather than as the one species of federalism accepted in modern times, namely, federation'.[14] These more broadly defined *federal political systems* include confederations, federacies, models of associated statehood, constitutionally decentralized unions, condominiums, leagues, joint functional authorities, and less formal asymmetrical federal arrangements.[15] These systems are distinct from unitary states by departing from a structure of government with a single source of authority, but they vary in the locus of sovereignty and political authority. Whereas federations share sovereignty such that neither tier of government is subordinate to the other, the balance of sovereignty and authority within confederations, for example, rests with the member states, with only limited powers and responsibilities lent to a common government. Federacies and associated states have very high levels of political autonomy within their own extensive areas of jurisdiction, but enjoy limited influence within the larger unit—which may or may not be federal—with which they are associated. In constitutionally decentralized or regionalized systems, ultimate authority rests with central government and parliament. Regional governments within such systems can exercise varying and sometimes considerable degrees of decision-making autonomy, but their powers are defined by, and derived from, central government or parliament and, at least in theory, can be withdrawn.

Drawing on these distinctions, we may conclude that the United Kingdom is not a federation, although it has been described by some as a 'quasi-federal' state,[16] at least with respect to the non-English territories. It certainly has some federal features. The Scottish Parliament, in particular, has a relatively high degree of self-rule, and as discussed below, the level of political autonomy this affords is not far behind the constituent units of many formal federations. The Scotland Act 2012 and the Scotland Bill 2015 will increase the level of self-rule still further. The Northern Ireland Assembly also has a high degree of self-rule, incorporating a broader spectrum of policy competences than its Scottish counterpart, including social security and energy. Its self-rule, however, is constrained

[13] N. McEwen and B. Petersohn, 'Between Autonomy and Interdependence: The Challenges of Shared Rule after the Scottish Referendum' (2015) 86 *Pol Q* 192–200.

[14] D. J. Elazar, 'From Statism to Federalism: a Paradigm Shift' (1995) 25 *Publius: The Journal of Federalism* 5–18.

[15] Elazar (nn 4 and 14); Watts (n. 9).

[16] See C. Picker, '"A Light Unto the Nations": The New British Federalism, the Scottish Parliament, and Constitutional Lessons For Multiethnic States' (2002) 77 *Tulane Law Review* 1–90; V. Bogdanor, *The New British Constitution* (Hart Publishing Ltd 2009).

by fiscal and policy dependence on Whitehall and a complex constitutional settlement which encompasses consociational government and shared sovereignty with and between the United Kingdom and the Republic of Ireland. The National Assembly for Wales has always been the weakest of the three devolved institutions, but has seen its powers and structures reformed and enhanced gradually in recent years with two additional devolution Acts in 2006 and 2014 and a referendum conferring primary legislative powers within twenty broad fields of domestic policy and extending limited revenue-raising capacity. The February 2015 St David's Day Agreement promises to extend Welsh self-rule further, albeit without fully meeting the recommendations of the Commission on Devolution in Wales (Silk Commission).[17] The Agreement also promised a 'funding floor' below which relative fiscal transfers to Wales would not fall, in the perhaps forlorn expectation that the Welsh Government will call a referendum on income tax devolution in the next parliament.[18]

Yet, in spite of devolution, it would be a stretch to describe the United Kingdom as 'characteristically non-centralized'[19]—a hallmark of federations and federal political systems. The status of Westminster and Whitehall as the continued source of legal sovereignty and considerable political authority remains evident, especially in the context of majority government. The constituent units established by devolution remain subordinate to and financially dependent upon the centre, although the Scotland Bill 2015 will extend Scottish fiscal autonomy considerably. Westminster parliamentary sovereignty is, of course, offset by the Sewel convention according to which the Westminster Parliament will not normally legislate in areas of devolved competence without the consent of the devolved legislatures. Although given expression within legislative consent motions, such parliamentary procedures mask an executive-led process of intergovernmental coordination and bargaining between Whitehall departments and the devolved governments in the preparation of UK legislation that affects the devolved nations.[20] Following the Smith Commission's recommendation, the Scotland Bill seeks to give statutory underpinning to the Sewel convention, alongside the provision to give statutory recognition to the 'permanence' of the Scottish Parliament and Government. These provisions are likely to be of more symbolic than legal significance, but

[17] Commission on Devolution in Wales, *Empowerment and Responsibility: Legislative Powers to Strengthen Wales*, March 2014; available at: <http://webarchive.nationalarchives.gov.uk/20140605075122/http:/commissionondevolutioninwales.independent.gov.uk/files/2014/03/Empowerment-Responsibility-Legislative-Powers-to-strengthen-Wales.pdf>.

[18] A. Evans, 'Out of Sight, Out of Mind? The St. David's Day Process and a Welsh Devolution Settlement' (*Centre on Constitutional Change blog*, 27 February 2015) available at: <http://www.centreonconstitutionalchange.ac.uk/blog/out-sight-out-mind-st-david%E2%80%99s-day-process-and-welsh-devolution-settlement>.

[19] Elazar (n. 4) at 34.

[20] C. McCorkindale, 'Echo Chamber: the 2015 General Election at Holyrood—a Word on Sewel' (*Scottish Constitutional Futures Forum blog*, 13 May 2015) available at: <http://www.scottishconstitutionalfutures.org/OpinionandAnalysis/ViewBlogPost/tabid/1767/articleType/ArticleView/articleId/5594/Chris-McCorkindale-Echo-Chamber-the-2015-General-Election-at-Holyrood-a-word-on-Sewel.aspx>.

the House of Lords Select Committee on the Constitution has suggested that they may signal a move in a federal direction, 'attempting to crystallize by way of statute, if not a written constitution, the status and powers of the devolved institutions in a way that has hitherto not been the case'.[21]

The United Kingdom also appears less federal when one considers the relative weakness of shared rule.[22] In contrast to self-rule, which focuses on the decision-making autonomy of constituent units within a federal system, shared rule concerns the input and influence of those constituent units in decision-making at the centre. Shared rule can be understood as a 'collaborative partnership through common institutions'.[23] These institutions may include a second chamber of the federal legislature providing for the representation of territorial interests, regional veto powers in concurrent policy spheres, or cooperation and co-decision within the intergovernmental arena. For Swenden, shared rule provides constituent units with a sense of co-ownership over central decisions that affect their interests.[24] In the United Kingdom, there is no region-specific input into UK legislation; the Sewel convention has evolved to become more a means of protecting self-government in areas of devolved competence than a way to exert influence over Westminster policy that affects the devolved territories. There is neither a territorial nor a representative element to the Upper House, with little prospect of Lords reform under the current Conservative Government. Representation in the House of Commons is on the basis of individual constituencies and is non-territorial beyond these constituency boundaries. The SNP may have all but swept the board in the 2015 election, but they remain only 56 out of 650 MPs in the House even if, informally, they can provide a vocal channel for the Scottish SNP Government in Westminster. The procedural and institutional mechanisms intended to give voice to territorial interests, most notably in the territorial select committees and the territorial ministries of state, are weakened by the expectation that they reflect the political complexion and balance of power within the UK Parliament and Government.[25] 'English votes for English laws' (EVEL), which is intended to provide to members of parliament representing English constituencies a veto over legislation deemed to apply to England only, may accentuate the lack of parliamentary shared rule. It will demarcate all MPs as from territorially distinctive

[21] House of Lords Select Committee on the Constitution, *Inter-Governmental Relations in the United Kingdom*, 11th Report 2014—15, HL Paper 146, para. 77.

[22] See W. Swenden and N. McEwen, 'UK Devolution in the Shadow of Hierarchy? Intergovernmental Relations and Party Politics' (2014) 12 *Comparative European Politics* 488–509; McEwen and Petersohn (n. 13).

[23] R. L. Watts, 'Typologies of Federalism' in J. Loughlin, J. Kincaid, and W. Swenden (eds), *Routledge Handbook of Regionalism and Federalism* (Routledge 2013) 20.

[24] W. Swenden, 'Territorial Strategies for Managing Plurinational States' in Loughlin et al (eds) (n. 23) at 69.

[25] In practice, this requirement has been modified in the select committees. To take the example of the Scottish Affairs Committee—of its eleven members, the SNP have four, the Conservatives have four and the Labour Party have three, leaving the balance of power tilted firmly towards the opposition. Prior to the election, the coalition parties had five members, the official opposition had five members, and the SNP had one, though the member in question boycotted the committee.

regions of the United Kingdom in a way that has not hitherto been recognized procedurally. At the same time, it will restrict the voting rights of those elected outside England, including on issues which could have financial and other policy implications for devolved matters.

Devolved governments do have an opportunity to try to influence central decision-making within the intergovernmental arena, not just in the operationalization of the Sewel convention as noted above, but when seeking to navigate the interdependence between devolved and reserved competences. As well as the informal, day-to-day interactions between senior and middle-ranking civil servants across administrations, more formal procedures have developed mainly within the Joint Ministerial Committee as well as in semi-formal bilateral and multilateral forums for ministers and officials. But from a comparative perspective, intergovernmental relations in the United Kingdom remain weakly institutionalized and more ad hoc than is the case in more established federal political systems, and provide only limited opportunities to participate in UK decision making.[26]

The one area of shared rule which has been recognized as present in the UK system—the informal veto over constitutional reform—is being tested in the ongoing reform processes. The constitution remains a reserved matter for all three devolved settlements, but the Sewel convention has in effect required the consent of the devolved parliaments and, in the case of Wales, the consent of the population in a referendum, to enact or implement new powers to Scotland and Wales. Moreover, the process of constitutional reform has been led from within Scotland and Wales, finding its genesis in the hastily arranged inter-party brokering within the Smith Commission, and the more reflective and thorough analysis of the Silk Commission. Yet, the Scotland Bill falls short of the expectations of both the SNP Government and the cross-party Scottish Parliament Devolution (Further Powers) Committee, while the St David's Day command paper[27] has implicitly rejected some of the recommendations of Silk II on further powers for Wales, most notably over policing and criminal justice. In the context of a majority UK Government, there have been limited opportunities to effect change to the legislation thus far, and it is not clear how Westminster would respond should the Scottish Parliament or the National Assembly for Wales withhold their consent to the legislation. That either the Scottish Parliament or the National Assembly for Wales would reject outright a Bill offering further devolution seems politically improbable.

Perhaps the most notable departure from federalism is the degree of asymmetry within UK territorial governance, which contributes to the absence of a federal spirit at the centre. Asymmetrical federalism—de facto or de jure—is not unusual in federal states. But the fact remains that the absence of devolution within England means that the United Kingdom's largest nation and 84 per cent

[26] Swenden and McEwen (n. 22); N. Bolleyer, *Intergovernmental Cooperation—Rational Choices in Federal Systems and Beyond* (Oxford University Press 2009).

[27] HM Government, *Powers for a Purpose; Towards a Lasting Devolution Settlement for Wales* (Cm 9020, 2015).

of the UK population continue to live within and be governed by a unitary state. Regional devolution on either the London or Manchester model does little to dilute the legislative authority that Westminster exercises over England. EVEL could have greater significance if it results in restructuring the way in which the UK Government is organized.[28] It is commonplace to note that successive UK Governments have hitherto changed very little of the way they conduct their business in response to devolution. The structure and organization of government for health, education, the environment, or any other area of policy which in Scotland, Northern Ireland, and Wales is, to a greater or lesser extent, devolved, continued much as before in spite of the UK Government acting as a de facto government for England. In part, this reflects a pattern of treating Scotland, Wales, and Northern Ireland as 'special status' regions, with varying forms of devolution developed for the 'periphery' as and when necessary, rather than conceiving of devolution as part of a coherent system of *UK* territorial governance of relevance for the state as a whole. The lack of a coherent territorial structure continues to be evident in the various reform proposals currently underway. But *if* EVEL compels the UK Government to reorganize itself so as to develop legislation which is more clearly 'England only', as has been suggested,[29] it *could* bring multilevel government to the heart of the UK Government, thus weakening the centralized nature of the UK state, if not being sufficient to make it 'characteristically non-centralized' in Elazar's terms. This could and should remove some barriers to the development of mechanisms through which the four UK territories can participate in systems of shared rule in areas of common interest. The proof, however, will be very much in the pudding.

There are other possible constitutional futures. Becoming more federal is not the only option, and may not even be the most credible. For Watts, the distinction between a federal and a unitary state is rooted in the location of ultimate political authority or sovereignty rather than the extent of policy areas decentralized.[30] So long as the biggest constitutional changes remain on the periphery, with separate bilateral arrangements vis-à-vis a centre that remains largely unchanged, then a more fully developed model of federalism seems unlikely. The structural asymmetries within UK territorial government and politics pose a challenge to a system of shared rule that could command legitimacy across the United Kingdom's territories. In this eventuality, we might expect further demands for greater self-rule on a federacy or confederal model, especially in Scotland, where the dynamics of territorial politics are also influenced by continued support for Scottish independence and the party which champions it.

[28] C. Jeffery, 'What does EVEL look like?' (*Centre on Constitutional Change blog*, 4 February 2015) available at: <http://www.centreonconstitutionalchange.ac.uk/blog/what-does-evel-look>; M. Kenny and D. Glover, *English Votes for English Laws: A viable answer to the English Question?* (Centre on Constitutional Change Research Briefing Paper, 2015), available at: <http://www.centreonconstitutionalchange.ac.uk/sites/default/files/papers/English%20Votes%20for%20English%20Laws_1.pdf>.

[29] This insight was derived from senior civil servants at a seminar in London on 14 July 2015.

[30] Watts (n. 23).

II. The most powerful parliament in the world? Evaluating Scottish devolution

The report of the Smith Commission proclaimed that the package of proposals agreed between the five main political parties would 'result in the biggest transfer of power to the Scottish Parliament since its establishment', and strengthen the ability of the parliament 'to pursue its own vision, goals and objectives'.[31] When draft clauses translating the Commission's proposals into proposed legislation were published in January 2015, the Prime Minister said they would make the Scottish Parliament 'one of the most powerful devolved parliaments in the world', a claim repeated when the Scotland Bill was introduced after the UK general election.[32] Much of the debate since then has focused on whether the legislation honours the spirit and substance of the Smith Commission's proposals. This is a largely futile discussion. The Smith process was primarily intended to broker a compromise agreement, at considerable speed, between the parties. We should not be surprised, then, that key sections of the report's recommendations relied upon forms of words that may have helped secure agreement between competing interests, but introduced an element of ambiguity to what precisely was being proposed. Consequently, in some areas, it is difficult to conclude with certainty that one interpretation is more accurate than another. Whichever version of Smith wins out, the new devolution settlement will result in a marked increase in the powers and responsibilities of the Scottish Parliament, the implications of which have largely evaded scrutiny in wider political debates.

Until now, most of the areas of devolved competence were previously under the administrative control of the Scottish Office. This latest round of devolution, and indeed the Scotland Act 2012 which at the time of writing is still to be fully implemented, take Scottish devolution on to new terrain. The Scotland Bill includes new powers over the conduct of elections to the Scottish Parliament, the management of the Crown Estate, *aspects of* equal opportunities policy, transport policy, tribunals, gaming machines, and consumer advocacy and advice. While energy policy remains a reserved matter, the Bill devolves power over licensing and access rights to onshore oil and gas, with some executive competence over fuel poverty/energy efficiency schemes, concurrent with the UK Secretary of State. But the biggest transfers of power are in the areas of tax and welfare. The Scottish Parliament will be responsible for raising 100 per cent of income tax levied on the earnings of Scottish residents, with the power to alter the rates and thresholds if it so chooses. In welfare, the Scottish Parliament will have legislative autonomy over several social security benefits, including benefits for people with disabilities and their

[31] Smith Commission, *Report of the Smith Commission for Further Devolution of Powers to the Scottish Parliament* (2014).

[32] See 'Will Scotland Have the Most Powerful Devolved Parliament in the World?' *Telegraph* (22 January 2015).

carers. The legislation will also provide the Scottish Government with executive competence to introduce flexibilities in the Universal Credit, the main reserved benefit for job seekers, as well as a capacity to 'top-up' any benefit which remains reserved to Westminster.[33] Though it may not make Scotland the most powerful regional parliament in the world (see below), this package of proposals represents a marked increase in Scottish self-government. However, the degree of decision-making autonomy—*self-rule*—will be constrained by the increased interdependence between the powers and responsibilities of the Scottish Parliament and the powers, authority, and legislative framework of the Westminster Parliament.

In the literature on federalism, territorial self-rule is reflected in the formal constitutional division of legislative, executive, and fiscal powers, such that each level has genuine autonomy in some policy spheres.[34] Whereas shared rule concerns the participation of substate nations or regions in decision-making processes at the centre, self-rule emphasizes the degree of political independence, with 'a sharp focus upon autonomy, separateness, independence, rule-making and the capacity to govern a political community'.[35] Federal political systems vary in the degree to which they emphasize self-rule or shared rule. In the United Kingdom, as in most other countries that developed federal political systems relatively recently, the emphasis has been more on self-rule than shared rule, often in response to substate nationalist demands for increased self-government. This implies a fairly clear separation of powers between levels of government, and often an asymmetric distribution of powers between regions, correlating with the strength and depth of demand. In Scotland, constitutional politics, at least since 1974, have been heavily centred on Scottish 'home rule', with relatively little attention paid to finding procedural routes to enhancing Scotland's influence through 'shared rule' with central government. Although none of the devolution settlements have diminished the sovereignty of the Westminster parliament in legal terms, in practice, they have resulted in progressively greater Scottish self-rule. This has resulted in a system of devolution which already positions Scotland among the most autonomous territories in Europe.

The Regional Authority Index (RAI) developed by Hooghe and others[36] helps to situate Scotland within a comparative framework. The RAI developed measures for both self-rule and shared rule, applying these measures to regional governments in eighty-one countries around the world. Self-rule is measured according to: institutional depth, that is, the extent to which a regional government is genuinely autonomous and not subject to central veto; the range of policy jurisdictions over which it has 'authoritative competence'; the level of tax-raising power and borrowing capacity; and the extent to which a region has an

[33] Scotland Bill 2015 *(as amended in committee)*, Available at: <http://www.publications.parliament.uk/pa/Bills/cBill/2015–2016/0048/16048.pdf>.

[34] See eg Pinder (n. 8); Burgess (n. 5). [35] Burgess (n. 5) at 184.

[36] L. Hooghe, G. Marks, A. H. Schakel, S. Chapman Osterkatz, S. Niedzwiecki, and S. Shair-Rosenfield, *A Postfunctionalist Theory of Governance. Volume I: Measuring Regional Authority* (Oxford University Press 2015).

independent legislature and executive. A separate index assessing the depth of shared rule includes the extent to which: regional representatives co-determine national legislation; regional government co-determines national policy in intergovernmental meetings; regional representatives co-determine the distribution of national tax revenues, subnational and national borrowing constraints; and regional governments, parliaments, or populations can co-determine constitutional change. These criteria produce a measure of self-rule ranging from a score of 0 to 18 and a measure of shared rule ranging from 0 to 12 (see the Appendix to this chapter for full details of the coding scheme).

Figure 10.1 below situates Scotland alongside other substate nations and regions within a selected range of federal political systems, including long-established federations, regionalized states and federacies, using the measures set out in the RAI.[37] It indicates the extent to which Scotland lacked self-rule prior to the establishment of devolution in 1999, scoring only one out of a possible eighteen. The 1999 devolution settlement (still largely in place in 2010) gave Scotland an independent parliament and executive, institutional depth (albeit as a result of delegated powers and constitutional convention rather than entrenched constitutional powers), and wide-ranging jurisdictional autonomy, though it lacked the fiscal autonomy and borrowing capacity of provinces and states within federations and federacies. The Scotland Act 2012 and the current Scotland Bill will increase Scotland's fiscal autonomy and should give the Scottish Government more autonomy with respect

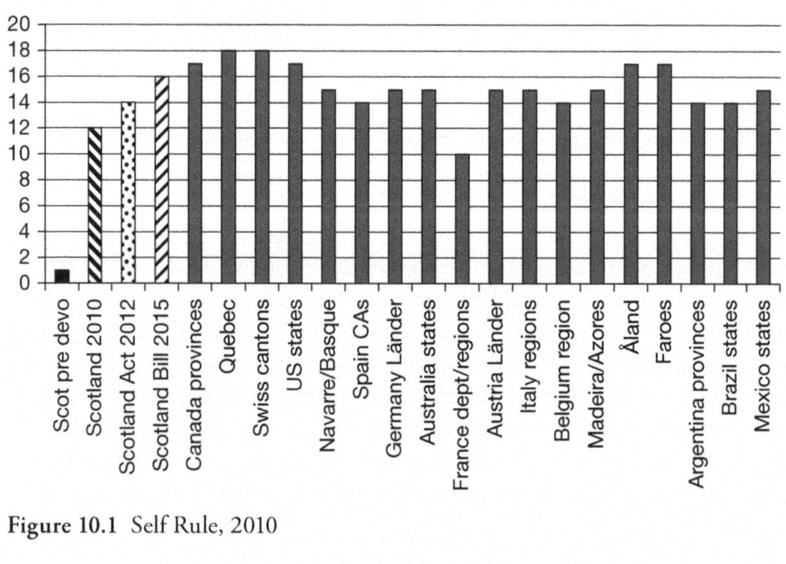

Figure 10.1 Self Rule, 2010

[37] The score accorded to the Basque country is my recalculation so as to combine regional and provincial autonomy. I have recoded the score for Scotland to provide what I believe to be a more accurate score for tax and borrowing, which reflects changes in the depth of autonomy over time.

to the capacity to borrow, albeit within the rules set out in the fiscal framework agreed bilaterally between the Scottish and UK Governments. Once the new devolution settlement is implemented, Scotland may still not enjoy the levels of self-government of the provinces and states of North America, the Swiss cantons, or federacies like Åland in Finland or the Faroe Islands, but it is a reasonable claim to suggest that it would be one of the most autonomous devolved systems in the world.

The authority of a substate nation or region is not only about having the autonomy to make policy and fiscal decisions. It is also about exercising influence, including over state-wide matters which directly or indirectly affect the nation or region in question. Agranoff argued that shared rule was a necessary complement to self-rule in order to manage jurisdictional boundaries, spillover effects and policy interdependence: 'self-rule can be formally introduced to a polity's governing arrangements but cannot be maintained without the working connections that tie central governments to those constituent units that enjoy measures of independent and interdependent political power, governmental control, and decision-making'.[38] Whereas devolution from the outset heightened Scottish self-rule, it was accompanied by rather less shared rule, in part because no significant player demanded shared rule and only the Liberal Democrats considered that devolution could be a step towards a fuller federal system. Consequently, there were no mechanisms through which the devolved institutions could be represented in the Westminster parliament, and only very weak intergovernmental procedures, with no rights to co-determine UK policies or the distribution of UK taxes. Only in the area of constitutional change have significant rights emerged, albeit by convention rather than statute. The reallocation of powers to Scotland, as indeed to Wales, has largely been driven by internal dynamics, with the scope of powers determined by internal politics and compromises. The relative weakness of shared rule within the UK system of multilevel government is illustrated when placed alongside other federal political systems. As Figure 10.2 indicates, only the French regions and departments have a weaker system of shared rule on the measurement used here.[39] There have been growing demands from parliamentary committees,[40] commissions (Silk Commission on Devolution in Wales, Smith Commission),

[38] R. Agranoff, 'Autonomy, Devolution and Intergovernmental Relations' (2004) 14 *Regional and Federal Studies* 26–65.

[39] Once again, I have recoded Hooghe's score for Scotland, reducing it from 4 to 2.5. Whereas they scored 0 for law-making shared rule, I gave Scotland 0.5 for law-making (e) given the regular, if informal, consultation, and negotiation which takes place over national legislation affecting devolved competence (in line with the Sewel convention). I have reduced their score for constitutional shared rule from 4 to 2, though with some hesitation. I share the view that this is the most significant area of shared rule, but I am uncomfortable with the application of the coding scheme to the Scottish case, and in particular, the assumption that regional governments could *require* referenda or exercise *veto* rights over constitutional change. In any event, while my recoding reduces the score a little, it would be comparatively low even if using the original Hooghe et al score.

[40] See eg Scottish Parliament, Devolution (Further Powers) Committee, *Official Report*, Thursday 5 February 2015; Select Committee on the Constitution (n. 21).

and scholarly reports[41] for a more formal system of intergovernmental relations that could, in effect, increase shared rule. Although reviews are underway, no proposals have at the time of writing been presented from either the Scottish or UK Government which would lead us to assume that the Scotland Act 2016 would generate a higher score for shared rule than is currently the case, in spite of the increased interdependencies the new devolution settlement will engender.

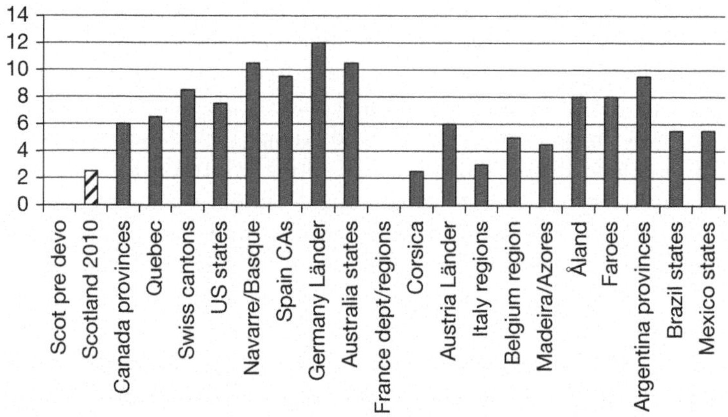

Figure 10.2 Shared Rule, 2010

The RAI provides a useful tool for comparative analysis, but understanding the impact of the new devolution settlement on Scottish self-government requires a closer examination of the specific powers embodied in the new legislation. Although the Scotland Bill increases significantly the fiscal autonomy of the Scottish Parliament, it places a heavy reliance upon income tax, and even then, the latter is not fully devolved. The Scotland Act 2016 will devolve 100 per cent of tax on earned income, affecting all rates and thresholds. However, the personal allowance, taxes on savings and dividends, capital gains tax, and national insurance—all of which interact very closely with income tax on earnings—will remain reserved. This creates several challenges and constraints. First, Scottish tax autonomy will be shaped by UK policy decisions over which the Scottish Government will have no control. For example, if the UK Government chooses to raise the personal allowance—effectively giving tax payers across the United Kingdom a tax cut—this would result in lower revenues accruing to the Scottish Government, which unlike its UK counterpart, would not be able to offset these lost revenues by raising other taxes to fill the gap.[42] Secondly, Scottish policy decisions can have perverse

[41] See in particular Bingham Centre for the Rule of Law, *A Constitutional Crossroads Ways Forward for the United Kingdom* (2015), available at: <http://www.biicl.org/documents/593_bingham_report_ constitutional_crossroads.pdf>.

[42] A. Hughes Hallett, *Comments on the Devolution of Further Powers after the Smith Commission*, (2015) written evidence submitted to the Scottish Parliament Devolution (Further Powers)

consequences as a result of the limitations placed on devolved competence. If, for example, the Scottish Government opted to support wealth redistribution by increasing only the higher rate of tax, the affected tax payers could shift their residence status, or divert their income into dividends or capital gains or benefit from some of the many other forms of tax allowance which are beyond the policy scope of the devolved institutions.[43] A third constraint emerges from the restrictions placed on the Scottish Government in setting tax rates, for which notification is expected to be given several months prior to the beginning of the tax year. The UK Chancellor of the Exchequer, by contrast, has discretion over the timing of his budgets, and often makes announcements affecting taxes and allowances just before the new tax year. This timing issue has generated concerns about the possibility of political 'gaming'. As Heald noted in his evidence to the Scottish Parliament Devolution (Further Powers) Committee, 'without appropriate constitutional machinery on intergovernmental financial relations, it would be possible for a UK Government to subvert the financial arrangements, for example, by significantly reducing income tax rates in England while increasing VAT'.[44] Thus, while the new devolution settlement will result in a formal increase in self-rule, the interdependencies between the new powers and those which remain reserved also, paradoxically, expose the vulnerability of the Scottish Government and Parliament.

The provisions within the Scotland Bill relating to social security also come with constraints. Because social security remains a reserved matter, the Bill creates exceptions by devolving specific benefits rather than policy functions. The Scottish Parliament could replace those benefits if it so chose, but it would have to do so within the criteria set out within this founding legislation. Social security devolution also creates new policy interdependencies. Decisions taken by UK ministers with responsibility for tax and social security will affect in fundamental ways new areas of devolved competence. For example, Universal Credit, which will remain reserved, affects other benefits, including Disability Living Allowance/Personal Independence Payments (DLA/PIP), which are to be devolved. The conditions attached to Universal Credit will intervene directly with the back-to-work employability schemes to be devolved to the Scottish government. Devolved and reserved benefits are also subject to 'passporting'—where entitlement to one benefit automatically generates entitlement to others—with passported benefits crossing devolved/reserved jurisdictions. Recognizing the increased complexity and spillover effects of the new devolution settlement, the Smith Commission stipulated that neither government should be adversely affected as a result of the policy decisions of the other, but if they are they should

Committee. Available at: <http://www.scottish.parliament.uk/S4_ScotlandBill Committee/General %20Documents/Andrew_Hughes_Hallett.pdf>.

[43] D. Philips, 'The Smith Commission's Proposals—How Big a Change Do They Represent? And What Questions Remain to be Addressed?' (Institute for Fiscal Studies Briefing Paper, 2014), available at: <http://www.ifs.org.uk/uploads/publications/bns/BN157.pdf>.

[44] D. Heald, *The Future Financing of the Scottish Parliament*, Written submission to the Scottish Parliament Finance Committee, 5 November 2015.

receive due compensation. Implementing the 'no detriment' principle in a way which is mutually agreeable for both the Scottish and UK Governments will be fraught with difficulty.

These new interdependencies are problematic when set against the weakness of shared rule, discussed above. Federal political systems which are designed to be interdependent tend to be accompanied by structures and processes nurturing collaboration and co-decision. The United Kingdom, by contrast, has retained very centralized decision-making and fiscal structures, with the authority of the Treasury particularly notable. As Muscatelli observed in his evidence to the Devolution committee, 'given the interdependence that is suggested in the fiscal structure that has been proposed by Smith ... it will be very difficult unless there is willingness on the part of the Treasury to share some of the power', something he suggested would require a psychological change in how the Treasury conducts its business.[45] As already noted, the Scottish and UK Governments have been negotiating the fiscal framework within which the devolution powers will be exercised, as well as the Memorandum of Understanding underpinning the relationship between the UK Government and all the devolved administrations. However, some of these features of territorial government which have inhibited the development of federalism in the United Kingdom—the asymmetrical distribution of power; the lack of meaningful devolution in England; and the lack of a federal mindset at the heart of the UK Government—as well as the diminished trust between the UK and Scottish Governments as a result of the referendum experience and the party political incongruence in the composition of these governments, suggest that the emergence of a more cooperative model of multilevel government any time soon is unlikely.

III Conclusion: The dynamics of constitutional change

The United Kingdom, then, faces a constitutional crossroads, and the direction of travel remains unclear. In Scotland, in particular, this latest round of devolution has all the hallmarks of a staging post rather than a final destination. It will, perhaps intentionally, herald a more interdependent system of devolution which, while heightening Scottish self-government may also increase the extent to which Scotland is affected by decisions taken at Westminster. The stability of such an interdependent system may depend on the capacity of the Scottish Government to influence those UK decisions, especially in tax policy, which will set the parameters within which new devolved competence is exercised. This would imply a marked strengthening of the mechanisms that could facilitate shared rule, as well as a will on the part of both governments to utilize them. That need not entail the development of a fully fledged federation—which this chapter has suggested is an unlikely path for the United Kingdom—but it would require a shift towards

[45] See Scottish Parliament, Devolution (Further Powers) Committee, *Official Report*, Thursday 5 February 2015 at 22.

a more federal mindset at the heart of central government, and a commitment to making such a system work from all governments concerned.

Beyond the institutional features and associated challenges of the new devolution settlement, broader political dynamics will shape the constitutional future of Scotland and the United Kingdom. Within Scotland, the referendum has clearly emboldened the SNP as a political party, as a government, and as a voice for Scotland in the Union. The party's recent electoral success, and the failure of its competitors, has allowed it to legitimately claim to represent Scotland in a way that the UK Government, with one MP from Scotland, simply cannot. The performance of the SNP in future elections, and the engagement of its opponents in the constitutional debate, will be crucial to strengthening or containing demands for further constitutional change. The referendum campaign also generated a nationalist movement which reaches deep into civil society, and can be mobilized should circumstances be conducive to demands for further self-government or a second referendum. Scotland's constitutional future will also be influenced by the nature and development of the United Kingdom in the coming years. Is the United Kingdom's future inside or outside of the European Union? Can the UK Labour Party become a credible alternative government which would have resonance and appeal within Scotland? Will fiscal austerity lead to a hollowing out of those *British* institutions, like the welfare state and the BBC, which for many Scots made the Union worth preserving, and if so, with what consequence for the United Kingdom's constitutional future? Only time will tell.

Appendix to Chapter 10

Regional Authority Index Regional Scores Codebook

SELF RULE

Dimension of Self Rule	Score	Detailed Measurement
Institutional depth	0–3	The extent to which a regional government is autonomous rather than deconcentrated: 0: no functioning general-purpose administration at regional level 1: deconcentrated, general-purpose, administration 2: non-deconcentrated, general-purpose, administration subject to central government veto 3: non-deconcentrated, general-purpose, administration not subject to central government veto.
Policy Scope	0–4	The range of policies for which a regional government is responsible: 0: very weak authoritative competence in (a), (b), (c), (d) whereby (a) economic policy; (b) cultural-educational policy; (c) welfare policy; (d) one of the following: residual powers, police, own institutional set-up, local government 1: authoritative competencies in one of (a), (b), (c) or (d) 2: authoritative competencies in at least two of (a), (b), (c), or (d) 3: authoritative competencies in (d) and at least two of (a), (b), or (c) 4: criteria for 3 plus authority over immigration or citizenship.
Fiscal autonomy	0–4	The extent to which a regional government can independently tax its population: 0: central government sets base and rate of all regional taxes 1: regional government sets the rate of minor taxes 2: regional government sets base and rate of minor taxes

SELF RULE		
Dimension of Self Rule	Score	Detailed Measurement
		3: regional government sets the rate of at least one major tax: personal income, corporate, value added, or sales tax 4: regional government sets base and rate of at least one major tax.
Borrowing autonomy	0–3	The extent to which a regional government can borrow: 0: the regional government does not borrow (eg centrally imposed rules prohibit borrowing) 1: the regional government may borrow under prior authorization (*ex ante*) by the central government and with one or more of the following centrally imposed restrictions: (a) golden rule (eg no borrowing to cover current account deficits) (b) no foreign borrowing or borrowing from the central bank (c) no borrowing above a ceiling (d) borrowing is limited to specific purposes 2: the regional government may borrow without prior authorization (*ex post*) and under one or more of (a), (b), (c), (d), (e) 3: the regional government may borrow without centrally imposed restrictions.
Representation	0–4	The extent to which a region has an independent legislature and executive.

SHARED RULE		
Dimension of Shared Rule	Score	Detailed Measurement
Law-making	0–2	0: a region or regional tier is not the unit of representation in a national legislature 0.5: a region or regional tier is the unit of representation in a national legislature 0: a regional government or regional tier does not designate representatives in a national legislature 0.5: a region or regional tier designates representatives in a national legislature 0: regions do not have majority representation in a national legislature based on regional representation 0.5: regions have majority representation in a national legislature based on regional representation 0: the legislature based on regional representation does not have extensive legislative authority 0.5: the legislature based on regional representation has extensive legislative authority 0: the regional government or its regional representatives in a national legislature are not consulted on national legislation affecting the region 0.5: the regional government or its regional representatives in a national legislature are consulted on national legislation affecting the region 0: the regional government or its regional representatives in a national legislature do not have veto power over national legislation affecting the region 0.5: the regional government or regional representatives in a national legislature have veto power over national legislation affecting the region
Inter-governmental co-determination	0–2	The extent to which a regional government co-determines national policy in multi-lateral or bilateral intergovernmental meetings.
Fiscal co-determination	0–2	The extent to which regional representatives co-determine the distribution of national tax revenues in multi-lateral or bilateral intergovernmental meetings.
Borrowing co-determination	0–3	The extent to which a regional government co-determines subnational and national borrowing constraints in multi-lateral or bilateral intergovernmental meetings

SHARED RULE		
Dimension of Shared Rule	Score	Detailed Measurement
Co-determination of constitutional change (i)	0–4	0: the central government or national electorate can unilaterally reform the constitution 1: a legislature based on regional representation can propose or postpone constitutional reform, raise the decision hurdle in the other chamber, require a second vote in the other chamber, or require a popular referendum 2: regional governments or their representatives in a national legislature propose or postpone constitutional reform, raise the decision hurdle in the other chamber, require a second vote in the other chamber, or require a popular referendum 3: a legislature based on regional representation can veto constitutional change; or constitutional change requires a referendum based on the principle of equal regional representation 4: regional governments or their representatives in a legislature can veto constitutional change.
Co-determination of constitutional change (ii)	0–4	0: the central government or national electorate can unilaterally reform the region's constitutional relation with the centre 1: a regional referendum can propose or postpone reform of the region's constitutional relation with the centre 2: the regional government can propose or postpone reform of the region's constitutional provisions or require a popular referendum 3: a regional referendum can veto a reform of a region's constitutional relation with the centre 4: the regional government can veto a reform of the region's constitutional relation with the centre

Source: L. Hooghe, G. Marks, A. H. Schakel, S. Chapman Osterkatz, S. Niedzwiecki, and S. Shair-Rosenfield, *A Postfunctionalist Theory of Governance. Volume I: Measuring Regional Authority* (Oxford University Press 2015). Codebook available at: <http://www.falw.vu/~mlg/rai/Codebook%20RAI%20 Regional%20Scores.pdf>.

11

The Territorial Constitution and the Future of Scotland

Neil Walker

I. The territorial constitution in question

This chapter considers the ways in which constitutional thought and practice may continue to shape the distinctiveness of Scotland as a political community in the post-referendum period. The emphasis is not just on the immediate future, nor on some ideal 'deep future'. Rather, its focus is on the foreseeable future. What are the candidate models—or rather, the candidate *orientations*[1]—and plausible pathways by which the future development of the territorial constitution might be pursued? What benefits and drawbacks are associated with different approaches and what are their prospects of success? In particular, what are the limits of accommodation of Scottish self-government within the framework of the UK state, and how, if at all, might such an accommodation be maintained in the face of continuing strong support for independence?

Our headline notion of the 'territorial constitution' provides a useful angle from which to approach these questions. The territorial constitution could signify one of three things. Most basically, it might refer to the overall constitutional order as conventionally understood. Here we use the 'territorial' part to describe the constitutional whole. We do so on the basis that our understanding of the constitutional form of the modern political system typically involves the geographical coincidence and mutual reinforcement of three fundamental elements—people, government, and territory itself—within the discrete container of the sovereign state.[2] As a defining property, and indeed the key 'locating' property of the state, the territorial descriptor here supplies a simple but telling shorthand for the more

[1] 'Orientation' is preferred to 'model' in acknowledgement of the fact that different approaches to constitutional development within our political culture are often assumed rather than explicitly named, sketched in broad brushstrokes rather than elaborated in detail.

[2] See eg M. Loughlin, 'In Defence of *Staatslehre*' (2009) 48 *Der Staat* 1; U. K. Preuss, 'Disconnecting Constitutions from Statehood: Is Global Constitutionalism a Viable Concept?' in P. Dobner and M. Loughlin (eds), *The Twilight of Constitutionalism?* (Oxford University Press 2010) 23–46.

encompassing idea. Yet, however familiar, and however suggestive as a conceptual anchor, this usage is of limited utility in unpacking Scottish constitutional distinctiveness. Indeed, in its tendency to reduce constitutional authority to the state alone, and, in particular, to the state's single root of constituent power, to its holistic conception of governmental organization, and to its supreme jurisdiction over internal and external affairs, this 'Westphalian' version of the territorial constitution stands in the way of an adequate appreciation of Scotland's situation and prospects in a more complex regulatory environment.

Instead, I want to introduce two applications of the idea of a territorial constitution that may be less familiar and less intuitive, but which are more promising for our purposes. One usage, which has recently gained ground,[3] treats the 'territorial' adjective as referring not to the constitutional whole but to just one dimension of a broader constitutional order, albeit an order that may still be understood in terms of the singular, holistic, and paramount authority of the sovereign state. That one dimension involves the geographical distribution of authority within the state. This is the usage with which we are mainly concerned in the present chapter. The other possible application to which we refer departs more radically from our conventional constitutional frame of reference. More than a matter of adjectival stress, instead it treats 'territorial constitution' as a compound noun—a distinct and separate species within the constitutional genus, and so as only one of a variety of constitutional orders applicable to any particular population.

What value lies in deploying these two alternative readings of the territorial constitution? An understanding of the territorial dimension as referring only to the geographically differentiated aspect of the sovereign whole has both analytical and practical worth. It pays an obvious analytical dividend in allowing us to identify those matters of primary concern to us. It is also of practical use in allowing us to think through the forms and limits of *partial* constitutional reform in the United Kingdom. The debate over the prospects for resolving the Scottish question turns on systemic considerations and on matters of process as well as on questions of substance. It is a matter of deep contention not only whether and to what extent reform short of independence involving further acquisition of legislative, executive, and fiscal power should take place, but also whether and to what extent it should do so on a unilateral and highly asymmetrical basis, or accompanied by a more multilateral settlement of a federal, consociational, or otherwise Union-reordering variety. How, if at all, might the balance of constitutional authority between Scotland and the central state be

[3] See eg A. McHarg, 'The Constitutional Implications of the Rise of the SNP' (*UK Constitutional Law blog*, 29 April 2015) <http://ukconstitutionallaw.org/2015/04/29/manifesto-watch-aileen-mcharg-the-constitutional-implications-of-the-rise-of-the-snp/>; A. Trench, 'The UK at a Constitutional Crossroads' (*Centre for Constitutional Change*, 21 May 2015) <http://www.centreonconstitutionalchange.ac.uk/?q=blog/uk-constitutional-crossroads>; M. Moran, 'Devolution: it's a constitutional issue' (*Manchester Policy blog*, 15 July 2015) <http://blog.policy.manchester.ac.uk/featured/2015/07/devolution-its-a-constitutional-issue/>; P. Scott, 'The Upper Chamber and the Territorial Constitution' (*UK Constitutional Law blog*, 22 July 2015) <http://ukconstitutionallaw.org/>.

renegotiated without deciding on the internal balance of authority between state and nations more generally, and without also deciding on matters such as the coherence of executive and administrative power between the various levels of government, the form of the central Parliament, the electoral system, the protection of fundamental rights, and the relationship between the state and supranational and international organizations? The prospects of the various reform orientations clearly depend, therefore, not only on the balance of Scottish aspirations, but also the extent to which the territorial dimension of the constitution, so conceived, is capable, as a matter of institutional logic, of being addressed by discrete means without the need for wider systemic reform, as well as the extent to which the methods and processes of constitutional initiative allow or require more or less discrete treatment of the parts.

With regard to the more radical notion of the territorial constitution as an entity distinct from other constitutional forms, the exercise in reframing is broader and has wider ramifications. So understood, the territorial constitution is just one of a number of specialist constitutional orders or systems, each of which might also be rendered as a compound noun.[4] It follows that our overall constitutional condition is defined by the combination and interaction of these specialist orders—the security constitution, the market constitution, the monetary constitution, the social or social welfare constitution, perhaps the environmental constitution, as well as the territorial constitution. As the tentative character of this listing indicates, these various specialist constitutional orders lack sharp definition and clear boundaries. Yet that should not cause us to discount the value of this approach. It is just because they are understood in terms of their material remit, rather than the crisp logic of formal legal pedigree, that these specialist constitutional orders take less precise shape. For the point of adopting this alternative perspective is to gain a deeper appreciation of the range and interrelationship of the different functional projects and jurisdictions that regulate our lives. Here the territorial constitution continues to refer to the basic complex of territorially rooted and focused general governing institutions and representative arrangements under which we live—or what is sometimes called the 'political constitution'.[5] Yet now it is just one normative framework governing our lives alongside other deep regulatory codes that perform an equivalent constitutive role in their specific domains.

[4] For two related but distinct approaches, see: G. Teubner, *Constitutional Fragments: Societal Constitutionalism and Globalization* (Oxford University Press 2012); K. Tuori, 'The Many Constitutions of Europe' in K. Tuori and S. Sankari (eds), *The Many Constitutions of Europe* (Ashgate 2010) 3–30.

[5] See eg N. Luhmann, *Law as a Social System* (Oxford University Press 2004) for the original treatment of the idea of a political constitution in the systems-theoretical manner later favoured by Teubner, and to a lesser extent Tuori (n. 4). In the British tradition of constitutional thought the idea of a political constitution also focuses on the idea of holding power to account through general political processes and institutions, but here the term is often deployed not only as a tool of sociological observation, as in the systems approach, but also as an object of normative approval; see eg G. Gee and G. Webber, 'What is a Political Constitution?' (2010) 30 *OJLS* 273.

The picture revealed through this fresh lens, then, is of a doubly differentiated constitutional order. On the one hand, the territorial or political constitution of general governing institutions is itself highly geographically differentiated—spread over substate national, state, and—acknowledging the increasing breadth of competence of the European Union (EU) and other regional and global organizations—even supranational sites. On the other hand, each functionally specific constitution also has its own particular centre, or, more likely, *centres*—of gravity. For example, as regards the market constitution, the United Kingdom supplies one level of constitutive framing and regulation through its basic system of private economic and enterprise law, but is also located within the wider legally constituted internal market of the EU, which in turn is located within the world market-making framework of the World Trade Organization. In their different way the security and the social constitution also operate on a multilevel basis, although with more emphasis on domestic institutions, while the monetary constitution is split between UK-centred sterling and EU-centred euro currency areas, but with an additional element of common regulation.

Even within this doubly differentiated perspective, close connections between the territorial constitutional order of general governing institutions and the other specialist constitutional orders remain. Importantly, however, unlike the Westphalian model of state sovereignty, this perspective does not assume that the territorial constitution can be reconciled into a singular source and holistic framework of authority, or that its authority over each functional domain is paramount. The relationship between the territorial levels is looser, the product of a number of intersecting claims and compacts rather than an overarching state-centred settlement. Contributing to this complex geographical dispersal of institutional power, the relationship between these various loosely coupled sites of territorial authority and the different functional projects of governance is itself variable. As is best illustrated by the evolving example of the European Union—host to powerful monetary and market constitutions—these functional projects, while they may originally have been allocated between sites and levels in accordance with state-centred pedigree norms, whether in federal-style settlements or, in this particular case, state-sourced international treaties, over time they become embedded and develop in ways which conform to their own specific institutional logic, growing more independent of—and perhaps resistant to—the steering capacity of the territorial constitution.[6]

No privileged status is claimed for this alternative reading of the territorial constitution. It is just one other way of thinking about our constitutional way of being—what we might call a *post-sovereign* orientation[7]—and somewhat at odds with the various more state-centred orientations. But it is an approach that responds to certain objective trends in the development of a multilevel national,

[6] See eg I.-J. Sand, 'Constitutionalism and the Multi-Coded Treaties of the EU: Changing the Concepts of Constitutionality' in Tuori and Sankari (n. 4) 49–67.

[7] See eg M. Keating, *Plurinational Democracy: Stateless Nations in a Post-Sovereignty Era* (Oxford University Press 2001).

state, regional, and global architecture—trends that inevitably affect the lived constitutional experience and aspirations of citizens and subjects.[8] As such, it supplies an important supplementary outlook on the distinctiveness of Scotland as a political community. It alerts us to the fact that the Scottish piece has to fit a larger regulatory jigsaw, and that it would be unduly reductive to measure the distinctiveness of Scottish self-government only in terms of Scotland's relationship to the state known as the United Kingdom. The range of possibilities may be better understood, not to mention less divisively pursued, if less rigidly framed by the binary logic of sovereign statehood.

The following sequence of discussion reflects an attempt to think about the future of the territorial constitution in these broader terms. We focus on various interrelated dimensions of ordering, each supplying an important section of the constitutional mosaic that frames Scottish distinctiveness, and ask how these are addressed through different constitutional orientations. We begin with the question of the extent and intensity of Scottish self-government considered in its own terms (sections II and III). Short of independence, what are the intrinsic limits to the constitutional autonomy of the substate part? We then proceed to discuss various particular problems and possibilities of Scottish self-government that arise from its relationship to the British state (section IV) First, there is the question of *symmetry* or otherwise of treatment of the other territorial parts with which Scotland retains a constitutional connection. To what extent is treatment of Scottish distinctiveness influenced by and influential of the treatment of other nations and regions of the United Kingdom? Secondly, there is the broader question of *common architecture*. What forms of common governing institutions at the UK level may be required to accommodate substate distinctiveness or to provide countervailing measures of integration? Thirdly, there is the question of the locus and terms of *constitutional initiative*. Who gets to decide on constitutional changes relevant to the question of Scottish distinctiveness, and with what implications for the orientation and feasibility of reform?

Whereas the themes of symmetry and common government address the systemic implications of greater Scottish self-government, the theme of constitutional initiative addresses the related procedural pathways and obstacles. In both cases, the primary concern is with the territorial constitution in the first of the two alternative senses introduced above. The last dimension of ordering to which we refer in conclusion (Section V), namely the question of constitutional *re-imagination*, returns us briefly to the other and more radical reworking of the idea of the territorial constitution. Taking account of developments under the previous heads, but also of wider movements in the global constitutional landscape, we ask what are the prospects and the implications of the Scottish question coming to be viewed through the new type of constitutional optic referred to above—one that no longer treats territorial sovereignty as *the* master key to the preservation of the constitutional legacy or the unlocking of constitutional potential.

8 See eg N. Walker, *Beyond the Holistic Constitution?* in Dobner and Loughlin (n. 2) 291–308.

II. The shifting frontiers of Scottish self-government

A. Devolution and beyond

Until recently Scottish self-government developed within a framework of 'devolution' built upon two features of the unwritten British constitution that exist in some tension; namely, its flexibility and its conservative quality. On the one hand, the progress of devolution has been open-ended. It has been 'a process rather than an event'[9]—a series of measures developed piecemeal in accelerating response to varied circumstances across the United Kingdom rather than according to a fixed and uniform constitutional design. From the earliest stages of the 1707 Union the continuing distinctiveness of Scottish affairs and the need for separate forms of government was recognized. Yet until the late twentieth century this was largely accommodated by means of administrative devolution—given settled institutional form through the founding of the Scottish Office and the position of Secretary for Scotland—later the Secretary of State for Scotland—in 1885, as well as in the emergence of a expanding corpus of Scottish legislation at Westminster. Following the failure of a first statutory scheme for a Scottish law-making Assembly in 1978 to reach the high implementation threshold of 40 per cent popular support demanded by a reluctant UK Parliament,[10] no further legislative plan for devolution emerged until 1998. On that occasion, the New Labour Government's initiative carried broader political support and was emphatically endorsed by referendum. Yet even such a radical institutional innovation involved significant continuity. The core areas of devolved competence to the new Scottish Parliament and Government were similar to those previously administered by the Scottish Office. They included agriculture, arts, culture, education, health, justice, and transport, with defence, foreign policy, currency, macro-economic policy, economic regulation, and social security retained by Westminster. The Scotland Act 2012 extended the legislative and executive jurisdiction of the new Scottish institutions at the margins,[11] but, as we shall see, in laying the groundwork for a more extensive framework of fiscal devolution, it foretold a further radical departure.

On the other hand, devolution chimes with a very old constitutional story. To understand the territorial spread of legal and political authority, however extensive, through the prism of devolution, is to adhere to the traditional conception of the British state as a sovereign unity. In the dominant Diceyan orientation, it is not 'the people', still less 'the peoples' of the United Kingdom who supply the *pouvoir constituant*. Rather, the Westminster Parliament, predating the Union with Scotland and absorbing the constitutional prerogatives of its erstwhile neighbor,

[9] As famously described by Ron Davies, the former Secretary of State for Wales.

[10] See eg I. MacWhirter, *Road to Referendum* (Cargo Publishing 2014) ch. 9.

[11] Scotland Act 2012, Part 1 (including aspects of the administration of elections, airguns, speed limits, and drink-driving limits).

is the source from which all authority flows. Devolved power, then, is merely delegated power, and unlike the constitutionally guaranteed allocation of competence to the parts of a federal state, the grant and continued enjoyment of such devolved power remains within the gift of the central state.[12]

Today, however, the framework and methods of devolution, and the distinctive mix of constitutional flexibility and conservatism underwriting this, appear increasingly inadequate in understanding the forms and dynamic of Scottish self-government. Two other powerful orientations now also compete to frame the debate about Scottish distinctiveness. On the one side, the idea of the United Kingdom as a 'Union state' is acquiring a new prominence. The concept of Union in the British political imagination is much older than the compact of 1707, assuming and shedding various nuances of meaning in different legal, political, and ecclesiastical contexts.[13] A contemporary strain, already evident in the Claim of Right and the Scottish Constitutional Convention of the pre-reform phase of the late 1980s and early 90s, and developing in range and intensity over the referendum period and beyond,[14] focuses more closely than earlier variants on Scotland's distinctive *constitutional* condition and prospects. This idea of Union implies an understanding of the constitutional order less hierarchical than under the sign of Parliamentary sovereignty, but also less ordered in its distribution of power than under a founding federal compact. Instead it relies upon a narrative in which the original national components retain—or at least reclaim—a measure of constitutional autonomy, and in which the integrity of the UK body politic depends upon the continuing mutual accommodation of these national constituencies. From this perspective, the legitimacy and perhaps even the formal authority[15] of the developing system of Scottish self-government flows not from a 'top-down' grant of powers but from the 'bottom-up' assertion and negotiated settlement of the parties to the Union.

On the other side of the new debate, there is, of course, the increasingly tangible prospect of independence. The strength of this orientation closely mirrors the rise of the SNP as a powerful force in Scottish political life since its early electoral success in the 1970s. The goal of independence has emerged intact from—apparently even fortified by—the unexpectedly narrow loss of the first referendum in September 2014.[16] According to the nationalist vision, the legitimacy of the developing system of Scottish self-government, including the new steps

[12] See eg B. Hadfield, 'Devolution: A National Conversation?' in J. Jowell and D. Oliver (eds), *The Changing Constitution* (Oxford University Press, 7th edn 2011) 213–37.

[13] See in particular C. Kidd, *Union and Unionisms: Political Thought in Scotland, 1500–2000* (Cambridge University Press 2008).

[14] See eg MacWhirter (n. 10), chs 10–16; C. Kidd, 'The Defence of the Union: Ironies and Ambiguities' in G. Hassan and J. Mitchell (eds), *After Independence* (Luath Press 2013) 45–54.

[15] See eg G. Anderson et al, 'The Independence Referendum: legality and the contested constitution; widening the debate' (*UK Constitutional Law blog*, 31 January 2012) <http://ukconstitutionallaw.org/2012/01/31/gavin-anderson-et-al-the-independence-referendum-legality-and-the-contested-constitution-widening-the-debate/>.

[16] See eg I. MacWhirter, *Disunited Kingdom: How Westminster Won a Referendum but lost Scotland* (Cargo Publishing 2014).

proposed by pro-Union parties in the wake of the referendum, remains essentially instrumental and incomplete. All measures accommodating Scottish distinctiveness within the existing British state, however beneficial in their own terms, are in the final analysis merely holding positions and intermediate rungs on the ladder to Scottish statehood.

The two orientations—Union state and nationalist—vie with one other, but they also feed off one another. From the Union state perspective, the endorsement of a free union of autonomous parts is critical of the categorical force of legal and political separation implied by independence. Yet it is also challenged by the nationalist vision, and provoked by it to conceive of Scottish constitutional autonomy in increasingly expansive terms. In particular, the maturing Union state perspective has come to accept the same basic ethic of Scottish self-determination as the nationalist vision, even as it insists that independent statehood is not needed to satisfy that ethical aspiration. From the nationalist perspective, the Union state perspective may be criticized as superficial or insufficient. Across a broader political spectrum, in fact, promotion of the idea of Union still suffers from association with certain historical forms of Union*ism*—most vividly in the Northern Ireland context—that, far from offering a vision of progressive power-sharing, instead involve a vigorous defence of the unitary UK state.[17] Yet many of the autonomy-enhancing measures of more progressive Union state thinking undeniably open the route towards independence. Indeed, nationalist politicians and thinkers have often been to the fore in contemplating new self-governing architecture *within* the Union state.[18] And, of course, nationalist interest in the Union state's progressive dispersal of authority is far from confined to the drawing board, for the post-1998 institutions of Scottish Parliament and Government also provide an active platform from which an increasingly electorally successful nationalist movement has been able to promote its wider objectives.

B. New terms of debate

The shift in the terms of debate from a traditional sovereigntist and Westminster-centric orientation towards devolved power to one in which constitutional authority is locally sourced and pursued in either Unionist or nationalist directions is reflected in the new reform agenda. From the Calman Commission,[19] which provided the impetus for the Scotland Act 2012, through the pre-referendum projections and blueprints of the main players and the 'Vow'[20] of the Better Together

[17] See eg Kidd (n. 14).

[18] Not least in their original suggestion of a third 'devo-max' option in the 2014 referendum ballot, and in their active involvement in the post-referendum Smith process. See s. IIB below. See also S. Tierney, 'Reclaiming Politics: Popular Democracy in Britain after the Scottish Referendum' (2015) 86 *The Political Quarterly* 226.

[19] Commission on Scottish Devolution, *Serving Scotland Better: Scotland and the United Kingdom in the 21st Century* (Final Report, June 2009) available at <http://www.commissiononscottishdevolution.org.uk/uploads/2009–06-12-csd-final-report-2009fbookmarked.pdf>.

[20] Published in the *Daily Record* newspaper on 16 September 2014; available at <http://www.dailyrecord.co.uk/news/politics/david-cameron-ed-miliband-nick-4265992>.

partners at the eleventh hour of a campaign marked by a late surge in support for Scottish independence, to the proposals of the subsequent all-party Smith Commission[21] and its legislative expression in the new Conservative government's 2015 Scotland Bill,[22] we are witnessing new frontiers of discussion and contestation. With so many areas of policy, especially in the traditional public services, devolved under the 1998 Act, and the list already somewhat expanded by the 2012 Act, aside from some significant exceptions in matters such as broadcasting and the regulation of telecommunications, transport, and energy,[23] attention has turned from the general flow of competence from London to Edinburgh towards certain more specific areas of concern which inevitably loom large as self-government tests its outer limits, and which, therefore, will set the terms of debate for the foreseeable future. These are three in number. First, there is the general constitutional standing of a mature self-government system. Secondly, there is the matter of fiscal autonomy. And thirdly, there is the related question of social welfare and its relationship to economic self-government. Each theme raises challenging questions for all candidate constitutional visions.

1. Constitutional standing

The question of constitutional standing directly confronts the limitations of the traditional understanding of Scottish devolution as the mere delegation of central authority. The Vow, the Smith Commission, and the Scotland Bill each advanced the claim that the Scottish Parliament and Government, though established by Westminster legislation, be regarded as possessing an authority no longer within the exclusive gift of the London Parliament. Instead, reflecting the growing overlap in nationalist and new Union state understandings of the roots of constitutional authority, the Scottish people, in the words of Smith, should be acknowledged as possessing 'the sovereign right ... to determine the form of government best suited to their needs'.[24] So it was proposed in the new Scotland Bill that the 'permanent' character of these Scottish institutions be affirmed[25] in

[21] Report of Smith Commission for Further Devolution of Powers to the Scottish Parliament (November 2014) available at <https://www.smith-commission.scot/wp-content/uploads/2014/11/The_Smith_Commission_Report-1.pdf>.

[22] Scotland Bill 2015–16 (HC 48); for the amended version of the Bill brought from the Commons and introduced to the House of Lords in November 2015, see Scotland Bill 2015–16 (HL 73); available at <http://www.publications.parliament.uk/pa/bills/lbill/2015-2016/0073/15073.pdf>. The Scotland Bill was preceded by the Coalition Government's White Paper: *Scotland in the United Kingdom: An Enduring Settlement* (Cm 8990, 2015) <https://www.gov.uk/government/uploads/system/uploads/attachment_data/file/397079/Scotland_EnduringSettlement_acc.pdf>.

[23] Smith Commission (n. 21) paras 36–41.

[24] Smith Commission (n. 21) para. 20.

[25] Scotland Bill ss 1–2. The original Scotland Bill introduced in the Commons 'recognized' the permanence of the Scottish Parliament and Government, unlike the Smith Commission before it. In the subsequent Lords' version of the Bill, the term 'recognized' was dropped from the wording of Clause 1 but retained for the affirmation of the Sewel Convention in Clause 2. Importantly, however, the revised Clause 1 does reinforce the commitment of the UK Parliament and Government to permanence in a more practical manner; by making abolition of the Scottish political institutions dependent upon a referendum of the Scottish people.

new Westminster legislation, and that similar recognition be given to the Sewel Convention by which the United Kingdom refrains from legislating in devolved areas without the consent of the Scottish Parliament. In additional acknowledgment of the elevated constitutional standing of the Scottish institutions and a general shift towards political self-government, the Scottish Parliament should gain the power to legislate by special majority for the conduct of its own elections, and to regulate the operation of the Scottish system of government more broadly.[26]

Yet the reliance on Westminster legislation—the highest form of law known to the UK constitution—to overcome some of the constitutional restrictions associated with that very same form is at one level paradoxical. Given the pure doctrine of Parliamentary supremacy, according to which a later Parliament can always unmake the legislation of its earlier incarnation, any attempt to entrench in strictly legal terms the permanence of devolved institutions and any asserted prohibition of unilateral legislative override of devolved powers is bound to fail, or at least be the subject of continuing doubt.[27] It was, indeed, precisely in acknowledgment of this normative limitation that the declaratory language of 'recognition' was resorted to in the original version of the 2015 Scotland Bill (though continuing uncertainty and controversy over the strength of the commitment to permanence thereby implied resulted in that language being subsequently dropped).[28] Absent legally binding guarantees, it certainly remains arguable that the better assurance of any constitutional arrangement lies in the political force of established convention or common accord. Yet, if that is so, it is not clear how much, if anything, is gained on balance by any *statutory* reference to these conventional or agreed standards. A reminder in such a solemn register may be of some expressive significance in affirming commitment to the practical settlement, but, viewed through sceptical eyes, its effect may equally be to draw unwanted attention to the lack of justiciable legal underpinning of that settlement.

More generally, in seeking to capture the political complexities of the current settlement over Scottish self-government, resort to the formal method of Westminster legislation, with its laconic and reductive style and UK-centred frame of reference, is as contentious for what it does not say as for what it does. The Sewel Convention's requirement of Scottish consent is generally understood to extend beyond Westminster legislation in the devolved areas to include amendments to the powers of the Scottish Parliament and the Scottish Ministers.[29] Yet

[26] Including the size of the Scottish Parliament and the electoral system to be used. Smith Commission (n. 21) paras 21–7.

[27] See eg Scottish Parliament, Devolution (Further Powers) Committee, *An Interim Report on the Smith Commission and the UK Government's Proposals*, 3rd Report, Session 4 (2015), SP Paper 720, paras 36–61.

[28] See Scotland Bill 2015–16 (HL 73), s. 1; see further (n. 25) above.

[29] See Devolution Guidance Note 10: Post Devolution Primary Legislation Affecting Scotland <https://www.gov.uk/government/uploads/system/uploads/attachment_data/file/60985/post-devolution-primary-scotland.pdf>.

early attempts in the post-Smith process to express the Convention in terse legal form made no mention of this second Sewel limb, prompting concerns that it might be undermined or downgraded by legislative silence.[30] Even more conspicuous by its omission from a statutory scheme intended to make a politically resonant statement about the constitutional standing of self-government is any explicit reference to Smith's agreed basic premise of an emerging right to Scottish self-determination, or any indication of the circumstances, terms, and conditions of its legitimate future expression.

The overall emphasis, then, is on constitutional conservation rather than transformation; on protecting the system of Scottish self-government established since 1998 rather than the continuing right of the Scottish people to decide on the nature and scope of that system. That emphasis may be as much a reflection of the unsuitability of the conservative legal source and method of Westminster legislation to convey a more open-ended constitutional scenario as it is an indication of the pro-Union constitutional end-state favoured by the majority of the parties represented on Smith. But, in any event, the result is a somewhat crabbed and one-sided depiction of the current constitutional standing of Scottish self-government. If the Scottish people are now in principle sovereign, then the highest legislative authority of a polity that embodies a quite different conception of sovereignty appears an awkward and, arguably, inadequate vehicle through which to express that popular vision.[31]

2. *The financing of self-government*

If we turn to the other central themes of fiscal autonomy, social welfare, and the scope of economic self government more generally, the ideological lines, at least at first sight, appear more clearly drawn. In its initial post-referendum repositioning the SNP government called for full fiscal autonomy as a second best alternative and as its optimal stepping stone to independence. This means that all onshore and offshore taxes would be designed and set in Scotland, including tax rates, allowances, thresholds, and the tax bases.[32] In addition to the full range of tax powers, the Scottish institutions should also have access to other macro-economic levers, such as employment policy and aspects of immigration. More generally, full fiscal autonomy necessarily implies that the Scottish Parliament and Government would take responsibility for *all* key elements of domestic expenditure, including social welfare. A direct payment would be made from Scottish revenues to London to cover only certain residual services Scotland receives from the remaining part of the United Kingdom. These would include agreed amounts for defence, security, foreign policy, and the servicing of historic debt interest.

[30] See eg (n. 27) paras 51–61. [31] But see further section V of the text below.

[32] See eg Scottish Government, *More Powers for the Scottish Parliament: Scottish Government Proposals* (October 2014) <http://www.gov.scot/Publications/2014/10/2806/0>; Scottish Government, *Further Devolution Beyond the Smith Commission* (May 2015) <http://www.gov.scot/Resource/0047/00479299.pdf>.

Full fiscal autonomy, and its accompanying wide-ranging legislative and executive jurisdiction, countenances a level of substate self-regulation unknown even in the most federalized of modern state polities.[33] Yet the transfer of fiscal powers is already underway, and in the wake of the referendum, the scope for further development short of full fiscal autonomy is significant. Replacing the unutilized three-pence maximum variation of UK basic rate income tax under the original 1998 scheme, the Scotland Act 2012 requires the Scottish Parliament from April 2016 onwards to make an open-ended determination of a Scottish rate of income tax to supplement the UK basic rate, which will be held 10 per cent lower for Scottish taxpayers than for other UK taxpayers.[34] The power to set new Scottish property transaction and landfill taxes further augments the fiscal authority of the Scottish Government,[35] which will see the block grant from the UK Government under the Barnett formula reduced to take account of enhanced domestic tax-raising capacity.

But even before these provisions have been fully implemented, Smith promises to go significantly further. One of its key agreed objectives is to enhance the accountability of the Scottish Parliament for the consequences of its decisions by increasing its independent revenue-raising capacity and aligning this more closely with its service delivery and spending obligations.[36] According to this prospectus, the Scottish Parliament will move beyond a supplementary brief to assume responsibility for setting all income rates and bands on earned income for Scottish taxpayers above the common UK floor. Air Passenger Duty and Aggregates Levy will also be devolved, and the first ten points of VAT raised in Scotland assigned to the Scottish Parliament.[37] Excise duties, corporation tax, national insurance, and all capital taxes, on the other hand, will remain the preserve of the UK Parliament. Yet even with these reservations, over half of the money spent by the Scottish Parliament will now either be raised by it or received by direct transfer from source rather than the Whitehall block grant.

Notwithstanding these innovations, the SNP government is a reluctant subscriber to the credibility of Smith's vision of a Scottish Parliament that would possess a 'sufficiently substantial and cohesive package of powers enabling the delivery of outcomes that are meaningful to the people of Scotland'[38] to accompany its new constitutional standing. The nationalist view is that Smith caps Scottish fiscal powers at a level bound to frustrate its own purported ambitions to make the Scottish institutions capable of achieving and answering for a coherent overall programme of government. Strengthened by success in the 2015 general election, the SNP government has, therefore, petitioned strongly for further specific fiscal powers, in particular over employers' national insurance contributions, corporation tax, and capital gains tax. These additional powers, it argues, together

[33] See eg Bingham Centre for the Rule of Law, *A Constitutional Crossroads: Ways Forward for the United Kingdom* (British Institute for International and Comparative Law 2015) para. 3.7.

[34] Scotland Act 2012, ss 25–7.

[35] Scotland Act 2012, ss 28–31.

[36] Smith (n. 21), Foreword p. 4.

[37] Smith (n. 21) paras 75–79, 86–91.

[38] Smith (n. 21) para. 7.

with control over personal allowances and other tax reliefs, would provide the essential tools with which to develop a 'substantial and cohesive' policy package different in kind from that emanating from the central government in London—particularly focused on an alternative economic strategy for growth and tackling inequality.[39]

3. Social Welfare

The same charge of undelivered promises and a lack of 'joined up' competence to deliver an alternative strategy of government has been levelled by the nationalist government against the Smith proposals in the adjacent areas of welfare and employment policy. While pensions, child benefit, and all aspects of working age benefits under the universal credit scheme other than housing benefit and associated tax credits are retained at Westminster, benefits for disabled and other dependent persons and their carers are to be devolved, and the Scottish Ministers granted additional powers to make discretionary payments or develop new benefits in areas related to their existing devolved responsibilities.[40] But in this aspect of the Smith Agreement more than any other, the UK Government stands exposed to the charge that its legislative proposals fail to deliver even on their stated terms.[41] Any implementation deficit is in part a product of the technical difficulty of disentangling a tightly interwoven tapestry of legal provisions on the treatment of individual need under the welfare state, but that integrated legacy is also indicative of a deeper ideological obstacle. For many who adopt a Union state orientation, common allegiance to an encompassing system of social welfare is vital to the conception of the United Kingdom as a social union committed to pooling and sharing risks and resources.[42] As such, it is viewed as just as key to the continuing viability of the United Kingdom as a political community as are the fundamentals of common security and defence, or a common currency and a single market. From this perspective, even the modest devolutionary steps mooted by Smith are viewed with great caution.

But while defenders of the Union remain reluctant to treat social welfare as divisible, the nationalist position relies upon mirror claims about the indivisibility of key elements of effective self-government to argue for significant advances on the concessions made by Smith. They ask for an additional transfer of responsibility for all benefits in relation to children and working age benefits in general. And to complete their vision of an integrated approach to economic self-government to match Smith's recipe for political self-government, the nationalists seek a

[39] Scottish Government (n. 32). [40] Smith (n. 21) paras 42–56.

[41] See eg Scottish Parliament (n. 27) paras 230–339; Scottish Government, *Scottish Government Response to the Interim Report From the Devolution (Further Powers) Committee on the Smith Commission and the UK Government's Proposals* (June 2015) <http://www.gov.scot/Resource/0047/00478767.pdf> 9–11.

[42] See eg Bingham Centre (n. 33) para. 4.1; G. Brown, *My Scotland, My Britain: A Future Worth Sharing* (Simon & Schuster 2015) ch. 6. See further Gallagher, Ch. 6 in this volume.

significant extension of powers in the employment field; in particular, jurisdiction over the minimum wage, and employment law more generally, including trade union law and health and safety regulations, as well as the full transfer of employment support programmes.[43]

III. Self-government in the shadow of independence

Examination of these emerging terms of debate over Scottish self-government indicates a number of factors shaping and restricting its further extension. As noted earlier, some constraints derive from the relationship of Scotland to the wider UK polity and beyond, and these are addressed in subsequent sections. The present section concentrates on certain intrinsic factors impacting upon the self-governing potential of a substate nation in which independence stands as a vibrant but contested alternative to an evolving Union state vision. The first two such factors we define as the problems of *approximation* and of *auditioning*. These involve complex considerations of political strategy, challenging the common assumption that the cause of independence is necessarily best served, or is even understood by its proponents to be best served, by all increases in powers of self-government short of independence. The third factor is the problem of *detachment*. This raises the deeper and more general question of the limits beyond which *any* system of regional or (substate) national self-government becomes so extensive in its own terms, and, therefore, so detractive of the potential of the wider polity as a community of shared purpose, that it may no longer be reconciled with membership of that larger polity. Unlike the first two factors, this line of discussion *does* indicate why advances in self-government beyond a certain threshold might jeopardize the Union and serve the cause of independence.

A. Approximation

The problem of approximation refers to the ways in which the distinction between self-government within the Union state and independence may become less significant, even blurred, as we approach the threshold of sovereign statehood, and how this may affect the political stakes in the debate over Scotland's constitutional future. Proximity to independence in the form of the most developed system of substate self-government, for all its temptations, carries certain dangers for nationalists, some engendered by their opponents and others a by-product of their own shifting vision.

As is apparent from the Vow and the Smith Commission process, and, indeed, from the earlier history of devolution, the Union's supporters may reckon that the attractiveness of independence will recede to the extent that its benefits are already available in a robust regime of self-government. This calculation has a

[43] Smith (n. 21) para. 57.

material and a symbolic dimension. In material terms, the delivery of a wide range of competences over domestic policy, together with a degree of fiscal autonomy, may be judged to satisfy the significant range of Scottish opinion that, according to recent evidence, is attracted to an intermediate if underspecified position of so-called 'devo-max'.[44] In symbolic terms, the affirmation of an autonomous constitutional status short of independence, as in Smith's proclamation of the Scottish political institutions as permanent, offers at least some measure of the recognition of distinct political community that nationalist sentiment demands. What is more, even as it seeks to seduce nationalist opinion, this kind of expressive commitment remains distinctly double-edged. For a vow of permanence might imply both sides of a 'durable'[45] solution. It offers not only a guarantee of irreversibility but also the suggestion of constitutional finality—and with it abandonment of the ultimate goal of sovereignty.

The erosion of a sharp distinction between an advanced form of self-government and independence also proceeds from the other side of the argument. The increasingly candid commitment of a mature nationalist movement to retaining Scottish involvement in many of the other longstanding unions that have accompanied the United Kingdom's legal and political Union, including the monarchical union, the sterling currency union, the European Union, and the wider defence union associated with NATO, may enhance the attractiveness of its case by acknowledging the practical limitations of national sovereignty in an interdependent world.[46] A position so qualified, however, also becomes susceptible to the charge of offering a version of 'independence-lite' whose differences from 'devo-max' become marginal and unstable. The problem of approximation, then, cannot be simply attributed to the decreasing distance of progressive Union state thinking from a fixed target of independence. It is also about the elusiveness of any such fixed target, and an emerging awareness that the tactical approaches underpinning the different constitutional options sponsored by new Union state and nationalist thinking alike means that they increasingly appear as more or less adjacent points on the same spectrum rather than as categorically distinct.

B. Auditioning

The attraction of any national independence movement is inherently aspirational.[47] It is predicated upon the contrast between an inhibited present, where the institutions of self-determination are inadequate and much of the cultural energy that would animate these institutions remains untapped, and a liberated

[44] J. Curtice, 'So Where Does Scotland Stand on More Devolution?' (Scotcen 2013), reporting that in 2013 slightly more Scots (32 per cent) supported 'devo-max' than independence (31 per cent) <http://www.natcen.ac.uk/media/282285/ssa13-devo-max-briefing-report.pdf>.

[45] Smith (n. 21) para. 17.

[46] See eg Neil Walker, 'Independence in an Interdependent World' in Hassan and Mitchell (n. 14), 30–44.

[47] See eg A. Smith, *Nationalism and Modernism* (Routledge 1998) ch. 1.

future where the resources of self-government are abundant and aligned to a richer sense of common political community. In order to draw this contrast effectively where, as in Scotland, partial self-government is already in place and political momentum favours its further development, promoters of independence must strike a delicate balance. On the one hand, if their vision of independence remains in the realm of the counterfactual—posited as a complete departure from current self-governing arrangements rather than a series of improvements upon these arrangements—they become vulnerable to the charge of disengaged utopianism. They must, therefore, indicate the concrete promise as well as the limitations of existing mechanisms of self-government. On the other hand, if they focus too much on the here and now in their attempts to extrapolate the virtues of full self-government, and in so doing draw excessive attention to the dangers and pitfalls involved in the task ahead, their appeal may founder on the opposite ground. They may fail to persuade their audience how an attractive version of independence might follow from the trials of its emergence. In other words, just as by adopting a utopian outlook they may seem to promise too much, by being too 'realistic' they may seem to offer too little.

The SNP's occupation of the seat of government in Scotland, first as a minority administration in 2007 and, since 2011, as the majority party, has allowed it to answer the charge of utopianism through demonstrating, by example, how the promise of self-government might begin to be fulfilled. In so doing however, alert to the danger of underselling the benefits of sovereign self-determination, the SNP has asked its performance to be assessed not as a full-blown rehearsal for independence but in light of its still limited control of the levers of self-government, and so as a more modest form of auditioning for a future role.[48] In turn, this approach has given rise to contestation with the parties of Union over what might be plausibly achieved within existing powers, and what additional powers might be required to achieve broader governmental objectives. Predictably enough, as devolved capacity has begun to expand the nationalists have been as emphatic in their insistence that they remain significantly handicapped by a deficit of powers as the supporters of Union have been robust in their claims that existing powers already make generous but underexploited provision for self-government.

That debate has reached a new pitch of intensity with the emergence of the post-Smith agenda of economic self-government. Here the problem of auditioning crystallizes as a special case of the problem of approximation. Nationalist post-referendum support for full fiscal autonomy is qualified not merely by concern that this comes to be widely regarded as so significant a concession as to make the case for independence redundant, but also because it might place in harsher relief some of the challenges attendant upon fuller self-government. Especially in view

[48] For example, the approach of the Yes campaign's pre-referendum manifesto was to distinguish clearly in each policy area between what was achievable under existing devolved powers and the higher goals accessible under independence: Scottish Government, *Scotland's Future—Your Guide to an Independent Scotland* (November 2013) available at: <http://www.scotreferendum.com/reports/scotlands-future-your-guide-to-an-independent-scotland/>.

of projected shortfalls in oil-related tax dividends, the precipitous grant of such powers could embarrass a future Scottish Government seeking to match revenue to committed expenditure priorities and levels.[49] It could, therefore, leave the nationalist custodians of self-government poorly positioned to supply a foretaste of the benefits of independence at the very point where the constitutional conditions strike a broader public audience as sufficiently developed and so conducive to effective self-government to support, even require, a proper trial. As we have seen in the increasingly fractious debate about the precise circumstances under which fiscal autonomy might be sought and granted, with the Unionist parties publicly doubting how committed the nationalists are in their claimed desire for full tax-raising powers and the nationalists responding that no such grant of powers is genuinely contemplated by the Unionist parties, both sides face a significant dilemma.[50] Nationalist concerns about being victims of premature judgment vie with a desire to press ahead, and to be seen to press ahead, towards their ultimate goal, while Unionist temptations to subject the nationalist case to advance scrutiny vie with their concern to draw a firm line in the sand beyond which self-government within the British state should be considered no longer viable.

C. Detachment

The problem of detachment concerns just that line in the sand. It covers two closely interconnected trends. On the one hand, it speaks to the objective tendency of an expanding institutional framework of substate self-government to develop remotely from the central authority of the state and at its expense, thereby undermining the state's capacity to maintain a governmental regime of shared purpose. On the other hand, it speaks to a growing attitude of subjective detachment, which both feeds and feeds off the objective trend towards institutional detachment. For to the extent that the Scottish *demos* comes to consider itself as the primary community of political attachment, its members may become progressively detached from the United Kingdom as a wider community of belonging and commitment.[51]

We have noted that both sides in the independence debate accept that the continued viability of the UK state requires at least a common system of security and defence, as well as the legal framework of a common currency and common market. Where disagreement arises is over the requirements of 'social union'. The conviction of Union state supporters that the nations must pool and share risks

[49] See eg D. Philips, 'Full fiscal autonomy delayed; The SNP's plans for further devolution to Scotland' (Institute for Fiscal Studies, April 2015) available at: <http://www.ifs.org.uk/publications/7722>.

[50] This has been a consistent theme of debate in and beyond the Houses of Parliament over the new Scotland Bill.

[51] See eg Curtice (n. 44); A. Henderson, C. Jeffery, and R. Lineira, 'National Identity or National Interest? Scottish, English and Welsh attitudes to the Constitutional Debate' (2015) 86 *The Political Quarterly* 265–74.

and resources to underwrite a basic bond of social solidarity clearly has implications for the broad framework of Scottish fiscal autonomy and for various specific areas of welfare provision. Sufficient central tax-raising capacity must be reserved to maintain a common pool to distribute as geographically unequal needs and resources require, whether in accordance with Barnett's rigid formula or a more flexible needs-sensitive approach. But the precise level of permissible fiscal autonomy is unclear, and there is a range of views about the appropriate package of taxes to be reserved or devolved.[52] In specific areas of social welfare, however, disagreement between Unionists and nationalists is more focused. The current Scottish scheme is quite typical in permitting a high level of self-government in services such as health, education, social housing, social transport, and environmental services. These have a redistributive dimension, but are also public goods, with significant economies of scale and diffuse benefits across the particular community targeted. The case for self-government tailored to local requirements in these sectors, therefore, is relatively uncontroversial. As regards individually targeted benefits such as pensions and social security, different considerations apply. Here the relevant risks and resources are a direct function of economic capacity, and, as is reflected in the Smith conclusions, the argument for a wider tax base and continued state-wide provision, and for the promotion of a culture of mutual concern sufficient to justify the continued sharing of resources across the nations, is correspondingly stronger.[53]

Even if we disregard how the directly opposing long-term aspirations of Unionists and nationalists in the face of the forces of fragmentation influence their claims, the limits of manageable detachment within the Union state remain highly contentious. In part, this is a matter of definitional latitude, and also of predictive uncertainty in the face of novel circumstances. There is, in the final analysis, no gold standard of viable statehood. We may develop persuasive arguments about the conditions necessary to retain the type of solidarity we have come to associate with the state considered as a social union, but that does not necessarily exhaust the category of sovereign statehood. Especially in a context of developing multilevel governance, with unprecedented supra-state forces of social and political integration, we may envisage looser arrangements between substate parts—the nationalist's intermediate option of full fiscal autonomy within a security and monetary union a case in point. These may remain perfectly compatible with the legal form of the Union state, even if the desirability or long-term practical stability of such arrangements is in considerable doubt.[54]

[52] See eg Gallagher, Ch. 6 and Scott, Ch. 7 in the present volume.

[53] See eg Bingham Centre (n. 33) ch. 6.2.

[54] In Chapter 8 in the present volume Sionaidh Douglas-Scott considers the case of Greenland, which remains part of the sovereign territory of Denmark despite having 'seceded' from the EU in 1985. Whatever we think of the merits of this arrangement, or of its adaptability to other national contexts, that part of a sovereign state can leave the EU without the sovereign integrity of the state being destroyed supplies one vivid illustration of the growing flexibility of the idea of statehood in the multilevel context.

But contention over the limits of viable statehood is also about a broader picture of institutional complexity. For the growing detachment of Scottish self-government is not the only slippery slope we face in considering the continuing viability of the British state. Just as important are factors external to the Scottish institutions and concerning the wider territorial constitution of the United Kingdom; in particular the relationship of Scottish self-government to other forces of self-government within the Union, and the challenge of providing adequate mechanisms for co-ordination of the parts at the UK centre in response to the expansions and encroachments of substate jurisdiction. It is to these systemic factors, and also to the question of the available mechanisms for initiating relevant constitutional reforms, that we now turn.

IV. Self-government and the British state

A. Territorial self-government all-round: The problem of symmetry

When David Cameron declared from the steps of Downing Street the morning after the Scottish referendum that the increased self-government 'vowed' to Scotland must be accompanied by a similar settlement for the other parts of the United Kingdom, and in particular, by engagement with the 'missing'[55] question of English self-government, he took us to the heart of the problem of asymmetry. A longstanding feature of the Union state has been the strikingly uneven arrangements for governing the parts, reflecting the distinctive histories of Scotland, England, Ireland, and Wales. All three Celtic nations received significant new grants of self-government in 1998, but the background, form, and likely trajectory is very different in each case. The creation of a new power-sharing Assembly and Executive in Northern Ireland responded to a repeating pattern of sectarian and national conflict in the North since the violent birth of an independent Irish state in 1922.[56] The forging of a Welsh Assembly, and its subsequent assumption of fuller legislative powers[57] began to reverse a long history of near assimilation into the English political system. The Scottish story sat somewhere between these two options, neither the object of internal colonization and locus of periodic political violence as in the Irish case, nor largely eclipsed by English political institutions as in the Welsh case. Yet, as already noted, however we might assess the formative

[55] UK Government, Scottish Independence Referendum: statement by the Prime Minister (19 September 2014) available at <https://www.gov.uk/government/news/scottish-independence-referendum-statement-by-the-prime-minister>.

[56] See eg B. Dickson, 'Devolution' in J. Jowell, D. Oliver, and C. O'Cinneide (eds), *The Changing Constitution* (Oxford University Press, 8th edn 2015) 249, 264–8; C. Bell, 'Constitutional Transitions: The Peculiarities of the British Constitution and the Politics of Comparison' (2014) *PL* 446.

[57] Commission on Devolution in Wales, *Empowerment and Responsibility: Legislative Powers to Strengthen Wales* (2014); see also Dickson et al (n. 56) 259–63.

conditions of our contemporary Union, a continuing capacity to respond flexibly to the varied conditions of a 'plurinational state'[58] is often claimed as a distinguishing virtue of its unwritten constitutional settlement. That flexibility, indeed, and the corresponding absence of a canonical agreement, also reflects and reinforces the longstanding absence of a federal orientation within the British constitutional narrative, with its tendency towards a fixed and uniform formula for power-sharing.[59]

Nevertheless, as Cameron's intervention suggests, asymmetry now threatens constitutional stability. As with the growing detachment of Scottish self-government, there are both objective and attitudinal factors at work. Objectively, asymmetry raises particularly difficult questions about the accommodation of England within the Union. England has around 84 per cent of the United Kingdom's population, compared to Scotland's 8.5 per cent. Demographically, therefore, the United Kingdom is much more heavily weighted towards a single component than any federal state.[60] That imbalance invites opposing attitudes of response, both problematic.

A first would be the continuation of a conservative approach in which neither England nor any of its parts boast devolved institutions or any similar recognition of constitutional distinctiveness. The absence of historical support for English self-government, whether in the existing pattern of constitutional asymmetry or as part of formal federal arrangements, indicates the lack of significant longstanding local dissatisfaction over this state of affairs. The expectation that English voters, represented by over 80 per cent of MPs, will normally have the UK Government of their collective choice, has tended to cushion principled objections. In particular, it has meant that the 'West Lothian' anomaly of Scottish MPs voting on English policies over which they have no responsibility to their own Scottish constituents, could be cabined as a minor irritant.

As Scottish self-government expands, however, the question of the adequacy of English representation is less easily dismissed. A new English-centred strain of political discourse, exemplified by Cameron's own intervention, both responds to and amplifies these concerns. In particular, recent evidence suggests an assertion of English political identity[61] to meet two linked challenges; first, to answer and match the effective channelling and articulation of national political and financial self-interest north of the border through the devolved institutions; and secondly, to argue for some recognition of English policy-making autonomy in the sphere of powers—ever-widening and unconstrained by any constitutional specification of an untouchable 'federal' core—devolved to Scotland and the other nations.

This shift in attitudes has led to broad reconsideration of the previously passive approach, and in particular, has produced a raft of proposals for 'English votes for English laws' (EVEL) in the House of Commons, culminating in a firm

[58] Keating (n. 7).

[59] See McEwen, Ch. 10 in the present volume; see also D. Torrance, *Britain Rebooted: Scotland in a Federal Union* (Luath 2014).

[60] See eg Bingham Centre (n. 33) ch. 3.6.

[61] See eg C. Jeffery, R. Wynn Jones, A. Henderson, R. Scully, and G. Lodge, *Taking England Seriously: The New English Politics* (The Future of England Survey 2014).

commitment from the new Conservative government.[62] The underlying basic principle is that legislative bills or provisions with a 'separate and distinct' effect for England should not pass the Commons without the consent of a majority of English MPs. Neither institutionally nor procedurally would this amount to the creation of an English Parliament, since such measures would also continue to require scrutiny and consent by the whole House. Yet the proposal threatens to erode still further the sense of a central political system dedicated to the common UK interest. What counts as 'separate and distinct' will continue to be fiercely contested by Scottish nationalists concerned about being excluded from voting on England-centred policy decisions which, under the Barnett formula, will continue to have consequences for the level of devolved Scottish grant. And if a significant number of provisions are designated in the new English category, then our main legislative chamber for the entire Union will be transformed into a body that devotes much of its attention to just one of its geographical parts.

Not all initiatives responding to movements elsewhere in the asymmetrical pattern of self-government need threaten the integrity of the Union. The recent pattern of Welsh devolution, for example, has often drawn on Scottish precedent, and the latest development under the so-called St David Day process[63] signals a commitment to emulate the Scottish and Northern Irish example of a model of devolved competence based on an open-ended grant rather than a list of conferred powers. Viewed in isolation, this initiative could suggest a pattern of convergence towards a quasi-federal model as much as it could the gradual unravelling of the fabric of the state. In England, too, recent proposals for a form of city-region devolution deliverable through the combination of existing local government areas have offered an alternative, less destabilizing reply to increases in Scottish and Welsh self-government than EVEL.[64] Yet it remains undeniable that some responses, with EVEL to the fore, do possess a competitive, even retaliatory element, with nations or regions increasingly conscious and defensive of their separate interests, whether or not this translates into an explicitly pro-independence agenda. To the extent that such a dynamic prevails, the Union state risks fragmenting by chain reaction as much as by design.

B. Central architecture

The growth in substate self-government has long raised wider questions about the adequacy of the central architecture of the state even as a basic means of

[62] Building on the 2013 Mackay Report, the coalition parties each put forward detailed plans, and these have been further developed by the new Conservative government following its election success; see Mackay Commission, *Report on Consequences of Devolution for the House of Commons* (2013); Cabinet Office *English Votes for English Laws: Revised Proposed Changes to the Standing Orders of the House of Commons and Explanatory Memorandum* (July 2015). On 22 October 2015 the Commons finally approved an amended version of the Conservative government's plans over vociferous SNP objections. See <http://www.bbc.co.uk/news/uk-politics-34599998>.

[63] HM Government, *Power for a Purpose: Towards a Lasting Devolution Settlement for Wales* (Cm 9020, 2015).

[64] See eg Bingham Centre (n. 33) ch. 5.3.

coordinating the disparate parts, still less in supplying a separate 'federal' level of shared competence. This issue arises most directly with regard to relations between central and devolved executives. Tellingly, the intergovernmental machinery introduced following the devolution settlements of 1998 was of uncertain constitutional status.[65] In particular the Joint Ministerial Committee (JMC), designed to bring together all the devolved administrations with the UK Government, has no statutory basis. Instead it is the product of an instrument more familiar in the environment of international law, namely the Memorandum of Understanding. More generally, the texture of relations between the different levels of government has tended to be highly informal, and to involve very limited terms of engagement. Most dealings take place below ministerial level and on a bilateral basis, between officials of a civil service still formally a singular entity but increasingly divided between a UK civil service and what is now a separate Scottish civil service in all but name. And to the extent that active relations are maintained in the more formal bodies, with the exception of JMC (Europe), which is required to decide and manage UK policy positions on EU matters, these are knowledge-sharing and grievance-airing rather than policy-making forums.

These defects are widely acknowledged. Smith and the SNP government agree that a wider range of JMC and bilateral forums is required to keep pace with expanded self-government, that these should proactively engage with policy coordination and implementation as well as providing for more efficient dispute resolution, that their workings should be transparent and accountable to both Parliaments, and that the Parliaments themselves should collaborate on matters of joint interest.[66] Yet while this speaks to the urgency of such reforms, there are structural and cultural reasons why these are unlikely to meet claimed aspirations. Structurally, the lack of a federal template as the ordering framework of the British constitution means that there is no developed institutional format or vision of two-level authority within which a central level of executive authority can be securely located, just as there is no clear role for a federal legislature. We lack the formal constitutional language of federal administration, or even of a thinner framework of consociational power-sharing,[67] precisely because our dominant constitutional orientations, and the evolved pattern of government with which they are associated, recognize no such institutional logic. Instead, as so often in the Union state, we tend to revert to the older language of unity—of legislative and administrative hierarchy and a single civil service. This means that new quasi-federal elements, if recognized at all, may still be viewed as untidy 'add-ons'; and, ironically enough, the dual system of power to which these elements refer, because it has not been processed within any internal constitutional vision, is instead conceptualized in

[65] See R. Rawlings, 'Concordats of the Constitution' 116 *LQR* 257.

[66] Scottish Government (n. 32).

[67] See eg C. Bell, 'Separation or Sharing? The Critical Choice for the Union (and Smith)' (*Scottish Constitutional Futures Forum blog*, November 2014) <http://www.scottishconstitutionalfutures.org/OpinionandAnalysis/ViewBlogPost/tabid/1767/articleType/ArticleView/articleId/4568/Christine-Bell-Separation-or-Sharing-The-Critical-Choice-for-the-Union-and-Smith.aspx>.

a more rather than a less differentiated fashion—and so evocative of the external architecture of international relations.

Culturally, the absence of a federal or consociational template for a more coherent framework of intergovernmental relations in any case tends to reflect the deeper mutual ambivalence of the two levels of authority within today's Union state. The notions of comity, reciprocal trust, and complementary authority we associate with a settled multilevel state are more elusive in a context where is no entrenched division and interdependence of powers and where power-holders may have quite different aspirations concerning the long-term prospects of the polity. Quite simply, cooperation across levels is likely to remain uneven, reactive, and a matter of qualified commitment in an environment where the very future of the entity dependent upon such cooperation is a matter of dispute.

Similar considerations apply if we look beyond the executive to other aspects of the common architecture of the state. To take two key examples, a regionally representative Upper House and a common framework of rights are also generally treated as staples of a federal system. Regional representation provides a way of ensuring that central legislative decisions take into account regional interests, while a Bill of Rights provides a common floor of individual freedom and well-being that government institutions at state and substate level alike must respect. But again, the absence of a federal orientation and vision means that these integrative features are hardly recognized as such in the British debate. In the first case, reform of the unelected House of Lords has long been compromised by the wish of successive governments to maintain a monopoly of power in the Commons. Those proposals that have won favour, promoting the principle of patronage over the principle of heredity, have marginalized the dimension of territorial representation.[68] In the second case, even after the Human Rights Act 1998 the culture of common rights in the United Kingdom remains a fragile achievement, as likely the victim of reform of the territorial constitution as a stabilizing force. Revealingly, the new Conservative government's plans to replace the European Convention of Human Rights (ECHR) catalogue with a British Bill of Rights, though now postponed, have appeared insensitive to the ways in which the ECHR norms have been inscribed as common Union-wide standards in the various devolution settlements.[69]

C. Constitutional initiative

It is no coincidence that the most volatile period in the modern history of Scottish self-government has been accompanied by much talk but little prospect of wholesale constitutional reform at the UK level.[70] We have seen that the pace and scale of Scottish reform creates profound systemic pressures towards new forms of

[68] See eg P. Norton, 'Parliament: A New Assertiveness?' in Jowell et al (n. 56) 187–91.

[69] See eg C. O'Cinneide, 'Human Rights and the UK Constitution' in Jowell et al (n. 56) 67.

[70] See eg V. Bogdanor, *The Crisis of the Constitution* (Constitution Society 2015) <http://www.consoc.org.uk/wp-content/uploads/2015/02/COSJ2947_The-Crisis-of-the-Constitution_WEB_FINAL.pdf>.

constitutional recognition in other national contexts, most urgently in England, and also towards the reinforcement of the state's central steering mechanisms. Yet that very state system appears trapped in a 'paradox of initiative',[71] for the divisions and centrifugal political forces that make 'joined up' constitutional reform so pressing also make it very unlikely to happen. The unwritten British constitution has always lacked mechanisms for its own transformation other than through the 'top-down' direction and establishment bias of a sovereign Parliament, and that structural shortcoming is reinforced by a political culture in which the parts increasingly lack the common cause to reinvest in the whole.

We should not be deceived by appearances here. Scottish self-government and its ripple effects, reinforced by a broader agenda of 'constitutional unsettlement'[72] over questions such as EU membership and human rights reform, have brought us to a position, quite unprecedented, where each of the major pro-Union political parties claims to be in favour of or at least open to the establishment of a Constitutional Convention.[73] But even if a constitution-making process and agenda could be agreed between those ostensibly well disposed, the supporters of independence in Scotland and the other constituent nations would have little or no interest in participating in such a project. For whatever benefits it might bring to their cause in the short term, it would have the unwanted consequence of affirming the integrity and entrenching the form of the polity from which they seek to depart.

Yet failing a documentary settlement, other candidate forms of constitutional initiative also face significant difficulties in accommodating the demand for Scottish self-government. One approach, which we might term 'constitutionalism-lite' and which is closely associated with the new strain of Union state thinking, acknowledges the difficulties of mounting a formal constitution-making process and seeks other methods for delivering an integrated package of constitutional reform. Its distinctiveness is twofold. First, there is a quite specific focus on the *territorial* constitution understood in the strong adjectival sense of a normative project that, while not covering all aspects of the constitutional settlement, addresses the geographical distribution of authority in the round; in particular, the articulation of general principles of a Union of common values and shared purpose, and the specification of intergovernmental machinery and other basic protections of the integrity of the state.[74] Secondly, these provisions are deliberated and decided through constitutional surrogates—via parliamentary committees and ad hoc Commissions, and in the form of instruments such as statute-based charters or codified conventions—rather than through a formal

[71] N. Walker, 'Our Constitutional Unsettlement' (2014) *PL* 529, 542.

[72] Walker (n. 71) 542.

[73] The 2015 election manifestos of the Labour and Liberal Democrat Parties contained a commitment to establish a Constitutional Convention, while the Conservative Party did not rule out such an option.

[74] See eg Bingham Centre (n. 33) ch. 4 (A Charter of Union); its basic protections included provisions regulating secession referendums.

constitutional convention or constituent assembly.[75] But such approaches are caught in a double bind. Where they might seek to be inclusive in their deliberations and decisions they suffer from the same paradox of initiative as the more formal processes, yet where they might exploit their more informal constitutional standing to bypass those constituencies reluctant to participate, the legitimacy and authority of their conclusions are likely to be undermined.[76]

Alternatively, and more plausibly, reform of the territorial constitution may continue to unfold as a series of episodes in which the constituent nations each treat separately with the central state in pursuit of their aspirations of self-government. This approach, as we have seen, has gained traction as the Union state orientation has begun to converge with nationalist thinking in attributing sovereignty, and so the ultimate power of self-determination, to the people. It is an approach that both contributes to and is reinforced by the lack of a robust central constitutional capacity. It is also an approach, as the example of EVEL indicates, that is apt to produce a ratchet effect, with each national constituency framing its claims in terms of its discrete collective interest in response to a constitutional landscape disturbed by a sequence of previous such claims.

Critics of the British system have long bemoaned the absence of dedicated procedures for constitutional reflection and reform, and how this has often led either to stasis or to piecemeal reform restricted to the ordinary tools of parliamentary government.[77] The recent fluctuations of the territorial constitution, however, suggest a different dynamic. Here, the lack of a canonical constitutional method leads neither to gridlock nor simply to an unsystematic and opportunistic steering from the centre, but also, and increasingly, to a multipolar framework of initiative where change is driven more from the parts than the whole.

V. Re-imagining the territorial constitution: A convergence of horizons?

The picture painted above suggests that, confronted with the momentum of Scottish self-government, the territorial constitution of the United Kingdom is close to breaking point. The dominant orientation of the British constitution may once have been one of Diceyan unitary sovereignty, but today more decentred approaches vie for ascendancy. The new Union state approach speaks more authentically to the plurinational history and current form of the British state

[75] See eg House of Commons Political and Constitutional Reform Committee, *Do we need a Constitutional Convention for the UK?* (2013) HC 371; and see now House of Lords Constitution Committee, *The Union and Devolution, call for evidence* (2015) <http://www.parliament.uk/business/committees/committees-a-z/lords-select/constitution-committee/inquiries/parliament-2015/the-union-and-devolution/>.

[76] See Walker (n. 71) 542–8; A. McHarg, 'Reforming the United Kingdom: Constitutional Law, Convention, Soft Law' (2008) 71 *MLR* 853.

[77] See eg House of Commons (n. 75).

than do any varieties of federalism, but significantly, it lacks the stabilizing symmetry of regional government, the clear demarcation of central jurisdiction and the reserved capacity for coordinated constitutional initiative we associate with federalism. These deficits make the Union state approach less able to resist the claims of an independence-focused nationalism, all the more so as it comes to share with the nationalist perspective a commitment to a nation-centred conception of popular sovereignty.

Yet these considerations are far from making a Scottish state inevitable. The success of the cause of Scottish independence is ultimately a matter of the sustained weight of popular support. The effective and timely mobilization of that support is certainly influenced, and mostly encouraged, by the range of ideological, systemic, and procedural factors we have discussed, but it is not determined by these factors. However propitious the broad circumstances and however impressive the levels of backing for independence at any particular point, it remains unpredictable when support might peak or how well it might be maintained over another lengthy political campaign.

We may point to three considerations in particular, all linked to the fragility and volatility of popular sentiment, which continue to lend uncertainty to the endgame of Scottish self-government. In so doing, these interconnected considerations invite a somewhat less negative conclusion regarding the future prospects of the UK state as a container—however light—of Scottish self-government. They are, in turn, strategic, structural, and symbolic.

In strategic terms, we have indicated how the perils of approximation and auditioning may slow the pursuit of new measures of self-government. Nationalists must remain alert to the twin dangers of the appetite for independence being sated by too generous a prior grant of powers, and of their long-term vision being judged prematurely and unflatteringly on the basis of their political performance under the terms of that prior grant. But if the anxiety here is about incremental drift, anxiety also attends precisely the kind of decisive intervention that would prevent or curtail drift.

The detailed terms on which any second referendum on Scottish independence would take place remain controversial, including the timing, the trigger test, and the appropriate source and vehicle of regulation.[78] Yet there is little doubt, despite claims on all sides during the first campaign that the result should settle matters for the foreseeable future, that the maintenance of the unprecedented levels of electoral support for the nationalist cause that have emerged in the post-referendum phase will supply an earlier mandate for a new vote. Such a conclusion from new political circumstances seems to in follow in principle from the broad affirmation in both nationalist and new Unionist circles of a continuing Scottish claim of popular sovereignty. Clearly, however, unlike its predecessor, the result of a second referendum *would* be decisive for the foreseeable future. In practice, it is difficult to see how the political momentum for independence could survive

[78] See eg Bingham Centre (n. 33) ch. 4.2.

another 'No' vote. And in principle, defenders of the Union state could legitimately argue, as they have in the case of Northern Ireland,[79] that the minimal terms of stability of the United Kingdom would henceforth require that the will of the Scottish people only be tested at reasonable intervals and in accordance with a settled formula. In light of these considerations, the nationalist leadership, while insistent that the option not be ruled out, are understandably reluctant to petition for a second referendum until confident of success.

It seems, then, that considerations of constitutional strategy may lead to hesitation in nationalist quarters as regards both available routes to their final destination—the single step of a second decisive vote as much as the longer road of incremental progress, and so in the short term may stall or slow momentum towards independence These chilling factors assume greater significance when we reconsider the multidimensional character of our constitutional condition.

Recall from our opening discussion that the territorial constitution, recast as a compound noun to refer only to the framework of general political institutions, speaks to the doubly differentiated character of our structure of governance. On the one hand, within the territorial constitution itself, significant authority is dispersed from Westminster both downwards to the substate nations and upwards to the EU, while the substate and supranational levels also enjoy direct connections through overlapping competences, resource transfer and mechanisms of representation.[80] On the other hand, the EU also illustrates the second layer of differentiation, forming a key part of other functionally specific constitutional regimes in the organization of the market, in its role as a currency union and, increasingly, as a social union and a security union, and also as an area of environmental protection. But in these other functional areas other international institutions such as the UN, the WTO, NATO, and the various elements that make up the global climate change regime[81] join the EU. Importantly, these all remain independently moving parts of the constitutional mosaic. The Paris Climate Change Summit of 2015 and the United Kingdom's EU membership referendum scheduled for June 2016, for example, stand out as key events in the contemporary regulation of our constitutional condition regardless of whether, when or how the question of Scottish self-government might finally be settled.

This wider domain of constitutional unsettlement can do much to shape perspectives on the Scottish question. To begin with, it can considerably alter the stakes for as long as the question of independence remains alive and unresolved. It appears, for instance, that a vote against continuing British membership in the

[79] Northern Ireland Act 1998, s. 1 and Sched. 1 (setting a minimum period of seven years between referendums).

[80] See eg N. Burrows, 'Scotland in Europe; Empowerment or Disempowerment?' in A. McHarg and T. Mullen (eds), *Public Law in Scotland* (Avizandum 2006) 45; Walker (n. 46); M. Keating and M. Harvey, *Small Nations in a Big World* (Luath 2014); A. Page, *Constitutional Law of Scotland* (Sweet & Maxwell 2015).

[81] See eg D. Bodansky and L. Rajamani, 'The Evolution and Architecture of the Global Climate Change Regime' SSRN, January 2015 <http://papers.ssrn.com/sol3/papers.cfm?abstract_id=2168859>.

EU referendum would encourage many to opt for an independent Scotland in Europe over an isolationist United Kingdom, while a vote in favour would offer less reason to pursue the course of independence. Equally, as the first referendum illustrated, the adoption of a more or less encouraging attitude by the EU to the vexed question of Scotland's continuing membership as the seceding part of an existing member state also affects domestic opinion about the prudence of leaving the United Kingdom.[82] In addition, the broader constitutional current can divert attention from the unresolved Scottish question towards other key moments and movements. Ongoing exposure to these other fast moving parts, especially if the domestic debate enters a phase where reform no longer seems imminent and its immediate prospects no longer dominate the political landscape, may bring a new sense of proportion to the Scottish question. Rather than the key decision from which all else flows and on which the overall quality of our constitutional condition depends, the Scottish question may become more widely viewed as just one frame of reference and just one part of a wider decision-making complex.

None of this will necessarily make the Union state orientation more attractive as a means of satisfying the demand for Scottish self-government. What it does, however, is to alter the symbolic import of the constitutional choice for or against independent statehood, in some ways reducing the significance of the decision for one sovereignty rather than another.

For the nationalist, the value of sovereignty as an expression of deepest political identity is likely to be affected by the shift in its material significance brought about by changing global circumstances—a shift that reinforces the tendency to approximation discussed earlier. Part of the historical attraction of the state sovereignty prize was its ostensibly categorical character. In the modern tradition, it suggested an unconditional authority; a clean break from and clear alternative to the previous order, and an affirmation of political identity to match that decisive shift in the locus of normative power.[83] To the extent that today's transnational regulatory terrain is one of divided authority, the prize of independence loses some of its material weight. For if we compare the nationalists' long-term attachment to European, monarchical, and currency unions and their cautious approach to fiscal autonomy with the loose asymmetry of national treatment that a Union state approach tuned into the attractions of 'devo-max'[84] may countenance, we can see how strategic recognition on both sides of the inevitability of a graduated system of authority in a multipolar constitutional environment is narrowing the material gap.

The expressive value of sovereignty, therefore, will increasingly reside in its affirmation of a more fluid form of entitlement*; namely, an inalienable native right to negotiate the terms on which a trade-off between autonomy of national voice and*

[82] See eg Douglas-Scott, Ch. 8 in this volume. See also (n. 54).

[83] See eg N. Walker, 'Late Sovereignty in the European Union' in N. Walker (ed.), *Sovereignty in Transition* (Hart 2003) 3.

[84] See Curtice (n. 44).

the inevitable pooling of influence and capacity in an interdependent regional and global context should be struck, and to retain ultimate control of the operation and further amendment of the self-governing national institutions that emerge from that trade-off.[85] Such an approach suggests a more reflexive form of nationalism. It is one that involves an ongoing and adjustable relationship between a Scottish 'people' and a set of institutions in which, unlike the teleological vision associated with the conventional version of the national sovereignty prize, collective goals are viewed as provisional rather than final, cumulative rather than predetermined, relative rather than absolute.[86]

This clearly remains an attractive claim to many, and, indeed, there is a sense in which the reduced material significance of the claim to national sovereignty may even amplify its expressive value as the reaffirmation of a familiar mode of political identity and belonging in altered circumstances. But it is also a claim that new Unionist thought can do much to accommodate. For if the immediate momentum towards independence is interrupted or paused in the ways suggested above, then advocates of a renewed Union can continue to explore the wider margins of what may be conceivable in the British state in ways that approximate the nationalist vision not only in material terms, as we have noted above, but also and increasingly, in these symbolic terms.

We have seen that the outer boundaries of new Unionist thought already recognize in principle a native Scottish right to formulate and negotiate the terms of the basic self-government trade-off. As an expression of the primacy of Scottish political identity, therefore, new Unionism differs from the more reflexive form of nationalism only in the absence of the insurance policy of Scottish sovereign ownership of the institutional architecture that results from that trade-off. But that, too, need not be an insurmountable difficulty to many who want to assert or safe guard their Scottish political identity within a Union state container. The point of the insurance policy of sovereign ownership is twofold. It is a guarantee against backsliding by the British state, but also of a continuing Scottish entitlement to renegotiate the terms of the national compact in a manner that may increase Scottish autonomy. Yet an enhancement of the Smith affirmation of the 'permanence' of the Scottish institutions could begin to address both issues. This would require the existing bald and Westminster-sourced and centred commitment to be augmented to include broader procedural mechanisms, such as referendums and joint parliamentary consent provisions, both as checks against regression and as standing devices for progression.[87]

Modest headway has already been made on the symbolic front. Amendments made during the passage of the Scotland Bill have witnessed significant

[85] See eg Walker (n. 46).

[86] For a fuller discussion of the distinction between teleological and reflexive nationalism, see N. Walker, 'Scottish Nationalism for and against the Union State' in N. Walker (ed.), *MacCormick's Scotland* (Edinburgh University Press 2012) 163–90, see 181–90.

[87] See Smith (n. 21), and section IIB(1) of the text. See also Scottish Parliament (n. 27) paras 36–61 for discussion of various reform options.

development in securing the first if not the second of these expressive guarantees of Scottish political identity.[88] The possibility beckons, therefore, of a constitutional future for Scottish self-government that inhabits an as yet poorly charted 'post-sovereign' ground between positions that have often been too easily coded and too stridently pursued as polar opposites.

[88] See Scotland Bill 2015–16 (HL 73) Clause 1 (ruling out abolition of the institutions of Scottish self-government unless approved in a referendum of the Scottish people); see further (n. 25) above.

12

The Referendum Debate, the Democratic Deficit, and the Governance of Scotland

Alan Page

A casual observer of the referendum debate might have been forgiven for thinking that what mattered most was whether Scotland would be financially better or worse off as an independent country, with one side claiming that Scotland could be as much as £5 billion a year better off within fifteen years of independence,[1] and the other that it would benefit from a 'UK Dividend' of £1,400 per person per year were it to remain part of the United Kingdom.[2] The casual observer might well have been right, but as was observed on the setting up of the Royal Commission on the Constitution in 1969, in response to the upsurge in support for nationalist parties in Scotland and Wales, 'more is involved in the constitutional development of Scotland, or indeed of any country, than the most convenient economic and fiscal arrangements. More is at stake than an efficient reorganisation of local government.'[3] There is also the question of what today is commonly referred to as 'governance', an effective system of which, within a constitutional democracy, requires a balance between 'the ability to conduct the business of government effectively and the limitation of the executive power of government in order to avoid abuse of power or loss of democratic consent'.[4]

Had Scotland voted Yes in September 2014, the SNP government's intention was that the Scottish Parliament elected in May 2016 should be required to establish a constitutional convention to prepare a permanent written constitution for

[1] Scottish Government, *Outlook for Scotland's Public Finances and the Opportunities of Independence* (2014) 48.

[2] HM Treasury, *Scotland Analysis: Fiscal Policy and Sustainability* (Cm 8854, 2014).

[3] A. W. Bradley, 'Some Constitutional Aspects of Scottish Development' in J. N. Wolfe (ed.), *Government and Nationalism in Scotland: An Enquiry by Members of the University of Edinburgh* (Edinburgh University Press 1969) 41.

[4] J. Elvidge, 'Governance and the Institutional Framework' in A. Goudie (ed.), *Scotland's Future: The Economics of Constitutional Change* (Dundee University Press 2013) 268; other desired characteristics of an effective system of governance, identified by Elvidge, include clarity of accountability and of responsibilities, and a balance between representativeness of society and the availability of high levels of expertise in the matters with which government is concerned.

Scotland.[5] A written constitution would distinguish an independent Scotland from the United Kingdom which, it was said, was the only country in the European Union, and the only country in the Commonwealth, which did not have either a written constitution or constitution act.[6] In the meantime, the Scottish Independence Act 2015, an Act of the Scottish Parliament, would have put in place an 'interim constitution' which, together with a 'refreshed' Scotland Act, would provide the basis for the governance of Scotland until such time as a written constitution was agreed 'by or on behalf of the people of Scotland'.[7]

Scotland's written constitution featured to a certain extent in the referendum debate, not least as an opportunity to remind voters of those aspects of the governance of the United Kingdom to which the SNP government was opposed—the presence of nuclear weapons on the Clyde, cuts in welfare spending, and the 'illegal' invasion of Iraq amongst others.[8] The governance of Scotland under the devolution settlement, or as it would have been between independence and the written constitution, by contrast, featured hardly at all. As one commentator remarked of the former, 'the campaign was conducted without any close examination of the record of the devolved parliament or of the quality of its elected representatives; it was almost as if Scotland had no devolved powers or that it had never used them.'[9] This chapter examines the governance of Scotland as it would have been, had the Scottish Government's proposals been implemented, in the interval between independence and the written constitution coming into force. Before doing so it recalls the main features of the governance of Scotland under the devolution settlement. It concludes by outlining some of the respects in which the governance of Scotland may change, and the challenges it faces, following enactment of the Scotland Bill currently before the UK Parliament at Westminster.

I. The devolution settlement

The devolution settlement is based on the Scotland Act 1998, which established the Scottish Parliament and Scottish Government and defined the limits to their powers. The Scottish Parliament is elected by a form of proportional representation, the additional member or mixed member system, rather than the first-past-the-post system used at Westminster, which was meant to prevent any single party gaining an outright majority, but which in the event did not prevent the SNP winning an overall majority in 2011, making inevitable a referendum on Scotland's constitutional future. The Scottish Government, which was originally called the Scottish Executive in an unsuccessful attempt to distinguish it from

[5] Scottish Government, *Scotland's Future: Your Guide to an Independent Scotland* (2013) 332; Scottish Government, *The Scottish Independence Bill: A Consultation on an Interim Constitution for Scotland* (2014) s. 33.

[6] A. Salmond, 'The People's Constitution', speech in Campbeltown, 28 August 2013.

[7] *The Scottish Independence Bill* (n. 5) s. 4(1).

[8] A. Salmond, speech to the Foreign Press Association, 16 January 2013.

[9] K. Roy, *The Invisible Spirit: A Life of Post-War Scotland 1945–75* (Birlinn, 2nd edn 2014) 518.

the UK Government, is drawn from the Scottish Parliament, on the Westminster model, and accountable to it for the devolved governance of Scotland.[10]

A. Limits

The Scottish Parliament has the power to make laws, 'to be known as Acts of the Scottish Parliament'.[11] In contrast to the 'sovereign' UK Parliament, however, its legislative competence is limited. Among the restrictions on its legislative competence, it has no power to legislate in relation to the matters reserved to Westminster by Schedule 5 to the Scotland Act.[12] As well as a number of general reservations, which include the constitution, defence, and foreign affairs, these include a long list of specific reservations, ranging from fiscal, economic, and monetary policy, with exceptions for devolved taxes and local taxes to fund local authority expenditure, to the regulation of activities in Antarctica.[13] It also has no power to modify the enactments listed in Schedule 4 to the Act,[14] which include the Human Rights Act 1998, the provisions of the European Communities Act 1972 which give effect to EU law in the United Kingdom, and the Scotland Act itself. It thus has no power to amend its constituent instrument. Nor does it have the power to legislate incompatibly with the European Convention on Human Rights (ECHR) or EU law.[15] Should the Scottish Parliament legislate contrary to the ECHR, the courts have the power to strike down its legislation as *ultra vires* or unconstitutional. They are not confined to making a declaration of incompatibility as they would be in the case of an Act of the UK Parliament,[16] which would then leave the Parliament to decide whether the offending legislation should be amended to bring it into line with the Convention.[17]

The Scottish Government is subject to essentially the same restrictions as the Scottish Parliament, save that it may take executive action, including make subordinate legislation, in relation to reserved matters where authorized to do so by or under a UK Act of Parliament.

B. Organizational v. constitutional autonomy

Under the devolution settlement, Scotland enjoys a high degree of autonomy over its organizational arrangements. With the principal exception of criminal prosecutions, which are a matter for the Lord Advocate,[18] the arrangements for

[10] The re-branding of the Scottish Executive as the Scottish Government was given formal legal effect by the Scotland Act 2012, s. 12.

[11] Scotland Act 1998 (SA 1998), s. 28(1).

[12] SA 1998, s. 29(2)(b).

[13] SA 1998, Sched. 5 Part III ss A1 and L7.

[14] SA 1998, s. 29(2)(c).

[15] SA 1998, s. 29(2)(d).

[16] Human Rights Act 1998 (HRA 1998), s. 4.

[17] Under the Scotland Act 1998, s. 102(1), the courts have the power to make an order removing or limiting the retrospective effect of a finding of invalidity, or suspending its effect in order to allow the defect to be corrected, but the making of such an order is at the court's discretion; see eg *Salvesen v Riddell* [2013] UKSC 22.

[18] SA 1998, s. 29(2)(e).

the exercise of devolved functions are a matter for the Scottish Government and, to the extent that its approval is required, the Scottish Parliament. Scotland's constitutional arrangements—the principal institutions of devolved governance and the relationships between them—by contrast, are beyond the reach of the Scottish Parliament. If they are to be altered it can only be by the Westminster Parliament, with the agreement of the Scottish Parliament under the Sewel convention. The Scottish Parliament itself has no power to alter them.[19]

The Scottish Government and Scottish Parliament have made extensive use of their powers over the organization of devolved governance. At the level of central government, the departmental structure inherited from the former Scottish Office has been abolished as part of the adoption of an 'outcomes based' approach to government. Public bodies have undergone two waves of rationalization, much of it involving 'the amalgamation of bodies without substantive change in functions'.[20] The judicial system has been extensively revised.[21] And in a move which led to widespread criticism of what were seen as the centralizing tendencies of the majority SNP government elected in 2011, Scotland's eight regional police forces were merged to form a single national police force.[22]

C. Local government

Scotland's constitutional arrangements as prescribed by the Scotland Act do not include Scotland's thirty-two local authorities. The Scottish Constitutional Convention, on whose recommendations the Scotland Act was based, wanted the devolution legislation to include a provision committing the Scottish Parliament to securing and maintaining a 'strong and effective system of local government', and to embody the principle of subsidiarity 'so as to guarantee the important role of local government in service delivery'.[23] In the White Paper that preceded the Act, however, the Labour Government confined itself to saying that it did not expect the Scottish Parliament and its Executive 'to accumulate a range of new functions at the centre which would be more appropriately and efficiently delivered by other bodies within Scotland', adding that it believed that 'the principle that decisions should be made as close as possible to the citizen holds good within Scotland as it does within the United Kingdom'.[24]

[19] Hence the complaint soon after devolution that the Scottish Parliament was unable to appoint a temporary additional deputy presiding officer without asking Westminster to amend the Act. The omission was repaired by the Scotland Act 2012, s. 4, which empowered the Parliament to appoint additional deputies.

[20] Elvidge (n. 4) 280.

[21] Judiciary and Courts (Scotland) Act 2008; Courts Reform (Scotland) Act 2014.

[22] Police and Fire Reform Scotland Act 2012; the criticism was given added force by the rationalization of Scotland's thirty-two colleges of further education to form seventeen 'college regions' under the Post-16 Education (Scotland) Act 2013.

[23] Scottish Constitutional Convention, *Scotland's Parliament, Scotland's Right* (1995) 16.

[24] Scottish Office, *Scotland's Parliament* (Cm 3658, 1997) para. 6.4.

Notwithstanding the lack of direct constitutional recognition, the status of local government has been recognized in various ways since devolution. The Accounts Commission, for example, has retained control of local authority audit—but not of health authority audit—in recognition of 'the autonomy of local government as a separate democratically accountable tier of government';[25] while the general restructuring power taken in the Public Services Reform (Scotland) Act 2010 may not be used to remove functions from local authorities or to make any structural change in relation to local government.[26] The removal of school education from local authority control, for example, which has sometimes been suggested as a means of reducing the dependence of local authorities on central government funding,[27] would thus require primary legislation.

D. Accountability

The Scottish Constitutional Convention expected the Parliament to provide through its practices and procedures 'a form of government in whose accountability, accessibility, openness and responsiveness the people of Scotland will have confidence and pride'.[28] Accountability was not conceived solely in terms of parliamentary (or judicial) accountability, but the Parliament was expected to play a prominent part in holding the Scottish Executive to account. The Consultative Steering Group (CSG), which was set up by the Secretary of State for Scotland to recommend the procedures the Parliament might be invited to adopt, was thus 'careful' to develop procedures designed to ensure that the Scottish Executive was 'fully accountable' to the Scottish Parliament for its actions.[29] Recommending the CSG principles to the Parliament, Henry McLeish, the former chair of the CSG, claimed that the Scottish Executive would be 'much more accountable to the Parliament in Scotland than the Government is to the Parliament in Westminster'.[30]

At the heart of the Parliament's procedures are its committees, which combine the roles of select and public bill (formerly standing) committees at Westminster, the idea being to enable MSPs to develop expertise in particular areas and to bring an informed view to the consideration of legislation and the scrutiny of government. Almost from the outset, however, the Parliament's committees struggled to match the expectations held of them. In the first two sessions (1999–2007), lack of time together with the breadth of their remits made it

[25] Scottish Office, *Principles of the Scottish Parliament's Financial Procedures: Final Report of the Financial Issues Advisory Group* (1999) para. 6.41.

[26] Public Services Reform (Scotland) Act 2010, s. 14(5).

[27] Elvidge (n. 4) at 283.

[28] *Scotland's Parliament, Scotland's Right* (n. 23) at 24.

[29] Scottish Office, *Shaping Scotland's Parliament: Report of the Consultative Steering Group on the Scottish Parliament* (1998) s. 2, para. 25 and s. 3.4, para. 1; accountability was one of the key principles on which the CSG's proposals were based: 'the Scottish Executive should be accountable to the Scottish Parliament, and the Parliament and the Executive should be accountable to the people of Scotland.'

[30] Scottish Parliament Official Report 9 June 1999, col. 367.

difficult for some committees to cover the ground, with the demands of legislative scrutiny in particular reducing the scope for some committees to undertake their own inquiries.[31] The slackening of the legislative pace in the third session (2007–2011), however, when a minority SNP government was in power, was not accompanied by any noticeable increase in scrutiny, the political focus by then having shifted to the chamber, and Labour and Liberal Democrat MSPs being at the same time reluctant to revisit their own record by way of post-legislative scrutiny. The sometimes rapid turnover of members also meant that committees did not build up the expertise anticipated.

Faced with an avalanche of criticism at the end of its third session,[32] the Parliament embarked on what was billed as a 'thorough MoT' of its performance.[33] Question time was adjusted to increase the opportunity for more topical questions, and committee conveners were said by the Parliament's Presiding Officer to have 'enthusiastically endorsed a reform agenda that should enable parliamentary committees to increase their agility, responsiveness and focus'.[34] After three years, however, and with the referendum imminent, the Conveners Group's 'programme for change' seemed to be more about securing favourable publicity for the work of committees than improving their effectiveness in holding government to account.

The courts, as we have seen, occupy a powerful position in the devolved constitution. Should the Parliament exceed the limits on its competence, they have the power to strike down its legislation as unconstitutional, a power they do not possess in relation to UK Acts of Parliament, being confined to making a declaration of incompatibility with Convention rights or, in the case of incompatibly with EU law, to denying effect to the offending legislation. Without this power the only check on the Parliament's potential for 'arbitrary and oppressive action'[35] would have been political—in the form of UK ministerial intervention—which would have been a recipe for intergovernmental conflict as well as affording individuals no guarantee of effective redress. Despite its novelty, constitutional review of legislation has not so far proved controversial. There have been only two

[31] In its Session 2 legacy paper, the Conveners Group singled out the difficulty in achieving a balance between legislative scrutiny and other essential scrutiny work as one of the most significant issues faced by committees in that session: Conveners Group Legacy Paper, 2nd Session (2007) para. 4.

[32] See eg 'Lord Foulkes Attacks "Pathetic" Scottish Parliament' *Telegraph* (21 September 2010); Jackson Carlaw, 'It's Time to Realise the Potential of the Scottish Parliament' (October 2010) available at <www.scottish.parliament.uk/S4_StandardsProceduresandPublicAppointmentsCommittee/Inquiries/Jackson_Carlaw.pdf>; Jack McConnell, 'Why the "Pedestrian" Scottish Parliament needs Overhauling' *Telegraph* (24 November 2010); 'Holyrood's "Three Wise Men" Back Parliament Overhaul' *Telegraph* (24 November 2010); 'Veteran MSP in Call for Shake-up of Parliament' *Herald* (23 May 2011); Bruce Crawford, 'All Parties Need to Help Change Holyrood' *Scotland on Sunday* (12 June 2011).

[33] Standards, Procedures and Public Appointments Committee 2nd Report, 2011, *Reform of Parliamentary Business Inquiry Phase 1 Report: Remodelling the Parliamentary Week* (SPP 57) para. 6.

[34] Letter from the Presiding Officer to all members, 8 July 2011.

[35] T. Daintith, 'The Kilbrandon Report: Some Comments' in H. Calvert (ed.), *Devolution* (Professional Books 1975) 31.

cases in which the courts have struck down a provision of an Act of the Scottish Parliament, in both cases on grounds of incompatibility with Convention rights, rather than reserved matters grounds, and neither provoked an outcry.[36] Where controversy did arise, it was between the Scottish Government and the UK Supreme Court, led by its Scottish members, rather than between the Scottish Government and the Scottish courts, over the implications of the ECHR for the Scottish criminal justice system, leading to the restriction of the Supreme Court's recently acquired jurisdiction in Scottish criminal cases by the Scotland Act 2012.[37]

II. The referendum debate

A. Scotland's written constitution

In a speech to the Foreign Press Association in London on 16 January 2013, a date apparently chosen because it was the anniversary of the approval of the Articles of Union by the Scottish Parliament in 1707,[38] the First Minister announced that one of the 'first, most fundamental and exciting tasks' of the first independent Scottish parliament elected in May 2016 would be 'to establish the process for Scotland's first written constitution through a constitutional convention'. The description of the constitution as a 'written' constitution was at first glance curious, given that a constitution prepared by a constitutional convention would by its very nature be a written constitution—a work of 'conscious art' rather than the result of 'natural growth'.[39] The contrast, however, was with the United Kingdom's—and hence Scotland's—'unwritten' constitution, which represented, in the First Minister's view, a 'democratic deficit' an independent Scotland should not repeat.[40] The SNP government was 'just one voice in the process', but among the measures that might be included in a written constitution were constitutional rights to education and vital social services, a constitutional ban on the possession of nuclear weapons, and parliamentary and constitutional safeguards in respect of the deployment of Scotland's armed forces.

The Scottish Government's views on what Scotland's written constitution should include were set out more fully in the independence White Paper, *Scotland's Future: Your Guide to an Independent Scotland*, which was published in November 2013. Among the long list of provisions it would propose for consideration by the constitutional convention were: guarantees of equality of opportunity and

[36] *Cameron v Cottam* [2012] HCJAC 31; *Salvesen v Riddell* [2013] UKSC 22.

[37] The story is recounted in A. Page, *Constitutional Law of Scotland* (W Green 2015) paras 9–15–9–23.

[38] Union with England Act 1707 (c. 7).

[39] L. Wolf-Philips, *Comparative Constitutions* (Macmillan 1972) 32.

[40] Elvidge (n. 4) at 269 questioned the desirability of a written constitution, pointing out that, like the statutory framework for devolution, it would place the domestic courts in a more significant position within the overall governance structures than would otherwise be the case.

freedom from discrimination and prejudice; entitlements to public services and to a standard of living that, as a minimum, secured dignity and self-respect and provided the opportunity for people to realize their full potential both as individuals and as members of wider society; protection of the environment and the sustainable use of Scotland's natural resources to embed Scotland's commitment to sustainable development and tackling climate change; a ban on nuclear weapons being based in Scotland; controls on the use of military force and a role for the Scottish Parliament in approving and monitoring its use; the existence and status of local government; rights in relation to healthcare, welfare, and pensions; children's rights; and rights concerning other social and economic matters, such as the right to education and a youth guarantee on employment, education, or training.[41]

B. The constitutional platform

In his January speech to the Foreign Press Association, the First Minister announced that the 'constitutional platform' for independence—'preserving continuity in key areas, but providing the first independent Scottish Parliament with the tools to make Scotland a better place'—would be established before the next Scottish Parliament elections in May 2016. Like the referendum itself, the Scottish Government's intention was that the constitutional platform—or the leading part of it—should be 'made in Scotland'.[42] Under it the Scottish Parliament would have the power to declare 'independent statehood for Scotland in the name of the sovereign people of Scotland'; bring Scotland fully into the European mainstream on the protection of human rights by giving the ECHR the same legal force for reserved matters as it already had for devolved matters; provide for the continuity of the monarchy in Scotland; provide for a transparent and democratic system for ratification of treaties; provide for continuity of laws; define entitlement to Scottish citizenship; provide for the Supreme Court of Scotland; and place on the Scottish Parliament a duty to establish a constitutional convention to prepare the written constitution.[43] The constitutional platform—or that part of it that would have been made in Scotland—was published for consultation three months before the referendum in the form of a draft Scottish Independence Bill.[44] Together with a 'refreshed' Scotland Act, the Bill once enacted would have constituted the founding legislation of an independent Scotland.

C. The Scottish Independence Bill

The Scottish Independence Bill, published in June 2014, was framed in terms of 'higher-level principles and values' with the technical detail being relegated

[41] *Scotland's Future* (n. 5) at 353; see also Scottish Government, *Scotland's Future: From the Referendum to Independence and a Written Constitution* (2013) para. 1.10.
[42] *Scotland's Future: from the Referendum to Independence* (n. 41) at paras 2.12–2.13.
[43] *Scotland's Future* (n. 5) at 338–40.
[44] *The Scottish Independence Bill* (n. 5).

to the refreshed Scotland Act, a summary of which was provided in the consultation document on the draft Scottish Independence Bill. The Bill had been drafted to be 'accessible, straightforward and concise', in the hope that this would enable the people of Scotland to see clearly the 'most important principles, rights and structures of government' on which the SNP government believed an independent democratic Scotland should be founded.[45] Foremost among those principles was the 'sovereignty of the people of Scotland'—'In Scotland, the people are sovereign'[46]—which would replace the sovereignty of the Westminster Parliament as 'the predominant constitutional principle in an independent Scotland.'[47]

Under the 'interim constitution', set out in Part 2 of the Bill, the constitutional arrangements of the new state would remain essentially unchanged.

> Scotland already has many of the institutions that a modern independent state requires: a parliament elected by the people, a government accountable to that parliament, an impartial civil service, an independent judiciary and an autonomous legal system. These institutions will continue on independence, underpinned by new constitutional arrangements reflecting Scotland's new constitutional status.[48]

The Scottish Parliament and Scottish Government would thus assume full powers and responsibility as the Parliament and Government of an independent State, while the High Court of Justiciary and the Court of Session in their appellate capacities would together become Scotland's Supreme Court. The jurisdiction of the UK Supreme Court in Scotland would cease.[49]

D. The revised Scotland Act

As for the technical detail, the Scotland Act would be 'refreshed and rewritten' so that it could function effectively in the context of an independent Scotland.[50] Several provisions would be repealed as no longer relevant to an independent state, including section 28(7), which provides that the Scottish Parliament's power to make laws for Scotland 'does not affect the power of the Parliament of the United Kingdom to make laws for Scotland', and Schedule 5 which sets out the reserved matters on which the Scottish Parliament cannot legislate. Others would be amended in the light of independence with references to the Prime Minister and the UK Supreme Court, for example, being removed. Many provisions, however would be retained, including the electoral system for the Scottish Parliament. The current franchise would also continue except that, as in the referendum, it would be extended to include 16- and 17-year-olds.[51]

[45] *The Scottish Independence Bill* (n. 5) at Foreword.
[46] *The Scottish Independence Bill* (n. 5) s. 2.
[47] *The Scottish Independence Bill* (n. 5) at 27.
[48] *Scotland's Future* (n. 5) at 354.
[49] *The Scottish Independence Bill* (n. 5) at 34.
[50] *The Scottish Independence Bill* (n. 5) at 50.
[51] A change now made by the Scottish Elections (Reduction of Voting Age) Act 2015.

E. Limits

The sovereignty of the people of Scotland was an obvious starting point for the interim constitution, given its historical resonance, real or imagined,[52]and the contrast frequently drawn between it and the unlimited sovereignty of the Westminster Parliament, which Lord Cooper had famously described in *MacCormick v Lord Advocate*[53] as a 'distinctively English principle which has no counterpart in Scottish constitutional law'. A Scottish Parliament, however, needs limiting as much as any other.[54] Under the interim constitution the Scottish Parliament (and Scottish Government) would have continued to be bound by EU law and the ECHR.[55] It would not have been bound, however, by the interim constitution: the SNP government rejected the 'rigidity' of hard entrenchment or a special amending formula as not appropriate for what were intended to be temporary arrangements.[56] Although, according to the independence White Paper, the founding legislation of an independent Scotland would not be subject to 'significant alteration' pending the preparation of a permanent constitution by the constitutional convention,[57] it would thus have been open to a future Scottish Government to amend the interim constitution by ordinary process of legislation until such time as it was replaced by the written constitution—at which point it would depend on what the written constitution provided. The courts meanwhile would have had the power to declare future legislation invalid if it was incompatible with EU law or the ECHR, but not if it was contrary to the Scottish Independence Act or renewed Scotland Act.[58]

The interim constitution also included, in line with the SNP government's views on what the written constitution should provide, a series of broad brush obligations and entitlements—in respect of nuclear disarmament, equality, children's wellbeing, the needs of island communities, the environment, and the use of Scotland's natural resources.[59] It would have been left to the courts to decide to what extent these were judicially enforceable, whether alone or in combination with other requirements. In some cases, for instance, nuclear disarmament, the view almost certainly would have been that the obligation to pursue negotiations with a view to securing nuclear disarmament, and the safe and expeditious removal from the territory of Scotland of nuclear weapons based there, was one for which ministers were answerable to the Parliament rather than the courts. It was only where legislation was incompatible with EU law or the ECHR that the courts would have had the power to declare it invalid.[60]

[52] *The Scottish Independence Bill* (n. 5) at 27; for a sceptical view of the 'ancient Scottish constitutional tradition', see Page (n. 37) at para. 1–02 and references cited therein.

[53] *MacCormick v Lord Advocate* 1953 SC 396, 411.

[54] B. Crick and D. Millar, *To Make the Parliament of Scotland a Model for Democracy* (John Wheatley Centre 1995) 7.

[55] *The Scottish Independence Bill* (n. 5) ss 24, 26.

[56] *The Scottish Independence Bill* (n. 5) at 63.

[57] *Scotland's Future* (n. 5) at 341.

[58] *The Scottish Independence Bill* (n. 5) at 63.

[59] *The Scottish Independence Bill* (n. 5) ss 23 and 28–32.

[60] *The Scottish Independence Bill* (n. 5) at 63.

F. Restructuring the Scottish state

In terms of the organization of government, a future SNP government would retain the unified structure of central government adopted in 2007, which, it was said, had been 'successful in delivering joined-up thinking and co operation and provide[d] a firm basis for taking on the full range of policy and functions of an independent national government.'[61] A number of new bodies would be required, including a welfare agency, an expanded tax collection agency, a debt management agency, a security and intelligence agency, a Scottish defence headquarters, a Scottish Civil Service Commission, a Scottish Passport Agency, and a Scottish Border and Migration Service, amongst others.[62] The majority of transferred functions, however, would be absorbed by existing bodies or else continued on a shared basis, 'where it makes sense to do so, and where it is in the interests of both Scotland and the rest of the UK',[63] prompting the UK Government to point out that the United Kingdom did not share public services, tax administration, pensions systems, or its currency arrangements with any other states, and that there were no states in existence that provided their neighbours with shared access to their public institutions on the scale the SNP government was promising on behalf of the continuing United Kingdom.[64] The UK Government, however, scored something of an own goal with its claim that the costs of setting up new institutions could be as high as £2.7 billion[65]—a figure arrived at by taking the estimated cost of setting up a UK central government department and multiplying it by the number of new bodies required regardless of the scale of their responsibilities. But if £2.7 billion was too high, the SNP government's estimate of £200 million was almost certainly too low.

G. Local government

Under the interim constitution there would also 'continue to be local government in Scotland'.[66] Local government would thus achieve the constitutional status it had been denied under the devolution settlement, although its powers and responsibilities would continue to be a matter for the Scottish Parliament. A future SNP government would also argue for the status and rights of elected local governments to be recognized in the written constitution.[67] This would enable Scotland to fully implement the European Charter of Local Self-Government, which provides for the recognition of the principle of local self-government in domestic legislation, and, where practicable, in the constitution. In the absence of a written constitution, the SNP government argued that it would be impossible to provide this

[61] *Scotland's Future* (n. 5) at 362.

[62] *Scotland's Future* (n. 5) at 362–4.

[63] *Scotland's Future* (n. 5) at 364.

[64] *United Kingdom, United Future: Conclusions of the Scotland Analysis Programme* (Cm 8869, 2014) para. 1.15.

[65] Cm 8854 (n. 2) para. 2.4 Box 2.B.

[66] *The Scottish Independence Bill* (n. 5) s. 17.

[67] *Scotland's Future* (n. 5) at 368.

degree of constitutional recognition to local government, but there is nothing in the Scotland Act to prevent the entrenchment of local government in the constitutional arrangements of the devolved Scotland should that be thought desirable.

H. Accountability

In terms of the accountability of government, the interim constitution would make it explicit that the Scottish Government was accountable to the Scottish Parliament, and the Scottish Parliament to the people of Scotland.[68] The principle was said to be implicit within existing arrangements—when it fact it had been explicit from the outset[69]—but the SNP government believed that one of the advantages of moving to a written constitution was that such 'basic and fundamental democratic principles can, and should be, expressly stated.'[70] Accountability, it acknowledged, had been identified by the Consultative Steering Group as one of the key principles on which the operational needs and working methods of the Scottish Parliament should be based, and it was appropriate this should be reflected in the constitution.[71]

There was no mention of the criticisms of the Parliament's performance in holding government to account, which on the contrary 'had set an example within the UK on how a modern legislature should operate. In line with its founding principles of power sharing, accountability, access and participation, and equal opportunity, the Parliament had successfully put into practice the principles on which it was founded.'[72] The debate itself, however, did little to allay fears of a 'one party state', with protests by the minority in the run up to the referendum that the SNP government was using its majority to close down inquiries and to edit out criticisms of government policy.[73]

Under the interim constitution, as we have seen, the courts would retain the power to strike down Acts of the Scottish Parliament which were inconsistent with EU law or incompatible with the ECHR.[74] There would be no Scottish equivalent of the declaration of incompatibility procedure under the Human Rights Act for Scottish Parliament legislation in the former reserved areas, which the SNP government argued would 'bring Scotland fully into the European mainstream on the protection of human rights by giving the [ECHR] the same legal force on reserved matters as it already has for devolved matters'.[75] European mainstream or not, it would have been open to the Scottish Parliament to set aside a judicial decision that was not to its liking

[68] *The Scottish Independence Bill* (n. 5) s. 12.
[69] *Shaping Scotland's Parliament* (n. 29).
[70] *The Scottish Independence Bill* (n. 5) at 33.
[71] *The Scottish Independence Bill* (n. 5) at 33.
[72] *Scotland's Future* (n. 5) at 355.
[73] See eg Public Audit Committee 3rd Report, 2014, *Police Reform* (SPP 496); Finance Committee 5th Report, 2014, *Appointments to the Scottish Fiscal Commission* (SPP 558); European and External Relations Committee 2nd Report, 2014, *Report on the Scottish Government's proposals for an independent Scotland: Membership of the European Union* (SPP 530).
[74] *The Scottish Independence Bill* (n. 5) ss 24, 26.
[75] *Scotland's Future* (n. 5) at 340.

in the absence of any form of entrenchment of the interim constitution. The Scottish Parliament would thus have escaped, even if only temporarily, the confines of the devolution settlement, leaving a majority Scottish Government in effectively the same position as a majority UK Government under the UK's unwritten constitution—a curious outcome, even if only a temporary one, for a process that took as its starting point the 'outdated and profoundly undemocratic Westminster system'.[76]

III. After the referendum

A. The Smith Commission

There was only one question on the ballot paper for the independence referendum on 18 September: 'Should Scotland be an independent country?' As part of the negotiations over the referendum, the SNP government had sought a second question on further powers for the Scottish Parliament, but the UK Government was adamant that only once the question of Scotland's future within the United Kingdom had been settled could there be any consideration of further devolution. With a UK general election set to take place in May 2015, the assumption was that work on further powers in the event of a No vote would only begin after the UK general election, by which time the countdown to the Scottish Parliament elections in May 2016 would already have begun. In the final days of the referendum campaign, however, with the polls suddenly narrowing, the leaders of the three main political parties at Westminster 'vowed' to deliver 'extensive new powers' for the Parliament 'by the process and according to the timetable announced by our three parties, starting on 19 September',[77] a vow widely regarded, rightly or wrongly, as having sealed victory for the No campaign.

On the morning of 19 September, once the results of the referendum had become clear, the Prime Minister announced that Lord Smith of Kelvin had agreed to oversee a set of cross-party talks with the purpose of agreeing a package of new powers to be devolved to the Scottish Parliament. By its terms of reference, which were published on 23 September, the Commission was required to:

> convene cross-party talks and facilitate an inclusive engagement process across Scotland to produce, by 30 November 2014, Heads of Agreement with recommendations for further devolution of powers to the Scottish Parliament. This process will be informed by a Command Paper to be published by 31 October and will result in the publication of draft clauses by 25 January. The recommendations will deliver more financial, welfare and taxation powers, strengthening the Scottish Parliament within the United Kingdom.

[76] A. Salmond, speeches on 16 January 2013 (n. 8) and 28 August 2013 (n. 6).
[77] *Daily Record* (16 September 2014).

The 'Smith Commission Agreement', which was published on 27 November,[78] followed by draft clauses on 22 January 2015,[79] forms the basis of the Scotland Bill currently before the Westminster Parliament.

B. The Scotland Bill

In terms of the governance of Scotland, the Bill's significance is threefold. First, it seeks to entrench the Scottish Parliament and Scottish Government as 'a permanent part of the United Kingdom's constitutional arrangements',[80] and in so doing to accord them the same 'in all time coming' status as was accorded the Court of Session by the Acts of Union three centuries before.[81] The Bill states that the purpose of the entrenching provision is to 'signify the commitment of the Parliament and Government of the United Kingdom to the Scottish Parliament and the Scottish Government', in view of which commitment they 'are not to be abolished except on the basis of a decision of the people of Scotland voting in a referendum.' Constitutional theorists will doubtless continue to argue that Westminster retains the power to abolish the Scottish Parliament and the Scottish Government without a referendum, but the political reality, which the Bill reflects, is that the Scottish Parliament and Scottish Government *are* part of the United Kingdom's constitutional arrangements, and will continue to be so for so long as Scotland remains part of the United Kingdom.

Second, the Bill recognizes that the Parliament of the United Kingdom 'will not normally legislate with regard to devolved matters without the consent of the Scottish Parliament'.[82] This provision gives statutory backing to the 'Sewel convention' which, as set out in the Memorandum of Understanding that governs relations between the UK Government and devolved administrations, provides that 'the UK Government will proceed in accordance with the convention that the UK Parliament would not normally legislate with regard to devolved matters except with the consent of the devolved legislature.'[83] As applied in practice, the convention extends to Westminster legislation altering the Scottish Parliament's legislative competence and the executive competence of the Scottish Ministers, as well as with regard to devolved matters. Were such changes to be made by order under the Scotland Act the consent of the Scottish Parliament would be required. Their inclusion within the scope of the convention thus ensures the need for the Parliament's consent regardless of whether they are made by primary or secondary legislation. The United Kingdom Government, however, has resisted amendments

[78] *Report of the Smith Commission for Further Devolution of Powers to the Scottish Parliament* (2014).

[79] *Scotland in the United Kingdom: an Enduring Settlement* (Cm 8890, 2015).

[80] Scotland Bill, cl. 1, inserting new s. 63A(1) in Scotland Act 1998.

[81] Union with England Act 1707, art. XIX; Union with Scotland Act 1706, art. XIX.

[82] Scotland Bill, cl. 2, inserting new s. 28(8) in Scotland Act 1998.

[83] *Memorandum of Understanding and Supplementary Agreements between the United Kingdom Government, the Scottish Ministers, the Welsh Ministers, and the Northern Ireland Executive* (2013) para. 14.

to the clause which would reflect the convention's application in practice, possibly with a view to not tying its hands in future arguments over whether the replacement of the Human Rights Act by a British Bill of Rights would require the Scottish Parliament's consent under the convention.

The repeal of section 28(7) of the Scotland Act, which affirms the continuing powers of the United Kingdom Parliament to make laws for Scotland, was not canvassed during the Smith Commission process, but the combined effect of these two provisions once enacted will be to set the seal on a federal or near federal relationship between Scotland and the rest of the United Kingdom, in which the 'devolution' settlement cannot be amended or legislation enacted with regard to devolved matters without the Scottish Parliament's consent.

Third, although the focus of the Smith Commission process was on financial, welfare, and taxation powers, the Scottish Parliament will also gain powers over 'all matters relating to the arrangements and operations of the Scottish Parliament and Scottish Government, including powers over the overall number of MSPs or the number of constituency and list MSPs, and powers over the disqualification of MSPs from membership and the circumstances in which a sitting MSP can be removed'.[84] Scotland will thus gain a substantial measure of control over its institutional arrangements as prescribed by the Scotland Act, and with it a measure of constitutional autonomy for the first time. Acknowledging the risk that a future Scottish Government might seek to revise those arrangements to suit its own ends, Scottish Parliament legislation amending the franchise, the electoral system or the number of constituency and regional members for the Scottish Parliament will require to be passed by a two-thirds or 'super' majority of the Scottish Parliament.[85]

These powers have attracted little in the way of discussion so far, but most interest is likely to centre on the possibility of their use to increase the number of MSPs, not least given the challenges the Parliament will face in terms of the scrutiny of government as a result of the further increase in its powers, following on from those conferred by the Scotland Act 2012. It must be open to question, however, whether an increase in the Parliament's size is in the realm of practical politics. It is perhaps noteworthy in this respect that, in the consultation on the draft Scottish Independence Bill, the SNP government said that it did not propose increasing the number of MSPs, which it considered 'appropriate for a country of Scotland's size'.[86]

The other major candidate for reform is the Parliament's electoral system, which the Arbuthnott Commission on Boundary Differences and Voting Systems recommended should be reviewed after the 2011 Scottish Parliament elections, a recommendation endorsed by the Calman Commission.[87] In the consultation on

[84] (n. 78) para. 26; Scotland Bill, cl. 11, amending Scotland Act 1998, Sched. 4, para. 4.

[85] Scotland Bill, cl. 10, inserting new ss 31A and 32A in Scotland Act 1998.

[86] *The Scottish Independence Bill* (n. 5) at 51.

[87] Commission on Boundary Differences and Voting Systems, *Putting Citizens First: Boundaries, Voting and Representation in Scotland* (2006) para. 4.8; Commission on Scottish Devolution, *Serving Scotland Better: Scotland and the United Kingdom in the 21st Century* (2009) para. 5.19.

the draft Scottish Independence Bill, the SNP government also said that it did not propose altering the Parliament's electoral system.

C. The Human Rights Act

An early test of the federal character of the relationship between Scotland and the rest of the United Kingdom may arise as a result of the Conservative government's manifesto commitment to replace the Human Rights Act with a British Bill of Rights (which may have been included in its manifesto as a bargaining counter in negotiations with possible coalition partners rather than as a cast-iron commitment which might have to be implemented). Although it might be argued that the Act's replacement relates to reserved matters, and hence does not require the Scottish Parliament's legislative consent, it is difficult to imagine such a reform being taken forward without the Scottish Parliament's consent—as a matter of practical politics if not of constitutional convention.[88] As things stand, there seems little question either that the Scottish Parliament's consent would not be forthcoming, leaving the Conservative government, if it decides to go ahead, with an uncomfortable choice between legislating in breach of the convention, by then enshrined in statute, or else not repealing the Human Rights Act so far as Scotland is concerned.[89] If the Scotland Act 2012 is a reliable guide, the Conservative government will prefer to proceed by agreement rather than publicly test the limits to the Sewel convention.

D. Local government

The Scotland Bill has no bearing on the position of local government, which remains a matter for the Scottish Parliament. Local government, however, made full use of the opportunity presented by the referendum debate to press the case for greater powers. In his foreword to the Smith Commission agreement, Lord Smith recorded 'a strong desire to see the principle of devolution extended further with the transfer of powers from devolution to local communities.' Acknowledging that this was an issue that would require 'significant further thought and discussion', he welcomed 'the enthusiasm of all parties for greater empowerment of our communities. The Scottish Government should work with the Parliament, civic Scotland, and local authorities to set out ways in which local areas can benefit from the powers of the Scottish Parliament.'[90]

[88] For the argument that the Scottish Parliament's consent would be required under the Sewel convention, see I. Jamieson, 'HRA Watch: Reform, Repeal, Replace? The Repeal of the Human Rights Act and the Sewel Convention in Scotland' (*UK Constitutional Law blog* 11 June 2015) available at <http://ukconstitutionallaw.org>.

[89] Replacement of the Human Rights Act by itself would not alter the obligation on the Scottish Parliament and the Scottish Government to refrain from acting incompatibly with the Convention rights, which derives from the Scotland Act, ss 29, 53, and 57(2), rather than the Human Rights Act.

[90] *Report of the Smith Commission* (n. 78) at Foreword.

Whether this recommendation will be acted upon, and if so in what form, remains to be seen. Shortly before the referendum, the Convention of Scottish Local Authorities' Commission on Strengthening Local Democracy called for a fundamental review of the structure, boundaries, functions, and democratic arrangements for all local governance in Scotland.[91] Since the referendum the Scottish Government has appointed a Commission on Local Tax Reform to consider alternatives to the council tax system—the second review of local government finance since devolution—and published a consultation paper on greater autonomy for Scotland's island areas by way of follow-up to the 'prospectus' for island communities published during the referendum campaign.[92]

E. Accountability

The further increase in its powers as a result of the Smith Commission process and the Scotland Bill represents a major challenge for the Scottish Parliament in terms of the scrutiny of government. Lord Smith, who saw the Parliament's increased powers as 'demanding' improvements in parliamentary scrutiny, recommended that the Parliament's Presiding Officer continue to build on her work on parliamentary reform by undertaking an 'inclusive review' that would produce recommendations to run along alongside the transfer of additional powers.[93] In October 2014 the Presiding Officer asked the Standards, Procedures and Public Appointments Committee to consider whether committee conveners should be elected by the whole Parliament on the model of the House of Commons. In its Session 3 legacy paper, the Conveners Group had drawn attention to the growth of 'assertive' parliamentary committees over the last thirty years at Westminster, and recommended that the Standards, Procedures and Public Appointments Committee consider introducing a system of election of committee members and conveners.[94] The Standards, Procedures and Public Appointments Committee noted that elected chairs seemed to have enhanced the status and authority of committees in the House of Commons, but was not persuaded that the election of conveners was the right starting point for reform of the Parliament's committee system. 'Instead there should be a focused and practical discussion about the steps needed to strengthen committees' ability to scrutinize legislation and policy and hold the government to account.'[95] The Committee agreed therefore to undertake an inquiry into the operation of committees with a view to enabling the Parliament to decide what changes were needed before the end of the current session in March 2016.

[91] Commission on Strengthening Local Democracy, *Effective Democracy, Reconnecting with Communities* (2014).

[92] Island Areas Ministerial Working Group, *Empowering Scotland's Island Communities* (2014); Scottish Government, *Consultation on Provisions for a Future Islands Bill* (2015).

[93] *Report of the Smith Commission* (n. 78) at Foreword.

[94] Convenors Group Legacy Paper—Session 3 (2011) paras 7–9.

[95] Standards, Procedures and Public Appointments Committee 6th Report, 2015, *Elected Conveners* (SPP 767) para. 27.

IV. Conclusion

The Scottish Parliament was not just about the 'the sovereign right of the Scottish people to determine the form of government best suited to their needs.' It was also about the subjection of the government of Scotland to democratic scrutiny and control, a theme which runs through Scotland's constitutional history from the criticisms levelled at that 'Pooh Bah, the Secretary of State for Scotland' in the 1920s, to the Claim of Right adopted at the inaugural meeting of the Scottish Constitutional Convention in 1989. Reflecting on the referendum debate, however, it is difficult to avoid the conclusion that it was more about powers than accountability and control—the tools the Scottish Parliament needed to make Scotland a better place than the governance of Scotland. The Yes campaign's answer to the governance question amounted to little more than its repeated insistence upon the need to 'eliminate the democratic deficit', be it in the form of governments Scotland did not vote for or the UK's unwritten constitution.[96] It was an issue the No campaign chose not to address, mindful no doubt of the risk of being seen to 'talk down' Scotland. The more extensive the Parliament's powers, however, the more demanding of a fuller answer the question of governance will become.

[96] *Scotland's Future* (n. 5) at 41.

13

Devolutionary Federalism Within a Westminster-derived Context

*Nicholas Aroney**

An inquiry into the source whence the law derives its authority in a community, if prosecuted too far, becomes merely metaphysical. But if a theoretical answer be adopted by a system of law as part of its principles, it will not remain a mere speculative explanation of juristic facts. It will possess the capacity of producing rules of law.[1]

[A] claim of popular sovereignty by a sub-state national society can emerge as an alternative story to rival the dominant statal narrative of the foundational constitutional moments in the history of a plurinational state.[2]

For Australia, Canada and New Zealand the starting point of constitutional reasoning now is that the United Kingdom Parliament and Government are not part of the internal legal systems of those countries. Their basic constitutional instruments were law because they were enacted by a superior law-maker. They are now law because they are accepted as fundamental legal rules of their respective systems and the basic constitutive documents of their communities.[3]

When the referendum really comes, the sovereign Parliament must go. But whether for good or for evil, the referendum, in principle at least, seems to be coming.[4]

* The support of Australian Research Council Future Fellowship grant FT100100469 is gratefully acknowledged. My thanks are also due to Jim Allan, Nick Gaskell, Paul Johnston, and Stephen Tierney for comments on an earlier version of this chapter and Twana Hassan for his capable research assistance.

[1] O. Dixon, 'The Statute of Westminster' in *Jesting Pilate and Other Papers and Addresses* (Law Book Company 1965) 82.

[2] S. Tierney, *Constitutional Law and National Pluralism* (Oxford University Press 2004) 137, n. 23.

[3] L. Zines, *Constitutional Change in the Commonwealth* (Cambridge University Press 1991) 27.

[4] C. H. McIlwain, *The High Court of Parliament and Its Supremacy* (Yale University Press 1910) xv.

I. Introduction

The Scottish independence referendum was always going to have a tremendous impact on the United Kingdom, whether the answer was Yes or No. Referendums are appeals to the opinion and authority of 'the people', and when the people speak, politicians have to listen.[5] Undertakings given by the leaders of the Conservative, Liberal Democrat, and Labour Parties prior to the referendum made further changes to the devolution system virtually inevitable,[6] and the UK Government has shown itself willing to adhere to those undertakings.[7] The only question is exactly what those changes will be and how far they ultimately will go. The separation of Scotland remains a possibility,[8] but what seems more likely is a substantial increase in the devolved autonomy of Scotland in both legislative and financial terms,[9] possibly accompanied by corresponding changes to the constitutional position of Wales, Northern Ireland, and even England. So much so, that a 'federal' future for the United Kingdom is now seriously being discussed.[10] While debate about such a possibility is certainly not new,[11] and while the likelihood of a fully-orbed federal system emerging is still remote,[12] there appears in the United Kingdom to be a renewed interest in the way that other countries,

[5] See S. Tierney, Ch. 3 in the present volume.

[6] 'David Cameron, Ed Miliband and Nick Clegg Sign Joint Historic Promise Which Guarantees More Devolved Powers for Scotland and Protection of NHS if We Vote No' *Daily Record* (15 September 2014).

[7] Smith Commission, *Report of the Smith Commission for Further Devolution of Powers to the Scottish Parliament* (2014); UK Government, *Scotland in the United Kingdom: An Enduring Settlement* (Cm 8990, 2015). Although see the criticisms in Devolution (Further Powers) Committee, *New Powers for Scotland: An Interim Report on the Smith Commission and the UK Government's Proposals*, SP Paper 720, 3rd Report, Session 4 (2015).

[8] J. Chapman, 'SNP Chief Nicola Sturgeon Threatens New Independence Referendum if Britain Votes to Leave the EU in 2017' *Daily Mail* (21 April 2015).

[9] The Scottish Government has called for 'full domestic economic and fiscal autonomy', under which all taxes in Scotland would be set and collected by the Scottish Government, with payment to Westminster for reserved services: Scottish Government, *More Powers for the Scottish Parliament: Scottish Government Proposals* (The Scottish Government 2014) ch. 4.

[10] See eg A. Blick and G. Jones, *A Federal Future for the UK: The Options* (The Federal Trust 2010); Home Rule and Community Rule Commission, *Federalism: The Best Future for Scotland* (Scottish Liberal Democrats 2012); D. Melding, *The Reformed Union: Britain as a Federation* (Institute of Welsh Affairs 2013); D. Torrance, *Britain Rebooted: Scotland in a Federal Union* (Luath Press 2014).

[11] M. J. C. Vile, 'Federal theory and the "New Federalism"' (1977) 12 *Politics* 1 at 1: '[N]ow we are witnessing something that would have seemed almost impossible a few years ago, a serious discussion taking place in the United Kingdom about the possibility, and the desirability, of the introduction of a federal, or "quasi-federal" system there.' See also M. Burgess, *The British Tradition of Federalism* (Leicester University Press 1995); J. Kendle, *Federal Britain: A History* (Routledge 1997).

[12] S. Tierney, 'Is a Federal Britain Now Inevitable?' (*UK Constitutional Law blog*, 27 November 2014); S. Tierney, 'Can the Union Survive the Election?' (*UK Constitutional Law blog*, 9 May 2015), both available at <http://ukconstitutionallaw.org>. See also N. Aroney, 'A Federal Constitution for the United Kingdom? Constitution-Making within a Westminster-Derived Context' (2012) 9 *Jus Politicum: Revue de Droit Politique* 1.

especially federations, manage the constitutional relationship between multiple orders of government within a territorial state.[13]

Two particular categories of federal system bear important analogies to the system of devolution as it currently exists in the United Kingdom. The first category involves federal systems that have come into existence through processes of devolution of a formerly unitary state, such as Belgium and Spain. The second category concerns federal systems that have come into existence under the authority of the UK Parliament, such as Australia and Canada.[14] The British system of devolution is similar to the federal systems of Australia and Canada in that they each owe their legal establishment to statutes of the UK Parliament, while it is also similar to Belgium and Spain as these are federal or quasi-federal systems that have come into being through the disaggregation of formerly unitary states.[15] At the same time, the British system has characteristics that distinguish it from these two types of federal system: it is dissimilar to Belgium and Spain (as well as Australia and Canada) because these countries possess written constitutions, and it is dissimilar to Australia and Canada because these countries, especially Australia, came into being through constitutive processes that were substantively aggregative, that is, through an agreement to federate negotiated between mutually independent self-governing colonies. In this last respect, Australia and Canada resemble the federal systems of the United States and Switzerland, which came into being through the aggregation of formerly independent states.[16] All of these similarities and differences have important implications for the constitutional mechanisms by which each federal or federal-like system is constructed.

The focus of this chapter is a comparison of the British system of devolution with the federal systems of Australia and Canada. As Westminster-derived polities, all three systems have had to grapple with the problem of combining the principle of parliamentary sovereignty with the principle of federalism, in both its devolutionary and aggregative senses. While the specific circumstances of each country is different, in all three the constitutive authority of the UK Parliament has had to be accommodated to the claims and aspirations of local communities

[13] See eg the workshop organized by the Edinburgh Centre for Constitutional Law entitled *How Federal is Britain?* (Edinburgh Law School, 23 April 2015). See also Melding (n. 10); Torrance (n. 10).

[14] India and especially Malaya (now Malaysia) might also be considered here. The Federation of Malaya came into existence through the Federation of Malaya Independence Act 1957 (UK), the Federation of Malaya Agreement 1957, and the Federal Constitution Ordinance 1957 (Mal).

[15] In certain respects the United Kingdom is better characterized as a 'union' than a 'unitary state', principally because the Acts of Union 1706/7 preserved the Scottish church, Scottish law, and Scottish courts as a condition of the Union. However, the Acts also consolidated the authority of the Scottish and English Parliaments into the one UK Parliament, which exercises final legislative authority throughout the United Kingdom. It is this consolidated authority of the Parliament which makes the United Kingdom relevantly analogous to unitary states in general.

[16] The aggregation of the Swiss cantons into the modern federation of Switzerland occurred over a very long period reaching back to the thirteenth century. The aggregation of the American states to form the United States of America occurred in two initial iterations pursuant to the Articles of Confederation in 1780 and the United States Constitution in 1788, and with the gradual addition of new states over the following two centuries.

to self-government and constitutional self-determination. Through a careful comparison of Australia and Canada with the United Kingdom, it is possible to be more precise about the extent to which the current system of devolution in the United Kingdom already resembles a federation, the ways in which it might possibly become more federal, and the constitutional issues that would have to be addressed for it to do so.

II. The structure of federal constitutions

Vernon Bogdanor has argued that devolution has already given the United Kingdom a quasi-federal system of government.[17] His argument rests on the view that a federation exists where there is a 'legal division of powers' between two or more levels of government. This is to adopt a definition of federalism similar to those proposed by A. V. Dicey, K. C. Wheare, and William Riker. Dicey said that a federation is a polity which aims to reconcile 'national unity' with 'state independence' through a 'distribution of limited, executive, legislative, and judicial power among bodies each co-ordinate with and independent of the other', effected through a 'supreme constitution', which is authoritatively interpreted by the courts.[18] Wheare proposed that a federal government exists where there is an 'association of states' in which powers are 'divided' between 'general' and 'regional' governments in such a way that the general and regional governments are each, within their respective spheres, 'co-ordinate and independent'.[19] Riker similarly considered that a federation involves two or more levels of government which rule the same territory and people, each level having at least one area of action in which it is autonomous, with some guarantee of the autonomy of each government in its own sphere.[20]

Bogdanor's argument is based on four characteristics of British devolution: first, the existence of directly elected legislatures and responsible governments in Scotland, Northern Ireland, and Wales; secondly, these legislatures and governments exercise independent powers of government over particular matters; thirdly, these powers are conferred by devolution statutes which the UK Parliament is politically unable to amend without the consent of the devolved governments; and, fourthly, the distribution of powers is enforced by the Supreme Court as the final adjudicator of disputes concerning such matters.[21] Even though as a matter of formal law the UK Parliament may be able to amend the devolution statutes by ordinary statute, as a matter of practical politics, devolution has been

[17] V. Bogdanor, 'Constitutional Reform in Britain: The Quiet Revolution' (2005) 8 *Annual Review of Political Science* 73 at 81–5.

[18] A. V. Dicey, *Introduction to the Study of the Law of the Constitution* (Macmillan, 8th edn 1915) 136, 140.

[19] K. C. Wheare, *Federal Government* (Oxford University Press, 4th edn 1963) 10. Compare M. J. C. Vile, *The Structure of American Federalism* (Oxford 1961) ch. 10.

[20] W. H. Riker, *The Development of American Federalism* (Kluwer Academic Publishers 1987) 13.

[21] Bogdanor (n. 17) at 84.

approved by popular referendums and is highly unlikely to be changed fundamentally without substantial support from the devolved political communities and their governments.[22]

At this level of analysis, Bogdanor's argument is compelling. If federalism means an effectively-entrenched, judicially-enforced division of powers, the UK already has a federal system. But, of course, it is not quite as simple as this. Ronald Watts, building on analyses of Alan Trench and others, has catalogued several ways in which British devolution is different from most mainstream federations.[23] Most prominent among these is the absence of a supreme written constitution, binding both the UK Parliament and the devolved legislatures.[24] The devolution statutes are binding on the devolved legislatures by virtue of the authority of the UK Parliament. It may be politically impossible for the Parliament to amend the devolution statutes without the agreement of the relevant constituent political communities, but it remains within the Parliament's legal power to do so, and could certainly happen in extraordinary circumstances, as has occurred in Northern Ireland.[25] Secondly, while constitutional asymmetry is a characteristic of many federal systems, British devolution is asymmetrical in a deep and very fundamental sense. Each devolution statute is uniquely tailored to the particular constitutional and political conditions of each of the three devolved communities. However, England, which represents 84 per cent of the population of the United Kingdom, has no devolved institutions of its own, but is governed directly by the UK Parliament and UK Government.[26] As a consequence, the people of the devolved communities elect representatives to the UK Parliament who have the right to vote on laws affecting only England, whereas laws enacted by the devolved legislatures remain matters for representatives elected by the people of Scotland, Northern Ireland, and Wales respectively. And yet, none of the devolved communities are entitled to special territorial representation within the UK Parliament as such, unlike most federations.

The definition of federalism used by Bogdanor is a narrow one. While it identifies most of the countries of the world conventionally considered to be federations,

[22] The Sewel Convention in respect of Scotland, and similar understandings for Northern Ireland and Wales, stipulate that in all usual circumstances the UK Parliament will not legislate in relation to devolved matters, or vary the legislative competence of the devolved legislatures, without their consent: P. Bowers, *The Sewel Convention*, SN/PC/2084 (London: House of Commons Library 2005) 2; *Memorandum of Understanding and Supplementary Agreements between the United Kingdom Government, the Scottish Ministers, the Welsh Ministers, and the Northern Ireland Executive Committee* (2013) para. 14.

[23] R. L. Watts, 'The United Kingdom as a Federalized or Regionalized Union' in A. Trench (ed.), *Devolution and Power in the United Kingdom* (Manchester University Press 2007) 239, drawing principally on A. Trench, 'The Framework of Devolution: The Formal Structure of Devolved Power' in A. Trench (ed.), ibid, at 48. Note that these analyses were published prior to the Scotland Act 2012 and Wales Act 2014.

[24] Watts (n. 23) at 250, see also 263–4.

[25] Northern Ireland (Temporary Provisions) Act 1972 (UK); Northern Ireland Constitution Act 1973 (UK). Devolution was also suspended in Northern Ireland for various periods in the 2000s, including from October 2002 to May 2007.

[26] That is, putting aside the system of local government in England.

it suffers from problems of under-inclusiveness and explanatory weakness. It is under-inclusive because it does not include Switzerland and Ethiopia: the former does not have judicial review of federal legislation, while the latter does not have judicial review at all.[27] It is explanatorily weak because it does not account for several other features commonly associated with federal systems. This latter problem is significant not only theoretically, but also practically. A theory has explanatory power when it is able to illuminate both the broad characteristics and the specific features of particular phenomena. The Diceyan theory of federalism used by Bogdanor can do little of this: it describes the distribution of powers in very abstract terms but supplies no account of the various ways in which such distributions are implemented in federal systems and offers no explanation at all for other features of federal systems, such as the processes by which such systems come into being (for example, by aggregation or devolution), the provision for representation of constituent political communities within the governing institutions of the federation (eg through a Senate or Bundesrat), and the mechanisms by which the federal arrangement can be altered in the future (eg through formal processes of constitutional amendment).

Bogdanor's definition proposes a relatively simple picture of federalism that cannot account for many of the similarities and differences between existing federal systems. An adequate theory needs to be able to explain not only the central cases and common features of federal systems, but also the peripheral cases and unique features of particular federal, and federal-like, systems.[28] Understanding the British system of devolution poses a difficult theoretical question because it involves particular characteristics that are not shared by most federal systems. What is needed is a theory that can account for more of the specific characteristics of British devolution, explain how and why they are similar to and yet differ from characteristics of other federal systems, and suggest ways in which the British system might evolve constitutionally in the future.

It is better to think about the similarities and differences among federal systems as concerning four related elements, namely the formation of the federal system, the governing institutions operating within the federal system, the distribution of governing powers among those institutions, and the alteration of the federal system. All federal constitutions have to deal with these issues, and they usually deal with them in this order, in part because it reflects the federating logic upon which they are constructed. This is because the constitutional context and method by which a federal system comes into being tends to have a systemic effect on the

[27] See A. Lienhard et al, 'The Federal Supreme Court of Switzerland: Judicial Balancing of Federalism without Judicial Review' and G. Hessebon, 'The Federal Supreme Court of Ethiopia: Federalism's Bystander' in J. Kincaid and N. Aroney (eds), *Courts in Federal Countries: Federalists or Unitarists?* (University of Toronto Press, forthcoming, 2016).

[28] Daniel Elazar and Ronald Watts have proposed an important set of distinctions between 'federalism', 'federal system', 'union', 'federation', 'confederation', and so on. These distinctions, although very important for some kinds of analysis, are not crucial to the points being made here. On the distinctions, see D. J. Elazar, *Exploring Federalism* (University of Alabama Press 1987) and R. L. Watts, *Comparing Federal Systems* (McGill-Queen's University Press, 3rd edn 2008).

governing institutions, distribution of power, and amendment processes that are adopted thereunder, while the construction of each of these latter elements has implications for the construction of the others.[29] It is important, therefore, to begin by being clear about the different ways in which federal systems can come into being, such as whether they are Westminster-derived, and whether their formative logic is devolutionary or aggregative.

As usually understood, a federation is formed by aggregation when previously independent polities agree to the establishment of a federal polity of which they will become constituent polities, whereas devolution occurs when a formerly unitary polity transforms itself into a federal or quasi-federal polity by establishing and devolving power to several component polities. The difference, it might be said, is between a political whole that is divided into parts, and several political parts that are formed into a whole, but with the result in both cases that the whole and the parts both continue to exist as constitutionally-related political communities.

The distinction between aggregation and devolution is significant. As Alfred Stepan has argued, the two types of federation display a 'completely different historical and political logic'.[30] In aggregative federal systems, which Stepan calls 'coming together' federations, the federal system comes into being through an agreement or compact between independent political communities,[31] and the form of the federation is shaped by the motivating objectives of the federating parties. In devolutionary systems, on the other hand, which Stepan calls 'holding together' federations, a federal-like distribution of powers is devised to hold divergent parts of a formerly unitary state together, granting them political autonomy to induce them to stay. As such, the distinction between aggregation and devolution is primarily about the formation of the system. However, the distinction also has important implications for the construction and design of the governing institutions, distribution of powers, and alteration of the federal arrangement.

It may seem, on first analysis, that aggregation and devolution are clear-cut categories that exhaust the possible ways in which a federal system might come into being. Either there is a whole that is divided into parts, or there are parts that are formed into a whole.[32] However it is not as simple as this. A formative process may

[29] I expand on this in: N. Aroney, 'Formation, Representation and Amendment in Federal Constitutions' (2006) 54(1) *American Journal of Comparative Law* 277 at 278–82 and 320–35; N. Aroney, *The Constitution of a Federal Commonwealth: The Making and Meaning of the Australian Constitution* (Cambridge University Press 2009) chs 1–3.

[30] A. Stepan, 'Toward a New Comparative Politics of Federalism, (Multi)Nationalism, and Democracy: Beyond Rikerian Federalism' in *Arguing Comparative Politics* (Oxford University Press 2001) 315, 320.

[31] It is no coincidence that the term 'federal' is derived from a Latin root *foedus*, which means 'compact', 'covenant', or 'treaty'. The corresponding German term *Bund* (cf. *Bundesstaat, Staatenbund, Bundesrepublik, Bundesrat, Bundestag*) is likewise derived from roots that convey the sense of binding or being bound by law or covenant.

[32] Thinking about the formation of federal systems in terms of 'wholes' and 'parts' is not quite accurate. In aggregative systems the constituent polities were not 'parts' prior to the creation of the federation.

be partly aggregative and partly devolutionary. As Ronald Watts has pointed out, one way this can occur is where the formative process simultaneously involves both devolutionary elements (ie, division of a pre-existing unitary polity into distinct constituent units) and aggregative elements (ie, addition of other previously separate polities).[33] This occurred in British North America in 1867: the existing province of Canada was *divided* into the provinces of Ontario and Quebec, and these two newly-created provinces were in turn federally *united* with the pre-existing provinces of Nova Scotia and New Brunswick to form the Dominion of Canada as a federation of the four provinces.[34] Another way it may occur is a consequence of the fact that political and constitutional independence is often a matter of degree. In some situations, the constituent polities may be only relatively autonomous, or they may already be bound together in a relatively weak federal arrangement which they agree to make stronger. This occurred in Australia in 1900: the six self-governing and mutually independent colonies *agreed* to unite under a system of government in which each colony would retain the vast bulk of its self-governing powers while also establishing a federal level of government that would exercise governing powers within its agreed sphere of operation.[35]

As Westminster-derived systems, Australia and Canada are thus especially relevant to understanding the extent to which the current system of devolution in the United Kingdom resembles a federation, the ways in which it might possibly become more federal, and the constitutional issues that would have to be addressed for it to do so. To undertake such a comparison, it will be convenient, in the remainder of this chapter, first to consider the three systems as they currently exist, and then to consider the extent to which what is currently being contemplated for the United Kingdom might transform it into something resembling a fully-orbed federal system. As will be seen, three matters are especially relevant to this analysis: first, the application of the principle of parliamentary sovereignty within the United Kingdom and within the Empire as a whole; secondly, the existence of aspirations to local self-government and constitutional self-determination within the United Kingdom, Canada, and Australia; and, thirdly, the gradual acquisition of political autonomy and constitutional independence within the three countries.

III. Legal foundations of Westminster-derived constitutions

A. Parliamentary sovereignty within the United Kingdom and the Empire

The constitutional premise of the British system of devolution is the establishment of the United Kingdom as a union of England, Wales, Scotland, and Northern Ireland through the successive effect of measures such as the Law in Wales Acts 1535/1542, the Acts of Union 1706/1707, the Acts of Union 1800, and the Irish

[33] Watts (n. 28) at 65. [34] See section III of this chapter.
[35] See section III of this chapter.

Free State Constitution Act 1922.[36] These statutes, and the treaties they implemented, created a political union governed ultimately under the authority of the Parliament at Westminster. According to orthodox English legal theory, the UK Parliament is the sovereign law-making institution within the United Kingdom. On this view, although United Kingdom is a union of once independent nations, the Union is governed by a Parliament possessing effectively sovereign legislative power.[37] Devolution in the United Kingdom is accordingly premised on the authority of the Westminster Parliament to establish the devolved legislatures and governments and to bestow powers upon them. The constitutive documents of British devolution are statutes formally enacted in accordance with the ordinary legislative processes of the Parliament.[38] The original power of the Parliament to legislate for the United Kingdom of Great Britain and Northern Ireland is taken for granted, and its continuing power to legislate for Wales, Scotland, and Northern Ireland is explicitly affirmed,[39] with the consequence that amendments to the devolution statutes also have to be enacted by the UK Parliament, save to the extent that a devolved legislature has been granted power to amend them directly.[40] These features of the British system of devolution bear important analogies with the Westminster-derived federal systems of Canada and Australia.[41]

Following the cession to the United Kingdom of Great Britain of several French possessions by the Treaty of Paris in 1763, a succession of British statutes provided for the establishment, reorganization, and governance of British possessions in North America.[42] This culminated in 1867 when the provinces of Canada, Nova Scotia, and New Brunswick were 'federally united' into 'One Dominion' by force of the British North America Act 1867 (UK). Like the British devolution statutes, the premise of the Act of 1867 was the original and continuing authority of the UK Parliament to legislate for its Canadian colonies. Consistent with this, no general local power to amend the Act was conferred on or claimed by the Canadians.[43] Future amendments to the British

[36] Laws in Wales Act 1535 (Eng); Laws in Wales Act 1542 (Eng); Union with Scotland Act 1706 (Eng); Union with England Act 1707 (Scot); Union with Ireland Act 1800 (UK); Act of Union (Ireland) 1800 (Ire); Irish Free State Constitution Act 1922 (UK).

[37] J. Goldsworthy, *The Sovereignty of Parliament: History and Philosophy* (Clarendon Press 1999) 165–7.

[38] eg Government of Ireland Act 1920 (UK); Northern Ireland Constitution Act 1973 (UK); Northern Ireland Act 1998 (UK); Scotland Act 1978 (UK); Scotland Act 1998 (UK); Scotland Act 2012 (UK); Government of Wales Act 1998 (UK); Government of Wales Act 2006 (UK); Wales Act 2014 (UK).

[39] Scotland Act 1998, s. 28(7); Northern Ireland Act 1998, s. 5(6); Government of Wales Act 2006, s. 93(5).

[40] eg Scotland Act 1998 (UK), Sched. 4, para. 4. Note that Scotland Act 1998 (UK), s. 30(2), also authorizes the Queen by Order in Council to make modifications to Scheds 4 and 5 of the Act.

[41] Two leading accounts are D. Creighton, *The Road to Confederation: The Emergence of Canada, 1863–1867* (Macmillan 1965) and J. A. La Nauze, *The Making of the Australian Constitution* (Melbourne University Press 1974).

[42] eg The Quebec Act 1774 (UK); The Constitutional Act 1791 (UK); The Union Act 1840 (UK).

[43] Only limited powers of amendment were conferred. See eg British North America Act 1867 (UK), s. 92(1) (amendment of the Provincial constitutions except in relation to the Office of Lieutenant Governor); British North America Act 1949 (UK), inserting a new s. 91(1) into the

North America Act had to be enacted by the UK Parliament itself. As imperial statutes, the British North America Act and its subsequent amendments operated in Canada by their own paramount force and any Canadian or provincial statute found to be inconsistent with the British Act would necessarily be void for repugnancy.[44] This meant that the British North America Act functioned as a kind of constitution for the Dominion of Canada, defining and limiting the powers of the federal and provincial institutions of government and providing a basis for a functioning system of judicial review, initially by the Judicial Committee of the Privy Council and, later, the Supreme Court of Canada. In all of these fundamental respects, Canadian federalism was plainly Westminster-derived. Indeed, when the Canadian constitution was eventually 'patriated' in 1982, this also occurred in a manner that preserved legal continuity with the Westminster origins of the system. It was again a UK statute, the Canada Act 1982 (UK), by which the legislative authority of the UK Parliament over Canada was brought to an end and a local power to amend their own constitution was conferred upon Canadians.[45]

A similar story can be told about the constitutional origins and evolution of the Commonwealth of Australia. From the time that the Crown annexed the eastern coast of Australia in 1770, a succession of British statutes provided for the government of the territory. By Order in Council of 6 December 1786, His Majesty's territory of New South Wales was declared to be a place for the reception of 'felons and other prisoners' pursuant to the Transportation Act 1784 (UK), governed under the authority of autocratic governors.[46] At its maximum extent New South Wales extended over some two-thirds of the continent, but in the course of time separate colonies were established under statutory authority: Van Diemen's Land (Tasmania) in 1825, Western Australia in 1829, South Australia in 1836, Victoria in 1851, and Queensland in 1859.[47] A succession of British statutes provided for the establishment of governing institutions in each of the colonies, consisting of governors, legislative councils, and eventually legislative assemblies.[48] As in Canada, when the six Australian colonies were formed into a federation in 1901 this also occurred through an imperial statute, the Commonwealth of Australia Constitution Act

British North America Act 1867 (amendment of the constitution of Canada, except as regards matters coming within the exclusive powers of the Provinces, etc).

[44] A. B. Keith, *Imperial Unity and the Dominions* (Clarendon Press 1916) 138–42.

[45] Canada Act 1982 (UK), s. 2; Constitution Act 1982 (UK), ss 38–48. Section 1 of the Canada Act gave force to the Constitution Act, the text of which was set out in Sched. B to the Canada Act. The name of the British North America Act 1867 (UK) was also changed to the Constitution Act 1867.

[46] For a discussion, see D. Neal, *The Rule of Law in a Penal Colony: Law and Power in Early New South Wales* (Cambridge University Press 1991) ch. 2.

[47] Imperial Act 21 Geo III c 56, 1784 (UK); Imperial Act 4 Geo IV c 96, 1823 (UK); Imperial Act 10 Geo IV c 22, 1829 (UK); South Australian Colonisation Act 1834 (UK); Australian Constitutions Act 1850 (UK).

[48] eg New South Wales Courts Act 1787 (UK); New South Wales Act 1823 (UK); Australian Courts Act 1828 (UK); Australian Constitutions Act (No. 1) 1842 (UK); Australian Constitutions Act (No. 2) 1850 (UK); New South Wales Constitution Statute 1855 (UK); Victoria Constitution Statue 1855 (UK); Order in Council (Qld), 5 June 1859; Western Australia Constitution Act 1890 (UK).

1900 (UK) which contains the Constitution of the Commonwealth of Australia. At the time of its enactment the Constitution Act operated in Australia by paramount force and is the basis upon which the Privy Council and High Court of Australia have exercised the power of judicial review to ensure that the governing institutions of the Commonwealth and the constituent States are kept within constitutional bounds. Likewise, when the UK Parliament eventually abdicated its power to legislate for Australia, this was accomplished, from a UK point of view, through the enactment of the Australia Act 1986 (UK).[49]

B. Local self-government and constitutional self-determination

In these important respects, the British system of devolution and the federal systems of Canada and Australia are fundamentally Westminster-derived. But this is not the whole story. In all three cases Westminster was moved to action by local community leaders who agitated for change. The development of local political institutions enabled the inhabitants to advocate and sometimes initiate constitutional reform, such as by organizing conventions, moving resolutions, preparing draft bills, holding referendums, and petitioning the UK Government to accede to their demands. Once powers of local self-government were granted, local political leaders often pressed for the expansion of those powers, not only in matters of everyday politics, but also concerning the constitutional evolution of the political system as a whole.

The statutes that eventually granted home rule to Ireland and Northern Ireland, for example, were enacted by the Parliament in response to local agitation.[50] Indeed, such was the effectiveness of Irish resistance during the Irish War of Independence that the United Kingdom was forced in 1921 to enter a form of treaty with representatives of the nascent Irish Free State to bring the hostilities to an end. These events gave rise to competing interpretations of the nature of the Constitution of the Irish Free State (1922),[51] an Irish interpretation attributing its binding force to its adoption by the self-professed Third Dáil Eireann sitting as a constituent assembly and a British interpretation according it legal force by virtue of its enactment as a schedule to the Irish Free State (Constitution) Act 1922 (UK).[52] The Anglo-Irish Treaty and the Irish Free State (Agreement) Act 1922 (UK) also gave Northern Ireland the right to opt out of being part of the new Irish Free State, which it exercised. In the context of continuing troubles in Northern Ireland, British statutes granting devolved powers of self-government to

[49] It was somewhat more complicated than this, as explained below.

[50] Government of Ireland Bill 1886 (UK); Government of Ireland Bill 1893 (UK); Government of Ireland Act 1914 (UK); Government of Ireland Act 1920 (UK); Irish Free State Constitution Act 1922 (UK); Irish Free State (Consequential Provisions) Act 1922 (UK); Northern Ireland Constitution Act 1973 (UK); Northern Ireland Act 1998 (UK).

[51] The Constitution was enacted as a schedule to the Constitution of the Irish Free State (Saorstat Eireann) Act 1922 (Ire).

[52] *State (Ryan) v Lennon* [1935] IR 170; *Moore v Attorney-General for the Irish Free State* [1935] AC 484.

Northern Ireland have even allowed that Northern Ireland may cease to be part of the United Kingdom and become part of a united Ireland with the consent of the majority of its people voting in a plebiscite.[53]

Scottish devolution was also fomented by local agitation, led by organizations such as the Scots National League, Scottish Nationalist Party, Scottish Covenant Association, Campaign for a Scottish Assembly, and Scottish Constitutional Convention. Documents prepared by the last two of these organizations, *A Claim of Right for Scotland* (1988) and *Scotland's Parliament, Scotland's Right* (1995), set out the case for devolution in radical terms. The first document contained an outright assertion of 'the sovereign right of the Scottish people to determine the form of government best suited to their needs' and committed its signatories to the project of agreeing on 'a scheme' for a Scottish Parliament, mobilizing 'Scottish opinion', securing 'approval of the Scottish people', and asserting 'the right of the Scottish people' to ensure its implementation. The second document presented a blueprint for Scottish devolution which crystallized the resolve of the UK Government to develop a White Paper on the topic, *Scotland's Parliament* (1997), and to press through with the enactment of the Scotland Act in 1998 following the positive result of a referendum on devolution held in Scotland in 1997.

The use of referendums to enable the people of each of the devolved communities to express their 'sovereign' will on questions of devolution and independence has become an established practice in the United Kingdom, with referendums held in Scotland in 1979, 1997, and 2014, Wales in 1979, 1997, and 2011, Northern Ireland in 1973 and 1998, and North East England in 2004, in addition to referendums on membership of the European Community in 1975 and the European Union in 2016. Arguments made by the Scottish Government that it was within the competence of the Scottish Parliament to hold a referendum on Scottish independence,[54] and the willingness of the UK Government to facilitate the referendum that was held in 2014, are recent illustrations of the way in which local politics within the United Kingdom has influenced the exercise of the sovereign powers formally vested in the UK Parliament. The undertakings given by the leaders of the three main political parties before the independence referendum, the report of the Smith Commission and the Scotland Bill currently before the Parliament offer yet further evidence of how agitation for rights to local self-government can sometimes precipitate considerable constitutional change.

Local political activism also played an important role in the development of Canadian and Australian federalism. In the eighteenth and nineteenth centuries, British policy in North America had to respond to local nationalist agitation, including rebellions in Upper and Lower Canada in 1837 and 1838, and demands for responsible government for the British provinces of North America, which were acceded to in the late 1840s and 1850s. The confederation of the colonies of Canada, Nova Scotia, and

[53] Northern Ireland Constitution Act 1973 (UK), s. 1; Northern Ireland Act 1998 (UK), s. 1.

[54] I discuss this in N. Aroney, 'Reserved Matters, Legislative Purpose and the Referendum on Scottish Independence' [2014] *PL* 422.

New Brunswick, although formalized by the enactment of the British North America Act 1867 (UK), was largely a Canadian initiative. Political leaders of the colonies met at Charlottetown and Quebec in 1864 to negotiate the terms of proposed federal union. The design of the federal union was based on a series of resolutions agreed to by the delegates, and the text of the Act was negotiated between the Canadians and British officials, following a further conference held in London in 1866.

By the time that the federation of the Australian colonies was seriously being discussed in the 1890s, most of the colonies had been enjoying the privilege of responsible government and exercising the power to amend and reform their own constitutions for several decades.[55] The political leaders in the Australian colonies took a very active role in the formation of the Australian federal constitution, drafting the entire text of the statute under which they proposed to be governed and forwarding it to the British authorities with the expectation that it would be enacted exactly as drafted.[56] The drafting was undertaken by a directly elected convention in which each Australian colony was equally represented and prior to its referral to the UK Parliament the draft was submitted to the voters in each colony for approval by referendum. The Commonwealth of Australia Constitution Act 1900 (UK) consists of 9 sections (commonly known as covering clauses), the last of which contains the Constitution of the Commonwealth, which itself consists of 128 sections. While at the time the covering clauses of the Constitution Act could only be amended by the UK Parliament, a local power to amend the Constitution by referendum was conferred by section 128 and a capacity to exercise the powers of the UK Parliament within Australia was conferred on the Australian Parliament acting upon the request or with the consent of the State legislatures pursuant to section 51(xxxviii) of the Constitution. By drafting a constitution that had these characteristics, even though the drafting vehicle was a Westminster statute, the Australians were purporting to grant themselves almost complete constitutional independence. As Andrew Inglis Clark, one of Australia's leading constitutional lawyers, said at the time:

> [the draftsmen] knew what they were doing.... They told the Convention what they were doing, and it agreed with them.... They did not hold anything back. They faced the position that they were going in for absolute legislative independence for Australia as far as it could possibly exist consistent with the power of the Imperial Parliament to legislate for the whole Empire when it chose.[57]

While constitutional autochthony was not claimed, Australian judges tended from the very beginning to interpret Australian constitutional law in a manner that

[55] Each Australian colony had its own variation of a Constitution Act which it was able to amend by local statute pursuant to powers conferred by each colony's founding statutes as well as the Colonial Laws Validity Act 1865 (UK).

[56] Only very limited changes were made in London by the Imperial crown law officers before enactment: B. K. de Garis, 'The Colonial Office and the Commonwealth Constitution Bill' in A. W. Martin (ed.), *Essays in Australian Federation* (Melbourne University Press 1969) 94.

[57] J. Reynolds, 'A.I. Clark's American Sympathies and His Influence on Australian Federation' (1958) 32 *Australian Law Journal* 62 at 66.

emphasized its Australian origins. In one case, the Chief Justice of the High Court of Australia likened the Privy Council's approach to interpreting the Australian Constitution to that of an 'astral intelligence' forced to rely on 'the aid of a dictionary'.[58] Privy Councillors, Griffith CJ reasoned, would not necessarily be 'familiar with the history or conditions of the remoter portions of the Empire', nor have 'any sympathetic understanding of the aspirations of the younger communities which had long enjoyed the privilege of self-government'.[59] By comparison, Australian judges were in a position to understand the 'local history' that lay behind the Constitution,[60] and accordingly the Australian Court, not the Privy Council, must be the final authority on questions of 'purely Australian domestic concern', such as the respective limits of the powers of the Commonwealth and the States.[61] In another case, the High Court insisted on a distinctly Australian understanding of the nature of the State constitutions. Although in form an ordinary statute of the State legislature, the Court held the Constitution Act of the State of Queensland to be a kind of fundamental law that could not be amended merely by implication of an inconsistent statute, but only explicitly and directly.[62]

C. Political autonomy and constitutional independence

This independent attitude was expressed by other self-governing colonies within the Commonwealth. At an Imperial Conference held in 1926, political leaders of several of the colonies, now called Dominions, unanimously agreed to a statement, commonly known as the Balfour Declaration,[63] which acknowledged and declared that such countries, including Canada, Australia, and the Irish Free State:

> are autonomous Communities within the British Empire, equal in status, in no way subordinate one to another in any aspect of their domestic or external affairs, though united by a common allegiance to the Crown, and freely associated as members of the British Commonwealth of Nations.[64]

Soon thereafter the UK Parliament enacted the Statute of Westminster 1931 (UK), which affirmed, among other things, that no Act of the Parliament would henceforth apply to a Dominion unless it was expressly declared that the Dominion had requested and consented to its enactment and that no law of a Dominion would be void or inoperative on the ground that it was repugnant to

58 *Baxter v Commissioners of Taxation (NSW)* (1907) 4 CLR 1087, 1106, 1109, 1111.

59 *Baxter* (n. 58) 1111–12.

60 *Baxter* (n. 58) 1109, 1112–17, 1122–4, 1126–8.

61 *Baxter* (n. 58) 1117–20.

62 *Re McCawley* [1918] QSR 62; *McCawley v The King* (1918) 26 CLR 9. The High Court's interpretation of the Queensland constitution was overturned on appeal by the Privy Council, which held that the Constitution Act could be amended as easily as a 'Dog Act': *McCawley v The King* [1920] AC 691; (1920) 28 CLR 106, discussed in Nicholas Aroney, 'Politics, Law and the Constitution in McCawley's Case' (2006) 30 *Melbourne University Law Review* 605.

63 The declaration was drafted by the Inter-Imperial Relations Committee of the Imperial Conference under the Chairmanship of Lord Arthur Balfour (1848–1930), a former Prime Minister, Foreign Secretary, and at the time Lord President of the [Privy] Council.

64 Inter-Imperial Relations Committee, *Report, Proceedings and Memoranda* (Imperial Conference, 1926).

the law of England or to an Act of the UK Parliament.[65] While the Statute of Westminster applied immediately to Canada, Ireland, and South Africa, it did not apply to Australia, New Zealand, or Newfoundland until adopted by them. The Australian Parliament enacted the Statute of Westminster Adoption Act in 1942, which gave the Statute of Westminster retrospective operation from 3 September 1939, to coincide with the commencement of the Second World War.

The Statute of Westminster gave the Parliament of each Dominion power to legislate inconsistently with any British statute in so far as it was part of the law of the Dominion,[66] except that this power did not extend to the British North America Acts 1867–1930 (UK) or the Commonwealth of Australia Constitution Act 1900 (UK) in order to preserve their functioning as a kind of constitutional law for the two countries.[67] It was also necessary to ensure that the Parliaments of Canada and Australia, being federal legislatures which shared legislative power with their constituent Provinces and States, would not be able to legislate with respect to matters within the authority of those Provinces and States. This was relatively straightforward in Canada, where the subject matters falling within the legislative powers of the Provinces are specifically identified and exclusive in nature.[68] Maintaining the division of power in Canada simply required a stipulation that the powers conferred by the Act on the Dominion and the Provinces would be restricted to matters within their respective competences.[69] In Australia, however, the legislative powers of the States are general, not specific, and are held concurrently with those of the Commonwealth, not exclusively.[70] This is because the underlying logic of the federation is aggregative: the States understood themselves to be agreeing to the formation of a federal system in which they would continue to exercise their general legislative powers subject only to the specific powers conferred upon the Commonwealth.[71] The Statute of Westminster therefore had to prevent the Commonwealth from enacting laws on matters within the legislative authority of the States without giving rise to the inference that those matters consist of an explicitly defined set of topics.[72] Somewhat convoluted language was considered necessary to achieve this.[73]

[65] Statute of Westminster 1931 (UK), ss 2, 4.

[66] Statute of Westminster 1931 (UK), s. 2(2). This was extended to the Canadian Provinces by s. 7(2).

[67] Statute of Westminster 1931 (UK), ss 7(1), 8. Also protected was the Constitution of the Commonwealth contained within the Commonwealth of Australia Constitution Act 1900 (UK).

[68] Constitution Act 1867 (UK), s. 92.

[69] Statute of Westminster 1931 (UK), s. 7(3).

[70] Australian Constitution, ss 51, 52, 106, 107.

[71] Aroney (n. 29) chs 9 and 10.

[72] To do so would have suggested that the states possess a specific set of 'reserved powers', a view that was maintained by the High Court of Australia until its landmark decision in *Amalgamated Society of Engineers v Adelaide Steamship Co Ltd* (1920) 28 CLR 129. See N. Aroney, P. Gerangelos, S. Murray, and J. Stelios, *The Constitution of the Commonwealth of Australia: History, Principle and Interpretation* (Cambridge University Press 2015) ch. 3.

[73] Statute of Westminster 1931 (UK), s. 9(1): 'Nothing in this Act shall be deemed to authorise the Parliament of the Commonwealth of Australia to make laws on any matter within the authority of the States of Australia, not being a matter within the authority of the Parliament or Government of the Commonwealth of Australia.'

The most far-reaching step in the development of the constitutional autonomy of Canada and Australia came in the 1980s, when the UK Parliament finally abdicated all authority to legislate for the two countries. Again, the impetus and initiative came from political leaders in the two countries. When the possibility of the 'patriation' of the Canadian constitution was being debated in the early 1980s,[74] the question arose whether the necessary request and consent required by the Statute of Westminster (and the inter-governmental convention to which the Statute gave effect) was a matter for the Parliament of the Dominion only, or would require the request and consent of some or all of the Provinces as well. In the *Patriation Reference*, decided in 1981, a majority of the Supreme Court of Canada held that, as a matter of law, the two houses of the Dominion legislature could simply request the UK Parliament to enact the relevant constitutional amendments, without reference to the Provinces.[75] However, a different majority also held that a constitutional convention constrained the Dominion from requesting the patriation of the constitution without a 'substantial measure' of provincial consent.[76] As a consequence of the decision and accompanying political pressure, the Dominion government was forced to seek and obtain the requisite provincial agreement, and in the event nine out of the ten Provinces (Quebec dissenting) concurred in the patriation of the Canadian Constitution on the terms contained in the Canada Act 1982 (UK).[77]

The objectives of patriation were several. As noted, the Statute of Westminster had affirmed the power of the UK Parliament to legislate for Canada while limiting it to circumstances where the Canadians requested and consented to the enactment of the legislation,[78] and had affirmed the power of the Canadian legislatures to enact laws inconsistent with British statutes while preserving the constitutional status of the British North America Acts 1867–1930.[79] The patriation scheme introduced by the Canada Act 1982 took this significantly further. In relation to the constitutional foundations of the system, its primary objective was to bring the authority of the UK Parliament to legislate for Canada to a decisive end,[80]

[74] The path to patriation was a long one. See P. C. Oliver, *The Constitution of Independence: The Development of Constitutional Theory in Australia, Canada, and New Zealand* (Oxford University Press 2005) chs 5–7.

[75] *Reference re: Amendment of the Constitution of Canada (Patriation Reference)* [1981] 1 SCR 753 at 762–809. The premise of this finding was the proposition, accepted by the Court, that the proposed amendments would affect federal-provincial relationships and the constitutional rights of the Provinces.

[76] *Patriation Reference* [1981] 1 SCR 753 at 874–910. The existence of the convention was adduced from a practice of consultation on the long series of British amendments to the Canadian Constitution. For a critique, see P. W. Hogg, 'Comment' (1982) 60 *Canadian Bar Review* 307.

[77] P. W. Hogg, 'Formal Amendment of the Constitution of Canada' (1992) 55 *Law and Contemporary Problems* 253 at 254; W. C. Hodge, 'Patriation of the Canadian Constitution: Comparative Federalism in a New Context' (1985) 60 *Washington Law Review* 585 at 632. Quebec's argument that its consent was required as a matter of convention was also rejected: *Reference re Amendment of Canadian Constitution (Quebec Veto Reference)* [1982] 2 SCR 793.

[78] Statute of Westminster 1931 (UK), s. 4.

[79] Statute of Westminster 1931 (UK), ss 2(2), 7(1), and (2).

[80] Canada Act 1982 (UK), s. 2.

while nonetheless preserving the British North America Acts as the foundational core of Canada's constitution. To achieve this, section 52 of the Constitution Act 1982 (contained as a Schedule to the Canada Act 1982) declared that:

(1) The Constitution of Canada is the supreme law of Canada, and any law that is inconsistent with the provisions of the Constitution is, to the extent of the inconsistency, of no force or effect.
(2) The Constitution of Canada includes
  (a) the *Canada Act* 1982, including this Act;
  (b) the Acts and orders referred to in the schedule; and
  (c) any amendment to any Act or order referred to in paragraph (*a*) or (*b*).
(3) Amendments to the Constitution of Canada shall be made only in accordance with the authority contained in the Constitution of Canada.

This made clear that, even though the UK Parliament had abdicated its authority to legislate for Canada and the Canadian legislatures had the power to enact laws inconsistent with Imperial statutes, the constitutional status of the British North America Acts 1867–1975, the Canada Act 1982, and the Constitution Act 1982 would be preserved. Moreover, this was achieved, not by relying on the background doctrine that colonial statutes repugnant to Imperial statutes are void or inoperative (as the Statute of Westminster had done),[81] but by declaring that the Constitution of Canada is the supreme law of Canada and can only be amended in accordance with the terms of the Constitution itself. This ensured that the ordinary legislative powers of the Dominion and provincial legislatures would not extend to the amendment of Canada's constitutional statutes.[82]

As part of the patriation package it was also necessary to provide for some mechanism by which the Canadian Constitution could be amended. Just as patriation had depended upon the request and consent of the Dominion with the agreement of nine of the ten Provinces, the federal nature of the system suggested that the new constitutional amendment process would have to involve the active participation of the Dominion and the Provinces, without enabling either to change the fundamental terms of the federation unilaterally. The Constitution Act 1982 accordingly contained provisions which gave the Dominion and provincial legislatures a jointly shared power to amend the Constitution, the exact level of agreement to be secured depending on the nature of the proposed amendment.[83] The primary provision allows the Constitution to be amended by proclamation issued by the Governor General where so authorized by resolutions of the Senate, the House of Commons, and the legislative assemblies of at least two-thirds of the Provinces that have, in the aggregate, at least 50 per cent of the population of all the Provinces.[84] However, any proposed amendment

[81] Compare ss 2(2) and 7(1) of the Statute of Westminster 1931 (UK).
[82] P. W. Hogg, 'Supremacy of the Canadian Charter of Rights and Freedoms' (1983) 61 *Canadian Bar Review* 69.
[83] Constitution Act 1982, ss 38–48.
[84] Constitution Act 1982, s. 38(1).

that derogates from the legislative powers, proprietary rights, or other rights or privileges of the legislature or government of a Province will not have effect in a Province the legislative assembly of which has expressed its dissent thereto by resolution supported by a majority of its members prior to the issue of the proclamation.[85] In addition, amendments concerning particular matters of intrinsic interest to all of the Provinces require the support of the Senate, the House of Commons, and the legislative assembly of every Province.[86] In this way, each provincial legislature was given a guaranteed role in the amendment process, including a capacity to veto any change affecting the powers, rights, or privileges of the government or legislature of the Province.[87] Despite the protection these procedures gave to the Provinces, they remained unacceptable in some quarters, especially in Quebec, so by way of further protection, the Canadian Parliament has since also enacted a law that prevents a Minister of the Crown from proposing a constitutional amendment without first obtaining the consent of each of Ontario, Quebec, British Columbia, two or more of the Atlantic provinces, and two or more of the Prairie provinces.[88]

The patriation of the Canadian Constitution, although contested by Quebec at numerous points, has resulted in the confirmation and deepening of the federal nature of the system in several fundamental respects.[89] While preserving legal continuity, the Constitution has been transformed from something almost entirely Westminster-derived into the fundamental law of a system that recognizes the rights to constitutional self-determination of the Canadian people organized federally in their respective Provinces. The transition affected by patriation was Westminster-derived, and did not depend on a revolutionary assertion of independence or autochthony, but the change was nonetheless initiated by Canadians, and profound in its effects.[90] By enacting the Canada Act 1982 in response to Canada's request, the UK Parliament simultaneously established the constitutional foundations of an independent Canada, abdicated its own authority to legislate for Canada, and conferred on Canadian political institutions an independent, federal, and democratic means of undertaking constitutional amendments in the future.

The process that occurred in Australia was comparable to the Canadian, but reflected the subtly different constitutional status enjoyed by the Australian Commonwealth and States. When the authority of the UK Parliament to legislate for Australia was brought to an end in 1986, two substantively identical Australia Acts were used, one enacted by the UK Parliament upon the request and consent of the Australian Parliament, the other enacted by the Australian Parliament upon the request and consent of all of the State legislatures pursuant to s 51(xxxviii)

[85] Constitution Act 1982, s. 38(2), (3). [86] Constitution Act 1982, s. 41.
[87] Constitution Act 1982, ss 38(2) and (3), 41, 43.
[88] An Act Respecting Constitutional Amendments (SC 1996, c. 1).
[89] *Reference re: Secession of Quebec (Quebec Secession)* [1998] 2 SCR 217 at 244–5, 250–2.
[90] Notably, the amendment clause appears in the Constitution Act 1982 (UK), not the main body of the Canada Act 1982 (UK).

of the Australian Constitution.[91] Like the Canada Act 1982, the Australia Acts provided for the termination of the authority of the UK Parliament to legislate for Australia.[92] Just as the Statute of Westminster had affirmed the power of the Canadian and Australian federal legislatures to make laws inconsistent with Imperial statutes, the Australia Acts affirmed the capacity of the Australian State legislatures to make laws inconsistent with Imperial statutes.[93] But as in Canada, once the Commonwealth and States legislatures were freed from Imperial restraints, it was necessary to preserve the binding authority of the Commonwealth of Australia Constitution Act and the Constitution of the Commonwealth it contains.[94] It was also necessary to specify how the Australia Acts, and the relevant provisions of the Statute of Westminster, might be amended in the future. Consistent with the enactment of the Australian version of the Australia Act on the basis of the section 51(xxxviii) procedure, the Australia Acts provide that they and the Statute of Westminster can be amended by the Commonwealth Parliament at the request or with the concurrence of all the State legislatures.[95]

Several Australian judges have suggested that, although at the time of federation the Australian Constitution owed its binding force to the sovereign authority of the UK Parliament, after the passage of the Australia Acts the Constitution must be conceived as deriving its binding force from autochthonous sources, in particular the ratification of the Australian Constitution by the voters in the Australian colonies in the 1890s.[96] Some have even gone so far as to say that 'ultimately sovereignty' now rests in the Australian people.[97] Notably, however, the process by which the Australian Constitution was patriated, as well as the new constitutional provisions enacted as part of the patriation package, reflect the fact that Australia is a federal commonwealth composed of constituent States.[98] In both Canada and Australia, the formative basis of the country's constitution and the required procedures for its amendment have thus been shaped profoundly by the federal nature of the polity. Both constitutional systems may be Westminster-derived, but as the authority of the UK Parliament has receded, the federal features of each system have been affirmed, and in important respects strengthened.

[91] Australia Acts 1986 (UK) and (Aust.). This gives rise to an interesting but unresolved question as to which of the two statutes is primarily effective, from the point of view of Australian law, to bring the powers of the UK Parliament over Australia to an end. See *Sue v Hill* (1999) 199 CLR 462 at 490–503 (Gleeson CJ, Gummow, and Hayne JJ), relying on the Australian version; see also 526–8 (Gaudron J).

[92] Australia Acts 1986 (UK) and (Aust), s. 1.

[93] Australia Acts 1986 (UK) and (Aust.), s. 3.

[94] Australia Acts 1986 (UK) and (Aust.), s. 5.

[95] Australia Acts 1986 (UK) and (Aust.), s. 15.

[96] See G. Lindell, 'Why Is Australia's Constitution Binding? The Reasons in 1900 and Now, and the Effect of Independence' (1986) 16 *Federal Law Review* 29. The Canadian debate on this issue has an interestingly different character. See P. H. Russell, *Constitutional Odyssey: Can Canadians Become a Sovereign People?* (University of Toronto Press, 2nd edn 1993).

[97] *Australian Capital Television v Commonwealth* (1992) 177 CLR 106 at 138 (Mason CJ); *Theophanous v Herald & Weekly Times Ltd* (1994) 182 CLR 104 at 171, 180 (Deane J); but see *McGinty* (1996) 186 CLR 140 at 274–5 (Gummow J).

[98] *Commonwealth of Australia Constitution Act* 1900 (UK), preamble, s. 3. For a fuller account, see Aroney (n. 29); N. Aroney, 'A Public Choice? Federalism and the Prospects of a Republican Preamble' (1999) 21 *University of Queensland Law Journal* 205.

IV. Constitutional futures of British devolution

The constitutional experience of Canada and Australia demonstrates that Westminster-derived systems of government can secure substantial degrees of constitutional autonomy and independence, and that this can occur through processes that do not involve an abrupt revolutionary assertion of autochthony. It also demonstrates that such processes can establish the ensemble of institutions, powers, and procedures necessary for a functioning federal system, including a binding, written constitution. British devolution resembles such systems in so far as it establishes elected legislatures and responsible governments in Scotland, Northern Ireland, and Wales, which exercise independent powers of government over particular matters, pursuant to devolution statutes which the UK Parliament is practically unable to amend without the agreement of the devolved institutions and the application of which is authoritatively determined by the Supreme Court.[99] The British system is, however, significantly different from the Canadian and Australian federations in that it does not have a legally entrenched written constitution, there are no devolved institutions of governance for England, and there is no system of territorial representation of the constituent nations of the United Kingdom within the UK Parliament. Yet proposals for reform in the aftermath of the Scottish independence referendum seem to have the effect of moving the British system distinctly closer to the Canadian and Australian systems. Indeed, many of the disagreements about exactly what changes should be implemented concern features that these federal systems have and the British system lacks.

As to the constitutive foundations of the system, while any future changes to the devolution arrangements in the United Kingdom will depend upon enactments of the UK Parliament, well-established constitutional conventions require that such laws will not be enacted without the consent of the devolved legislatures. The right of the peoples of Scotland, Wales, and Northern Ireland to determine their constitutional destinies is thus acknowledged, but it is also recognized that the UK Government and Parliament, representing the people of the United Kingdom as a whole, also have an essential role in settling the fundamental features of the UK constitution. In this respect, the situation in the United Kingdom resembles that of Canada and Australia prior to the enactment of the Statute of Westminster 1931 (UK). At that time, the sovereignty of the Imperial Parliament was accepted, but it was conceded that the Parliament would not legislate for Australia and Canada without their request and consent. The Statute of Westminster was a statutory recognition of the convention that had come to regulate the constitutional relationship between the United Kingdom and its self-governing Dominions.

The very day after the Scottish independence referendum, the UK Prime Minister announced the establishment of a Commission under Lord Smith of Kelvin the aim of which was to secure an agreement among all of the parties

[99] Bogdanor (n. 17) 81–5.

represented in the Scottish Parliament concerning further powers to be devolved to Scotland. The first two recommendations of the Smith Commission were that the devolved institutions of government in Scotland be recognized as 'permanent' institutions and that the Sewel Convention be placed on a statutory footing.[100] A similar proposal to recognize the permanent constitutional status of the Welsh National Assembly and to formalize the Legislative Consent Motion procedure for Wales was recommended by the Silk Commission on Devolution in Wales.[101] Notably, the recommendations of the Smith Commission were premised on 'the sovereign right of the people of Scotland to determine the form of government best suited to their needs'.[102] They propose to do for Scotland something of what the Statute of Westminster did for Canada and Australia by inserting into legislation the conventions and understandings that already existed between the respective governments.

The UK Government has shown itself generally willing to implement the recommendations of the Smith and Silk Commissions in relation to these matters.[103] However, the Scotland Bill drafted and introduced into the Parliament by the Government states only that the Scottish Parliament and Government are to be 'recognized as' permanent parts of the United Kingdom's constitutional arrangements and similarly provides that it 'is recognized' the United Kingdom Parliament will not 'normally' legislate with regard to devolved matters without the consent of the Scottish Parliament.[104] This has given rise to the concern, expressed by the then Devolution (Further Powers) Committee of the Scottish Parliament, that this wording would weaken the effect of the clauses.[105] In evidence to the Committee, the Law Society of Scotland maintained that the permanency clause merely acknowledged or declared a 'matter of fact' rather than constituted a positive enactment having legal force.[106] Tellingly, the relevant provision of the Statute of Westminster was similarly careful, indeed elliptical, in its language, rather than baldly purporting to cut down the sovereign legislative authority of the Imperial Parliament. It stated that no future Act of the UK Parliament would extend or be deemed to extend to a Dominion 'unless it is expressly declared in that Act that the Dominion has requested, and consented to, the enactment thereof'.[107] By comparison, the

[100] Smith Commission (n. 7) [21]–[22].

[101] Silk Commission on Devolution in Wales, *Empowerment and Responsibility: Legislative Powers to Strengthen Wales* (2014), [13.3.23], R.54(a), [13.3.30], R.56.

[102] Smith Commission (n. 7) at para. 20.

[103] UK Government (n. 7) at paras 1.2–1.4; UK Government, *Powers for a Purpose: Towards a Lasting Devolution Settlement for Wales* (Cm 9020, 2015) para. 2.2.4. See also Smith Commission (n. 7) at paras 23–7; and see also Scotland Bill 2015, cls 3–11, in relation to Scottish elections and the composition and operation of the Scottish Parliament and Government.

[104] Smith Commission (n. 7) at paras 20–22, 48; UK Government (n. 7) at para. 1.2; Scotland Bill 2015, cls. 1, 2.

[105] Devolution (Further Powers) Committee (n. 7) at paras 47, 61.

[106] Quoted in Devolution (Further Powers) Committee (n. 7) at para. 41. The Deputy First Minister of Scotland also seemed to express the view that the Sewel clause did not succeed in giving the Convention legally enforceable effect: quoted (n. 7) at para. 58.

[107] Statute of Westminster 1931 (UK), s. 4.

Canada Act 1982 (UK) and the Australia Act 1986 (UK) were much more categorical: they unequivocally declared that no future British statute would 'extend to' Canada or Australia as part of its law.[108]

The task of replicating a similar effect within the realm of the United Kingdom is complicated by two important factors. One is that by the time that the Canadian and Australian constitutions were patriated, the jurisdiction of the Privy Council to hear appeals from Canada and Australia had been brought to an end, making Canadian and Australian courts the final judicial authorities within their respective jurisdictions.[109] Even if UK courts might be required to give effect to a British statute purporting to amend or repeal the Canada Act or the Australia Act, Canadian and Australian courts would not be so obliged and have in fact indicated that they regard the authority of the UK Parliament to have been permanently extinguished and the theoretical foundation of their respective constitutions to be virtually autochthonous.[110] This state of affairs does not exist within the United Kingdom, where the Supreme Court remains the court of ultimate appeal from the courts of England and Wales, Scotland, and Northern Ireland. The second and more fundamental complication lies in the continuing role of the UK Parliament, not only as the general legislature for the United Kingdom, but as the sovereign legislature upon which the entire British system of devolution depends. As evidence received by the Devolution (Further Powers) Committee of the Scottish Parliament emphasized, unless some alternative mechanism for the amendment of the devolution statutes were to be introduced, the constitutive authority of the UK Parliament must continue. It is thus one thing for the authority of the UK Parliament to be discontinued in respect of its overseas Dominions, it is another for it to be discontinued or modified within the realm of the United Kingdom itself.

In this respect it is noticeable that the local constitutional amendment processes established in Canada and Australia were considered to be essential components of the patriation of their respective constitutions. In Canada, the new amendment process not only acknowledged the federal-democratic principles that underlie Canadian politics, but also converted these principles into a set of legally enforceable rules that must be complied with in order to amend the constitution. In Australia, the prescribed process for the amendment of the Constitution that already existed required proposed changes to be approved by a majority of the people of the Commonwealth and a majority of the people in a majority of the States.[111] On a literal reading of the relevant constitutional provisions, there is no

[108] Canada Act 1982 (UK), s. 1; Australia Act 1986 (UK), s. 1.

[109] Oliver (n. 74) at 50–3, 95–6. In relation to appeals from the courts of the Australian States, the Privy Council's jurisdiction was effectively terminated by the Australia Acts 1986 (UK) and (Aust.), s. 11.

[110] *Sue v Hill* (1999) 199 CLR 462 at paras 63–4; *Durham Holdings v New South Wales* (2001) 205 CLR 399 at para. 9; *Attorney-General (WA) v Marquet* (2003) 217 CLR 545 at paras 66–7; *Mitchell v M.N.R.* [2001] 1 SCR 911 at para. 129.

[111] Australian Constitution, s. 128.

specific rule laid down for the amendment of the preamble and covering clauses of the Commonwealth of Australia Constitution Act 1900 (UK), and there is therefore doubt about exactly what procedures would be required should the preamble or covering clauses ever need to be amended.[112] However, it is considered unthinkable that an Australian-based process of some kind would not exist.[113]

The enactment of the Sewel Convention into law would go some way towards legally prescribing a special process for the amendment of the Scotland Act. There are many other special procedures that might be adopted, such as the requirement of a supermajority within the UK Parliament.[114] However, as evidence to the Scottish Committee acknowledged, any such procedures contained in a British statute presumably could themselves be amended by an ordinary enactment of the Parliament.[115] A similar problem has arisen in Canada and especially Australia, where the State constitutions are contained in ordinary statutes enacted by the State legislatures. In order to prevent some of the more important elements of the Australian State constitutions from being amended by simple majorities within the State legislatures, the relevant provisions in the State Constitution Acts are protected by 'manner and form' provisions, which lay down special procedures for the amendment of the relevant sections of those Acts. The effectiveness of these procedural requirements originally depended upon an Imperial statute, the Colonial Laws Validity Act 1865 (UK), which stipulated that every representative legislature in a colony would have full power to make laws respecting the constitution, powers, and procedure of that legislature, provided that such laws were passed in such manner and form as was required by any relevant law, including any such law enacted by the colonial legislature itself.[116] At the time of patriation it was considered necessary to make similar provision in the Australia Acts to ensure the effectiveness of the manner and form requirements contained in the State constitutions.[117] It is also recognized in Australian law that manner and form provisions must themselves be entrenched so that they cannot be amended unless the same (or some other) manner and form procedure is followed.[118] Otherwise, the manner and form provision could be avoided by first repealing it by ordinary legislation and then proceeding to amend the substantive sections of the Constitution Act.

[112] I discuss this in Aroney (n. 98).

[113] *Polyukhovich v Commonwealth* (1991) 172 CLR 501 at 638 (Dawson J); *Final Report of the Constitutional Commission* (Australian Government Publishing Service 1988) para. 3.104.

[114] Notably, there are some provisions of the Scotland Act that can already be amended by the Scottish Parliament. See Scotland Act 1998 (UK), Sched. 4, para. 4; The Scotland Act 1998 (Modification of Scheds 4 and 5 and Transfer of Functions to the Scottish Ministers etc.) Order 2015, arts 3 and 4. In addition, the Smith Commission has recommended that the Scottish Parliament be given power to amend by special procedure those parts of the Scotland Act dealing with the Scottish Parliament franchise, electoral system, and membership: (n. 7) at para. 27.

[115] Devolution (Further Powers) Committee (n. 7) at para. 45.

[116] Colonial Laws Validity Act 1865 (UK), s. 5.

[117] Australia Acts 1986 (UK) and (Aust.), s. 6.

[118] *Attorney-General (NSW) v Trethowan* (1931) 44 CLR 394; *Attorney-General (WA) v Marquet* (2003) 217 CLR 545.

Much the same technique of 'double entrenchment' could be used to help protect any special process laid down for the amendment of the devolution statutes within the United Kingdom. However, double entrenchment might not be enough. In Australia, manner and form provisions are given force by the Imperial statutes that established and conferred legislative power on the State legislatures, but this line of reasoning is not available in respect of the UK Parliament itself. If the matter were ever litigated in the United Kingdom the question of the nature of the sovereignty of the Parliament might have to be confronted, and the question is likely to turn on considerations similar to those that arose in *Jackson v Attorney General*.[119] While much of the reasoning in *Jackson* suggests that such a procedure might well be effective, it is not possible to be certain of this, as the Parliament Acts 1911 and 1949 (UK) only bypassed the House of Lords; they did not detract from but rather enhanced the authority of a majority within the House of Commons. This uncertainty about the nature of parliamentary sovereignty contributes to the view, expressed by some, that a more final settlement of the constitutional fundamentals of British devolution will require a constitutional convention and a ratifying referendum to establish a written constitution for the United Kingdom.

Reasoning along these lines, the Devolution (Further Powers) Committee of the Scottish Parliament recommended that to overcome the limiting effect of the doctrine of parliamentary sovereignty, the permanency of the Scottish institutions of government would have to be underwritten by a Scottish referendum and the support of the Scottish Parliament.[120] The Silk Commission on Devolution in Wales further observed that a constitutional convention might be the pathway by which a United Kingdom constitution might be developed which would function as a 'vehicle for making permanent the existence of the three devolved legislatures'.[121] When the Scotland Bill 2015 was being debated on its introduction to the House of Commons, several amendments were proposed to address these issues. The amendments included proposals to:

- render the declaration of the permanency of the Scottish Parliament and Government more categorical by removing the words 'is recognised as' and inserting 'shall be';[122]
- make the enactment of the Sewel Convention more categorical by removing the word 'recognise' and further providing that the United Kingdom Parliament will 'never' (rather than 'not normally') legislate with regard to devolved matters or the powers of the Scottish Parliament and Government

[119] *Jackson v Attorney General* [2005] UKHL 56; [2006] 1 AC 262 at para. [81] (Lord Steyn), at para. [113] (Lord Hope), at paras [161]–[163] (Baroness Hale).

[120] Devolution (Further Powers) Committee (n. 7) at para. 50. See, similarly, Scottish Government (n. 9) at 28.

[121] Silk Commission (n. 101) at para. 16.8.3.

[122] Scotland Bill 2015, Amendments 16, 17, 18; United Kingdom, *Parliamentary Debates*, House of Commons, 15 June 2015, col. 24.

without the consent of the Scottish Parliament and following consultation with the Scottish Government;[123]

- prevent repeal of the clauses establishing the Scottish Parliament and Government as permanent parts of the United Kingdom's constitution without the consent of the Scottish Parliament and the Scottish people voting in a referendum;[124]
- establish constitutional conventions to review and make recommendations in relation to the UK Constitution and future governance arrangements for the United Kingdom, including voting rights in the House of Commons, democratic reform of the House of Lords, further sub-national devolution within England, and codification of the constitution;[125]
- provide that the Scotland Act 1998 (UK) be cited as 'The Written Constitution of Scotland' and require the establishment of a standing Scottish Constitutional Convention to conduct reviews and make recommendations to the Scottish and UK Parliaments.[126]

Further expanded legislative and fiscal powers were also proposed, including 'full fiscal autonomy',[127] as well as provision for territorial representation in the House of Lords by empowering the Scottish Parliament to nominate persons to represent Scotland in the House of Lords broadly in proportion to the population of Scotland within the United Kingdom.[128]

Following lengthy debate during the committee stage of the Bill, these amendments were generally either negatived or withdrawn, but they may resurface at later stages as they capture the way in which the problem of entrenching the constitutional position of Scotland within the United Kingdom is being conceived and debated. As one participant observed, at the heart of the issue is the question of sovereignty. Even a clause which stipulated that the Scotland Act could only be amended by referendum might not be enough, as the clause itself could always be got around by a simple repeal. What is needed, he argued, is a 'fundamental change in the way we do things', and this can only be achieved through a written constitution formulated by a constitutional convention.[129] Several other

[123] Scotland Bill 2015, Amendments 4, 19, 20, 39, 41, 45, and 56, and New Clause 10; United Kingdom, *Parliamentary Debates*, House of Commons, 15 June 2015, cols 96–8.

[124] Scotland Bill 2015, Amendments 58 and 59; United Kingdom, *Parliamentary Debates*, House of Commons, 15 June 2015, col. 24. There was also a proposed amendment to the Parliament Act 1911 (UK) to require that any amendment to the permanency of the Scottish institutions and the enactment of the Sewel Convention must be passed by both houses of the UK Parliament: Scotland Bill 2015, New Clause 7; United Kingdom, *Parliamentary Debates*, House of Commons, 15 June 2015, col. 26.

[125] Scotland Bill 2015, New Clauses 2 and 9; United Kingdom, *Parliamentary Debates*, House of Commons, 15 June 2015, cols 25, 26–7.

[126] Scotland Bill 2015, New Clause 6; United Kingdom, *Parliamentary Debates*, House of Commons, H C Deb, Vol. 597, 15 June 2015, col. 26.

[127] Scotland Bill 2015, Amendment 89 and New Clause 3; United Kingdom, H C Deb, Vol. 597, 15 June 2015, cols 25–6.

[128] Scotland Bill 2015, New Clause; United Kingdom, H C Deb, Vol. 597, 15 June 2015, col. 26.

[129] United Kingdom, H C Deb, Vol. 597, 15 June 2015, cols 28–9 (Alistair Carmichael); see also cols 71–2 (Pete Wishart).

participants also observed that what was being contemplated was a movement to a 'more federal arrangement'.[130] Indeed, full fiscal autonomy, if made a general principle of devolution, would give the British system characteristics which resemble the relatively loose 'confederations' that existed in the United States, Switzerland, and Australia before their modern 'federal' constitutions were established, for it would make the constituent devolved governments the primary taxing entities and the central government in some respects dependent upon them for its financial resources.[131] However, the fiscal, political, and constitutional barriers to such developments remain formidable. For the moment, a halfway house seems more likely.[132]

A Commission established by the Bingham Centre for the Rule of Law has called for the enactment of a Charter of Union that would lay down a set of judicially-enforceable principles of UK constitutional law as a significant first step towards a written constitution.[133] These principles include the following propositions:

- The United Kingdom is a voluntary union of four component nations.
- It is for each nation of the United Kingdom to determine the form of government best suited to its needs.
- Each nation of the United Kingdom enjoys autonomy in the exercise of its lawful powers, just as the United Kingdom as a whole enjoys autonomy in the exercise of its lawful powers.
- The purpose of devolution is that the body best able to respond to the wishes of the people and provide a particular service should be the body that carries out that task.[134]

The Bingham Centre Commission drew attention to the important role of referendums as the means by which the 'sovereign will' of the people of each of the constituent nations might express their voluntary consent to form part of the United Kingdom.[135] It also noted that the Liberal Democrats and the Labour Party have endorsed the idea of a constitutional convention to advance the reform agenda.[136] However, recognizing the practical difficulties of establishing a constitutional convention, the Commission proposed only that the new Charter of Union be enacted by the UK Parliament rather than first developed by a constitutional convention and then submitted to a referendum.[137]

[130] See eg United Kingdom, H C Deb, Vol. 597, 15 June 2015, cols 32, 38, 47–8, 52, 75, 91 (Jim Cunningham, Edward Leigh, Ian Blackford, Graham Allen, Tommy Sheppard, Alistair Carmichael).

[131] F. K. Lister, *The Later Security Confederations: The American, 'New' Swiss, and German Unions* (Greenwood Press 2001).

[132] See eg the UK Government's resistance to a constitutional convention and its insistence on the sovereignty of the UK Parliament as the UK's alternative to a written constitution: United Kingdom, H C Deb, Vol. 597, 15 June 2015, cols 90–1, 105–6 (David Mundell).

[133] Independent Commission, Bingham Centre for the Rule of Law, *A Constitutional Crossroads: Ways Forward for the United Kingdom* (British Institute of International and Comparative Law 2015) para. 1.

[134] Bingham Centre (n. 133) at para. 4.1.

[135] Bingham Centre (n. 133) at para. 4.2.

[136] Bingham Centre (n. 133) at para. 5.1.

[137] Bingham Centre (n. 133) at para. 4.1.

V. Conclusion

The UK constitution has always been in a state of evolution and development. However the nature and rate of constitutional change has been very considerable in recent decades, and the pace of change shows little sign of abating. There are several important proposals on the table. Many of them have met with some resistance, however. The House of Lords Select Committee on the Constitution has questioned the sidelining of the UK Parliament's role in contributing to the development of the Smith Commission proposals.[138] While maintaining that the proposed changes are only political and symbolic and place no legal constraints on the sovereign powers of the UK Parliament, the Select Committee has expressed concern that such provisions may create misunderstanding or conflict in the courts and has pointed out that they 'appear to be moving the United Kingdom in a federal direction, attempting to crystallize by way of statute, if not a written constitution, the status and powers of the devolved administrations'.[139] Although the Smith Commission recognized that the interests of the United Kingdom and its other component parts ought to be considered, its recommendations did not depend upon the conclusion of political negotiations elsewhere in the United Kingdom but rather focused on the particular needs and expectations of Scotland.[140] The Select Committee has called for a more inclusive and systematic approach to devolution generally, arguing that if an enduring constitutional settlement is to be reached 'it must be accepted by the UK as a whole and not simply one part of it'.[141] To this end, it has launched an inquiry that focusses on the constitutional needs of the United Kingdom as a whole.[142]

Such an enquiry, if genuinely inclusive and systematic, will not be able to avoid the question of England and the deep asymmetry that characterizes the British system of devolution. The possibility of a devolved legislature for England or the division of England into several regions each with its own legislature would have to be considered. However, it is not clear whether the people of England, or the people of the regions of England, are likely to want to this. The McKay Commission's proposal that UK bills dealing only with England (or England and Wales) must obtain the consent of the elected representatives of England (or England and Wales) may prove to be more practicable, although this too is not without its difficulties.[143] It would also be necessary to consider whether the

[138] House of Lords Select Committee on the Constitution, *Proposals for the Devolution of Further Powers to Scotland*, 10th Report, 2014—201, HL Paper 145, paras 35–43.

[139] Select Committee on the Constitution (n. 138) at 4–5, paras 56–77.

[140] Smith Commission (n. 7) at para. 7.

[141] Select Committee on the Constitution (n. 138) at paras 13–24, 127.

[142] <http://www.parliament.uk/union-and-devolution>. The Scottish National Party has, in turn, objected to the proposition that the Scotland Bill might be amended when it passes through the House of Lords.

[143] McKay Commission, *Report of the Commission on the Consequences of Devolution for the House of Commons* (2013) para. 109. See also UK Government, *The Implications of Devolution for England*

extent of the powers granted to the three devolved legislatures should be made more uniform, a non-trivial question given the very different political, social, and economic conditions of Scotland, Northern Ireland, and Wales, let alone England.[144] Moreover, because it is not possible to distribute governing powers into watertight compartments, it is becoming recognized that improved systems of intergovernmental cooperation are needed.[145] In this connection, the question will also arise whether some system of territorial representation in the House of Lords should be adopted.

When compared to the Australian and Canadian experience, it is difficult to avoid the conclusion that a reasonably stable settlement of the constitutional fundamentals of British devolution will require the full participation of all of the governments, legislatures, and peoples of the United Kingdom in a genuinely deliberative and inclusive process. But this is more easily said than done. The potential pitfalls are many.[146] Not least of them is the problem of reconciling the principle of parliamentary sovereignty with the principle of federalism. For Canada and Australia, the tension between these two principles was negotiated through a long period of constitutional evolution during which power was gradually transferred from the United Kingdom and distributed between federal and regional levels of government. Within the realm of the United Kingdom such a process is less easy to achieve, due largely to the deeply asymmetrical nature of the devolution settlement, under which the Parliament at Westminster functions simultaneously as the special legislature for England, the general legislature for the United Kingdom, and the sovereign legislature upon which the entire system of devolution depends. These functions of the Parliament are not easily unravelled and distributed without recourse to the idea that sovereignty is ultimately vested in the peoples of the United Kingdom, the kind of sovereignty that is ordinarily expressed in constitutive devices such as deliberative conventions and ratifying referendums. Certainly, this is the path that Canada and especially Australia have taken. As Charles McIlwain pointed out so many years ago: '[w]hen the referendum really comes, the sovereign Parliament must go'.[147] And yet today the question remains: when will the referendum finally come, if ever?

The successful drafting, approval, and enactment of the Canadian and Australian constitutions in the 1860s and 1890s were considerable achievements, as was their patriation in the 1980s. However, the obstacles encountered then, as well as by other ambitious constitutive and reconstitutive processes, such as the Convention on the Future of Europe in 2001, demonstrate how difficult it can be to make

(Cm 8969, 2014) 18–20. Changes to the Standing Orders of the House of Commons to secure EVEL have been proposed: UK Cabinet Office, *English Votes for English Laws: Revised Proposed Changes to the Standing Orders of the House of Commons and Explanatory Memorandum* (2015).

[144] Already the Scottish and Northern Irish legislatures possess an extensive array of powers, and many more are being proposed for Scotland, including far-reaching fiscal powers: Smith Commission (n. 7) at paras 75–93.

[145] Smith Commission (n. 7) at paras 28–30.

[146] For a list of objections to the establishment of a federal system in the United Kingdom, see McKay Commission (n. 143) at paras 69–71.

[147] McIlwain (n. 4) at xv.

major constitutional decisions in a manner that is fully democratic and inclusive, especially when the goal is to integrate a diversity of independently-minded nations and peoples into a stable federal-like relationship. Although Canada and Australia were successful in establishing and patriating their Westminster-derived federal constitutions, the period of the 1990s was a time of constitutional turbulence and indecision for Canada, while efforts to reform Australian federalism have repeatedly encountered what appear to be perennial and insurmountable obstacles.[148] Reforming federal systems is an arduous undertaking, and much is to be learned from the successes, and the failures, of such efforts in countries that face similar challenges of reconciling unity and diversity.[149]

[148] I discuss this in N. Aroney, 'Federalism and Subsidiarity: Principles and Processes in the Reform of the Australian Federation' (2016) 44(1) *Federal Law Review* (forthcoming).

[149] See eg A. Benz and F. Knüpling (eds), *Changing Federal Constitutions: Lessons from International Comparison* (Barbara Budrich Publishers 2012).

14

The Technical Jekyll and the Political Hyde

The Constitutional Law and Politics of Scotland's Independence 'Neverendum'

Andrew Tickell

I. A disaster averted, a tension unresolved

On 15 October 2012, the UK Supreme Court was deprived of one of its landmark constitutional cases, its *Secession of Quebec* reference.[1] In St Andrew's House in Edinburgh, Prime Minister David Cameron, Secretary of State for Scotland Michael Moore, and First and Deputy First Ministers Alex Salmond and Nicola Sturgeon put their names to the *Agreement between the United Kingdom Government and the Scottish Government on a Referendum on Independence for Scotland*. The product of private, backroom negotiations between the two governments, what became known as the 'Edinburgh Agreement' ended months of uncertainty and legal debate over whether Holyrood had the competence to legislate for a referendum on Scottish independence. Paving the way for a 'legal, fair and decisive' poll, the two governments agreed that Westminster would intervene to 'put it beyond doubt that the Scottish Parliament can legislate for that referendum'.[2]

This memorandum was accompanied by a draft Order under section 30 of the Scotland Act 1998, which set out how the devolution legislation would be amended to achieve these ends. Holyrood would be invested with a categorical but time-limited power to legislate for a referendum on Scottish independence.[3] This legal security was purchased with a series of policy concessions to the coalition government's constitutional agenda, ruling out a multi-option referendum including a second question about further devolution, and involving the Electoral Commission in the poll's scrutiny and regulation. The Agreement also set out principles which would shape the Scottish Parliament's subsequent legislation, modelling the referendum on the Political Parties, Elections and Referendums

[1] [1998] 2 SCR 217.

[2] *Agreement between the United Kingdom Government and the Scottish Government on a referendum on independence for Scotland* (2012) 2.

[3] The Scotland Act 1998 (Modification of Schedule 5) Order 2013 No. 242.

Act 2000,[4] and devolving responsibility to Holyrood for determining the franchise, the campaign finance rules, and the precise referendum question and the timing of the poll.[5]

Politicians on both sides of the national question, civil servants, and anybody anxious not to see the referendum embroiled in potentially protracted litigation breathed a sigh of relief. Only constitutional lawyers might—privately—admit to any professional disappointment that the lively *vires* debate which had crackled for months on airwaves, in print, parliament, universities, and on blogs would not now be tested before the UK Supreme Court. The crux of the dispute concerned the interpretation of the Scotland Act 1998. The Scottish National Party had been re-elected in 2011 with a majority of MSPs in the Scottish Parliament, having stood on a manifesto that:

> We think the people of Scotland should decide our nation's future in a democratic referendum and opinion polls suggest that most Scots agree. We will, therefore, bring forward our Referendum Bill in this next Parliament. A yes vote will mean Scotland becomes an independent nation and we can then begin the job of delivering the better country we all know Scotland can be.[6]

But did Holyrood enjoy the legislative competence to realize this manifesto commitment, democratically endorsed by the Scottish electorate? Under section 29(1) of the Scotland Act, Acts of the Scottish Parliament which are outside legislative competence are not law. Amongst other limits on Holyrood's power, including compatibility with Convention rights and the law of the European Union,[7] an Act will fall outside the Parliament's competence where it 'relates to reserved matters' set out in Schedule 5 of the Act.[8] Part 1 of the Schedule reserves 'aspects of the constitution' to Westminster, including 'the Union of the Kingdoms of Scotland and England'.[9] The Scotland Act provides guidance on how courts are to approach adjudication under this section. 'Whether a provision of an Act of the Scottish Parliament relates to a reserved matter' is to be determined 'by reference to the purpose of the provision, having regard (among other things) to its effect in all the circumstances'.[10] This test must be read alongside the interpretative duty imposed on the court by section 101, which provides that any Act of the Scottish Parliament 'which could be read in such a way as to be outside competence' must be 'read as narrowly as is required for it to be within competence, if such a reading is possible'.[11]

In the months preceding the Edinburgh Agreement, the Scottish Government claimed that its referendum bill could withstand the rigour of

[4] Incorporating some of the inadequacies of that Act. Cf. A. Tickell, 'Regulating #indyref: Social Media and the Scottish Independence Referendum Act 2013' (2014) 18 *Edinburgh Law Review* 406–10.

[5] S. Tierney, 'The Referendum on Scottish Independence: A Process as well as an Event' (2014) 18 *Edinburgh Law Review* 245–50.

[6] Scottish National Party, *Scottish National Party Manifesto* (2011) 28.

[7] Scotland Act 1998, s. 29(2)(d).

[8] Scotland Act 1998, s. 29(2)(b).

[9] Scotland Act 1998, Sched. 5, para. 1(b).

[10] Scotland Act 1998, s. 29(3).

[11] Scotland Act 1998, s. 101(1) and (2).

this test. They suggested the bill fell within legislative competence.[12] The bill's detractors, including independent legal analysts and scholars, the UK Government, and House of Lords and Commons committees, took the diametrically opposite view.[13] They argued that, having regard to its 'purpose and effect', any referendum bill would 'relate to' the reserved matter of 'the Union of the Kingdoms' and accordingly, fall outwith Holyrood's legislative competence. Professor Page summarized the critical arguments on the *vires* of any referendum Bill crisply:

> When regard is had to the effect of the legislation, including its effect on the reserved matter of the Union … it becomes clear in my opinion that its true purpose is not to solicit the views of people in Scotland on a proposal about the way Scotland is governed, but to further the Scottish government's aim of achieving independence. A referendum is not a disinterested exercise in opinion gathering. It is embarked upon for a purpose—in this case to mobilize Scottish opinion in support of independence.[14]

Also critical was the UK Supreme Court's (2011) decision in *AXA v Lord Advocate*.[15] Leading judgments from Lords Hope and Reed loosened Scotland's historically restrictive rules on standing,[16] which required petitioners to demonstrate 'title and interest' to sue.[17] In *AXA*, the Supreme Court liberalized the rules,[18] requiring litigants to demonstrate only a 'sufficient interest' to bring judicial review proceedings, to be determined on the facts and circumstances of individual cases.[19] While a petitioner might struggle to establish a particular 'title and interest' to review the *vires* of the referendum, a very large number of people could be seen as having a 'sufficient interest to do so'.[20] Litigation seemed inevitable.

The Edinburgh Agreement was an act of statesmanship by which potentially damaging and divisive court proceedings were avoided. Yet it represented only a temporary compromise between political claims of a right to Scottish

[12] Scottish Government, *Scotland's Future: Draft Referendum (Scotland) Bill Consultation Paper* (2010); Scottish Government, *Your Scotland, Your Referendum Consultation* (2012).

[13] See, amongst other examples, UK Government, *Scotland's Constitutional Future: Responses to the Consultation* (2012); Scottish Affairs Committee, *The Referendum on Separation for Scotland: making the process legal* (HC 2012–13, 542); J. Wallace, Advocate General, 'Approaching the Independence Referendum: The Legal Issues', Speech at the University of Glasgow (2 October 2012); J. Wallace, Advocate General, 'Looking Forwards: To a Legal, Fair and Decisive Referendum', Speech at Balfour and Manson, Aberdeen (24th May 2012); UK Government, *Scotland's Constitutional Future: A Consultation on Facilitating a Legal, Fair and Decisive Referendum on Whether Scotland Should Leave the United Kingdom* (2012); House of Lords Committee on the Constitution, *Referendum on Scottish Independence Report* (HL 2010–12, 263).

[14] Quoted in Scottish Affairs Committee, *The Referendum on Separation* (n. 13) at para. 29.

[15] *AXA General Insurance Ltd and Ors v the Lord Advocate* [2011] UKSC 46.

[16] See, generally, A. McHarg, 'Analysis: *Axa General Insurance Ltd v Lord Advocate*' (2012) 16 *Edinburgh Law Review* 224–60.

[17] *D & J Nicol v Dundee Harbour Trustees* 1915 SC (HL) 7.

[18] See also C. McCorkindale, 'Public Interest Litigants in the Court of Session' (2015) 19 *Edinburgh Law Review* 247–53.

[19] *AXA General Insurance Ltd and Ors v the Lord Advocate* [2011] UKSC 46 at paras 169–70.

[20] *AXA* (n. 19) at para. 147.

self-determination, and legal uncertainty about the Scottish Parliament's power unilaterally to embark on a democratic process resulting in independence. The 2012 pact left these tensions fundamentally unresolved. When the bells of Hogmanay tolled on 31 December 2014, the temporary authority extended to the Scottish Parliament lapsed, largely unmarked, unremarked, and unnoticed. If the Yes campaign had carried the day on 18 September 2014, these questions would be consigned to the tome of nice points of law forgotten to history. The relevance of the UK devolved and constitutional order would have receded. Negotiated independence would, in all probability, have followed. Scottish politicians would be working in early days of a different nation. Having voted to remain in the Union, however, the unresolved questions of 2012 are now of more than academic interest.

II. 2014: Legal, fair, but decisive?

Professor Jeffery has argued that 'it did not take long for some who had campaigned for Scottish independence to begin envisaging a second referendum'.[21] This diagnosis is arguably too limited. In the months that followed the vote, it did not take long both for proponents *and* opponents of Scottish independence to begin to discuss the possible timing, triggers for, and legitimacy of a second referendum on Scottish independence. The prospect of a 'neverendum' is now upon us. For some, this will be a source of considerable anxiety and unhappiness. For others, it is the object of lively anticipation. For most, it now seems inevitable. Social research by Survation, published on 8 July 2015, suggested that only 20.4 per cent of the Scottish populace wished never to see another independence referendum. Only 38 per cent of those who voted No in September 2014 told the pollster there should never be a second referendum.[22] The Scottish National Party's plans—or lack of plans—for a second plebiscite formed a central plank of the Labour Party's UK general election campaign in the spring of 2015. Scottish Labour sought to attract voters opposed to any rerun of the 2014 poll by arguing Scotland would be 'turbo-charged towards a second referendum' if significant numbers of SNP members were returned to Westminster.[23] In the wake of the 2015 general election, the unseated former leader of the Scottish Labour Party, Jim Murphy, claimed that 'there will be a second independence referendum' because 'David Cameron will stumble into giving the SNP the excuse for one'.[24] Scottish Conservative leader, Ruth Davidson, has said that 'if the SNP puts in its

[21] C. Jeffery, 'Constitutional Change—Without End?' (2015) 86 *Pol Q* 275 at 275.

[22] Survation, *Issues Poll Prepared on Behalf of the Scottish Daily Mail* (2015) 23 accessible at <http://survation.com/wp-content/uploads/2015/07/Full-SDM-tables-1c0d8h4.pdf> last accessed 29 November 2015.

[23] 'Murphy: Scotland will be turbo-charged towards a second indyref if over 50 per cent of Scots vote for SNP' *Herald* (28 April 2015).

[24] D. Maddox, 'Jim Murphy: There will be second indyref' *Scotsman* (15 June 2015).

manifesto that it has an intention to hold a second referendum, and if it wins an outright majority, I think it does have a mandate to hold one', arguing that 'in the longer term, Westminster saying "No you cannae" will not play well in Scotland, and I think that it would damage the unionist cause'.[25]

Despite repeated claims during the 2015 campaign that 'there is no second independence referendum on the immediate horizon', SNP leader Nicola Sturgeon was pressed by the media and her political opponents on the circumstances which, in her view, could justify calling a second referendum.[26] The First Minister maintained that 'something material would have to change in terms of the circumstances or public opinion before I think it would be appropriate to have a proposal for a referendum'—giving UK exit from the European Union as one example of a 'material change' of this kind.[27] In the months that have followed the SNP landslide, several SNP figures have identified different constitutional *causae belli* which might justify calling a second referendum, from renewing Trident, failing adequately to reflect their preferences in the third Scotland Bill, and changes to the standing orders of the House of Commons which curtail the voting rights of Scottish MPs concerning primary and secondary legislation designated by the Speaker as England or England and Wales only—English votes for English laws. At time of writing, the Scottish Government's public view on the possibility of holding another referendum has stabilized into the following formula:

> The timing of any future referendum is entirely a matter for the people of Scotland to decide—the people, not politicians, are in charge at every stage of the process. The First Minister has made clear we are not planning another referendum, but equally has made it clear that it is not in the gift of any politician and party to rule it out indefinitely.[28]

Those familiar with debates about the proper scope of self-determination and the right to secede under international law will recognize the fundamental structure of these two strains of argument, the one emphasizing triggering grounds for secession, the second emphasizing self-determination as an inherent, fundamental right which can be exercised irrespective of transient events and circumstances. Thus far, the case for a second referendum has been articulated in both formats. Parliamentary debates since the 2015 election, from all sides of the Westminster Parliament, have meditated on the Union's continuing frailty. Op-eds continue to be written and talking heads continue to talk as if a second independence referendum is inevitable, and all that remains to be determined is when the poll takes place. As Cairney has argued, it has become increasingly clear since September

[25] D. Aitkenhead, 'Ruth Davidson, Scottish Conservative leader: "Up here, you have to make more of an effort"' *Guardian* (12 June 2015).

[26] N. Sturgeon, *A Conversation With Nicola Sturgeon* (Council on Foreign Relations 2015).

[27] BBC News, 'Election 2015: Sturgeon says only "material change" could spark Scots referendum' (8 April 2015) accessible at <http://www.bbc.co.uk/news/election-2015-scotland-32222806> last accessed 1 June 2015.

[28] 'SNP MP asks Scottish Secretary: do you have any contingency plans in case second indyref is held' *Herald* (20 July 2015).

2014 that the 'result was not decisive and did not settle the matter'—even for the short and medium term.[29] The prospect of a Scottish 'neverendum', or at least expectations that a second referendum can and will be held at some point in the none-too-distant future, are mainstream.

Curiously absent from this political speculation and argument, however, is any reflection on the fraught process which laid the legal foundations for the 2014 poll, and the constitutional tensions it expressed. Fundamental questions about the legal and constitutional status of Scottish secession referendums, deferred but not resolved by the Edinburgh Agreement of 2012, now return with a vengeance. Can the Scottish Parliament lawfully hold a referendum on its own authority? What conjunction of circumstances might justify a second referendum? And who decides? Sunstein characterizes constitutions as 'precommitment strategies, designed to foreclose debate over certain fundamental questions'.[30] As Mac Amhlaigh has suggested, unless the Scotland Act is radically reordered to put the question beyond doubt, the legality of future referendums remains 'an archetypical "hard case"'.[31] Yet it is a hard case which Westminster currently seems disinclined to answer in any decisive way. In contrast with the Canadian Clarity Act of 2002, which explicitly anticipated the prospect of future Québécois secession referendum, specifying when the Canadian federal government would consider such a poll binding upon it, the United Kingdom now seems determined to maintain the ambiguous *status quo* and to avoid 'pre-commitment' to the legality, or conditions for the legality, of a future referendum of any kind on the national question. Why? *Cui bono?*

III. Against constitutionalizing a right to secession

One influential defence of rejecting legal and constitutional pre-commitments to the legality of secession polls can be found in the writings of the American constitutional scholar, Professor Cass Sunstein. Writing as the rubble of the Berlin Wall settled, as the Soviet Union unravelled, and new constitutional orders emerged in the Caucuses, the Baltic republics, and the Balkans, in 'Constitutionalism and Secession' Sunstein is preoccupied by questions of constitutional design in multi-ethnic and multinational states. His point, however, is not a parochial one. Drawing on the American constitutional experience of federation and subsequent civil war, Sunstein argues that 'whether or not secession might be justified as a matter of politics or morality, constitutions ought not to include a right to secede'

[29] P. Cairney, 'The Scottish Independence Referendum: What are the Implications of a No Vote?' (2015) 86 *Pol Q* 186–91.

[30] C. R. Sunstein, 'Constitutionalism and Secession' (1991) 58 *University of Chicago Law Review* 633 at 635.

[31] C. Mac Amhlaigh '... yes, but is it legal? The Scottish Independence Referendum and the Scotland Act 1998' (*UK Constitutional Law blog*, 1 December 2012) accessible at <http://ukconstitutionallaw.org/2012/01/12/cormac-mac-amhlaigh-yes-but-is-it-legal-the-scottish-independence-referendum-and-the-scotland-act-1998/> last accessed 29 November 2015.

and 'courts should not find such a right to be implicit in constitutions'.[32] Why not? 'To place such a right in a founding document', he argues, would

> increase the risks of ethnic and factional struggle; reduce the prospects for compromise in deliberation in government; raise the stakes of day-to-day political decisions; introduce irrelevant and illegitimate considerations into those decisions; create dangers of blackmail, strategic behaviour, and exploitation; and, most generally, endanger the prospects for long-term self-governance.[33]

Sunstein is particularly concerned about the emergence of a national politics, framed by what Weinstock has described as 'trigger-happy secessionists',[34] where 'a threat to secede could under certain conditions be plausible at any given time, allowing the exit of the subunit from the nation to be a relevant factor in every important decision'.[35] A decade on, a number of the multi-ethnic, multinational states Sunstein discussed had already disintegrated. In short order, Yugoslavia unravelled into Croatia, Slovenia, Macedonia, Bosnia and Hezegovina, Serbia, and Montenegro. Nevertheless, Sunstein reiterated his earlier analysis, contending that 'the mere existence of a secession right would fuel secessionist impulses—making the claim for secession more credible, and more frequent'.[36] Sunstein is not hostile to independence movements as such. He recognizes, for example, 'in some cases, a right to secede will be fully justified as a matter of political mortality', but defends 'a strong presumption against a constitutional right to secede' as a threat to the integrity of states, and a distorting influence on their democratic decision-making.[37]

The concept of the 'constitutional' in Sunstein's argument grafts neatly onto the United States' experience of codification, and the constitutional drafting which was being undertaken in post-Soviet republics of the early 1990s. He defines a constitutional right to secession as 'an explicit textual provision guaranteeing such a right' or 'an implicit understanding that the constitution creates' such a right, accompanied by 'a willingness to enforce that right by a court capable of granting and enforcing a subunit's request to secede despite the objections of the central government'.[38] However, these definitions, and their implications, sit much less comfortably in the modern British constitution, and the challenges of legitimate self-determination it faces. Sunstein's argument against constitutionalizing secession relies on a sharp distinction between constitutional recognition and non-recognition of secession. But what does 'constitutional recognition' mean, in a state in which the constitution is uncodified and politically contested?[39] In the

32 Sunstein, 'Constitutionalism' (n. 30) at 634.
33 Sunstein, 'Constitutionalism' (n. 30) at 634.
34 D. Weinstock, 'Constitutionalizing the right to secede' (2001) 9 *The Journal of Political Philosophy* 182 at 202.
35 Sunstein, 'Constitutionalism' (n. 30) at 648.
36 C. R. Sunstein, 'Should Constitutions Protect the Right to Secede? A Reply to Weinstock' (2001) 9 *The Journal of Political Philosophy* 350 at 354.
37 Sunstein, 'Constitutionalism' (n. 30) at 653.
38 Sunstein, 'Constitutionalism' (n. 30) at 647.
39 Sunstein, 'Constitutionalism' (n. 30) at 635.

wake of the 2014 referendum, and the legal and political constitutional ideas embodied in the process, are the advantages of rejecting constitutional 'pre-commitment' available to the United Kingdom at all?

This chapter argues the category of the *constitutional* remains essentially politically contested and unstable in the United Kingdom. Questions of the legality, constitutionality, and justifications for calling a second referendum on the national question must be understood in that context. Examining first the proceedings of the Smith Commission, the origins of devolution in 1998, and finally the Scottish Government's strategic, limited engagement with the question of whether the 2011 referendum Bill was technically *intra vires*, this chapter argues that constitutional law is not an exhaustive repository of legitimating and delegitimating constitutional values. Considering both the technical and the political constitution, the constraints of the Scotland Act, and the dominant concept of Scottish popular sovereignty, the prospect of a 'neverendum' is much like the 2014 poll: primarily, and ultimately, a negotiated, contested, and ongoing question of constitutive politics.

IV. Deciding not to decide: The Smith Commission

The hastily assembled Smith Commission report, and subsequent Scotland Bill based on its recommendations, are silent on the legal regulation of future referendums. At the insistence of its pro-independence members, Smith's final report recognized that 'nothing in this report prevents Scotland becoming an independent country in future should the people of Scotland so choose,' but said nothing about whether, when, and if such a choice might be expressed.[40] Although the issue was largely missing from the agendas of Smith's elite, exclusive, and narrow plenary sessions, several individual submissions received—and largely ignored—by the Commission were preoccupied with the prospect of a future referendum, and anxious that the question should be regulated by law. Interestingly, this preoccupation was not limited either to supporters or opponents of Scottish independence, and equally tellingly, submissions articulating both points of view characteristically appealed to the idea of 'the sovereign right of the Scottish people to determine their constitutional future' to justify their preferences.[41] For example, the pro-independence Yes East Ayrshire group submitted that 'the current Scottish Claim of Right signed in 1989 should be legally enacted, enshrining the Sovereignty of the People of Scotland in Law',[42] while the sceptical Stay United Scotland group insisted that 'all parties must accept that the "Sovereign will of the Scottish People" is to remain part of the UK' and accordingly:

[40] Smith Commission, *Report of the Smith Commission for Further Devolution of Powers to the Scottish Parliament* (2014) para. 18.

[41] Yes Largs, *Submission to the Smith Commission* (2014) 2.

[42] Yes East Ayrshire, *The Smith Commission Scotland's Constitutional Settlement Response* (2014) para. 1.1.

No further referendum on Scottish Independence should be allowed by the UK Government unless it is supported by an Act of Parliament or a specific vote in Westminster approved by two thirds of all UK MPs. Such a requirement is demanded in Spain, Australia etc because of the consequential damage to the whole of those countries from the departure of a part.[43]

Public submissions did little to shape the substantive Smith Commission agenda. These are, however, telling fragments of 'popular constitutional consciousness', to adapt Ewick and Silbey's celebrated phrase.[44] In these largely neglected fragments, expressing ordinary people's earnest and deeply felt understandings of the law and the constitution, it is striking how the discourse of Scottish 'popular sovereignty' unites both Yes and No campaigners. Nothing better exemplifies the hegemonic status this idea now enjoys in Scottish—and arguably British—public life.[45] This language was also used in the final Smith Commission report itself, legitimating the hurried consensus the political parties reached in November 2014:

Reflecting the sovereign right of the people of Scotland to determine the form of government best suited to their needs, as expressed in the referendum on the 18 September 2014, and in the context of Scotland remaining within the UK, an enhanced devolution settlement for Scotland will be durable, responsive and democratic.[46]

In its submission to the Smith Commission, the Scottish Government argued that 'the sovereign right of the people of Scotland to determine their form of government should be enshrined in law'.[47] This proposal was briefly revived by the SNP delegation at the third reading of the Scotland Bill in the House of Commons in November 2015, but was defeated. Defending the amendment, which would have invested the Scottish Parliament with the power to call another independence referendum without resort to the UK Parliament or Government, the party's Westminster leader, Angus Robertson MP, invoked the idea of Scottish popular sovereignty, arguing that:

there should only be another referendum on Scottish independence when the people of Scotland indicate that they want one, but it is right that the Scottish Parliament—the people of Scotland's Parliament—should hold the power to react to the wishes of the people of Scotland.[48]

[43] Stay United Scotland, *Submission to the Lord Smith Commission* (2014) 1–2.

[44] P. Ewick and S. S. Silbey, *The Common Place of Law: Stories from Everyday Life* (Chicago University Press 1998).

[45] J. Mitchell, 'Shibboleths and Slogans: Sovereignty, Subsidiarity and Constitutional Debate', *Scottish Government Yearbook 1992* (Unit for the Study of Government in Scotland, University of Edinburgh, 1992) 98–113; N. MacCormick, 'Sovereignty: Myth and Reality' (1995) 11 *Scottish Affairs* 1–13; J. Mitchell, 'The Narcissism of Small Differences: Scotland and Westminster' (2009) *Parliamentary Affairs* 1; M. Goldoni and C. McCorkindale, 'Why We (Still) Need a Revolution' (2013) 14 *German Law Journal* 2197–228.

[46] Smith Commission (n. 40) at para. 20.

[47] Scottish Government, *More Powers for the Scottish Parliament: Scottish Government Proposals* (2014) 2.

[48] HC Deb, 9 November 2015, Vol. 602, col. 71.

The UK Government voted down the Nationalist amendment, but has otherwise been unwilling to revisit constitutional questions temporarily foreclosed by the Edinburgh Agreement. In its submission to the Smith Commission, the Scottish Conservatives argued that 'as a nation, we must avoid future damaging and divisive debates on separatism'.[49] However, the new Conservative government, elected in May 2015, has shown no enthusiasm for using the law, and their Commons majority, legally to foreclose that debate. The constitutional door has—just—been left ajar.

V. The origins of uncertainty: The Scotland Bill 1998

UK politicians were not always so reluctant to consider the questions which animated Lord Smith of Kelvin's correspondents. Delving back into the parliamentary proceedings concerning the Scotland Act 1998 reveals that the prospect of an independence referendum, and Holyrood's constitutional authority to organize such a poll, preoccupied framers of the Act. This question is not only of historical or political interest. It also informs a critical legal question: in 1998, did the UK Parliament intend to give Holyrood the legislative competence to call an independence referendum on its own authority? Paragraph 1 of Schedule 5 reserves 'the Union of the Kingdoms' but nowhere does the Scotland Act directly or explicitly establish that referendums on independence are *ultra vires*. Referendums are not listed as a reserved competence. Accordingly, under the Act's reserved powers model, competence to organize referendums is generally devolved to Holyrood. But what about organizing a more specific poll about the Union's future? To answer that question, we must consider whether the referendum 'relates to the reserved matter' of the 'Union' having regard to the referendum provision's 'purpose and effect in all the circumstances'.

Investigating the Scotland Bill proceedings in 1997 and 1998, what did Westminster intend in passing the Scotland Bill? Did it envisage that Holyrood would have the power to organize an independence referendum? That investigation produces ambiguous evidence. The first draft of the Scotland Bill, presented to Parliament by Tony Blair's Labour government after the referendum victory on 17 December 1997, had proposed a much more widely drawn restriction on Holyrood's competence over 'constitutional' matters. Paragraph 1 of Schedule 5 initially provided that 'the constitution, including the Crown, the succession to the Crown and a regency and the Parliament of the United Kingdom, are reserved matters'. In the final text adopted by parliament, however, this provision was narrowed significantly. The Scotland Act 1998 listed only '*aspects* of the constitution which are reserved matters', including 'the Union of the Kingdoms of Scotland and England', the 'Parliament of the United Kingdom'—and so on.[50]

[49] Scottish Conservative Party, *Commission on the Future Governance of Scotland* (2014) 1.
[50] Scotland Act 1998, Sched. 5, para. 1.

Given the logical structure of the Act, where powers not reserved are devolved, the clear implication of this paragraph is that there is no general reservation of power to Westminster over every issue which might be considered 'constitutional' in character.

During Commons proceedings on the Bill, the Secretary of State for Scotland, Donald Dewar, was to some extent evasive on the *vires* of a referendum canvassing public attitudes to Scottish independence, as opposed to unilateral legal measures purporting to tear Scotland from the United Kingdom. On 12 May 1998, Dewar was pressed on the question by MPs. Tory constitutional spokesman, Michael Ancram, put the central point clearly:

> the Secretary of State mentioned the Union of the United Kingdom being a reserved matter. Does that mean that a referendum on the union also will be a reserved matter and not available to the Scottish Parliament?[51]

Dewar emphasized the Scottish Parliament's limited authority to enact changes to the UK constitution unilaterally. 'It is clear that constitutional change—the political bones of the parliamentary system and any alteration to that system—is a reserved matter. That would obviously include any change or any preparations for change,' he said.[52] Ancram, devolution-sceptic Labour MP Tam Dalyell, and Tory MP Dominic Grieve QC pressed Dewar for a more categorical statement. Dalyell suggested Dewar's 'charm, wit and verbal facility disguise that there has been no answer to a fundamental question' of whether the Scottish Parliament could, of itself, initiate a referendum on independence.[53] The Secretary of State responded:

> it is not in the power of the Scottish Parliament to change the constitutional arrangements. Scotland will of course have the right to enter into any debate about these matters in the United Kingdom Parliament, and there will be Scottish representatives to do so. That is as it should be.

Detecting 'a certain tendency to shy away from the specific question', it fell to future Attorney-General, Dominic Grieve, to prompt the clearest comment from the minister on the question of legislative competence.[54] Grieve noted that 'a referendum in itself would not be a constitutional change but a mechanism of consultation'—on that understanding, 'would the holding of a referendum be within the competence of the Scottish Parliament?'[55] 'A referendum that purported to pave the way for something that was *ultra vires* is itself *ultra vires*,' Dewar concluded.[56] Even this statement—to some extent—hedges.

By contrast, government ministers in the Lords sketched out a more decisive position. Resisting an amendment from Lord Rowallan which would have specified

[51] HC Deb, 12 May 1998, Vol. 312, cols 256–7.
[52] HC Deb, 12 May 1998 (n. 51) at col. 257.
[53] HC Deb, 12 May 1998 (n. 51) at col. 258.
[54] HC Deb, 12 May 1998 (n. 51) at col. 258.
[55] HC Deb, 12 May 1998 (n. 51) at col. 258.
[56] HC Deb, 12 May 1998 (n. 51) at col. 258.

that 'the Union of the Kingdoms Scotland and England, including the holding of referendums on questions relating to the maintenance of that Union' are reserved matters,[57] Lord Sewel was categorical:

as the Bill stands the Scottish parliament will not be able to legislate to hold a referendum on independence as the union of the kingdoms is already a reserved matter under Schedule 5. Explicit reference along the lines proposed by the noble Lord, Lord Rowallan, is just not needed. In determining what relates to a reserved matter, the government amendments table to Clause 28 are of help here, because they indicate that we must look at the purpose of what is being done. If the parliament passed an Act to hold a referendum about whether the Union should continue, it would thus clearly be legislating in relation to the reserved matter of the Union. Any such Act would be about the continuation of the Union and it would therefore be beyond the parliament's competence and would not be law.[58]

This position was reiterated in similarly uncompromising terms by the Lord Advocate.[59] Significantly, this interpretation of the Bill was not accepted by the Conservative constitutional spokesman in the Lords. At the Committee stage, Lord Mackay of Drumadoon maintained that 'notwithstanding the argument explained by the Secretary of State in another place and repeated by the Lord Advocate':

it would be perfectly possible to construct a respectable legal argument that it was within the legislative competence of the Scottish parliament to pass an Act of Parliament authorising the executive to hold a referendum on the issue of whether or not those who voted in Scotland wished Scotland to be separate from the UK.[60]

Read in isolation, Lord Sewel's comments seem decisive against the legislative competence of any referendum bill. Read in context, however, the question remains more open. Which one of these diverse, sometimes Delphic, and conflicting statements should be treated as reflecting parliamentary intent? Although Lord Sewel's remarks were unqualified and unequivocal, his interpretation was rejected by opposition spokesman and supported in a less than full-throated way by the minister in the democratic house, despite being given several opportunities to make such a statement. It is also instructive to note that Lord Sewel anticipated that in interpreting the 'purpose and effect' test enshrined in section 29 of the Scotland Act, the courts would draw on the 'pith and substance' doctrine employed 'in dealing with cases arising from the Commonwealth constitutions and the Government of Ireland Act 1920'. As the former president of the Court of Session, Lord Clyde, pointed out in the subsequent debate, 'purpose, to my mind, is not the same as the pith and substance'—a judgment which was vindicated in the United Kingdom Supreme Court's leading authority on the interpretation of section 29, *Martin and Miller v Lord Advocate*.[61]

[57] HL Deb, 21 July 1998, Vol. 592, col. 850.
[58] HL Deb, 21 July 1998 (n. 57) at col. 854.
[59] HL Deb, 18 June 1998, Vol. 590, col. 1787.
[60] HL Deb, 21 July 1998 (n. 57) at col. 852.
[61] HL Deb, 21 July 1998 (n. 57) at col. 832.

Mackay's scepticism about the force of Lord Sewel's analysis draws strength from the imprecision of Sewel's analysis of the text of the Bill, and other important provisions of the legislation which he failed to mention. As the courts have subsequently recognized, the 'relates to a reserved matter' test cannot be parsed as referring to legislation which is 'about' reserved matters, but 'indicates something more than a loose, consequential connection' with them.[62] The analysis of parliamentary proceedings leaves the status of a referendum where it began: arguable, clearly strengthening the case of those who argue such a referendum would be unlawful, but with too many inconsistencies and ambivalences to answer the matter conclusively.

VI. The two constitutionalisms of Scottish Nationalism

Before proceeding to examine the constitutional ideas mobilized by the Scottish Government in 2012, and likely to be mobilized in support of any future referendum, it is instructive first to consider the Scottish National Party's more general constitutional politics, from which its referendum strategy emerged. For the Nationalist leadership, what does a good constitution look like? What characteristics does it have? Speaking at the Edinburgh Centre for Constitutional Law in June 2014, Nicola Sturgeon outlined her vision for the constitution of an independent Scotland:

> We believe that Scotland should have a written constitution, rather than the quilt work of statutes, precedent, practice and tradition that make up the constitution of the UK. A written constitution provides certainty and security for the citizens of a state. It defines and constrains the organs of the state. It describes where power lies and how those who wield it are chosen and scrutinized. As is well known, this is not always clear in the UK.[63]

In their criticism of the constitutional status quo in Britain, and preference for a codified, entrenched and judicially enforceable basic law, Sturgeon's remarks are characteristic of contemporary Nationalist constitutional thinking. In earlier remarks to the Foreign Press Association in January 2013, Alex Salmond explicitly tied claims of Scottish popular sovereignty to a critique of the United Kingdom's constitutional practices. Citing the 1320 Declaration of Arbroath and the 1989 Claim of Right as evidence of a 'centuries' old and 'distinct' Scottish constitutional tradition, Salmond argued:

> That tradition states that the people of Scotland are sovereign and that they have the power to determine the form of government best suited to their needs. It stands in contrast to the UK principle that parliament has unlimited sovereignty. That UK tradition is one of the reasons that the UK has no written constitution. That makes the UK highly

[62] *Recovery of Medical Costs for Asbestos Diseases (Wales) Bill: Reference by the Counsel General for Wales* [2015] UKSC 3 at para. 25 per Lord Mance.

[63] N. Sturgeon, 'The Constitutional Future of an Independent Scotland', speech given at the Edinburgh Centre for Constitutional Law, 16 June 2014.

unusual among Western democracies, and unique within the European Union. That deficiency is a democratic deficit that an independent Scotland should not repeat.[64]

Nationalist constitutional discourse has tended to emphasize the *precarious* legal status in which devolved institutions are left by the principles of Westminster sovereignty and non-entrenchment of the Scotland Act. Another Nationalist MSP, writing in a popular tabloid newspaper in 2015, exemplifies this attitude:

> The UK does not have a written constitution protecting the rights of the different countries that make up the Union. If it did, Scots could challenge a move to kill off their parliament as unconstitutional. As things stand, we are at the mercy of a House of Commons.[65]

What often goes unnoticed, however, is how far Nationalist politicians have employed the very constitutional flexibility they deride to *promote* their political ambitions within the United Kingdom since 1998. Aspirationally, Nationalist politicians may be legal constitutionalists. As cold-eyed pragmatists, however, the United Kingdom's political constitution has done a great deal more to accommodate their demands than any codified UK constitution which more definitively delimited the powers and privileges of Scottish institutions on the one hand, and shared UK institutions on the other. As Lord Reed held in *Imperial Tobacco*, 'the Scotland Act is not a constitution, but an Act of Parliament'.[66] While non-entrenchment must mean that Holyrood is, legally, vulnerable to abolition, it also means that the current limits to Holyrood's powers cannot be justified with reference to any higher law. They remain, always, a matter of political choice. An uncodified UK constitution cannot formalize the principle of 'Scottish popular sovereignty' invoked by Alex Salmond, but nor can it decisively exclude it. The category of the *constitutional* remains essentially politically contested, and unstable. This instability is reflected in the gradual elaboration of Holyrood's powers since 1998 by successive Scotland Bills, and most vividly of all, by the *volte face* which invested the Scottish Parliament with clear legal authority to organize a referendum on Scottish independence in 2014. The Scottish Government's arguments during this period are of more than historical interest. They sketch, in outline, the constitutional attitudes liable to inform any attempt to revisit the national question in a second referendum.

VII. Boxing shadows: The technical Jekyll and the political Hyde

The Scottish Government's substantive legal analysis of the *vires* of their various referendum questions remained inscrutable throughout debates on the legislative

[64] A. Salmond, 'Constitutional rights', speech given at the Foreign Press Association, London, 16 January 2013.

[65] J. McAlpine, 'Westminster can't be trusted with the Scottish Parliament' *Daily Record* (17 June 2015).

[66] *Imperial Tobacco v Lord Advocate* [2012] CSIH 9 at para. 71.

competence of the first referendum. Scottish Ministers proved consistently reluctant to recognize that the question of legislative competence was even open to question, arguing their proposals were *intra vires* while emphasizing broader claims of legitimate self-determination and democratic decision-making. Its 2010 *Scotland's Future: Draft Referendum (Scotland) Bill Consultation Paper* noted that:

Scottish Parliament legislation must conform to the provisions of the Scotland Act 1998. The Scotland Act has in-built flexibility so that the Scottish Parliament's powers can be extended over time. The Scottish Parliament has a role in such processes, for example in relation to orders made under section 30 of the Act. It is therefore legitimate for a referendum held under an Act of the Scottish Parliament to ask the people questions related to an extension of its powers insofar as this is within the framework of the Scotland Act.[67]

The later *Your Scotland, Your Referendum Consultation* (2012) observed that:

a wide range of opinion has been expressed about whether or not the Scottish Parliament has the power to hold a referendum consulting the Scottish people about independence. The Scottish Government has previously published a referendum question asking whether the powers of the Scottish Parliament should be extended to enable independence to be achieved. That question was carefully phrased to comply with the requirements of the Scotland Act 1998. Much independent legal opinion supports the Scottish Government's view.[68]

Notably, the Scottish Government failed to provide even a single example of legal opinion which supported the idea that what it was proposing fell 'entirely within legislative competence'.[69] The consultation included a grudging and carefully worded note of conciliation, observing that the SNP were 'ready to work with the UK Government to remove *their* doubts about the competence of the Scottish Parliament and to put the referendum effectively beyond legal challenge'.[70] The Scottish Government's legal analysis was never explained in public—a failure criticized by pro-Union Westminster committees. The Scottish Affairs Committee found 'the silence' of the Lord Advocate on the *vires* of the Bill 'remarkable', noting that while

it is well understood that Law Officers do not, save exceptionally, make their advice public, but, on a matter such as this, there is a very strong public interest in understanding the legal basis of the Scottish Government's approach to a process which will determine the future of the country.[71]

The House of Lords Select Committee on the Constitution found it similarly 'regrettable that the Scottish Government have not set out their legal position more fully'.[72] This reticence is not altogether surprising. Although this has never

[67] Scottish Government, *Scotland's Future: Draft Referendum (Scotland) Bill Consultation Paper* (2010) para. 1. 26.

[68] Scottish Government, *Your Scotland, Your Referendum Consultation* (2012) 4–5.

[69] Scottish Government, *Your Scotland* (n. 68) 5.

[70] Scottish Government, *Your Scotland* (n. 68) 5 (my emphasis).

[71] Scottish Affairs Committee, *The Referendum on Separation* (n. 13), at para. 25.

[72] House of Lords Select Committee on the Constitution, *Referendum on Scottish Independence* (n. 13) at para. 10.

been publicly confirmed, it is understood that the Scottish law officers advised ministers that the proposed referendum legislation would not withstand judicial scrutiny under section 29 and Schedule 5 of the Scotland Act and that Westminster cooperation would be necessary to escape the significant risk of litigation. One can understand why Scottish ministers were disinclined to meditate on these questions in public. This reticence extended to the Scottish Nationalists' decision not to deploy their majorities on critical Holyrood committees to pursue investigations to parallel the Lords and Commons reports on the *vires* of the referendum under the Scotland Act. Their tactical reasons for not doing so were twofold. Firstly, even in committees with SNP majorities, Holyrood committees were always more heterodox on the national question than their London equivalents. Given their cross-party membership, they could not be expected to fulfil the same partisan, campaigning function as the uniformly pro-Union committees of Scottish Labour MP, Ian Davidson, and Baroness Jay.

Secondly, public discussion of the legislative competence of the referendum would have cut against the SNP's wider, characteristically disciplined shadow-boxing strategy, which made no public concessions as to legislative competence whatever. Any fair-minded, evidence-based investigation of the *vires* questions would inevitably generate and publicize doubts about the competence of the referendum legislation, even if legal voices could have been produced to make the case that 'a plausible case can be made that such a Bill would be lawful'.[73] Ignorance was exploited and message-discipline maintained by ensuring that *vires* issues remained poorly ventilated and poorly understood. That this was even possible reflects the extent to which the devolution settlement in Scotland, and the role and powers of the courts within it, is poorly understood by the public, and indeed, by the political commentators who help shape legal and political consciousness through the national and local media.

This limited comprehension and regard for the limits of the Scotland Act perhaps explains the frustrated tone which characterized the numerous warnings advanced by the Advocate General for Scotland before October 2012. Warning in January of that year that 'wherever law ends, tyranny begins,' Jim Wallace invoked 'the importance of upholding the Rule of Law' in the referendum process, opposing the idea 'that legal technicalities' about reservations of power under the Scotland Act 'shouldn't get in the way of the Scottish Parliament going full steam ahead' with the referendum.[74] Although no prominent SNP politician had explicitly committed the party, the parliament, or the government to pressing on without Westminster consent, Wallace's warnings should be understood as a response

[73] G. Anderson, C. Bell, S. Craig, A. McHarg, T. Mullen, S. Tierney, and N. Walker, 'The Independence Referendum, Legality and the Contested Constitution: Widening the Debate' (*UK Constitutional Law blog*, 31 January 2012) available at <http://ukconstitutionallaw.org/2012/01/31/gavin-anderson-et-al-the-independence-referendum-legality-and-the-contested-constitution-widening-the-debate/>.

[74] J. Wallace, 'Looking Forwards' (n. 13).

to the public debate in the pages of newspapers and on social media in 2011 and 2012, which increasingly speculated on the possibility of Holyrood pressing ahead with a referendum, even if the coalition government in Westminster refused to come to terms.

But why did Nationalist politicians refuse, in public at least, to engage with these fundamental questions about the distribution of powers in the British constitution, and the perils of litigation? Their strategy—their constitutional *omertà*—arguably reflected a recognition that constitutional law is not an exhaustive repository of legitimating and delegitimating constitutional values. Nationalist politicians calculated, correctly, that the powerful 'political orthodoxy' of Scotland's right to self-determination would answer the significant, but ultimately politically indefensible, legal hurdle represented by an unfavourable interpretation of Schedule 5 of the Scotland Act, if not in the Supreme Court, then in Parliament and Whitehall.[75] The force of this political constitutional orthodoxy also helps to explain the strange absence of any technical constitutional debate from the ongoing, sometimes heated, political debate about the conditions which might provoke a second referendum on the national question. For all of the fanfare and coverage of the Edinburgh Agreement, it signally failed to entrench in the popular consciousness that the United Kingdom Government and Parliament had and has a legitimate, countervailing interest in whether and when referendums are held concerning the integrity of its territory.[76] In an entrenched constitution, with cumbersome or difficult amendment protocols, the UK Government might have found constitutional resources to resist the referendum. But if, as Lord Reed concluded, the Scotland Act is 'not a constitution' but only an emanation of Westminster's legislative will, constitutional recognition of the Scottish people's constitutive power becomes a matter of political choice.[77]

There is little evidence that pro-Union politicians ever seriously contemplated a strategy of constitutional resistance to Scottish demands for self-determination. As Colin Kidd has argued, the intellectual tradition of Scottish nationalism and Unionism should not be conceptualized as binary opposites, sharing nothing in common, but as overlapping traditions, sharing a number of political premises. Graeme Morton has identified a 'Unionist-nationalism', which favours the retention of the Union, but which emphasizes the importance of Scottish distinctiveness within its confines, rejecting conceptions of the Union as incorporating or producing a unitary state within which Scottish claims to distinctiveness are effaced.[78] A contemporary version of this conception of union was of fundamental

[75] A. Tomkins, 'Scotland's Choice, Britain's Future' (2014) 130 *Law Quarterly Review* 215 at 220.

[76] An argument advanced by N. Barber, 'After the vote: regulating future independence referendums' (*UK Constitutional Law blog*, 21 March 2014) accessible at <http://ukconstitutionallaw.org/2014/03/21/nick-barber-after-the-vote-regulating-future-independence-referendums/>.

[77] *Imperial Tobacco v The Lord Advocate* [2012] CSIH 9, per Lord Reed at para. 70.

[78] G. Morton, *Unionist-Nationalism: Governing Urban Scotland 1830–1860* (Tuckwell Press 1999).

importance to the broad consensus in 2012 on the legitimacy of Holyrood posing the national question. The Claim of Right was, after all, not a Nationalist document but a declaration to which a great number of Scottish independence's most inveterate opponents put their names in 1989. As Tomkins has argued, for adherents of the Diceyan tradition, 'as a matter of strict law the Claim of Right is heresy'.[79] In the popular constitutional consciousness, by contrast, it is orthodoxy and right-reason. The right to self-determination invoked by the Scottish Government in 2011 and 2012 was not novel, or essentially contested, but had already been politically mainstream and entrenched in Scottish public life for at least three decades, if not longer. The language of self-determination undergirded the decision to establish a Scottish parliament in 1998, and the role of a referendum in sanctioning its creation. By treating the referendum as self-evidently *politically* legitimate, the Scottish Government implicitly popularized the claim that it must be equally self-evidently *legally* legitimate—which is to say, lawful under section 29 of the Scotland Act.

Although cynical, and hardly candid, this was not an inherently unreasonable or unstrategic position for Nationalist politicians to adopt. After the Holyrood election of 2011, the attitude of the UK Government and Parliament to the legitimacy of the proposed poll could not entirely be taken for granted. Within living memory, during the Scotland Bill debates of 1997–8, UK ministers had envisaged that Holyrood would not, and should not, have the power to organize a referendum on its own authority. Scotland's right unilaterally to exercise self-determination remains open to question in international law.[80] It was not self-evident that ministers and MPs from across the United Kingdom would accept the SNP's democratic mandate for a poll and prove willing to take legislative steps to facilitate a referendum. Spanish attitudes to the plebiscite on Catalan self-government represented a salutary object lesson in the constitutional trench resistance which the United Kingdom might have exercised in defence of its territorial and political integrity. SNP politicians avoided making public concessions which could have proved damaging in any future legal proceedings, if the UK Government's broadly deferential approach to Scottish self-determination had not been maintained.

In 2000, the late Neil MacCormick argued that 'it is a very particular virtue of the Scottish national movement always to have discountenanced any apparent shortcuts. Instead, it has stuck doggedly to a democratic and constitutional path, whatever obstacles this involved in the way of electoral disadvantage under the dominance of hostile media'.[81] UK constitutional resistance to the 2014 referendum would have placed this commitment under unprecedented strain and have thrown open a constitutional and political Pandora's Box. During this period, the UK Advocate General, Jim Wallace, made several public interventions,

[79] Tomkins, 'Scotland's Choice' (n. 75) at 220.

[80] See Bell, Ch. 9 in this volume, at 200–3.

[81] N. MacCormick, 'Is There a Constitutional Path to Scottish Independence?' (2000) 53 *Parliamentary Affairs* 721 at 721.

arguing that the referendum was *ultra vires*. Would he use his authority under the Scotland Act to refer the matter directly to the Supreme Court to vindicate his view, striking down the Act and exposing him and his government to intense political pressure and criticism? Alternatively, would he await the efforts of a private citizen challenging the referendum, and the prospect of protracted and damaging litigation which that would inevitably entail? For Unionists, this was a nightmare scenario—a scenario which would inevitably have been taken less seriously, had the Scottish Government not robustly maintained its intention to press on with the poll, come what may. The UK Government was left with only two options: either facilitate a lawful poll, or face the prospect of trying (and probably failing) to prevent the Nationalists organizing the referendum anyway while exposing UK institutions to allegations of anti-democratic attitudes. In defence of constitutionalizing the right to self-determination, Daniel Weinstock describes the 'prudent constitution-makers', who make 'legal provision' for a poll as 'a way of controlling a process which would otherwise happen anyway in a much less manageable, and potentially more destructive manner'.[82] The Edinburgh Agreement process is an object lesson in this kind of prudential constitutional calculation.

In the light of this lopsided non-debate, it is perhaps unsurprising that contemporary mediations on the prospect of a future referendum tend to assume the attitude criticized by Jim Wallace in 2011, waving aside 'legal nit-picking' and nice questions of statutory interpretation.[83] Because of the Scottish Government's calculated reticence to embark on a detailed *legal* defence of its authority to call a referendum, the arguments in favour of an *intra vires* reading of a future referendum poll remain largely unventilated.[84] It is perhaps unsurprising, therefore, that the political debate and counter-debate about the rights, wrongs, calculations, and triggers informing a decision to hold another referendum continue to ignore the technical constitution almost entirely. Sunstein suggests that 'the mere existence of a secession right would fuel secessionist impulses—making the claim for secession more credible, and more frequent'.[85] However, the ongoing UK experience arguably vindicates Weinstock's more sceptical analysis of Sunstein's emphasis on the particular perils on constitutionalizing secession rights. 'Secessionist politics' Weinstock argued, 'will occur anyway, regardless of legal silences and prohibitions'.[86] Indeed, by having no groundwork of agreed legal principles, establishing a timeline and conditions on which another referendum might be held, arguably gives Scottish Nationalists greater scope to issue threats and menaces about precipitating a second referendum than might otherwise be the case.

[82] Weinstock, 'Right to Secede' (n. 34) at 202.

[83] Wallace, 'Looking Forwards' (n. 13).

[84] A point made eloquently at the time in an influential academic intervention by a number of contributors to this book: Anderson, Bell, Craig, McHarg, Mullen, Tierney, and Walker (n. 73).

[85] Sunstein, 'Reply to Weinstock' (n. 36) at 354.

[86] Weinstock, 'Right to Secede' (n. 34) at 196.

VIII. Navigating towards a neverendum, without a map or compass

The outcome of this meditation is in many ways paradoxical. Considered exclusively from a legal point of view, in terms of the technical constitution, the devolution legislation, and the Court's approach to the interpretation of the Scotland Act, the emphasis is on the 'never' in 'neverendum'. While a further secession poll is not explicitly banned under the Scotland Act, and an arguable case may still be constructed in defence of the legality of such a poll, any pro-independence future Scottish Government and Parliament faces—perhaps insuperable—legal hurdles unless Westminster consent and acts to facilitate another referendum.

However, constitutional law is not an exhaustive repository of constitutional values. In the wake of the 2014 referendum, we are left with an ambivalent combination of 'constitutional recognition' and non-recognition of Scottish secession rights.[87] At the time of writing, the new Scotland Bill remains under scrutiny, subject to amendment and change. But in the Bill's early months before parliament, there seems little appetite to anticipate what to many critics and commentators now seems inevitable, and to take the opportunity to pre-commit to the legality of a future independence poll. A conscious policy choice has been made to leave the question of the legality of any future referendum open, ad hoc, and uncertain. If the technical constitution is ambivalent about Scottish rights to self-determination, Unionist or nationalist, pro- or anti-independence—the political culture is not. The recognition of the 'sovereign right of the Scottish people to determine the form of government best suited to their needs'[88] may be 'extratextual and nonjusticiable',[89] yet it has, if anything, been more deeply entrenched by the 2014 referendum than it has been at any point in history before. This Jekyll and Hyde dyad leaves the constitutionality, if not the legality, of future referendums in the half-twilight, caught between a technical analysis of the Scotland Act and the powers it confers, and a largely uncontested political claim that the Scottish people have the right to decide how they are governed.

In Sunstein's terms, the right to secession is at once recognized and not recognized. This constitutional duality is perhaps an inevitable consequence of the United Kingdom's uncodified basic law. Having constitutionally legitimated ideas of popular Scottish sovereignty, that recognition is extremely difficult to reverse in the short and medium term, whatever technical restrictions are articulated in the Scotland Act. Yet the political behaviours Sunstein fears—using threats of secession as tools of political strategy, examining day-to-day policy decisions through the prism of national and constitutional questions—arguably *already* characterize post-referendum UK politics. This is reflected by the pervasive logic of 'triggers' for a second referendum,

[87] Sunstein, 'Constitutionalism' (n. 30) at 635.
[88] Smith Commission (n. 40) at para. 20.
[89] Sunstein, 'Constitutionalism' (n. 30) at 633.

transforming questions of European Union reform, or defence policy, into constitutionally provoking events. Yet in a constitutional sense, all of these debated 'triggers' are essentially transient factors whose importance can be contested. Woven together, they may contribute to the justificatory fabric of demands to revisit the national question in a national plebiscite. Yet *only* the idea of Scottish popular sovereignty represents a constitutional *sine qua non* for a second referendum.

So why leave the future regulation of independence referendums to chance? Why defer a political conflict which, to many, now seems inevitable? Lawyers are sometimes inclined to treat the idea of legal indeterminacy as inherently problematic, and to demand further codification, further clarification, greater legal 'pre-commitment'—as if these things are self-evident goods in statecraft and governance. Lord Bingham expressed the sense of jurisprudential forlornness in the absence of legal regulation particularly vividly. In an essay on written constitutions, he said 'constitutionally speaking, we now find ourselves in a trackless desert without map or compass'.[90] But is this legal maplessness the substantial problem which some lawyers may be tempted to claim? The limits of legal regulation may certainly be uncomfortable. It can precipitate crises. In 2011, after the election of a pro-independence majority in Holyrood, these dubieties in the law were undeniably problematic. Yet when the political mandate and political will to organize an independence referendum met the strictures and ambivalences of the Scotland Act—Westminster yielded. In response to legitimate political claims, politics (temporarily) remoulded the law.

This approach is at least defensible, both from pro-independence and pro-Union perspectives. By declining to put the matter beyond doubt, whether through caution, calculation, or principle, Westminster ensures that the legal, political, and constitutional question—can Holyrood ordain another referendum?—remains an open one until a concrete proposal materializes. The ambivalence of the status quo continues to afford a future Westminster government some leverage on question, timing, and terms. In parallel, the political domination of claims to legitimate self-determination mean that patient and impatient supporters of Scottish independence need not be too preoccupied by the non-recognition of secession rights in the Scotland Bill. The constitutional debate remains unforeclosed. This represents an uneasy kind of constitutional truce.

Perhaps this is as it should be. In a letter to James Madison in September 1789, Thomas Jefferson wrote that 'the earth belongs in usufruct to the living' and 'that the dead have neither powers nor rights over it'.[91] We can express this thought more simply: law cannot strip democratic politics of its inherent uncertainty and instability. Negotiation may be preferable, and less apt to generate insoluble political crises, than maladapted constitutional 'determinacy and rule-governedness'.[92]

[90] T. Bingham, 'A Written Constitution?' in *Lives of the Law: Selected Essays and Speeches* (Oxford University Press 2011) 97.

[91] Quoted in H. Sloan, 'The Earth Belongs in Usufruct to the Living' in P. S. Onuf (ed.), *Jeffersonian Legacies* (University of Virginia Press 1993) 281.

[92] H. Aronovitch, 'Seceding The Canadian Way' (2006) 34 *The Journal of Federalism* 541 at 560.

The spectre of a 'neverendum' rose immediately from the grave of the 2014 poll, as independence supporters were smarting, and as Better Together campaigners sighed relief. As Weinstock argues, in defence of the idea of constitutionalizing secession rights:

> there are occasions in the political history of a community when the fund of good will and trust is sufficient to make or amend a constitution in such a way as to incorporate a right to secede, and there are times when all suggestions will be viewed with suspicion.

In the wake of the 2015 general election, the necessary elements of trust and goodwill seem in short supply. But in our Jekyll and Hyde constitution, deferring these questions until tomorrow, dealing with them concretely rather than in the abstract, may ultimately be the most prudent, the most politically adroit, response to Scotland's changed politics and now unsettled constitutional will. For both proponents and opponents of Scottish independence, arguing their cases under the political constitution of the United Kingdom, 'the campaign continues, and the dream shall never die'.[93]

[93] BBC News, 'Scottish referendum: Salmond to quit after Scots vote No' (19 September 2014) accessible at <http://www.bbc.co.uk/news/uk-scotland-29277527> last accessed 29 November 2015.

Index

Page references to footnotes will be followed by the letter 'n' and number of note, while references to Figures and Tables will be in *italics* followed by the letters 'f' and 't' respectively.

The manufacturer's authorised representative in the EU for product safety is Oxford University Press España S.A. of El Parque Empresarial San Fernando de Henares, Avenida de Castilla, 2 - 28830 Madrid (www.oup.es/en or product.safety@oup.com). OUP España S.A. also acts as importer into Spain of products made by the manufacturer.
Printed and bound by CPI Group (UK) Ltd, Croydon, CR0 4YY
14/09/2026
02216288-0006